Unlikely Insider

Unlikely Insider

A West Coast Advocate in Ottawa

JACK AUSTIN WITH EDIE AUSTIN

McGill-Queen's University Press

Montreal & Kingston • London • Chicago

ISBN 978-0-2280-1624-3 (cloth)
ISBN 978-0-2280-1625-0 (ePDF)
ISBN 978-0-2280-1626-7 (ePUB)

Legal deposit first quarter 2023
Bibliothèque nationale du Québec

Printed in Canada on acid-free paper that is 100% ancient forest free
(100% post-consumer recycled), processed chlorine free

Funded by the Government of Canada   Financé par le gouvernement du Canada   Canada

Canada Council for the Arts   Conseil des arts du Canada

We acknowledge the support of the Canada Council for the Arts.
Nous remercions le Conseil des arts du Canada de son soutien.

LIBRARY AND ARCHIVES CANADA CATALOGUING IN PUBLICATION

Title: Unlikely insider : a West Coast advocate in Ottawa / Jack Austin with
    Edie Austin ; foreword by Paul Martin.
Names: Austin, Jack, 1932– author. | Austin, Edie, author.
Description: Includes bibliographical references and index.
Identifiers: Canadiana (print) 20220423466 | Canadiana (ebook) 2022042358X |
    ISBN 9780228016243 (cloth) | ISBN 9780228016267 (ePUB) | ISBN 9780228016250 (ePDF)
Subjects: LCSH: Austin, Jack, 1932- | LCSH: Legislators—Canada—Biography. |
    LCSH: Legislators—British Columbia—Biography. | LCSH: Politicians—
    Canada—Biography. | CSH: Cabinet ministers—British Columbia—
    Biography. | LCGFT: Autobiographies.
Classification: LCC FC626.A97 A3 2023 | DDC 971.064/4092—dc23

To every Canadian seeking a Canada of fairness,
social justice, economic equity, and opportunity for all

Contents

Photographs follow page 156

Foreword • *Rt Hon. Paul E. Martin*   ix

Introduction   3

1   Becoming a British Columbian   12

2   The Influence of Art Laing   26

3   Ups and Downs in a Resource Economy   45

4   Deputy Minister in the Eye of the Storm:
   An Oil Crisis, and More   57

5   Chief of Staff to the Prime Minister   82

6   The Evolving Senate   103

7   The Expo 86 Backstory   136

8   One Minister, Many Files   157

9   My Introduction to China   180

10   Building the Canada-China Relationship   201

11   The American Elephant and the Aztec Eagle   235

12   Recognition and Reconciliation   254

13   Travels with Pierre   284

Conclusion   311

Acknowledgments   319
Notes   321
Index   327

Foreword

THIS BOOK TELLS THE STORY of a young British Columbian who, through one unexpected opportunity after another, rose to high office in Ottawa. With a talent for getting things done, a first-rate mind, and a deep understanding of the challenges and the opportunities facing Canada and his home province, Jack Austin went on to make a lasting imprint on national affairs, beginning with the role he played in bringing the perspective and priorities of British Columbia into the national policy debate.

What Jack writes is that for many, British Columbia was for a long time the province beyond the mountains, facing the Asia Pacific, and, unfortunately, not seen in Central and Atlantic Canada as relevant to the classic issues of their concern, those relating to trade with Britain and the European continent and similar issues in Canada-US trade and security. In summary, British Columbia was expected to just go along. British Columbia's natural reaction was a rejection of eastern Canadian disinterest and what in British Columbia became known as fed-bashing, as provincial politicians harnessed this sense of alienation for partisan purposes.

As political minister for British Columbia in the Pierre Trudeau cabinet in the early 1980s, Jack worked as a tireless advocate for his province and its people to bring British Columbia to the centre of Canadian policy. His success in rescuing the failing Expo 86 world's fair by enhancing federal participation, including the construction of the iconic Canada Place as host pavilion – Vancouver's convention centre today – was the beginning of the end of fed-bashing. In the same vein, among Jack's many other achievements, he was a prime mover in the creation of the Asia Pacific Foundation of Canada and secured its headquarters in Vancouver.

Jack Austin first made an appearance on the federal scene in the early 1960s, when, as a lawyer and businessman, he brought to Ottawa a valuable combination of skills and experience. Under the leadership of my father, the Right Honourable Paul Martin, then secretary of state for external affairs, Jack joined the federal negotiating team as a legal adviser in the negotiations for the Columbia River Treaty. My father thought highly of Jack, and when my father set out to win the Liberal Party leadership in 1968, Jack took on the direction of his campaign in British Columbia. Others thought highly of Jack as well, recruiting him from Vancouver in 1970 to be Ottawa's deputy minister of energy, mines and resources (EMR), where he produced a major study on Canada's energy resources that led to the establishment of Petro-Canada. Following his service as deputy minister, he was appointed principal secretary (chief of staff) to the Right Honourable Pierre E. Trudeau and subsequently to the Senate of Canada, representing British Columbia.

Whether as a lawyer, businessman, civil servant, politician, or later in an academic setting, Jack has kept his focus on Asia and its importance to Canada, constantly reminding those at the "centre" that Canada is also a Pacific nation and British Columbia is its Pacific Gateway. He was president of the Canada China Business Council from 1993 to 2000 and created and managed the first Team Canada to China in 1994, headed by Prime Minister the Right Honourable Jean Chrétien, with 9 premiers and 2 territorial leaders, accompanied by more than 350 business executives. This created an era of increasingly productive Canada-China relations.

In his second cabinet career, as a member of my government as Leader of the Government in the Senate of Canada, Jack continued his focus on British Columbia's interests. He promoted and secured the federal government's commitment to invest in the Pacific Gateway Strategy whose objective was and is to create the best rail and other transportation facilities and capacities to move goods from Asia to eastern Canadian and US markets and to return North American exports to Asia. He accompanied me in 2005 to Japan and China in a highly successful mission to secure Canadian business interests. He also worked hard for the success of the Kelowna Accord, which, had it been implemented by the government that followed mine, would have greatly furthered reconciliation with Indigenous Peoples. Throughout his public career, Jack worked continuously for recognition of Indigenous rights and reconciliation with Indigenous Peoples, highlighted by his dedication to the passage in the

Senate, in the year 2000, of the final agreement with the Nisga'a people of northern British Columbia.

The Honourable Jack Austin is a passionate Canadian, a dedicated British Columbian, and an optimistic realist, as well as a long-time friend.

He taught us much and we are much the better for it.

RT HON. PAUL E. MARTIN
Prime Minister of Canada, 2003–06

Unlikely Insider

Introduction

WITHIN A FEW WEEKS of my appointment to cabinet in September 1981, I was faced with one of the most significant battles of my long political career. The stakes could not have been higher for my home province of British Columbia, and success was far from assured. My task was to persuade my more senior colleagues that it was essential for our government to increase the wholly inadequate level of support it was then offering for British Columbia's planned Expo 86. The transportation-themed world's fair, held on the north shore of Vancouver's False Creek, would go on to be a smashing success. With fifty-four nations participating, it welcomed 22 million visitors and benefited Vancouver and its residents in myriad ways, from providing a first job to putting the city on the international map. But at the time, Premier Bill Bennett, who saw the fair as a means to boost British Columbia's ailing economy, insisted that without a more significant federal contribution, the province wouldn't be able to afford the event. Bennett accused Ottawa of not caring about his province's welfare and was publicly threatening to cancel the fair.

With the support of my cabinet colleague and fellow British Columbian Ray Perrault, Leader of the Government in the Senate, I made a pitch to the economic development committee of cabinet for enhanced authority to negotiate a federal contribution large enough to ensure Expo's future. But our colleagues from Ontario, Quebec, and the Atlantic provinces did not see why we should be doing British Columbia any favours when the province had elected no Liberals in 1980 and the BC provincial government's favourite pastime, it seemed, was railing against the federal government, a practice so well established that it even had a name: "fed-bashing." The Bill Bennett government and most, if not all, of its predecessors since British Columbia's entry into Confederation in 1871 used Ottawa as a punching bag for their own political purposes, in the process exacerbating British Columbians' sense of alienation from the distant national capital.

After the economic development committee of cabinet rejected enhanced funding in the winter of 1982, dooming the Expo 86 project, I appealed the decision to the Priorities and Planning Committee (P&P), the inner cabinet, on the basis that there were government interests the committee had not appropriately taken into account. There, in the cabinet's most powerful decision-making body, I argued vehemently that federal support was essential, both on economic and political grounds. I had commissioned the background research, which showed that the BC economy, then suffering an economic depression, needed "jump start" federal support, and that Expo 86 would be an excellent way to provide it. However, minister after minister in P&P spoke against it, while the all-important minister of finance, Marc Lalonde, stayed silent.

Instead of taking the obvious path to follow the consensus, Prime Minister Pierre Trudeau adjourned the decision, reserving judgment, which I took as a signal to come to brief him. I called his office for an appointment and was quickly received. Leveraging the trust I had earned as a deputy minister in his government and then as his principal secretary (chief of staff), I argued that the federal government had a responsibility to assist provinces suffering serious economic problems, as British Columbia most certainly was. I also told him that if we didn't support Expo, all the efforts under way to rebuild the federal Liberal Party in the province would be wasted. We would have lost all credibility, both with party members and the general public. Further, if we did not deliver, my capacity to be effective as the cabinet's key interlocutor on BC files would be finished. British Columbians would no longer see me as having leverage in Ottawa. And it would be hard to persuade them that the Trudeau government was governing for all of Canada, including our Pacific province.

National unity was always a key concern for Trudeau and so was economic fairness; the fate of the Liberal Party in British Columbia was admittedly a lower priority. The prime minister thanked me for my comments without betraying a sense of his own view.

At a subsequent committee meeting of the inner cabinet, I was gearing up to continue my arguments, when Trudeau said he didn't see a need for further discussion and that unless there was some new objection, he had reviewed the issues and decided it was in the national interest to support Expo 86. The response was stunned silence. My first reaction was one of considerable relief followed by a surging respect for Trudeau's national vision. It was a pivotal, to say nothing of an incredibly dramatic and emotional, moment.

Trudeau's decision allowed the negotiations with British Columbia to proceed, and on 1 April 1982, we announced that as its main contribution to the fair, the federal government had committed $134 million to building a convention centre and cruise ship facility in Vancouver's inner harbour to serve as the Canadian host pavilion. The Canada Place structure situated on the waterfront, with its distinctive five sails, is now an iconic image of Vancouver, as well as an enduring symbol of the federal presence in the province. These achievements demonstrated to successive BC governments, and to the BC public generally, that there was more to be gained by working co-operatively with Ottawa than maintaining a hostile attitude.

Throughout my political career – one spent shuttling between Vancouver and Ottawa, which often seemed to be on two different planets – I was a persistent advocate for British Columbia's interests. From my 1963 debut in Ottawa as a young executive assistant to northern affairs and national resources minister Arthur Laing to my 2007 retirement from the Senate at age seventy-five, and not least during my service in cabinet under two prime ministers, my key mission has been to ensure my province's realities, perspectives, and priorities were known and included in national policy. There were, of course, many facets to this work. A major one has been to build relationships for Canada in the Asia Pacific region and to see to the adoption of policies facilitating those connections. No one has had to persuade me of Asia's economic importance both to my own province and to Canada as a whole. British Columbia's location as Canada's Asia Pacific gateway and its economic interests prompted an enduring fascination, which began in the late 1950s when I came to understand Japan's importance as a customer for our natural resources. China came into focus after Canada's exchange of diplomatic recognition in October 1970.

I played a minor role in the opening of Canada's relations with the People's Republic of China and visited the country the following year as part of Canada's first official delegation. We were received by none other than

Premier Zhou Enlai. I had been well aware of Zhou's stature in China and his reputation as a brilliant administrator, but what most struck me as I shook hands with the somewhat gaunt man, a foot shorter than myself and old enough to be my father, was the intensity of his penetrating focus as his eyes locked with mine. I felt he was studying me. Later, I mentioned this to the head of our delegation, industry minister Jean-Luc Pépin, and he told me he had made the same observation. During that groundbreaking visit, I saw a China vastly different from the one that exists today.

Over the years, I was to return many times as I worked to build the Canada-China relationship. A highlight of my time as president of the Canada China Business Council was the 1994 Team Canada mission, led by Prime Minister Jean Chrétien, which was a resounding success. At the time, it made Canada a leader in Western relations with China. At Chrétien's request, I later worked to broaden political relations with China as well, creating the Canada-China Legislative Association. This furthered exchanges of views and sharing of experience between Canadian MPs and senators on the one hand, and members of China's National People's Congress on the other, building mutual trust and knowledge.

The human element in these relationships is fundamental to their success. In Asia, business is not merely transactional. Underlying any business deal is a personal connection that builds confidence in the other party. In building that relationship, be it at the individual or national level, an understanding of the other side's perspectives and needs is essential. It's important to be aware of differences of values or priorities that are based on historical and cultural factors, and not naively or imperiously presume that others can be remade in our own image.

Despite the significance of Asia, it is our relationship with the United States that will always be our most important, because of our shared geopolitical interests, cultural affinities, and economic synergies. From my university days, I have understood the importance of getting to know the United States; at a time when many top Canadian students headed to Britain or France for graduate studies, I chose American universities for my master's and doctoral work. This afforded me a deeper understanding of the American legal and political systems, and their role in facilitating the exercise of US economic and political power globally.

Resources are a focal point of the Canada-US relationship, and as a British Columbian, it was only natural that I became interested in these issues early in my career. My work on the Columbia River Treaty and in the mining sector was an eye-opener. During my doctoral studies at Berkeley, I became familiar with the US government's 1952 Paley Commission report (*Resources for Freedom*), which focuses on gaining and maintaining access to the energy, minerals, and other resources that are the building blocks of a modern economy. This gave me a deeper understanding of the basis for US dominance in the Canadian oil and gas industry and the importance of US capital in resource development. While serving as deputy minister of energy, mines and resources (EMR) during the international oil crisis of the early 1970s, I advocated the creation of Petro-Canada and other measures to increase Canadians' participation and to elevate our role in our own resource industries.

Because of my energy policy initiatives, I became known as an economic nationalist. Perhaps paradoxically, I have been a continentalist on matters pertaining to trade. A growing awareness of Mexico, its historical struggle to avoid domination by the United States, and its enormous economic potential led to my involvement in trilateral organizations. I developed a strong belief in the possibilities of a trilateral North American community, one that would be better equipped to face global challenges than any of its members individually.

Canada's relationship with Indigenous Peoples has been another enduring focus of mine. Advancing the unfinished process of decolonization and reconciliation has been an abiding priority. My work as a young lawyer in the field of resource development had exposed me to the racism, dispossession, and marginalization Indigenous Peoples faced in my province and in the country at large. Working as executive assistant to Arthur Laing in the early 1960s opened my eyes still further. Laing had a great deal of interest in, and empathy for, Indigenous individuals and Peoples that were at odds with the prejudicial attitudes of the time. He encouraged my own interest and provided opportunities to speak with Indigenous people in the North. From them, I learned how resource development in their homelands, conducted without regard for their views or interests, had been deeply detrimental. In the early 1970s, as deputy minister of EMR, I pushed for the creation of the Mackenzie

Valley Pipeline Inquiry, suggesting the appointment of Tom Berger as its head. This marked the first time that Indigenous people in Canada were consulted about resource development. A decade later, as a member of the Senate, I served on the special joint committee on repatriating the constitution and was among those strongly arguing for the constitutional entrenchment of Aboriginal rights.

First Nations in British Columbia have led the way in asserting their rights and in taking steps to build their economies and regain political autonomy. In Ottawa, I acted in an advocacy capacity, whether securing funding for Indigenous-led economic development initiatives or ensuring passage through the Senate of key legislation. As a member of the Paul Martin government, I worked on what came to be known as the Kelowna Accord, which was one of Prime Minister Martin's highest priorities. Had it not been killed by the Harper government, for purely political reasons, it would have brought huge and tangible benefits to Indigenous people and been a highly significant advance for the process of reconciliation. The $5.1 billion initiative's objectives were to significantly reduce poverty and bring advances in education, health, housing, and access to clean water for Indigenous people. The programs were to be managed by Indigenous communities. The Kelowna Accord was to be another step away from the Indian Act.

To be frank, despite all the positive changes I have witnessed, Indigenous people have yet to be fully accepted as partners in building Canadian society. Of course, this is true across Canada, and not only in my home province. Public awareness continues to lag. In 2015, after hearing heartbreaking testimony that was widely reported in the media, the Truth and Reconciliation Commission published a six-volume report on the horrors experienced by Indigenous children at residential schools. But it took the discovery in 2021 of what appear to be the unmarked graves of 215 children in Kamloops for the enormity of Canada's assimilationist residential school policy to hit home to the broader Canadian public. Similar discoveries have been made in several other communities. As Canadians come to learn a more accurate version of their history, old prejudices are giving way to empathy, respect, and a growing acceptance of First Nations rights as articulated by the courts.

The Senate of Canada was my political home for more than three decades. During that time, I saw just how important a role is played by the much-maligned upper house of Parliament. Created in part to ensure that regional interests and minorities had a strong voice in government, it has evolved into a critical vehicle for even broader inclusion and diversity, both regional and demographic. As a British Columbian, however, I was keenly aware of how underrepresented my province was, and continues to be, in the Senate, our 6 seats disproportionately low. Throughout my service, an abiding priority was to obtain fairer and more appropriate representation.

In the Senate and throughout my career, I have been incredibly fortunate to have been able to work with many, many people who were no less devoted than I feel I have been to this nation and to the welfare of its citizens. Many of them are mentioned in these pages, not least prime ministers Paul Martin and Jean Chrétien; my early political mentors Arthur Laing and Paul Martin Sr; and extraordinary civil servants Michael Pitfield and Gordon Robertson.

No one, however, is a more important part of my story than Pierre Elliott Trudeau. He was the right leader for the times, both at home and abroad, meeting the challenge of Quebec separatism, patriating the constitution, and leading the international community in accepting the reality of China under communist leadership. Our professional relationship began in 1970, and we worked closely for many years. As chief of staff to Trudeau, and later, when I served in his cabinet, I found a leader passionate for national unity, social justice, and world peace. He ranged from ultimate idealist to cold pragmatist, but he always cared, and he expected the best from everyone.

He demanded no less of himself. His own work habits were excellent – he was systematic and very good at time management – and he was always on top of his files. At all our sessions, he demonstrated that he'd done his homework. His was an inquiring and penetrating mind. He expected that anyone meeting with him would be as prepared as he was, and he was unforgiving if he found that was not the case.

There were different facets to his personality, as with all of us, but he was basically someone who kept his distance from people until he was comfortable with them, and then he was forthright, even aggressive, in engaging. He would hold you to account for everything you said and did. When he went on the attack, rather than engage with his adversary's statement on its surface, he would home in on its underlying premise. This was his practice particularly with media "inquisitors," and it left many not knowing what had hit them.

In Ottawa, Trudeau had a small circle of personal friends, mostly fellow Quebecers like Jean Marchand, Gérard Pelletier, and Sen. Jacques Hébert, all of whom he had known in Montreal. But in his capacity as prime minister, he had no friends as such; rather than engage in any form of cronyism, he sought out those with talent and the ability to get things done. I certainly would never describe myself as a personal friend of Trudeau's while he was in office; afterward, however, when we travelled together in the late 1980s and early 1990s, to Pakistan, China, South and Central America, Indonesia, South Africa, Namibia, and Ethiopia, we grew closer. Travelling with Trudeau opened many doors. Those trips were fascinating not only for the remote places we saw and experienced and the incredible people we met, not least Nelson Mandela, but also for the opportunity to gain further insights into Trudeau himself and into some past events.

In 1996, a German artist presented Trudeau with four copies of a lithograph showing the same image of his face repeating in squares of many, many colours. Trudeau offered me one of the copies, saying, "Would you like this as a memento between us, and what would you like me to write?" And for reasons that encapsulate what I thought of him, I just suddenly said, "Please write, 'A man with many faces but one reality.'" He said, "That's very good." And that's what he wrote. That was my instinctive encapsulation of a lifetime of experience with him.

Once when we were in Asia, Trudeau said, in a quiet and reflective voice: "Do their leaders dream for their country and its people or only for themselves and their power?" There is no doubt that Pierre Trudeau's dream was for a better Canada, one of optimism, personal security, fairness to all, both diverse in makeup and united in purpose at home and abroad. It has been my dream, too, the North Star guiding my work.

While some of the episodes I relate in these pages took place decades ago, recounting them can help succeeding generations understand how we have arrived where we are now. The battles fought, decisions made, and policies implemented were unique to their period, but most of the fundamental problems and issues that were being addressed remain as current as today's headlines. To name a few: moving away from a colonial relationship with Indigenous Peoples, navigating Canada-China relations, navigating Canada's all-important relationship with the United States, assuring economic security for the nation and its citizens, defending Canada's sovereignty, and debating the future of the Senate. As William Faulkner wrote, "The past is never dead, it's not even past."

A theme that runs through this book is inclusion, an ongoing challenge for Canada. In spite of considerable progress, members of minorities, and especially racialized people, remain underrepresented in the highest echelons of policy-making and politics. I came of age in western Canada at a time when British Imperial culture was predominant and Jews were very much the "other." Members of my community faced barriers of various sorts. While today Canadian Jews are full participants in public life, I remain sensitive to the fact that Canada has yet to be a place of fairness and opportunity for all.

On a national scale, it remains essential for Canada's federal system to accommodate regional diversity and perspectives. In representing British Columbia in Ottawa, my goal was not only to ensure that the province received its due but also to help build a stronger, more inclusive nation, one that reflected the interests and aspirations of all Canadians.

This memoir, then, is not merely about my personal journey and accomplishments. More significantly, it is a reflection on events and people whose impact is still felt, and on the issues and continuing challenges – provincial, national, and international – that remain at the centre of Canadian life.

1 Becoming a British Columbian

LIKE SO MANY British Columbians, I was born elsewhere.

In my case, it was just on the other side of the mountains, in Calgary. My parents had each arrived in Alberta in the first decade of the twentieth century, as young children brought by their own parents from Eastern Europe. Their families came to Canada not only for the economic opportunity but also to escape anti-Semitic pogroms.

My paternal grandfather, born Gershon Zelig Arenstein or Arnstein, came to Canada from Ukraine just after the turn of the twentieth century, and then brought over my grandmother, Chava Sarah, née Kanefsky (known as Eva, once she was in Canada). According to the story I heard growing up – and I don't know whether this is fact or myth – he was originally from Vienna, but after his older brother had become the Kyiv manager of the Vienna-to-Kyiv railway, my grandfather went along with him to Ukraine. There, he had met and married my grandmother, who was from the Poltava area. Not long after his arrival in Canada, my grandfather anglicized the family name to Austin. He declared that his ancestors had taken a German name when they had lived in a German-speaking country, and now that he was in an English-speaking country, it was time for an English name. He also started going by the first name Jacob. On 5 October 1908, in Calgary, probably at the first opportunity, he naturalized himself and his family as British subjects; Canadian citizenship per se did not yet exist. This reflected his adamant desire to leave Europe behind.

I did not meet either of my paternal grandparents.[1] My grandfather died in July 1914. He had owned a general store in what is now the Bridgeland area of Calgary, as well as some other real estate. With the start of the First World War a couple of months after his death, the real estate market collapsed just as his assets were being liquidated. The family's economic fortunes tumbled. My father, Morris, finished high school and then worked, mainly as a truck driver, to help support his mother and three younger siblings. Eventually, he went into the fruit wholesale business, with a partner. Although my father had sought to enlist during the First World War, he had been rejected on compassionate grounds. At that point, he already had an older brother, David, serving overseas, and his eldest brother, Aaron, was away serving in the North West Mounted Police. My father was told to stay in Alberta to support his family. My grandmother died in 1931.

My mother's family hailed from the Kishinev area of Bessarabia (present-day Chişinău, Moldova). My grandfather Joseph Chetner, a religious scholar, arrived in Calgary in 1907, with my grandmother Fanny and their six children. My mother, Clara Edith Chetner, was the youngest. The Chetner family went to homestead near Sibbald, in southeastern Alberta close to the Saskatchewan border, on the Montefiore Colony there.[2] These were Jewish agricultural communities named for Sir Moses Montefiore (1784–1885), a Jewish-British philanthropist who helped Jews leave the pogroms of Eastern Europe to settle in other countries.

The Chetners were not successful as farmers. The land was dry and stony, and the fact that they arrived without any serious farming experience presumably did not help.[3] So they moved back to Calgary, opened businesses, and became active in the city's small Jewish community. My mother was an elementary schoolteacher, but only taught for a few years. In those days, female teachers were expected to resign once they married.

My parents wed in May 1931. I was born just a little more than nine months later, on 2 March 1932. They named me Jacob, after my paternal grandfather, in keeping with the Eastern European Jewish custom of naming children after deceased relatives, but I was always called Jack. My younger sisters, Eva and Josephine, were also named for our grandparents. I do not have a middle name. (I used to tell my own children that my parents were too poor to afford one.)

I would like to be able to say that I had a carefree childhood, but the truth is much harsher. Times were tough for our family during the Depression, as they were for many others. Before I was born, my father lost the fruit wholesale that he owned, I think because his customers couldn't pay him what they owed. He found some work at a different fruit wholesale, but there was not much money to be made. We ended up on welfare for a period of time, living in a tenement called the Commercial Block on 7th Avenue, sharing a bathroom with several other families. Although we were never actually hungry, I grew up drinking buttermilk we bought at the Union Dairy and eating boiled onions as well as oatmeal, the cheapest foods available. I am still fond of buttermilk.

It was during those difficult years that my mother instilled in me a love of reading. From the time I was about three or four years old, she would take me to the Carnegie public library and we would borrow books.

When I was about five, my father had a serious accident. As he jumped off a loading dock, a truck backed up, pinning him and leaving him with a broken pelvis, among other injuries. He wasn't expected to live, and then he wasn't expected to walk. After a long stay at the Calgary General Hospital, he finally came home. He went on to live to age ninety-two, but always walked with a cane.

Following the accident, he needed to find a job where he could sit down a lot. He was able to buy a small corner store, the North Star Grocery, at 940 2nd Avenue NW, in Sunnyside, north of the Bow River.[4] The grocery, which at that point had little inventory and was derelict, was run by an older woman who was ready to sell it. I believe my father made an arrangement to take over the store and pay out the purchase price by instalments. He obtained fruit and grocery inventory on credit and trust, as he was already well known in that industry, as was his accident. I attribute the store's success to hard work and the advent of the Second World War, which made supplies hard to get. Scarcity made income more secure as everything sold out almost immediately.

At first, we lived in one room in the back of the store. After a while, we were able to move to an apartment upstairs. Much later, my father built a house across the street.

Then another family tragedy struck. My mother was diagnosed with breast cancer. She died in 1946, when I was fourteen.

If my mother's legacy was her love of learning, my father's was his optimism. He had what can only be described as a difficult life. Yet, he met his disappointments with courage, and this left a profound impression.

I grew up working in the North Star Grocery, making deliveries, serving people in the store, and, when asked for credit, appraising their integrity as best I could. It was a hands-on education in the realities of a small business that would serve me well. Among the many skills I retain from those days is an ability to judge the ripeness of melons. Perhaps more importantly, I learned a lot about the behaviour of people.

Sunnyside was essentially settled by Scots, who hailed from the Glasgow shipyards and were brought over to work in the CPR repair shops in another Calgary district called Ogden. Consequently, I learned something of Scottish culture, history, and music. I also learned that the "sassanach"⁵ were not favoured people.

In my latter teenage years, I would run home every day at lunchtime, down North Hill from Crescent Heights High School, in order to allow my father to take a lunch break, and then run back up the hill to return to school. This served as my training for cross-country running, in which I competed in high school. I also somehow found time to play on the badminton team and once got as far as the Alberta junior semifinals. The championships were held at the Glencoe Club, which didn't accept Jewish members at that time, although no one stopped me from playing in the tournament.

While I was conscious of the existence of anti-Semitism in Canada – and of course was aware of the Holocaust – I did not generally encounter prejudice in my own day-to-day life. We were one of only a handful of Jewish families north of the Bow River at that time, and I was one of only three Jewish kids at our high school. I don't remember any unpleasant incidents, either at school or in our neighbourhood, where our store brought us into contact with a large number of area residents. This was the heyday of Social Credit in Alberta, whose unorthodox ideas about monetary policy were rooted in some rather toxic prejudices about supposed international Jewish banking conspiracies (the latter beliefs, at least, were renounced by those who came to power). Whatever our customers and neighbours thought of Social Credit and its founding ideology, it would have been hard to connect the struggling Jewish family they knew with international high finance. Some of our customers, who were mainly evangelical Protestants, seemed to want to try to save our souls; however, their interest was expressed kindly.

All to say that I grew up as part of the larger community, but also as part of a small Jewish community. While I was aware of being a member of a minority, I did not regard that as a problem. My upbringing did not leave me seeing identity as a zero-sum game; we were fully integrated, but not assimilated.

When I was not busy in the store, I read voraciously. At the Carnegie library, I found a treasure trove of insights addressing the unformed concerns of my youth, concerns that I can see now were rooted in our family's vulnerability and threats of all kinds that seemed imminent as the Second World War raged.

Among the most significant influences on me were the books of Upton Sinclair, an American writer of novels based on tales of social justice or the lack of it. *The Grapes of Wrath* by John Steinbeck also made an indelible mark, as did the music and personal story of Paul Robeson.

I wondered who had the power over our lives, to make or break us. What was the role of money and its relationship to power? How was wealth created? What determined how it was distributed? What was the role of government?

My interest in these questions only grew over time.

I did not want to spend my life working in the grocery store, nor was that what my father wanted for me. It was obvious that education held the key to other opportunities.[6]

Fortunately, I was a well-performing student. My teachers at Crescent Heights took an interest in me and encouraged my academic ambitions. In particular, I recall Mr Florentine, who taught history and social studies. I also recall Aylmer Liesemer, the teacher who led the Young CCF Club and was himself a former member of the Alberta legislature. While pursuit of social security and fairness was the goal presented to me, I found a strong atmosphere of mind control and pressure for conformity in the club's operations and communications. From an early age, I have rejected others' attempts to control me without rational debate. My increasing discomfort led to my departure from the Young CCF after a few months.

When the time came for university, I had a decision to make.

While in high school, I had read a story about the University of Chicago, its educational innovations, and its famous president and then chancellor Robert Maynard Hutchins. I was excited about the idea of going there. However, that dream came to a hard landing. Although my application was accepted and I was even offered a small scholarship, I did not have the money to attend.

The obvious thing for Calgarians in those days was to head north, to the University of Alberta in Edmonton, because at the time, post-secondary options in Calgary were limited. I did not relish the idea of harsh Edmonton winters. Moreover, I wanted to have a completely new experience and meet new people: most of my university-bound peers would be heading to Edmonton, so it seemed I would have been with a lot of the same people I had known for years. I talked things over with my cousin (and good friend) Harold Austin, who was in the same graduating class as I was, also at Crescent Heights. Together we decided to go to the University of British Columbia (UBC), in Vancouver. As it turned out, that was an excellent decision, and I congratulate the kids who made it.

When I arrived in Vancouver, enrolled in UBC's Bachelor of Arts program to study history and economics, I fell in love with the water and mountains, as so many people do. I concluded after just a few weeks in the city that I would make this my home. At no point after that did I ever consider moving back to Calgary, although I returned in the summers to work at Calgary Brewery washing bottles, cleaning tanks, and loading trucks, and to work in my dad's store. Harold and I roomed together for our first year at UBC and then went our separate ways.[7]

Once I was settled at UBC, a definite social pecking order emerged, certainly among the Jewish students, although I suspect it was not unique to them. I found my peers cliquey and some of the males a bit arrogant, dressing in expensive clothes and boasting about what cars their families had. While I did not face any discrimination on account of being Jewish, I did feel there was discrimination on the basis of wealth. Once people saw I was a strong student, I suddenly became more acceptable.

I wish I could provide a better picture of what Vancouver was like in the early 1950s, but my awareness of the city beyond the UBC campus was limited. My world was narrowly focused. I took my academic work seriously, and my social life was also based on campus. For sport, badminton was my passion.

I first dated and then, in 1953, married a fellow UBC student, Sheila Toban, whose family owned a chain of shoe stores and was prominent in Vancouver's Jewish community. Sheila consistently supported my educational and professional ambitions. She had been inclined to set aside the completion of her Bachelor of Social Work once we were married, but I in turn encouraged her to complete it, which she did. We would go on to have three daughters, Edith (Edie), Sharon (Shari), and Barbara, before deciding to part in the early 1970s.

In November 1976, I met Natalie Veiner Freeman, who was divorced with two teenage children, Richard and Jody. Originally from Medicine Hat, Alberta, she by then had been living in Vancouver for many years. She had an MA in political philosophy from UBC and had spent a year in doctoral studies at the University of California, then worked as a lecturer at UBC and as academic director at Antioch College's Cold Mountain Institute in Vancouver. I was immediately dazzled by Natalie's charisma and brilliance. We married in 1978. Over the ensuing decades, we learned to weave our challenging lives together into an enduring relationship. Independent and self-reliant, Natalie has followed her own passions as a successful businesswoman, writer, and traveller. I owe her a great deal for her support, insight, and companionship in public and, more importantly, in private life.

The Jewish community in Alberta was small, and it turned out that our fathers had been acquainted: as a truck driver, my father would pick up cattle from Natalie's father's cattle ranch to bring to the stockyards in Calgary. In fact, though, just about everybody knew Harry Veiner, a larger-than-life character who later served as mayor of Medicine Hat for twenty-two years and had several successful businesses. His mission was to make his town an attractive place in which to do business, and he promoted it around the world.

When I entered UBC, I had not been thinking of law. My great interests were history and economics. At some early point in my university education, I came to the realization that anyone who sought to understand a society's values and priorities and where its power resided needed to understand its law. One of my roommates was a law student. I started reading his casebooks, found them interesting, and I thought that law did not look so hard. After two years at UBC, I was accepted into the university's law school for the fall of 1952.

Studying law was a pivotal experience for me. It opened up an understanding of how society operated at the governance level through constitutional and administrative law, and how it operated in the wealth sphere through contracts, property law, and corporate law. I came to recognize that, among other things, law was the expression of a society's evolving understanding of its own norms.

I took to law like a duck to water. The Socratic method of teaching[8] was far more engaging than merely sitting down for lectures and note-taking. A newly constructed building for the law school had opened a year or so earlier, replacing the wartime huts that originally housed the faculty. Ours was a small class of about seventy students (only three of them were women, though in those days nobody found that startling). We were in the unenviable position of following an unusually strong class the year before us – it included two Rhodes Scholars – so by comparison our group was considered dull.

I developed an interest in an academic career and discussed this with some of my professors, who were encouraging. A particularly important mentor was Malcolm MacIntyre, a Harvard graduate who taught torts. He went out of his way to invite me to his office for chats and to his home for tea. I also got to know his son Jim, who later became a UBC law professor himself. Dean George Curtis also took an interest in me after I told him I was thinking of an academic career.

I finished at the top of my class in my first year. This surprised me, and I think it surprised everybody else. I ranked second in my second year and in the top five in my third year, 1955, probably not higher because of the time I spent serving as editor of ubc *Legal Notes*, as the law school's academic journal was then called.

I applied to Harvard University to do a master's degree in law (LLM) for the following year, 1955–56. My acceptance included two scholarships. Naturally, I was very excited.

In the spring of 1955, I was in the library studying for my final exams when Dean Curtis's secretary walked in, looking for me. The dean wanted to see me. I was instructed to accompany her back to his office. This was not a common occurrence, and I asked her why. She said she had no idea.

Dean Curtis told me there was a change of plan concerning my LLM. He had just been invited to teach at Harvard that fall to replace another visiting professor who had cancelled. He said he had agreed. It was already too late to find someone to replace him at ubc, and given that I had expressed an interest in teaching law, he had decided to have me teach his courses. Harvard would defer my acceptance and scholarships for one year. It was a done deal. It was also a fabulous opportunity. All I could say was, "Thank you very much."

So, I leapt from law student to law lecturer. I taught Dean Curtis's contracts course to the first-year law class and two other courses to the second-year law class, because there also were adjunct professors (practising lawyers) who were unavailable that year. I was younger than many of my students, so to establish my credentials, I opened my first lecture by pointing out that I had a law degree and they didn't.

It proved a remarkable year for me that led to new opportunities.

In the fall of 1955, the president of the university, Norman MacKenzie, suggested that he and I publish an article together on the law of the sea. He had previously taught international law. I drafted the article, and he edited it. We published it as one of the occasional pamphlets then issued by the university. He was delighted with our collaboration, as of course was I. It was not often that the youngest faculty member shared author-ship with the president of the university.

Another occasion brought me back to the president's office in the spring of 1956. President MacKenzie called me in to introduce me to General Andrew McNaughton, a well-known figure of the day. McNaughton had been a top Canadian general during the Second World War and had briefly become the unelected defence minister for Canada. At the time of our meeting, he was the Canadian co-chair of the International Joint Commission, a bilateral body with the United States set up under the Boundary Waters Treaty of 1909, designed to regulate and adjudicate on issues dealing with the management of the Great Lakes and rivers crossing the international boundary.

An issue before the commission at that time involved the Columbia River, which has its sources on the BC side of the Rockies, flowing first to the northwest, then turning south and crossing into Washington State and then flowing along the Washington-Oregon border into the Pacific. The Grand Coulee hydroelectric dam had already been built in Washington, in the 1930s, in violation of the Oregon Treaty of 1846, which had accorded the British (and therefore, in time, Canadians) the right to navigate the river from its headwaters all the way to the ocean. The Americans were interested in having Canada build dams on our side of the border for the purpose of flood control. In 1948, the Vanport Flood had washed out a town north of Portland, taking dozens of lives and causing property losses in the tens of millions of dollars. But what the Americans were prepared to pay for flood control was almost nothing.

General McNaughton was an engineer, and he and his team thought that flood control was worth a lot of money. More than that, evening out the flow of water through Grand Coulee and other dams would allow the Americans to produce much more power without having to invest any capital to build anything new. But true to form, the Americans were tough negotiators, and McNaughton was looking for some leverage. At our meeting, he told me he wanted a legal opinion on whether Canada could divert the Columbia into the Fraser-Thompson system. My first question was as to whether that was even possible. And he replied in the affirmative, that there was only a 145-kilometre distance between the two systems and that the Columbia was much higher; technically, he said, it would be easy enough to do.

I have to confess that in those days, it did not occur to me to ask about the environmental advisability of such a move, or what impact it might have on the Indigenous and other communities along the rivers, or on the salmon that inhabited those rivers. I simply delved into the legal question. In any case, though, I think McNaughton just wanted to hold up his end of some hardball negotiations with the Americans. Still, if Canada could reduce the flow of the Columbia River and divert it into the Fraser-Thompson system, and it was legal to do so under international law, who could judge how far Canada would really go?

I did my research and wrote a legal opinion for McNaughton that said, in effect, yes, Canada as the upstream riparian had every right to construct such a diversion. I used the same arguments that the US government had used with Mexico concerning the Colorado River, which at one time flowed into Mexico. The United States argued that as the upstream riparian, it could take all the water. Later, the Americans concluded a treaty with Mexico allowing the Mexicans some water flow but in fact they retained almost all of it.

In the summer of 1956, I travelled to Europe for the first time, after receiving a fellowship to study for a month at The Hague Academy of International Law. I also visited Dubrovnik, where I was a delegate to a conference of the International Law Association. Sheila and I bought rail passes, and we visited Italy and France. We chose not to visit Germany. The North Star Grocery and my early years in Calgary felt very far away.

That fall, I began my studies at Harvard accompanied by Sheila, who enrolled at Boston University for her Master of Social Work. The legal opinion I had written for General McNaughton served as the starting point for what became my master's thesis on the international law of international rivers, which was published, in abbreviated form, in the September 1959 *Canadian Bar Review*, the leading law journal of that time.

While at Harvard, I was offered a position with a significant Washington law firm whose practice included representing international governments and large business corporations and staffing the legal membership of congressional committees. It was a fork in the road. I debated briefly but deeply about whether to accept the offer, which would have led to becoming an American, or return to Vancouver and the Canadian path. I discovered I was a passionate Canadian and never looked back.

Dean Curtis had told me that if I wanted to come back to teach at UBC, there would be a place for me on the law faculty. I told him that while I would be happy to teach, I also wanted to be called to the Bar. That meant I needed to article.

I received a call from Nathan Nemetz QC when I was still at Harvard. He was a prominent labour lawyer in Vancouver, about twenty years older than I was. He said Dean Curtis had given him my name. Nemetz offered me an articling position, and I accepted, though I informed him that my intention was to teach afterward. "That's what George Curtis says, but I don't think you will," he replied.

I did not think too hard about the referral at the time, but given the prejudices of the day, Dean Curtis might have been concerned I would not find a suitable position, so took it upon himself to help me out by contacting Nemetz, who also was Jewish.

In 1957–58, I articled with Nemetz in the afternoons. In the mornings, I taught two classes at UBC law school, because as it turned out Dean Curtis was away again that year.

In my third year at law school, I had taken the foreign service entrance exams, along with my classmates Ted Lee and Maurice Copithorne. All three of us were accepted. Lee and Copithorne went on to become ambassadors and to hold other important posts. I asked for and received a deferment to teach law at UBC as requested by Dean Curtis, and then requested a second deferment, also granted, to attend Harvard Law School. I asked for a third deferment to remain at UBC to teach law in 1957–58 and be called to the British Columbia Bar. That, too, was accepted. After three deferments, with every courtesy given to me by external affairs, I finally decided in the summer of 1958 to stay in Vancouver and enter the practice of law.

Nathan Nemetz, who went on to become chief justice of British Columbia and also chancellor of UBC, was not one to offer pearls of wisdom. Instead, he taught by example, and I learned a great deal just by watching him. Nemetz was probably the most effective labour negotiator in the province at that time, known for his fairness as well as his concern for civil rights. He also seemed to know everyone in the Vancouver business community. He was one of the most competent small *p* political people I've ever met, and over the years, I've met quite a few.

In 1958, I was called to the Bar, and from then on we practised law together. Nemetz had a lot of confidence in me and assigned me big files very quickly. His introduction of me to the broader BC business community was invaluable. I continued to learn a great deal and I met a lot of people.

While I practised commercial law, my first three or four years included a court practice that saw me working with several of BC's most prominent lawyers as junior to senior counsel. One eminent lawyer with whom I worked was Sen. John Wallace de Beque Farris. Farris was a great storyteller. One evening at his home, after a successful appeal, he told me that when he was a young counsel he lost cases he should have won and when he became senior counsel he won cases he should have lost, so justice was served in the end. I have always come back to reflect on the life's lesson expressed there.

During those years, I developed an interest in resources law and started practising in that area, with Nemetz's blessing. Although he was skeptical of my first small client's ability to pay, he gave me the go-ahead to take the risk. As it turned out, his concern proved unfounded and the work led to other opportunities. I became a very successful lawyer specializing in resources law and the corporate and securities law that accompanied it. Before long, I had major clients like Placer Development and International Minerals and Chemicals (IMC), as well as many smaller ones.

We brought on board a third partner, Norma Christie, to specialize in litigation. Originally an Albertan, she had served in London as a senior officer in the women's navy during the Second World War. When the war was over, she was hired as an executive assistant to Vincent Massey, who was at the time high commissioner for Canada in London. Then she had been one of the stars of that remarkably strong UBC law class the year ahead of mine. Subsequently, we were joined in the partnership by John Bruk. Of Croatian background, he had escaped from Communist Yugoslavia in his late teens. At UBC law school, he had been a student of mine. A year later, David Huberman joined the firm as an articling student. He went on to serve as a professor at the UBC law school before practising corporate and tax law.

The law firm of Nemetz, Austin, Christie and Bruk was an exciting place to work. We had a varied and successful practice. It was to end in late 1963, with the appointment of Nathan Nemetz QC to the Supreme Court of British Columbia and my decision to remain in Ottawa as a member of the team negotiating the Columbia River Treaty. (More on that to come.)

Thus began my education, one that continues to this day. And thus began my life as a British Columbian.

2 The Influence of Art Laing

THE ARTHUR LAING BRIDGE links Vancouver and Sea Island, the site of the city's airport. Before Laing became synonymous with a bridge, he was my first political mentor, and someone who taught me a great deal about the human dimension of politics.

I first met Laing in 1959, when he attended a lecture I gave to the Vancouver chapter of the Canadian Institute of International Affairs. The institute had awarded me a Newton Rowell fellowship to help fund my master's degree at Harvard, and in return, I was to give a series of talks to four of their chapters in western Canada. The topic I had chosen was the Treaty of Rome, which created the European Economic Community, a forerunner of the European Union. After the lecture, Laing asked me what I thought were some remarkably astute and well-informed questions. (It turned out he was a regular reader of *Forbes*.) He must have liked my answers, because he then suggested we meet for lunch.

Superficially, at least, we did not have much in common.

I was a kid from Calgary, by then in my late twenties, with a master's degree in international law, practising natural resources law (or as we called it, "rocks and logs") in Vancouver with Nathan Nemetz. I was immersed in the world of ideas, and saw myself, perhaps, as headed for a career as a law professor or working in business law. Nemetz, an active member of the Liberal Party, had brought me along to party functions, where I met many of the key local Liberals of the day, not least James Sinclair, a long-time Liberal MP who had been a cabinet minister under Louis St-Laurent. I joined the Liberal Party in 1958, just as others were leaving in droves in the wake of that year's Conservative landslide. The party was a natural fit for me: I was neither a socialist nor a conservative, so what else would I be? But politics was not on my personal radar, certainly not in any serious way.

Laing, born on Sea Island to a family of Scots background, was three decades my senior. He had a wealth of practical experience, in business as well as in the political realm. After graduating from UBC with an agricultural science degree, he had worked as a manager for Buckerfield's, an agricultural supplies company. By the time we met, he had been active politically for many years, including as a federal MP and then in provincial politics as an MLA and BC Liberal Party leader. At that point, the Diefenbaker Progressive Conservatives commanded the federal scene, so it was not a great time to be a Liberal, and Laing was an unhappy man, though he was not one to complain. In Victoria, the Liberals had been swept into irrelevance by the Social Credit Party of W.A.C. Bennett. On top of that, Laing found himself on the outs with the local Liberal establishment of the day.

When we had lunch, I found him highly intelligent and deeply insightful, more conservative than myself but not unprogressive socially. That lunch set in motion events that were to change the course of my life, and shift my focus to public service. In retrospect, I became involved in politics the way many people do: by accident.

We kept in touch, and as the 1962 federal election approached, Laing called me. He was planning to run in Vancouver South and wanted me to be his campaign manager.

"Art, I've never run a campaign, I don't know anything about a campaign, you're crazy to ask me," I told him. Meanwhile, Nathan Nemetz tried to discourage me; many in the party establishment were trying to block Laing from getting the nomination. Nemetz was a supporter of his rival, Jack Nicholson. (As for James Sinclair, he was neither friend nor foe to Laing.) Quite a few people told me Laing was a has-been and a grouch. But I knew and liked him, and saw his depth. He was good at talking with what today would be called "real people" and had a reputation for straight talk. He also believed strongly in public policies that would reinforce small- and medium-sized enterprises, something I appreciated as the son of a corner store grocer.

For these reasons, although I had worked with Nicholson on a legal case, appearing with him at the Supreme Court of Canada, and got along well with him, I agreed to run Laing's campaign. Laing's electoral success had seemed improbable because of antipathy from local Liberals and especially given the Progressive Conservative incumbent

Ernie Broome's substantial majority in 1958. In the end, Laing not only won the nomination but the seat – by about 2,700 votes.

We had run a strong campaign, knocking on many doors and attracting a lot of attention with one particular gimmick. At the time, there was a popular tea marketed with the name The Tea that Dares to Be Known by Good Taste Alone. On small envelopes, we had printed, "The man who dares to be known by his good name alone." They bore a photo of Laing but not his name. Inside each envelope was a tea bag and a suggestion that the tea could be enjoyed while reading the Liberal campaign material we distributed along with it. I believe the tea bags significantly boosted Laing's cause. Nationally, the Progressive Conservatives were returned to office as a minority government.

In the winter of 1963, Laing called again to say a new election was imminent. He asked me to run his campaign once more. So I did. One event, a gathering held at our home in the Marpole neighbourhood, was particularly memorable. Laing made a short speech, standing on our flagstone fireplace so that he could be seen. When he had concluded, the voice of my daughter Edie, then almost five, could be heard asking her nearly three-year-old sister what Laing's first name was. Shari's reply – "Votefer" – elicited gales of laughter. In the April 1963 election, Art won by a much bigger margin – about 9,000 votes – than he had the previous year. Nationally, the Liberals were victorious but able to form only a minority government.

Prime Minister Lester B. Pearson appointed Laing to his cabinet as minister of northern affairs and national resources. Laing was thrilled with that portfolio.

The day of his appointment, Laing phoned to invite me to Ottawa as his executive assistant (a position that today is called chief of staff). I said, "What is that?" I had no idea what the role was, and like most British Columbians, had no intention or thought of ever going to Ottawa. Moreover, I had begun work on a doctorate, commuting to the University of California in Berkeley while still practising law in Vancouver, and had a young family.

However, there was an additional enticement. I had written my master's thesis on the international law of cross-boundary rivers, focusing on those crossing the Canada-US and US-Mexico borders. In the Diefenbaker period, Canada and the United States had begun negotiating the Columbia River Treaty, and although an initial treaty had been signed, further talks were needed before it could be ratified. I told Laing that if I could be involved in those negotiations as a legal adviser, I could justify coming to Ottawa and doing both jobs. Before long, I received a call from Paul Martin Sr, who had been named secretary of state for external affairs. He invited me to join his team, thus beginning another relationship that was formative for me. I agreed to go to Ottawa until the negotiations were over.

At one point in the discussions, I concluded that a US argument was sound, but accepting it would cost Canada $28 million in downstream benefits. During a break, I approached Martin and commented that the Americans had a good point. He replied, "Jack, I don't want to know that much." He never accepted the Americans' argument, and they eventually agreed to his offer of a compromise that left Canada with more than it deserved. I have never forgotten that lesson.

The treaty was ratified in 1964, but in June of that year I moved my family to Ottawa – I had been commuting to that point – where we stayed until the summer of 1965.

I told myself that I would return to my doctoral thesis in a couple of years. I never did.

A long-standing West Coast refrain is that while Vancouver is 3,000 miles from Ottawa, Ottawa is 30,000 miles from Vancouver. By April 1963, when I arrived in Ottawa, this essential truth had not changed. British Columbia's history in Confederation had been defined by isolation, federal indifference, and the domination of what political scientists today call the "Laurentian Consensus." Those who governed in Ottawa tended to see the western provinces as former colonies of Central Canada and not so much money makers as money losers. Canada's economic engine was Central Canada with its manufacturing, finance, forestry, and mining. Central Canada looked to the United States and Europe for its markets. There seemed to be no awareness at all that Canada was also a Pacific nation. Most of the time, the power brokers in Ottawa were oblivious to British Columbia's interests, and when they were aware of British Columbian perspectives, Central Canadian interests prevailed in any case.

British Columbians responded in kind. There was a widespread disdain for and resentment of what the distant elites were up to; in effect, the province cultivated its own feeling of alienation and seemed even to cherish its sense of isolation.

Of course, British Columbians were not the only Canadians who were feeling they were getting a raw deal. One of the first things I realized when I arrived in Ottawa was how little I knew about Quebec. I had some awareness of the repressive Duplessis years and the central role the Roman Catholic Church played there. But the Quiet Revolution under way at the time was a revelation to me – as was the deep sense of alienation felt by francophones who believed they had been equal partners in Confederation with English-speakers but were being treated as second-class citizens.

I had not heard much about these concerns in British Columbia, where the prism through which we viewed the country pitted east against west. And while anti-Quebec sentiments existed in other parts of the country, the prevailing attitude in British Columbia was simply indifference.

However, Quebec's dissatisfaction quickly came to my attention once I reached Ottawa, where it sometimes seemed that the province was the main topic of discussion: In July 1963, Pearson made good on an election promise to appoint a royal commission on bilingualism and biculturalism, putting these issues into the national spotlight. Among the commissioners was Jean Marchand, then a labour leader, who would before long enter federal politics and bring his friend and colleague Pierre Elliott Trudeau along with him.

By 1963, Premier W.A.C. Bennett, who had leveraged British Columbians' feelings of alienation for political gain and made fed-bashing into an art form, was in the process of redefining the federal-provincial relationship. He had caused the Diefenbaker government much consternation by rejecting their negotiation of the Columbia River Treaty. "Wacky" Bennett, as his detractors called him, was known for histrionics and had made a series of over-the-top declarations – for example, claiming all offshore jurisdiction for the province, from the low water mark halfway to Japan and suggesting that BC annex Yukon. Consequently, some people did not take him seriously, but at the very least he succeeded in getting attention, and in my view, his apparently erratic behaviour was in fact calculated. He was not merely a big talker: he expropriated BC Electric in order to proceed with the hydroelectric development he saw as essential to the province's economic growth. Although his assertion of provincial rights and BC interests as he saw them caused him to be viewed as a spoiler by those in Ottawa, he put British Columbia on the national agenda, which had the effect of empowering the province's federal ministers and caucus. This meant that Bennett and Laing found themselves as de facto allies, even though they did not particularly like each other.

I was lucky enough to also count Premier Bennett as a mentor. Keeping both Bennett and Laing as mentors was not easy. They were major political rivals, dating back to Laing's time in provincial politics, but, in fact, they had similar objectives for building British Columbia.

I had first met Bennett in 1961, in connection with the Peace River power development. One day, out of the blue, Nathan Nemetz told me to make plans to travel to Victoria, where I was to meet Premier Bennett on an important file. Next, I received a call from Bill Clancy, Bennett's chief assistant, who instructed me to rent a day room at the Empress Hotel in Victoria and order only ginger ale. (Bennett was famously a teetotaller.) When the premier arrived, he said that he wanted me to arrange a ten-year no-strike agreement, vital to control the costs of the Peace River project. This dam, later named for Bennett, was the major infrastructure project of its time and, unlike the projects that were to come on the Columbia, was entirely within provincial jurisdiction.

I replied, "Well, Premier Bennett, I'll start drafting the legislation right away."

To my surprise, he said, "I don't want legislation. Do you know what happened to Alcan at Kitimat? Rolling strikes, twenty-eight unions, one strike after another." In fact, both the unions and contractors used the lack of a comprehensive agreement to jack up costs and just about rendered that project uneconomic. What Bennett wanted from me was to figure out how to avoid history repeating itself. I went away to consider the problem, then wrote a legal opinion recommending that the contractors be grouped to form a single employer on the one side, and that unions also join together and bargain together on the other side, in order to be able to negotiate one comprehensive collective agreement. The proposal may sound obvious, but no one else seemed to have thought of it. As a result, BC Hydro created the Peace Power Constructors, and the government set up the Allied Hydro Council to bring together the unions, with their agreement. A ten-year no-strike, no-lockout collective agreement was signed in February 1962. Bennett was very pleased. I learned from him that the impossible is just a little bit harder.

In the Diefenbaker years, the Conservatives' senior BC minister Davie Fulton and Bennett were constantly at odds, quarrelling over jurisdiction and political credit for the Columbia River dam construction project. As an international waterway, the Columbia was federal jurisdiction, but Bennett came up with ways to claim provincial jurisdiction – though not so persuasively. Bennett seemed deeply suspicious of Fulton. I believe the premier feared Fulton was going to return to British Columbia and revive the provincial Conservative party as a serious rival to the Social Credit Party, popularly known as the Socreds.

Later, once the Liberals were in power in Ottawa, I occasionally served as a messenger between Paul Martin Sr and Premier Bennett as they forged a strong working relationship.

Martin wanted to get British Columbia onside in the Columbia River negotiations and was willing to see it BC's way, at least to a point; far from rigid, he was a "get things done" kind of guy. He saw the importance of renewing the bilateral relationship, and he asked me whether I knew Bennett. I told him I did. So, Martin asked me to introduce them. I contacted Bill Clancy and explained that Martin wanted to develop a direct relationship with Bennett so that they could move ahead jointly. Clancy signalled back that Bennett would take Martin's call. Bennett and Martin were two old pros, and they understood each other perfectly. In addition, Bennett seemed to appreciate that Martin had reached out.

Even though Bennett had considerably more strained relations with Laing – for instance, Bennett criticized Laing harshly and unfairly during the 1965 election campaign – the long-serving premier eventually came to appreciate his erstwhile rival. At Arthur Laing's tribute dinner in September 1974, when Prime Minister Pierre Trudeau announced the Ottawa-financed bridge over the North Fraser River at Hudson Street would be named in Laing's honour, Bennett, by then out of power, made a moving speech that has stayed with me about political rivals and friends and the greatness of British Columbia.

When I joined Laing as his executive assistant, a very different world opened up for me. In my two and a half years with him, I had the opportunity to travel around the North, to every part of British Columbia and western Canada, and even to the Soviet Arctic. I noticed how Laing talked to people, how he took an interest in their stories, and how he listened. Between the travelling and watching my mentor's interactions, an enormous education unfolded. For his part, Laing was a wonderful speaker. Long before it became fashionable, he spoke about the need for compassion in politics: he would talk about caring and compassion as the key to political responsibility.

There was a story that Laing liked to tell about his upbringing on Sea Island, a story I heard him repeat many times. His family was Presbyterian. The congregation they belonged to had a small church but couldn't afford a permanent minister. In those days, itinerant ministers would come from Scotland and elsewhere. Laing would recount when he was a boy of four or five, a minister from Scotland delivered a sermon, telling the congregation that if they sinned, the Lord would rain hellfire and brimstone down upon them, and they would be in great pain: "And you will cry out to the Lord, 'I dinno ken.' [I don't understand.] And the Lord will say to you, 'Well you ken noo.' [Well, you understand now.]" Laing's point was that he was raised in a denomination of Christianity with an unforgiving nature, but this was not the way society should be. He told this story to show where he came from and how politics had changed him over the years.

Caring and compassion were to be accorded to everyone. Through his travels around the province as a businessman and then while in provincial politics, Laing had become familiar with and open to the concerns of First Nations communities in British Columbia, particularly those on the coast and in Kamloops. While his jurisdiction as minister of northern affairs and national resources was limited to matters north of 60 degrees latitude insofar as Indigenous Peoples were concerned, he showed himself to be a passionate activist in reaching out in a respectful manner, with a view to including them as full participants in the political and economic development of the North.

Laing sought to advance the political evolution of Yukon and the Northwest Territories (which in those days included what is now Nunavut) and improve the social conditions of the First Nations and Inuit people there. He didn't have a lot of resources, but I watched and listened as he opened up dialogue. I had a socially conscious awareness before working with Laing, but it certainly expanded during that time. When Laing first became minister, deputy ministers were running Yukon and Northwest Territories from Ottawa. He worked to transfer authority and powers to territorial governments, appointing new commissioners who were required to be resident in their respective territories.

Laing also wanted to offer opportunities to First Nations people. That, and his belief in recognizing talent, led him to hire Len Marchand, a member of the Okanagan Indian Band, as an assistant. Marchand held a master's degree in forestry. He went on to his own distinguished parliamentary career: in 1968 becoming the first status Indian elected as a member of Parliament and in 1976 the first to be named to the federal cabinet. He later served in the Senate. Working with Marchand opened a window for me onto First Nations perspectives – and their humour. I have never forgotten his wry quip that when questions of European immigration to Canada arose, First Nations always had the wrong immigration policy.

One of the many things I learned during my travels in the North with Laing was that the Indigenous people who dealt with outsiders were not necessarily the people who were most important in their communities. They were the community members who happened to speak English.

Another lesson came when I first met Charlie Watt – many years later, we were to become colleagues in the Senate – who was then serving as a translator for his community of what was then Fort Chimo (now

Kuujjuaq), in northern Quebec. When Laing and I met with the elders, I noticed that after he would speak for several minutes, Watt would speak for only a few seconds when translating. Puzzled, I asked Watt about that. It turned out he was providing the elders with his own executive summary. "I told them that it is all bullshit," he replied. While I was taken aback by his frankness, I appreciated the lesson that Indigenous people resented politicians touching base just to serve their own political agendas, visits that all too often did not yield tangible results.

At the time, governments had yet to fully understand that it was essential to take Indigenous perspectives into account. Certainly, that was the case when the Lesage government of Quebec, under natural resources minister René Lévesque, called for the transfer of the Inuit residents in his province to provincial jurisdiction, as if the Inuit were just another jurisdictional issue rather than people who deserved a say in the matter. Laing and I succeeded in blocking this move on the grounds that such a transfer without the consent of the Inuit would be entirely illegitimate. Our stance was not only morally right but also a politically astute way to sidestep Quebec's request and defuse the situation. While Lévesque had no problem arguing with the federal government, it was much harder for him to argue against the democratic will of the people concerned.

In November 1964, Peter C. Newman wrote an article saying Art Laing was disappointing to Prime Minister Pearson and would be removed from cabinet. This story, published in the *Vancouver Sun*, came as an incredible blow to Laing. At my own initiative, I called Richard O'Hagan, a senior aide to Pearson. I told him if the story were true, Laing had no more use to the government, and as long as this perception hung over his head, Laing wouldn't be effective in British Columbia. I added that if the report was unfounded, it was essential for the prime minister to repudiate Newman's story at the earliest opportunity. I also asked Keith Davey, who was then national director of the Liberal Party and a senior party strategist, where the story had come from. Davey said he didn't know.

The next day, Pearson sent a statement to the *Vancouver Sun* bureau in the Parliamentary Press Gallery making it clear the Newman story about

Laing was a complete fabrication. He stated he continued to have confidence in his minister. O'Hagan also told reporters Pearson had called Laing "one of my most valued and esteemed colleagues."[1] At the end of the day, Laing had more credibility than he had started with. But the source of that story continued to be a mystery.

A decade or so later, I was having breakfast in Vancouver at the Bayshore Hotel, when Newman stopped by and introduced himself. He suggested we talk sometime. He followed up when we were both in Ottawa. When we met, I took the opportunity to ask him where he had got the Laing story. His response: Keith Davey!

I learned early on that in politics it's not only the opposition one has to worry about.

While both a sense of personal loyalty and my job description meant that I had Laing's back, he was more than capable of standing up for himself. Anyone who mistook the minister's kindness and consideration for weakness was in for a rude surprise. He believed strongly in doing what was right. Like any cabinet minister, Laing found himself at the centre of often-conflicting pressures from those seeking to have their interests served. For example, as the minister responsible for national parks, he came under heavy pressure because of his work to avoid over-commercialization. Laing felt strongly that national parks should not become merely large-scale commercial amusement centres. Park operators strenuously objected to their personal gain having been subordinated to public welfare. Another source of pressure arose from United States water interests wanting Laing to take an easygoing attitude toward the diversion of Canadian water to United States industry. At the time, there was an American proposal, known as the Parsons plan, to construct a transmission system to carry more than 120 million acre-feet of water annually from the Athabasca River for distribution throughout the United States. Laing opposed the project, because he considered fresh water to be Canada's most valuable and indispensable natural resource, and he believed Canada should not become a servant of the United States but rather its partner.

Laing's portfolio also put him on a collision course with certain provincial governments – not least that of his home province of British Columbia – seeking to extend their jurisdiction over natural resources in ways that encroached on the federal sphere. British Columbia in particular was claiming exclusive jurisdiction over offshore resources, apparently trying to take advantage of the minority government at the time. Laing took the national view and did not yield. He firmly believed these resources should be used by the national government for the benefit of all Canadians, and that giving in to provincial demands, while perhaps the easier path, would ultimately weaken and divide the country.

During my time with Art Laing, we criss-crossed the country and travelled extensively in the North. These trips afforded fascinating insights and opportunities to see a wide array of people and places. The most remarkable trip Laing and I made, however, was to the Soviet Arctic during the height of the Cold War, when the Iron Curtain was firmly in place. Of course, we were not unaware of the political context, and although the visit was hailed as a breakthrough in Canada-Soviet relations, our own objectives were primarily technical. The Soviets were far ahead of us in their development of their Arctic, and we felt there was much to be gained through scientific and technical exchanges.

Our invitation to the Soviet Union was the result of a chance encounter I had had with a Soviet diplomat at the Parliamentary Press Gallery's annual dinner in Ottawa. I had been invited by Gerald Waring, whose columns appeared in the *Vancouver Sun*. As fate had it, we found ourselves across the table from Vladimir Moltchanov, the first secretary of the Soviet embassy. Among other subjects, we chatted about the Soviet Arctic. I told him I thought it might be mutually advantageous for Canada and the Soviet Union, the world's leading Arctic nations, to exchange information about Arctic development. Moltchanov seemed highly receptive to the idea, but he was a diplomat, after all, so it was hard to know whether he was just being polite. I suggested we have lunch soon to talk further. In the meantime, of course, I informed External Affairs of our conversation and received the department's blessing to pursue the contact.

Several lunches later, Art Laing received an official invitation from the Soviet government. Waring later boasted that my ticket to the Press Gallery dinner was the best ten dollars he ever spent on account of the trip's modest contribution to decreasing Cold War tensions.

We departed from Ottawa on 16 May 1965. Art Laing led the delegation, and its other members, in addition to myself, included John Turner, later prime minister but then an MP and Laing's parliamentary secretary, and three senior civil servants. En route to the Soviet Union, we visited the United Kingdom and the Nordic countries to gather information about the development of resources, energy, transportation, and shipping facilities in the Arctic latitudes, and, in the Nordic countries, to discuss the role of the Sámi people in their economies.

On 25 May, we arrived in Moscow. Western visitors were not common in those days. We received red carpet treatment: chauffeured around in Zil limousines, taken to a performance at the Bolshoi Theatre, fed extremely well, and offered an array of strong alcoholic beverages.

We had a few days of background briefings from officials and academics in Moscow and Leningrad (as St Petersburg was then known) on such things as construction on permafrost. On 30 May we flew to Irkutsk in eastern Siberia, where we visited a hydroelectric station and an aluminum smelter. Our next stop was Bratsk, near Lake Baikal. We were the first Westerners to ever visit what was then the world's largest power dam. We discussed challenges around power transmission and construction of dams in discontinuous permafrost areas. Next, we went to the Tomponsky District of the Yakut Autonomous Soviet Socialist Republic (it didn't strike us as very autonomous, but it certainly was socialist). There we visited the coal mining community of Dzhebariki-Khaya and then continued to Yakutsk for a briefing about mineral resource development in eastern Siberia, discussions about the status of national minorities in the region, and visits to health and education facilities.

It was a serious working tour, but there were some lighter moments. In Yakutsk, we were hosted at a dinner given by the director of the Yakut branch of the Academy of Science. As was the custom at such gatherings, there was an exchange of toasts in the Yakut national drink, a fermented mare's milk served in special three-legged cups and made by a process that dated back to the days of Genghis Khan. It was incredibly fiery and foul-tasting. It got no farther than the tip of my tongue before I meekly asked for vodka instead. Fortunately, John Turner, who in Laing's absence that evening was the senior member of our group, was made of sterner stuff. It fell to him to make the formal response to the toast of friendship, after which he downed about three ounces of the milk without a visible wince, even if he did then seem to take on a greenish hue. Graham Rowley, an old Canadian Arctic hand who prided himself on being able to drink like the locals wherever he might go, also downed his drink, then asked for another and downed that. None of the rest of us could manage even one, but the Yakutis were so impressed by Turner and Rowley that Canada's honour was secure.

Drinking fermented mare's milk was not the only entertainment. The Yakut National Ballet put on an impressive program of folk dancing and singing. At another remote stop, Khandyga on the Aldan River, the demands made of us were musical. Our fellow guests at a luncheon serenaded us with some Russian songs, and we were invited to respond in kind. Ernest Côté, our department's deputy minister, led us in "Alouette," "Red River Valley," "O Canada," and a few similar numbers. We collectively may have been better singers than drinkers, but our standard was not a high one.

On 7 June, we travelled back to Moscow, and then on to Norilsk, becoming the first Westerners to visit this important nickel and copper mining and smelting centre on the 69th parallel. It was astonishing to see large buildings there, as many as nine storeys high, constructed on permafrost. At the time, the construction methods prevalent in Canada's North could not have been used to build such large buildings. The Siberia we saw was not a region of bleak exile or gulags, though those surely existed, but a place of enormous human energy and optimism about how the North could be developed.

A few days later, we were back in Ottawa, exhausted but exhilarated. It had been a remarkable tour, and we had learned a great deal.[2] Despite the obvious political differences between our countries, it was clear that on the technical side, there was much to be gained from exchanges and co-operation. A few months later, in August 1965, we hosted a reciprocal visit from a Soviet delegation that included stops in Whitehorse, Mayo, Inuvik, Yellowknife, and Hay River.

In the fall of 1965, Prime Minister Pearson called an election, hoping to win a majority government. By then, I was looking forward to returning to Vancouver, having already stayed longer in Ottawa than I had originally intended. I did not have any thought of running in the election. I wasn't looking to make politics a lifetime career; rather, I wanted to get back to practising law so that I could pay my bills.

I ended up being drafted. At an election strategy session focused on the Vancouver ridings, I had advocated the Liberals run a strong candidate in Vancouver Kingsway, which was located just to the east of the informal line dividing the east and west sides of the city. At the time, Burnaby, New Westminster, and the eastern part of Vancouver were NDP strongholds, while the Liberals held the ridings in the western part of the city. My thinking was that even if the Liberals had no hope of winning Kingsway, going on the offensive there would force the NDP to expend energy to defend that riding, and thus serve to protect the seats the Liberals already held. It turned out I was not the only one who thought this was a good strategy.

Soon after the election was announced, Pearson's scheduling assistant called to tell me the prime minister wanted to see me. I found that odd. Pearson would have been busy with the election and would have had neither reason nor time to see an executive assistant. When I walked into his office, the prime minister said to me, "Art Laing tells me you're going to run for us in Kingsway." This was news to me, but I said I would be honoured to run. Thinking on my feet, I asked one favour of Pearson: would he make a campaign appearance on my behalf in the riding? He promised he would.

At the Vancouver Kingsway nomination meeting held at Collingwood Community Hall, I was chosen by acclamation.

I received important support from external affairs minister Paul Martin Sr, Art Laing, and Ray Perrault. They agreed to appear at a public meeting, held in a large hall, at which we spoke about Canadian foreign policy. The Vietnam War was under way and although Canada was not a participant, there were many tough, sometimes hostile questions asked by opponents of the war about Canada's role. The event attracted considerable publicity. During the campaign, I also received valuable guidance from John Nichol, who was the federal Liberal election manager in British Columbia. Nichol later served in the Senate and, as national Liberal party president, served as chair of the 1968 Liberal leadership convention, which chose Pierre Elliott Trudeau.

Ray Perrault, at that time an MLA and leader of the provincial Liberals, was my honorary campaign chair. I did not have an actual campaign chair, just a group of assistants who took on various tasks. When one of those assistants, a practising Roman Catholic, advised me to pay a visit to Monsignor (later archbishop) James Carney, Perrault, a devout Catholic himself, facilitated the meeting and vouched for me. Carney and I chatted for about fifteen minutes. He asked about my views on politics, and then told me the most important question he had was whether I believed in God. I replied that of course I believed in God, in the Jewish understanding of God. He indicated that was a satisfactory answer. Though the visit was rather an odd experience, perhaps in a certain way, my being Jewish was helpful; as a Jew, I was mostly oblivious to the animosities and prejudices common between Protestants and Catholics in those times, and among Catholics coming from diverse European countries. In any case, it was a fascinating ground-level look at politics.

I would work with Perrault on many occasions over the course of my career: first in British Columbia, then when we were both in the Senate, and ultimately, when we served in the Pierre Trudeau cabinet together. We first met when he was running for the leadership of the provincial Liberal Party, a position he won in 1959. Perrault had approached me for my support. At the time, the federal and provincial Liberal parties were unified in British Columbia. Perrault and I both remained loyal Liberals through those difficult years, when many others left to join the dominant Social Credit Party. Not one to switch allegiance out of expediency, he spoke often of loyalty. Indeed, he taught me much about loyalty in times of political adversity. And as Liberals from British Columbia, we faced a great deal of political adversity!

I loved campaigning, with its combination of discussing ideas and meeting people. I spoke to a wide array of community groups, to students, and people in church halls. My team knocked on doors throughout the riding, hearing voters' concerns. Inspired by my success with distributing tea bags for Art Laing's campaign, I had our canvassers give out small envelopes containing a pair of Aspirin to "relieve the headache of minority government." Pearson indeed kept his promise, visiting one of my campaign events, a Halloween party for children, where he gave away presents. Of course, the parents were there, too. The event was a hit.

One day, when I was knocking on doors in Fraserview, a unionized woodworker in an undershirt and boxer shorts, with a beer in his hand – yes, that's a caricature, but my story is true – greeted me with, "A Liberal! You're wasting your time." I asked why. He said, "Because we all vote NDP." I repeated my question. He explained that it was necessary to keep the Liberals sensitive to the working people. He said he preferred a Liberal government, but he also needed to vote for a party that would keep the Liberals accountable.

Indeed, my main competition in the campaign was Grace MacInnis of the NDP. She was the widow of Angus MacInnis, who had held the riding or its forerunners for twenty-seven years, until 1957, first as an Independent Labour member and then for the CCF, the predecessor of the NDP. She was also the daughter of J.S. Woodsworth, a founder and the iconic first leader of the CCF. I had a great deal of respect for Mrs MacInnis, whom I considered a formidable opponent, not only because of her lineage but also because of her own political experience, which included a stint in the BC legislature, and her strengths as a campaigner. She, too, was an iconic member of the CCF, and later NDP.

I took a much dimmer view of the party MacInnis represented. Although I was a left-leaning Liberal and shared the NDP's commitment to social justice and humanitarian ideals, I believed the Liberal Party stood a better chance of translating those ideals into policies that would improve the lives of Canadians. It seemed to me the NDP had many ideas on how to slice the economic pie, but not a single idea on how to make the economic pie bigger. By contrast, the Liberals were focused on growing the economy and had managed the difficult but important task of encouraging investor confidence, while at the same time developing important programs in the area of personal security: pensions, education, and labour standards.

I also took issue with the NDP's rigidity and self-righteousness. There was little tolerance of opposing views, including within their own ranks.

As well, I absolutely detested the NDP's focus on class struggle and the party's fostering of class-consciousness in order to justify its existence. I found these aspects socially divisive. I also disagreed with what I saw as an emotional anti-Americanism coming from the NDP. To me, being pro-Canadian does not require adopting a hostile attitude toward our neighbours.

My experience in Ottawa with Art Laing had confirmed that the Liberal Party was my political home, and the campaign in Kingsway reinforced my perspective. Nationally, of course, our main rivals were the Progressive Conservatives. While their emphasis on freedom and individual responsibility was not unattractive, my observation was that in practice, such a system, if not complemented by policies in the public interest, lacked compassion, leaving too many people behind. As a child of the Great Depression, I had my reservations about unalloyed free-market capitalism. And as the son of a man who had suffered a serious industrial accident, I understood that people and families can fall on hard times through no fault of their own. Private businesses naturally have private objectives, and these are not always consistent with the public's view of the national interest. Liberals are prepared to use the role of the state in an interventionist way to direct or, where necessary, to limit the use of private power. On the other hand, public power and bureaucracy can dominate policy-making and decision-making in a way that is injurious to private initiative and private responsibility. I had found in the Liberal Party a proper balance between private and public sectors, where neither dominates. This, I believed, and still believe, is the best way to advance the general welfare.

My experience in Ottawa had also taught me about the key role the federal government played and the need for a proper balance between provincial interests and national ones. During the campaign, Premier Bennett came out swinging against the Liberal government in Ottawa, and not least against Art Laing, its senior British Columbia minister and his own long-time rival. It seemed as much as anything to be a tactical move to prevent Pearson from winning a majority; for Bennett, a minority government would leave the provinces in a relatively stronger position.

Election Day was 8 November. Nationally, although the Liberals did pick up a handful of additional seats, a majority government proved elusive. Laing was re-elected in Vancouver South, and hired as his new chief of staff Gordon Gibson Jr, a Vancouverite from a prominent Liberal family who went on to work as an assistant to Pierre Trudeau and later was himself elected to the BC legislature as leader of the BC Liberal Party.

In Kingsway, I finished second to Grace MacInnis, who became British Columbia's first female MP. I was both disappointed and relieved. Laing and I kept in touch, exchanging opinions on Ottawa policies and BC reactions.

3 Ups and Downs in a Resource Economy

RESOURCE INDUSTRIES – mining, natural gas, forestry, fishing, and the generation of hydroelectric power – have long been central to British Columbia's economy. When you're practising law, it's a good idea to practise within the confines of the principal economic drivers of the province where you live. I would like to be able to say that I made a calculated decision to that effect, but the truth is more complicated. It was a matter of taking opportunities as they presented themselves, one thing leading to another, as with most things in my life. At the same time, given my interest in the sources of wealth and power, my involvement in these fields was probably inevitable once I settled in British Columbia.

When I was studying law, it hadn't occurred to me to single out resources from other economic activities. My eureka moment came when General McNaughton asked for a legal opinion about the possible diversion of the Columbia River, drawing my attention to water as a resource, not only for such purposes as irrigation and municipal consumption but also as a means of generating hydroelectricity, all in the context of the unequal power relationship between Canada and the United States. Water is a finite resource that can be used for municipal purposes, industrial purposes, power generation, and agricultural purposes. The question is, with all those interests competing to be the primary user of the resource, how do you assign equity? Resource law, at its heart, is about resolving conflicts between competing claims, domestically and sometimes internationally, to finite resources. It combines political power, social justice, and legal principles in a fascinating array of issues and conclusions.

Practising with Nathan Nemetz, I became acquainted with the forest industry, a major export earner for British Columbia. In my early months with him, he was counsel in a provincial royal commission on forestry issues that was headed by Chief Justice of British Columbia Gordon Sloan. I did a lot of the background research for Nemetz. There, too, industry stakeholders – the companies, the loggers, the sawmillers, and others – had competing priorities. There were also conflicts between the industry and the province, the steward of the resource.

I became involved in mining and resources law on my own. The Nemetz law office was in the former Inns of Court Building on Howe Street, on the northeast corner of Howe and Georgia. Next to us was the office of Neil McDiarmid, a mining promoter and trained lawyer. Shortly after I started articling, he accosted me in the hall. He told me he knew that I had gone to law school about the same time as his son Neil Jr. I asked him what Neil was doing, received an update, and then after the small talk, he got down to business.

McDiarmid asked if I would act as counsel for Craigmont, a mining company he controlled. As I was just an articling student, I said I would have to talk to Nemetz. And Nemetz told me I was crazy to consider the offer. He said I would be paid in shares that we would prepare on our law firm typewriters, and they would certainly be worthless. I responded that I had to start somewhere and even if I ended up working for free for a few months, the opportunity would be educational and give me a background in mining law and the industry. Nemetz told me to go ahead.

Sure enough, when I went back to McDiarmid, he said he didn't have a lot of cash and asked how I wanted to be paid. I replied I would accept shares of Craigmont, and that would do for six months. He agreed, and I made sure that the shares were properly issued and registered. In order to do so, I needed to talk to the superintendent of brokers, Stewart Smith. I called his office in Victoria and was advised he was in Vancouver, at the bar of the Ritz Hotel, on Georgia (where the Grosvenor Building is now). I found him having a drink with some of his pals. I stated my business. He instructed me to write up the order and he would sign it. Things aren't done that way anymore.

While Nemetz's warning was well taken, as it turned out, assays a few months later showed there was a significant amount of copper at Craigmont's property in Merritt, British Columbia. That mine became highly successful, and the shares did prove to be of value.

Having audited a course in US securities law at Harvard, I had told McDiarmid that it was essential to respond quickly to this discovery by issuing new shares to ensure the company wasn't raided, so that he didn't lose control. However, he did not have the resources to buy any new shares and had decided to let events take their course. Under the circumstances, he said he would be satisfied with seeing his stock rise in value.

Indeed, once Craigmont announced its discovery hole, Noranda, Placer Development, and an American private investor named Vernon "Moose" Taylor started buying up shares. One day in the spring of 1958, Doug Little, an exploration geologist with Placer, asked to see McDiarmid, who referred him to me. Little alerted me that Placer, Noranda, and Taylor had more than half the shares and were acting together, meaning they effectively controlled Craigmont. I learned later that they had bought a substantial number of McDiarmid's shares.

Acting on behalf of the minority shareholders, I negotiated a successful agreement to transfer control to Placer, Noranda, and Taylor's company – seen as a highly significant deal at the time. The experience gave me a high profile in BC mining circles, even before I was called to the Bar.

Craigmont's new owners retained me as the outside corporate lawyer for the company. And so, for the next three or four years, I was extremely busy. I participated in the legal work for all the debt instruments related to the money the consortium borrowed out of New York to build the Craigmont mine, which went into production in late 1961. I travelled to Japan in 1958 to participate as the lawyer in the negotiations on a team led by Gerry Gordon, general manager of Canadian Explorations, a subsidiary of Placer, and conclude a contract to sell copper concentrates to Nippon Mining, a major player in Japanese mineral smelting.

It was my first trip to Asia. I was absolutely fascinated. We were in Tokyo for three weeks. At that time, Japan was struggling to rebuild its economy after the Second World War, and mineral products were essential to that endeavour. I was impressed by the masses of people – nowhere in western Canada could one ever see such crowds – and their upbeat attitude. When not busy with my work, I had a chance to stroll in the area around my hotel and was amazed by the arts and crafts set up on tables on the street, being offered for sale at incredibly low cost. Although I also admired the woodblock prints on rice paper from the eighteenth and nineteenth centuries, I decided not to buy any, calculating they would have no enduring value. What a mistake! They have become extremely valuable.

Following our work in Tokyo, Gerry Gordon had plans to head to Hong Kong. He suggested that if I had time, I do likewise to see a remarkable part of Asia. The three or four days I spent there ended up being the first of many over the years, though of course, I could not know that at the time. What I saw was a British colony with a great deal of poverty but a high level of human energy. I looked up some Canadians I knew there, who told me Hong Kong was headed for considerable economic success. They mentioned a few shares I might consider buying on the Hong Kong stock exchange. I decided it would be too risky an investment. Again, I missed one of the major investment opportunities of all time.

Still, few could have foreseen the rise of Asia back then. There was no reason for me to believe that part of the world would flourish to the extent it has. What did become apparent, though, was Japan's, importance to British Columbia as a market for its resources.

Another opportunity I had during that period was to represent Craigmont as a junior counsel to Evans Wasson, Placer's long-time senior legal counsel. We were defending against a lawsuit brought by another mining company that was challenging Craigmont's title and mineral leases. The case went to the Supreme Court of Canada. We won, as we had in the lower courts. This was my second appearance as legal counsel in the Supreme Court of Canada. Again, I was quite thrilled to be there.

In many ways, my involvement with Craigmont, from exploration to production and marketing, had been an education worthy of a PhD in geology, securities, and finance. My work had taken me to the site of the future mine, where I stayed in tents with geologists, as well as to fancy offices and restaurants in New York and Tokyo. One of those geologists was Norman Keevil Jr, who would play a key role in my career a decade later, when he was president of Teck Resources.

In fact, I had not given up on the idea of an academic career, and so I decided it was time to start work on an actual PhD. I enrolled at Boalt Hall, the law school at the University of California (Berkeley), in the fall of 1962. Commuting from Vancouver, I spent Tuesdays to Thursdays in Berkeley and continued to practise law with Nathan Nemetz on Mondays, Fridays, and Saturdays.

One of my objectives was to better understand the resource sector from a strategic point of view, which required an awareness of American theory and practice on resource issues. The United States was at that time far and away the world's biggest consumer of resources and was not shy to wield its economic power and its tax policies to improve its access to them internationally. The US strategies for ensuring a secure supply of resources had been set out in the 1952 Paley Commission report, *Resources for Freedom*, which a decade later was still the seminal document in the field. Any understanding of the Canada-US resource relationship was not really possible without having studied that report. Among other things, it provided the context in which US companies came to dominate the Canadian oil patch.

Additionally, during my work with Craigmont, I had been acutely aware of fluctuations in the price of copper, so I was curious to learn more about how a country might be able to stabilize such resource industries. Certainly, the price fluctuations so often seen with commodities made development of those industries more difficult, especially because huge capital investments were required at the front end, with a revenue stream coming only after the total investment had been made. Guessing at the revenue stream and how it would repay the capital and interest on debt was a major risk assessment exercise. At the time, international commodity agreements already existed for such products as tin, coffee, rubber, wheat, sugar, and, in Europe, wood. These served to stabilize prices and bring more predictability to the international market.

My PhD research focused on international commodity agreements and their enforcement. My program was a joint one between the university's law school and the Giannini Foundation of Agricultural Economics, also a unit of the University of California (Berkeley). I set out to compare the different arrangements and learn more about the international economic, political, and legal contexts in which they operated.

I moved to Ottawa in 1963 at the request of Art Laing, before I had finished my doctorate. I continued my education about the role of resources in the economy and society, albeit in a different fashion.

It was serendipitous for me that Laing had been given the northern affairs and national resources portfolio, which included responsibility for Yukon and the Northwest Territories. In addition to my work on the Columbia River Treaty, I now had the opportunity to familiarize myself with a wide range of resource issues and to learn from my travels around the Canadian North as well as the Soviet Arctic. At the time, there was significant mining under way in Yukon as well as in the Northwest Territories, where Imperial Oil had a small oilfield operating at Norman Wells.

One of Laing's key objectives was to advance economic development in the northern territories in order to enhance the welfare of their people and make the territories self-supporting and eventually self-governing. During an early visit, he had been struck by the number of civil servants there and their comfortable housing in contrast with the local Indigenous people, who lived in inadequate conditions. This asymmetry arose from the need to provide incentives to southern Canadians to go north and work for the federal government. But the smell of colonialism was strong.

In my time with Laing, I learned about the struggles of Indigenous Peoples, the negative effects outside intrusions imposed, and the indifference of most Canadians toward both.

There I was, with a background in commodity arrangements whose goal was to achieve equity between producers and consumers, and I was struck by the total lack of equity on the human side of resource development.

Before I had left for Ottawa, my work for Craigmont and other companies had fostered my reputation in Vancouver as a major mining lawyer, and I had developed a fine practice. When Laing hired me, I was regarded by the mining industry at that time as a friend and spokesman to the federal government for the BC mining industry because I was of and from that sector.

I returned to Vancouver in the fall of 1965, having enhanced my knowledge of federal government operations and policies, particularly in the resource sector, and with a deeper understanding of the impact of federal actions on the economic and social life of British Columbia. My involvement in various federal-provincial issues alongside Laing, the senior federal political minister for British Columbia, also deepened my understanding of Victoria, which I had first developed during my Peace River work for W.A.C. Bennett. However, I found the top law firms in Vancouver of that time were not interested in hiring me at the salary I believed I deserved. I received offers but found them too low either in compensation or the junior position proposed. So at the beginning of 1966, I set up my own law practice and had no trouble attracting clients, mostly smaller and medium-sized mining companies. Within three or four months, I was so busy that I had given up looking to join another practice.

Near the end of 1966, I was approached by Bryan Williams, who had been a first-year student of mine at UBC law school. (Later, he became chief justice of British Columbia.) On behalf of the partners of Andrews, Swinton, Margach and Williams, he asked me to join the firm. I accepted. My practice was in natural resources law, mining, forestry, oil and gas, and the securities work related to raising money for those industries. As well, I negotiated with my new partners the right to be a principal in mining companies. As I grew busy with my own business interests, I offloaded legal files to others in the firm.

Just before I joined Andrews, Swinton, I had been retained by what was known as the Brenda group and brought that work with me to the firm. Brenda had three principals: Bern Brynelson, a mining engineer who was vice-president of exploration for Noranda in western Canada, but he was allowed, if the company was not interested in an offered project, to do his own development on the side; a chartered accountant from Kelowna named Merv Davis; and Morris Menzies, who held a PhD in geology. I had met Brynelson and Menzies during my Craigmont days, when they were representing Noranda.

They had a prospective molybdenum property west of Kelowna, the Brenda property. It was a big area of low-grade molybdenum. Noranda had looked at it and told the Brenda group it was uneconomic. Other companies in Vancouver had said the same. Nonetheless, the three principals had said to me, "Can you help us?" They needed someone with the capital to invest in developing the mine.

I considered the request and offered to approach some people in the East with the geological reports and third-party reports. I said I would not charge them anything but expenses for my travel and hotels, but if I was successful, I would charge a considerable success fee: $25,000 (the equivalent of $200,000 today). They said they had nothing to lose.

I went off to Power Corporation in Montreal – Maurice Strong, with whom I had become friendly, was an executive there and was kind enough to help me get a meeting with Power Corp. president Bill Turner – and I outlined the project. He asked why his company would be interested if Noranda had turned it down and Placer wasn't interested. My reply was straightforward: because molybdenum is essential for steel, and the steel industry was at the time expanding dramatically. I noted those two companies wanted it for cheap, and they would get together as they did over Craigmont and take it over just as soon as the founders ran out of money.

I suggested Power Corp. contact people I knew at Newmont, a large American mining company, to have them appraise the Brenda property. They did. Newmont said it needed a lot of capital because it would be a big open pit,[1] there would be a lot of rock to move, but the market prediction seemed right: by the time the mine was in production, which would take three to four years, the price of molybdenum probably would have risen. As a result of having done the appraisal, Newmont was interested in developing the property, but only if they had a major Canadian capital partner. At this point, Turner expressed interest, and on behalf of the Brenda group, I concluded an investment agreement with Power Corp.

I had achieved everything the Brenda group had asked me to accomplish. What I didn't realize was that Brynelson would take that information back to Noranda to give them another chance, or perhaps because he knew they wanted to develop the project. What I had actually done was negotiate the price.

At this point, because there was already an agreement with Power Corp., Noranda, which had suddenly become more interested, paid a price for its original hesitancy because it now had to buy out Power Corp. A deal was made – I never did find out for how much – but as part of it,

I was paid my fee. And the Brenda group, once production was under way, made a significant amount of money through their shareholdings. The deal enlarged my reputation in Vancouver with mining clients and the local investment community.

As a result of all these events, Brynelsen, Menzies, and Davis invited me to join what then became known as the Brameda group. They pointed out that they now had money as a result of the transaction and wanted to assemble a new company, which would be named for the four of us. They had a mining engineer, an accountant, and a geologist. But they didn't have a lawyer. I agreed to join them.

My partners in Brameda and I aspired to build what would be one of Canada's major mining companies, based in Vancouver. We acquired interests in a series of properties: Churchill Copper, in northern British Columbia, close to the Yukon border; Hearne Copper Mine, an exploration project in the Northwest Territories; a nickel property in Quebec; and perhaps most significantly, some coal showings in the Tumbler Ridge area that Menzies was particularly passionate about. We did a financing on the whole package with Burns Fry, a Toronto blue chip firm.

The mining market was very hot in the late 1960s – Japan's demand for minerals was strong – and the stock took off for a period of time. By early 1969, it seemed we were well launched.

Meanwhile, I had set my sights on running my own mining company, apart from my role in Brameda, and looked for one that was already operating. Through my contacts with the Gibson family, whom I had originally come to know as supporters of Art Laing, I developed the idea of acquiring Giant Mascot. It was a nickel and copper producer near Hope, British Columbia, and the Gibsons were ready to sell their controlling interest. We negotiated a price; the deal was contingent on my ability to secure financing.

My bankers at the Bank of Nova Scotia weren't prepared to lend me as much money as I needed to close the deal on my own because I could not offer sufficient security guarantees. My Brameda partners were each willing to buy in and guarantee the loan. The bankers felt this was still insufficient; however, they informed me the Bronfmans were looking to invest in an operating mine. They arranged for me to meet Samuel Bronfman at the Seagram offices in Montreal.

When we met, Bronfman had his sons, Edgar and Charles, with him. Although I had sent the proposed deal in advance to give them a chance to study it, I made my pitch. I explained that Japan's demand for commodities was growing, and I had good contacts among Japanese trading company representatives in Vancouver from my Craigmont days. I shared my estimates about where nickel prices were going: upward. Bronfman asked some astute business questions, and his sons listened. We continued the conversation over lunch. When Bronfman asked what he could offer me to drink, no way was I going to ask for something that was not a Seagram's product. (I had anticipated the question – my contact at the bank may well have briefed me to expect it.) I asked for a Glenlivet, which was the best scotch they distributed (they bought the company a few years later). Samuel Bronfman approved of my choice. At the end of the lunch, he said, "Of course we'll do it." The Bronfmans took 40 per cent and the four of us in Brameda each took 15 per cent as individuals. The bank held the shares of the Brameda group as collateral.

The Giant Mascot purchase, made in late 1968, gave us and the Bronfman group control of the company. In January 1969, I became the company's president. Shortly thereafter, Lou Starck, a mining engineer who was the company's long-time general manager, and I set off for Japan to negotiate a new deal with Sumitomo for the sale of our concentrates. Although Giant Mascot already had a contract with Sumitomo to purchase its nickel and copper concentrate that agreement was about to expire. Under the new contract we were proposing, we would sell them about 75 per cent of the concentrates outright, in the usual way, but for the remainder, we would retain ownership and have Sumitomo sell the smelted product as nickel on the spot market. This would provide us with a higher return. It was an unusual proposal that had impressed Samuel Bronfman when I told him this was my plan. Our nickel was high grade and easy to process, which gave us some additional leverage with Sumitomo. Starck and I were able to negotiate the contract I wanted: three years, at the spot price. When nickel prices rose, as we had predicted, this gave Giant Mascot tremendous earnings.

By then, Japan was becoming a major industrial power, creating a world demand for raw materials. To a British Columbian, it was clear that our province's economic development opportunities would lie in doing business across the Pacific.

Although Giant Mascot was highly successful, the Brameda group had overextended itself and ran into trouble with its own holdings. The nickel property in Quebec proved to be impossible to treat at any economic level. I insisted we cancel it, which caused a fight between me and Brynelsen, Davis, and Menzies. The Churchill Copper property in northern British Columbia, meanwhile, should have been economic, but my partners proceeded to spend far more money than was justified on building the mill and concentrator. They built a Cadillac when a Chev would have been more than adequate, making the property uneconomic. I had had to trust their professional judgment about the required budget for the project and its cost of operations so had not in the first instance opposed their view of what was needed. My partners also leased an airplane, a move I had thought unnecessary and in which I had no part. I told them if they put it into the company, I would be gone. So, they contracted for it separately, though later tried to claim I shared liability for it.

We also had some exploration properties that did not come to anything. But the geology that Menzies was doing on the metallurgical coal properties by Tumbler Ridge did pay off significantly. We got development licences from the province for those coal measures. Shortly after us, there were one or two other companies that picked up properties in the area.

In late 1969 and early 1970, the mining industry was in a downturn. This made Brameda's overextension untenable. The four of us in the group were at odds – me versus the other three – about how best to handle what was left.

Burns Fry, which had a reputational risk in having backed us, decided to step in because the group was now short of cash and had bills that weren't being paid. In the crisis, Davis resigned as president and CEO; Burns Fry asked me to take over, with the approval of Brynelson and Menzies, to see whether I could get us out of this mess. I looked at the possibility of raising money by selling more shares, but the market was not interested in mining stocks at that time. It seemed the only option was to find somebody to take over Brameda and pay the bills.

Despite its troubles, the company had real assets, not least the coal properties in Tumbler Ridge. And these were of interest to Teck, a medium-sized mining company at that time, owned and run by Norman Keevil Sr and his son, Norman Jr. The Keevils saw the Japanese steel industry rising; the coal at Tumbler Ridge was metallurgical, and they understood its value. It turned out that the two coal properties were the making of Teck, as they developed the properties and sold coal to the Japanese, particularly Sumitomo. And Sumitomo ended up buying 17 per cent of Teck at one point. So, the Keevils built the next stage of their company on Brameda coal and went on to other things, including the purchase of metallurgical coal assets in southeast British Columbia, becoming Canada's leading met coal producer.

Essentially, what happened was that I made a deal with Teck with the support of Burns Fry. My three partners were obliged to agree to the deal, because Burns Fry declared it was this way or no way. We sold a lot of our shares to Burns Fry for a very small payment, which was the punishment the four of us took for the situation of Brameda. Burns Fry took control of Brameda and then sold the shares to Teck. The shares we retained were converted to Teck shares when they merged Teck with Brameda in 1979.

When my three partners and I lost control of Brameda, the Bronfmans saw an opportunity to control Giant Mascot outright and were interested in buying our shares. My Giant Mascot shares had been my security on my loan to purchase them, a personal loan, so when the bank called in my loan, I had no choice but to sell. (My three partners were in similar positions.) My proceeds went to pay most of my loan from the bank. It took a while for me to pay off the rest of my debt, but I did.

4 Deputy Minister in the Eye of the Storm: An Oil Crisis, and More

IN EARLY 1970, as I was in the latter stages of negotiating Teck's takeover of the Brameda group, out of the blue came a call from Gordon Robertson. As the clerk of the Privy Council he was the most senior civil servant in Ottawa. He had headed up the team of civil servants involved in our work on the Columbia River Treaty negotiations, when I had worked in Ottawa with Art Laing.

Robertson informed me that Prime Minister Pierre Trudeau had several vacancies for deputy ministers. Rather than go the traditional route of naming generalists educated at Oxford or Cambridge, Trudeau had decided to appoint people who had specialized knowledge of their particular fields. Robertson wanted to talk to me about the upcoming vacancy at EMR. He invited me to Ottawa to be interviewed for the job.[1]

I don't think Trudeau would have known who I was at that point. I had left Ottawa just before he arrived – he was first elected to Parliament in 1965 – and we moved in different worlds. I had no involvement in Quebec, and he had none in British Columbia or in the resources industry. In the Liberals' 1968 leadership race, I had been a supporter of one of his opponents, Paul Martin Sr. I've always assumed that it was Robertson himself who recommended me.

But of course, I knew who Trudeau was, and not only because he was the prime minister. In the early 1960s, I had heard him speak at a constitutional law seminar at Mont-Tremblant, Quebec, and he had made a lasting impression. He had driven up in his Mercedes sports car, wearing his buckskin jacket, an ascot around his neck, and sandals. I wondered, Who the heck is that? Frankly, I thought he looked like a flake. In those days, law professors wore tweed jackets and ties. But I changed my mind pretty quickly once he started to speak. It was clear there was a great deal of substance underlying his unorthodox style.

At the time of Robertson's invitation, I wasn't entirely sure I wanted to return to Ottawa – I enjoyed being back in Vancouver, as did my family. But the job certainly sounded fascinating, and after having worked in Ottawa, public policy had become a subject of real interest for me. The chance to chat with Trudeau was not something to pass up, so I told Robertson I was interested and would be delighted to come for an interview.

When I arrived in Ottawa, I learned the prime minister had to fly to Toronto but he would talk to me on his plane. I waited in Toronto while he completed his engagements, and then flew back to Ottawa with him. The interview was intense, and we got along famously. After a preliminary chat about our respective legal educations, experiences teaching law, and people we knew in common, I said, "Prime Minister, your time is short, what do you want accomplished if I take on this assignment? What are the principal priorities in the natural resources sector?" He responded that the Canadian government had no up-to-date knowledge of the country's energy resources. He wanted to know what we could produce economically and competitively, including the cost of delivery to market. He said that the government knew very little about our energy security, our security of supply, our dependence on foreign supply. Indeed, at the time, private US oil companies knew more about Canada's resources than the federal government did. We had a National Energy Board (NEB), but the members got their facts from Houston, when Houston cared to provide them. So we needed a white paper on a Canadian energy strategy, and I would have at my disposal whatever resources were needed to accomplish the task.

Then Trudeau asked me, "Why would *you* take this job?"

I said that based on my work in the field I had found that more than 90 per cent of our oil and gas properties were owned or controlled by foreign companies, and the remainder were not the significant deposits.

I told him that was why we had no information, and the government of Alberta liked it that way because they didn't want the federal government getting involved. With a domestic tax system that discouraged Canadian investment in the oil and gas sector, I didn't see how the Canadian investment community was ever going to be able to accumulate the capital to allow Canadians to be competitive with American investment in Canada, let alone elsewhere. I told him that I had in mind a state champion for Canada, that in the energy report, I would personally write the part on national oil companies, explaining why other countries had them, why there was a British Petroluem, Total in France, Ente Nazionale Idrocarburi (ENI) in Italy, and so on, what the policy reasons were, and whether they applied in a Canadian context.

He said, "I'm not an economic nationalist. You can write it, but don't think you have approval in advance. You'll have to talk me into this."

I weighed the choice I then faced between continuing to lead Giant Mascot for the Bronfmans or going through a completely different door.

I accepted the job as deputy minister of EMR in March 1970, and began in May. My family joined me in Ottawa after the end of the school year.

I realized that my activity in the mining industry up to that point would raise concerns about conflict of interest, so I moved proactively to ensure that no conflicts would arise. Prior to my appointment, I had, on my own initiative, declared my holdings in resource-based companies and placed all these interests and those of my family in a blind trust, where the trustees had full power to buy and sell assets. I was only to be informed periodically of the value of the trust but not of its contents. This was a groundbreaking move, over and above what was required by the rather primitive ethics guidelines of the time. The *Vancouver Sun* wrote an approving editorial when my trust arrangements were announced.

Prior to leaving British Columbia, and before my appointment had become public, I asked Bill Clancy to let Premier W.A.C. Bennett know. The premier called me personally to say he was pleased I would be taking the job. "You will be BC's ambassador in Ottawa," he said. To make the point explicit, he wanted me to have a Queen's Counsel designation from British Columbia. A few days later, I was officially informed by Attorney General Les Peterson that I would be accorded that honour.

Historically, EMR had been the Department of Mines and Technical Surveys. It was a department made up of scientists and technical people and had never acted as a policy unit. As far as calculating oil and gas reserves was concerned, that was done by the NEB, which also regulated pipelines. But the NEB in that era essentially represented the industry and was in the habit of advancing industry needs. To many people in the federal public service, the NEB often appeared to be in the pocket of the "oil patch," particularly Imperial Oil, which had far better analytic capability about everything related to petroleum and natural gas than the NEB or any other part of government. The Royal Commission on Government Organization, or Glassco Commission, in the early 1960s had recommended reorganization of the department to include a policy capacity and thus an advisory role to government on Canada's natural resources.

Upon my arrival in Ottawa to take up my assignment, I was met at the airport by Dr Jim Harrison, chief scientist and senior assistant deputy minister. His first question to me was, "What's a lawyer doing as head of a science department?" I told him the prime minister wanted a survey of Canada's energy resources, including the economics of exploration, discovery, and production, in order to determine Canada's security of supply and at what economic cost. I said my mandate was to produce a white paper recommending a Canadian energy strategy, and this would require policy analysis at a number of levels in the department. Harrison told me the department was not organized for policy work but rather it did scientific research and provided data for others to do policy research. My response to him was that I would need his support in explaining to the department the significant pivot in its role I was there to conduct. I added that if people in the department could not be policy advisers as well as scientists but instead wanted to remain "pure" scientists, then they should do their work in the universities.

With Harrison's assistance, the department and its personnel came around to accepting the new challenges, but there was significant debate and upheaval as senior officials took on the new mandate. There was also a subsequent upheaval within the oil and gas industry, because the industry, in order to attract capital, was less than forthright in representations to the investment community about how large and accessible the resources were. But that is another story for another book.

What I would like to underline here is the importance of a professional public service in assuring the effective functioning of government. Federal civil servants are sometimes the butt of jokes, particularly outside of Ottawa. This is not particularly fair and reflects both a misunderstanding of their vital role and an underestimation of the quality of the individuals in these roles.

While it's the job of the democratically elected political leadership to make the decisions, the quality of these decisions depends on the quality of the data and advice received. The role of the civil service is to master the factual background and understand the competing interests within society, and this on a continuing basis. Implementation of the government's policy decisions also depends on the civil service; here, too, its quality is vital. A merit-based, non-partisan public service is the bedrock upon which the stability of our system of government is based. Although our democratic leadership changes, the core competency must remain constant.

While I was privileged to work with many extraordinary civil servants over the years, Michael Pitfield was the most extraordinary of all. A member of a Montreal family prominent in finance, he was intellectually brilliant and fluently bilingual. He had attended university at a precocious age, graduating at sixteen, followed by earning a law degree. Then he had gone to Ottawa in 1959, at twenty-two, as an administrative assistant to Progressive Conservative justice minister Davie Fulton. Pitfield and I would go on to become friends and work closely together during my role as deputy minister, then after I became principal secretary to Trudeau in 1974 and he became clerk of the Privy Council, and again once we were both in the Senate.

Our first meeting, however, involved an argument.

It was in the fall of 1970, not long after I had assumed my post as deputy minister. At the time, Pitfield was working as an assistant secretary to Gordon Robertson in the Privy Council Office (PCO).

EMR included a water division accounting for about one-third of the department's personnel, which was responsible for the administration of policy and programs for much of the country's freshwater resources as well as our three oceans. Robertson had just informed me of a departmental reorganization in which responsibility for water was to be transferred to a newly created department of the environment. I argued that not only was I promised my department would be intact, but also it didn't make sense to pull resources out of the resources department.

I asked Robertson who was in charge of this reorganization. It was his assistant for policy development, Michael Pitfield. If I wanted to try to reverse the decision, he was the person to talk to. I knew I would not succeed in changing a decision already made at the cabinet committee level, but I decided to contest it in order to see how the department might be compensated.

Pitfield and I had an aggressive discussion at a high analytical level, debating, among other things, whether such a move was in conformity with the recommendations of the Glassco Commission.

I lost the argument, but on the bright side, the loss of responsibility for the water sector created momentum toward the national energy study. What I did get in return was agreement for staffing and funding for that study, which got under way in earnest. Among other objectives, it was to take a close look at Canada's energy supply; examine what had been a rapid growth of demand; consider how much of our energy should be reserved for Canadian requirements and what surplus would be available for export; investigate environmental issues that would be raised by possible oil and gas production, particularly in the North; look at foreign ownership; and consider the viability of state participation in the oil industry. The significant undertaking would require three years of work.

Meanwhile, I was faced with having to manage a crisis in the uranium industry.

Canada had started mining uranium mostly to serve the US market, which relied on Canadian production. By 1959, Canada had about two dozen mines in operation, most of them in Ontario, some in Saskatchewan, producing approximately 15,000 tons of yellowcake annually. Then, in 1964, the Americans abruptly stopped buying uranium from sources outside their own country. They cited national security reasons, but in fact, the move stemmed from pressure from US producers, who had by that time developed adequate production at home. It was probably the worst case of protectionism since the Second World War. By 1970, there were only three Canadian mines still in operation, and together their production was somewhere around 4,000 tons a year. To the Americans, Canadian resources were there to be used as a surge tank at their convenience; otherwise, they had no problem leaving Canadian producers in the lurch.

The US move left Elliot Lake – the centre of Ontario's uranium industry – a community in serious trouble. The Beaverlodge-Uranium City area of northern Saskatchewan did not fare much better. To support those communities, the Pearson government had bought and stockpiled uranium, under a five-year program that began in 1965. Once that program was drawing to an end, Denison Mines threatened to close down its Elliot Lake operation if it did not get further government help.

Energy minister Joe Greene asked me whether there was anything we could do. There was much at stake economically: entire communities were dependent on uranium, people's livelihoods were threatened, and if we were to close down the industry, starting it up again when needs changed in the future would be costly. As well, Eldorado Nuclear, involved in uranium mining in northern Saskatchewan, was a Crown corporation – one more reason for the government to take action.

I told Greene my doctoral work had focused on international commodity agreements, so I understood international practice and what the possible policy options were. I recommended we set up a new stockpile using a different system. This time, Denison and Rio Algom would pay a share of the cost, which would give the companies an incentive to assist in marketing their uranium in the future, as sales would be from the stockpile once the demand side of the industry picked up. I calculated that if we could keep the industry going for five years, then global demand would catch up with supply again.

At the same time, I suggested the first thing to consider was whether we could set up producer-supplier arrangements to stabilize the market.

These had been set up for various other commodities internationally, with the benefit that they provided predictability and the avoidance of sudden price fluctuations. Under such an arrangement, Canada and uranium buyers would agree on a sale price range for uranium for a period of time, and producers would bid within that range; therefore, they would be able to operate with a modest commercial rate of return.

Cabinet approved this plan.

I set out to talk to the main consumers.

First stop was Washington DC, where I visited the federal energy regulatory commission to transparently explain our problems and what we were trying to achieve. I was told Congress would never approve such a deal, nor would the major US buyers be interested; in their view, they could count on their government to protect them on supply and price, so there would be no reason to make such an arrangement. It also was made clear that Congress had not the slightest interest in changing the existing policy barring imports.

I then travelled to Japan with Joe Greene in December 1970 to meet with government officials and industry leaders. The Japanese weren't interested in any deal that would see them paying more than the world price for any commodity, even if we could offer them a secure supply and they could avoid price hikes when times of shortage would inevitably return. I warned them that Tokyo Electric's days of buying uranium below the cost of production as suppliers competed with each other in a race to the bottom were going to have to end, as this was not sustainable for the producers. The Japanese held firm to their position, concerned that any uranium commodity agreement would act as an inducement to suppliers of other concentrates to request similar action, with the possible consequence of an across-the-board higher cost to them for their commodity supplies.

In any international conversation I had, the people I talked to were quite familiar with such commodity arrangements, but the political situations in their respective countries meant agreements were not possible. Short-term thinking prevailed. The attitude taken by many was that in all likelihood, a return of higher costs would be the problem of their successors.

It became clear to me that the producers would have to make their own arrangement among themselves. At the time, the other major uranium producers were France (with mines in Niger and other former African colonies) and South Africa. Australia had reserves but was not yet producing.

I went to France to talk to officials at the French government's unit for atomic energy and production of uranium. I had first stopped in Spain to sell some Canadian uranium there, underbidding France and selling below the cost of production, an arrangement that was facilitated by Denison's Stephen Roman, who had connections in that country. We took this approach so that we could say to the French and South Africans that if we all race to the bottom, we will all be destroyed. In meetings in France and in South Africa, I proposed the negotiation of a producers' agreement. Then we went back to the consumers and gave them a last chance to enter into a producers-consumers deal. They still turned us down. They did not have the political capacity to agree to a deal that might serve them well in the future but would mean higher prices for them in the immediate term.

Ontario Hydro, as it was then known, also passed up the chance to sign a long-term contract with us, which would have mitigated the eventual rise in costs of the uranium they purchased for use in electricity generation. Although it was a provincial Crown corporation, Ontario Hydro took the position that the future of the uranium industry in the province was not their concern.

Thus was born the so-called "uranium cartel" that was to become the subject of so much breathless coverage in the press, coverage that often suggested the arrangement was scandalous and possibly illegal, when in fact it was neither. And while I was indeed the strategist behind the cartel's creation, I note that, notwithstanding some suggestions at the time, this was no one-man, cloak-and-dagger operation. Cabinet had signed off on the initiative, which involved gaining broad co-operation in the industry, and everything was done transparently.

Everything we did was within the law. The Combines Investigation Act did not apply to Crown corporations insofar as combination in restraint of trade was concerned. So we set up Uranium Canada as a Crown corporation, of which I was president and CEO and all shares were held by the minister of EMR. Uranium Canada became the entity that acted as the Canadian producer in the producers' arrangement.

In 1981, because of the price hikes to Ontario Hydro, federal prose-cutors laid price-fixing charges against six Canadian uranium compa-nies, two of which were Crown corporations; however, the case never came to trial. After a Supreme Court ruling that the Crown corporations could not be prosecuted, under the legal dictum that the queen can do no wrong, charges were dropped against the private companies in the name of fairness. I was disappointed at that turn of events. I had been looking forward to the arrangement's legality being vindicated by an eventual court decision.

And far from being shameful or scandalous, the arrangement was in the best interests of Canada. In the three years while the arrangement operated, it kept afloat the industry and the communities dependent on it. By the mid-1970s, there were multiple factors pushing uranium de-mand and prices upward, not least the oil shock brought about by the actions of the Organization of the Petroleum Exporting Countries (OPEC) cartel, so our producers' deal was allowed to lapse. Once there was an upswing in demand, the uranium that had been stockpiled found a mar-ket. At the end of the day, Canadian taxpayers got their investment back.

In mid-August 1971, the Nixon administration suspended the convertibil-ity of the US dollar into gold. This was an effort to rein in inflation in the United States, which was partly a consequence of the Vietnam War. At the same time, the administration levied a 10 per cent tariff surcharge on im-ports to protect US producers against an erosion of their competitive posi-tion as a result of the expected fluctuation in exchange rates, as well as to address growing economic competition from Japan and West Germany.

This came to be known as the Nixon Shock. It hit Canada hard.

Pierre Trudeau in 1969 had famously told a US audience, "Living next to you is in some ways like sleeping with an elephant. No matter how friendly or even-tempered is the beast, if I can call it that, one is affected by every twitch and grunt." Two years later, that elephant had not just twitched but rolled over onto us, and senior Canadian officials would be urgently dispatched to Washington to plead with the US government for an exemption from import duties. Exports to the United States were hugely important to Canada's economy, as they continue to be, and these moves would have a devastating impact on this side of the border. Moreover, there was no justification for the surcharge insofar as Canada was concerned because the Canadian dollar was already floating against the US dollar. In the end, the Nixon administration withdrew its most egregious provisions affecting Canada.

In September 1971, Joe Greene and I travelled to Tokyo, accompanied by several other officials, to meet with Japanese government officials and gather information about Japan's anticipated energy needs as part of the research for the energy policy study then in progress. This would help us to better anticipate global demand for oil, both in terms of understanding possible future markets and protecting our domestic requirements.

While we were in Tokyo, Greene suffered a stroke. He received emergency medical attention there, and then required a longer period of treatment and convalescence in Canada. Luckily, his wife had been with him on the trip, so she was immediately at his side in hospital. I was left to continue on my own to previously arranged visits to Tehran, Paris, and London.

It was in Tehran that I was fortunate to have some particularly fascinating discussions with Dr Parviz Mina, the director of international affairs for the National Iranian Oil Company, who shared insights into what directions OPEC was headed. Among other things, it was clear the Nixon currency decision would have an impact on oil prices, which were paid in US dollars. The oil producers would start raising their prices to compensate for the erosion of their earnings.

As it became evident that Joe Greene was not making a full recovery from his stroke, the prime minister decided to seek a new minister for EMR. I had very much enjoyed my relationship with Greene, who had first impressed me when as a candidate for the Liberal leadership in 1968 he had made an excellent presentation. After Greene's service in the EMR post, Prime Minister Trudeau appointed him to the Senate. Serving in the Senate is a less physically demanding job than cabinet, with its exceedingly long hours and considerable travel, but one where Greene could still make a valuable contribution. Later, on my first day in the

Senate, 5 November 1975, Greene offered warm words of welcome in a humorous vein. He told the Senate, "I was once his minister in energy, mines and resources, where he was my deputy minister, and as such, under our system, obviously my boss. Therefore, it is nice to have him here now where we can be equals."

A cabinet shuffle was in the offing for late January 1972, and Prime Minister Trudeau asked me whom I wanted as my minister. This was not a question deputy ministers were routinely asked.

I told him my preference would be Donald Macdonald, a Toronto MP known around Ottawa as Thumper, then serving as defence minister. I thought Macdonald would be the right person for the challenges ahead. He was essentially the delegate of the Ontario party elites – though not of the Toronto business elites – and was a powerful figure both in cabinet and in caucus.

Not long after I spoke with the prime minister, Macdonald phoned me to say, "I hear from the prime minister that you would like me to be minister of EMR. Can we get together?" He wanted me to tell him more about the department and why he should be interested in becoming minister.

We had a long lunch in the Canadian Grill, in the basement of the Chateau Laurier. Now long gone, it was the power lunch place of the day. And I told him why EMR was important, that it was a critical economic portfolio as well as critical to federal-provincial relations and important to international relations because of OPEC and the OECD oil committee.

My remarks about EMR's importance and centrality may have contributed to convincing Macdonald to accept the assignment. As it turned out, though, they were understated. Once the oil crisis hit in the fall of 1973, the department was truly at the centre of the action.

To understand what happened in the couple of years following that lunch at the Chateau Laurier – in terms of oil price increases, policy responses, and the reverberations on federal-provincial relations – it's important to know that at the time, Canada was split into two oil markets. This circumstance was a legacy of the Borden Commission of 1957–59 that recommended the drawing of a line (called the Borden line or Ottawa Valley line) just west of the Ottawa Valley, a policy the Diefenbaker government had adopted. To the east, Quebec and the Atlantic provinces relied on oil imported from the Middle East and Venezuela that was refined in Montreal into gasoline, home heating oil, and other products. To the west, the western provinces and most of Ontario consumed domestic oil, primarily from Alberta, refined in Sarnia and elsewhere. Western producers would also export their oil to the United States, as opportunities permitted. At the time, imported oil was cheaper than domestic oil. Canadians east of the line benefited from access to oil at the world price. Alberta benefited from having Ontario, with its relatively large population and industrial base, as a captive market (just as Albertans and other Canadians were a captive market for Ontario's industrial goods).

During 1972, however, world oil prices rose steadily, in large part because of the OPEC response to the previous year's Nixon Shock and the attendant lowering value of the US dollar –the currency in which oil is sold. Eastern Canadian consumers began to feel the impact. The increases did not initially affect the price of domestic Canadian oil, however, which at the time was subject to import restrictions and price controls in the United States, dampening US demand.

The first jump in the price of domestic oil came late in 1972. Around the same time, the NEB raised concerns about Canada's own growing demand for energy. As 1973 began, there was a second increase in the price of domestic oil along with rapidly rising US demand.

Ensuring that Canada would have enough oil for its own needs was essential. The federal government announced that Canada would place export controls on crude oil as of 1 March 1973. This was not a prohibition on exports. Rather, it meant they would be subject to tighter scrutiny on a security of supply basis. A short time later, the Americans lifted their import controls. Canadian oil was now viewed as a part of continental supply.

In the spring of 1973, Canada's export controls were extended to gasoline, due to mounting concerns about a possible shortage in Canada as a result of the huge increase in US demand. Suddenly, the US was concerned about its own security of supply and dependence on non-North American resources and also about the price escalation driven by the OPEC producers. Canada again became a "buddy."

It was in this context that *An Energy Policy for Canada*, EMR's comprehensive study, was published in June 1973. It could not have been timelier. It proved an invaluable resource for addressing the problems that arose in the months following. Nobody could say we were unprepared to deal with the energy crisis, which only intensified after the report's publication. Understandably, Trudeau was quite pleased with his own decision to initiate the study, his major priority for me when I was appointed. Requesting the study arose from his Cartesian approach: identifying a gap in knowledge and then taking steps to find the information.

While I was in overall charge of the energy policy white paper, I had many other responsibilities. It was the assistant deputy minister for energy, Gordon McNabb, who acted as general editor and brought the various pieces of the work together. I had first met him on the federal Columbia River negotiating team, where he was the lead adviser on the engineering studies. It was a delight to find him at EMR when I became deputy minister. He was an invaluable colleague and in due course became EMR deputy minister as well.

In its approximately 800 pages, the report provided a survey of Canada's energy resources, setting out what energy we could produce in all forms and at what price, including not only oil but also hydroelectricity, nuclear energy, and coal. It included price forecasts that were seen as high at the time but quickly proved far too conservative. Market analyses were also included with forecasts of what we needed to meet domestic requirements and ensure our supply was secure. The overall picture indicated Canada had sufficient energy reserves, but the days of cheap energy were over, not only because of rising prices internationally but also because some of Canada's reserves would be more costly to develop (for example, the oil sands). The report also noted that in any decision to develop resources in the North, where there was much potential, impacts on the ways of life of Indigenous people there had to be considered. As well, there was the chapter on state-owned national oil companies, which I personally wrote.

By and large, the report was descriptive, not prescriptive. That April, after my draft chapter recommending creation of a national oil company had been submitted for discussion, the cabinet had issued instructions that the report was to contain no policy recommendations, only policy options. The P&P committee of cabinet had called me in. After I presented my report, Charles "Bud" Drury, a veteran cabinet minister from Montreal who was identified with the business wing of the party, said to me, "I thought you were a businessman, and you turn out to be a socialist!" I replied, "I'm not a socialist, I'm pro-business, but there's a place for state enterprise in public policy." I added that I didn't see a national oil company as permanent but as transitional because there was a problem with foreign ownership and control that had to be addressed. Drury was an important and impressive minister. We had an excellent relationship, but his opposition to a state oil company reflected the consensus in cabinet at that time, which leaned centre-right. I was told the chapter could stay in the report, but it could not make any recommendations. It had to be written in a neutral and balanced way, simply setting out a national oil company as an option.

In order to prepare the chapter on state energy companies, I had needed research to be conducted and facts compiled. I called John H. McArthur, then a professor, and later the dean, at Harvard Business School, a British Columbian whom I had met when he had been an undergraduate at UBC. He was a person of astute judgment in the worlds of business and education.

Through McArthur, I met Bill Hopper, a Canadian geologist with an MBA who at the time was working for the well-known consulting firm Arthur D. Little, based in Boston. Hopper delivered what I had asked for, giving me a big picture of two contesting groups of major oil companies: the American private group and the European and other state enterprise group. Later that year, after the report was published, I hired him as assistant deputy minister for energy policy.

The election of October 1972 had left the Trudeau government with a minority, and an extremely narrow one at that. The Liberals had 109 MPs elected, and Robert Stanfield's Progressive Conservatives had 107. The balance of power was held by the 31 MPs of the New Democratic Party, led by David Lewis. He was a Rhodes Scholar from Montreal who as a young man held far-left policy convictions that included favouring the nationalization of the Canadian Pacific Railway. At the onset of the Trudeau minority, I saw Lewis as still holding his earlier principles, but as a practising politician, willing to be pragmatic.

I was involved in three minority governments – Pearson's in 1963–65, Trudeau's in 1972–74, and Paul Martin's in 2004–06 – and can say that most important to managing them is understanding the opposition parties' political strengths and weaknesses, obvious and hidden, and their relation to your positions and the positions of one another. This is not a static scenario. It changes by the hour sometimes and needs to be ceaselessly tracked. Also requiring focus are the personalities within each of those parties. They have internal policy differences and differences of ambition and interest. All to say that knowing what will be tolerated and for how long is critical to the survival of a minority government. So is knowing when you are ready to go to the people with confidence, and when the time is wrong. How Trudeau's 1972 minority government handled energy issues would have a major bearing on its survival.

After the publication of *An Energy Policy for Canada*, eight months into the life of the Liberal minority government, Lewis told the prime minister that he wanted him to create a Canadian Crown corporation in the oil patch – one policy option outlined in the report. Lewis made this a condition of his continued support. Trudeau, as he had warned me at my job interview, was not an economic nationalist. He had witnessed the agonies of the Pearson government's fights over economic nationalism, pitting the nationalist Walter Gordon against Mitchell Sharp, who stressed the importance of access to US capital and markets, and did not buy in. But by this time, Trudeau was open to the idea of creating a national oil company – what would become Petro-Canada – on pragmatic grounds, having seen the case made in the report, though he did not see it as a priority. Meanwhile, the Progressive Conservatives were against the idea of a national oil company from the beginning on the basis that they opposed a federal state presence in the Alberta oil and gas sector. The small Canadian oil independents, dominated by the large American companies that held the leases and those that provided the major oilfield services, not surprisingly shared the American industry's point of view. Alberta was against it, the American oil industry was against it, the Conservatives were against it, and so on.

As someone raised in Alberta, I was keenly aware of the culture of grievance held by many as a result of the withholding of ownership of natural resources at the time Alberta was admitted into Confederation, in 1905. Eastern Canadians saw the western provinces as economic colonies and felt that the resources of Alberta and Saskatchewan belonged to them. It took a great deal of political activity to make those two provinces resource owners, parallel to the entitlements of Ontario, Quebec, and the Atlantic provinces along with British Columbia and Manitoba. The legislation transferring ownership received royal assent on 30 May 1930, in the dying days of the W.L. Mackenzie King government, in anticipation of the election held on 28 July 1930. This history of resentment was something I spent hours explaining to my federal colleagues, whose reaction was more or less, "They should get over it."

Caught between the NDP, the Conservatives, and resistance in his own cabinet, the prime minister instructed me to meet with Lewis as many times as possible and to keep talking with him, without letting the issue of a state oil company mature into an election issue. In effect, my instructions were to rag the puck.

In August 1973, the price of domestic oil took another jump. An increase of forty cents per barrel, slightly more than 10 per cent, it was the biggest hike in twenty years and came on the heels of three other increases in less than a year. This only added to the prevalent concerns about inflation and its impact on prices to consumers, as well as on labour contract demands. Meanwhile, Canadians east of the Ottawa Valley line had to contend with rising international oil prices. The government faced considerable pressure, not least from the NDP, to tackle cost-of-living increases.

As it turned out, Parliament was recalled from its summer break on 30 August to respond to a rail strike. That meant the cabinet was in Ottawa, and in a good position to respond to the August oil price increase. The options had been set out in *An Energy Policy for Canada*, and it was up to cabinet to decide what to do.

On 4 September 1973, in the context of a broader anti-inflation policy, the prime minister announced in the House of Commons the government was asking the petroleum industry to refrain from further price increases to Canadian consumers before the end of the following January. He also stated that some kind of mechanism would be introduced to prevent this move from allowing the international price in the United States to push up the price of domestic oil in Canada. As well, he said the government now supported construction of a pipeline to bring Canadian crude oil to Quebec so that eastern Canada would no longer be dependent on imported oil.

Following up with more detail, several days later, Macdonald announced the government would be charging an export tax on oil. With oil prices rising in the United States (as well as internationally), Canadian producers were poised to make windfall profits from their exports to customers south of the border. After all, Canadian producers' costs were not increasing beyond inflation. Our motive was to be able to use some of this windfall for public purposes: to protect the country's industrial heartland and to subsidize consumers, including those in the East, for a transitional period, so that the adjustment to higher prices could be phased in. To say Alberta was not happy about this export tax would be an understatement.

As if things were not already difficult, they worsened with the Arab oil-producing states' response to the Arab-Israeli war the following month. Oil was used as a weapon against Western countries deemed to be supporting Israel; an embargo was declared against the United States. As well, OPEC raised its prices by 70 per cent (further price increases were to follow). While Canada was not directly targeted by the embargo, Canadians felt its impact, not only on prices but also on supply: The oil imported into Canada arrived in Portland, Maine by tanker, and then was transported by a pipeline to Montreal. The fact that the oil was ultimately destined for Canada and not the United States did not impress the Arab exporters, who had been providing about one-quarter of the oil imported into eastern Canada. (The biggest single source was Venezuela.) In November, the prime minster warned Canadians of the possibility of rationing at the wholesale level for fuel oil and gasoline during the coming winter. The severity and duration of any such rationing would depend on how well Canadians could restrain their demand by conserving energy. Meanwhile, Albertans were screaming that they were entitled to the global price for oil and had no responsibilities to protect the rest of Canada from the price rise.

Alberta viewed me as the architect of the problems they were having with the federal government. I was vilified, which was why cabinet decided to send me to Edmonton to explain federal policies. I had expected to see Premier Peter Lougheed, but, when I arrived, he refused to see me, delegating instead his energy minister, Don Getty.

Getty and I had a long talk. I reminded him about how Canada had subsidized Alberta's oil production for years through the tax system and through providing Alberta with a protected and subsidized market in western Canada and most of Ontario. That national policy needed to be adjusted. We also discussed revenue sharing and price management. Getty made it clear that Alberta disagreed with all I had to say, and the federal position was politically unsellable in his province. Alberta had the attitude that they didn't need to see things from the national perspective because the resources were theirs. Getty and I sat for three hours, and then I got back on the government plane and returned to Ottawa. It was a day trip. I reported back the next morning to the P&P committee of cabinet.

One day, in late November or early December 1973, David Lewis told me, "Enough talking, tell the prime minister if he doesn't commit to a state oil company, we will bring the government down early in the new year." If we had had a majority government, I am not sure we would ever have had a Petro-Canada.[2] I spoke to the prime minister, who replied,

"Okay, draft the damn speech." So I did. In the meantime, the Progressive Conservatives were planning a non-confidence motion, which made it all the more urgent to win NDP support for the government's continued existence.

Speaking in the House of Commons on 6 December 1973, Trudeau announced plans to create Petro-Canada as part of a new energy policy. Its purpose would be to promote Canadian energy self-sufficiency and develop purely Canadian expertise in the field independent of US companies. Petro-Canada would give the Canadian government a window on the oil industry that would allow its fiscal policies to be informed by a better understanding of industry realities. Additionally, the company would take risks in the public interest to develop the Alberta oil sands and find and develop new oil and gas reserves in the provinces, the North, and offshore – risks private companies did not see fit to take. Eventually, Petro-Canada would also get into refining and retailing. In sum, it would be a Crown corporation that would serve Canadian policy goals but was not intended to replace private enterprise. Trudeau's speech also unveiled plans to erase the Ottawa Valley line and make Canada into a single oil market, with eastern Canada consuming Alberta instead of international oil, as a means to achieve domestic energy self-sufficiency by the end of the decade.

The NDP were excited by their achievement. Their ambition to see state ownership in the oil industry was long-standing.

The prime minister in his 6 December 1973 speech expressed support for the construction of a Mackenzie Valley pipeline to bring Canadian and American natural gas discoveries to market – a project that had been proposed by Imperial Oil and its partners in Canadian Arctic Gas Pipeline Ltd. But Trudeau added a crucial qualifier: this would not be done by lowering environmental standards or by neglecting the rights and interests of Indigenous people in the area.

In reorganizing EMR, I had insisted on the right to hire an environmentalist to look at pipeline development issues and oil and gas issues. I had brought on board David Brooks, an American with a PhD. At the time, very few in the department and in the earth science field in general were sensitive to the social and environmental costs of resource extraction, so the reaction I got was, "What's *he* for?" The prevailing view of those in the department then, as well as of those in industry who had been their university classmates in resource engineering or geology, was that their role was to create wealth by advancing the development of the country's resources. Coming from a family of relative poverty, I thought the idea of creating wealth was a very good thing, but my own experience in mining and my observations about its impact on nearby communities had also left me sensitive to its destructive side effects. Like those in the department, I had thought the damage was a necessary evil, but I came to realize it wasn't necessarily necessary. I came to realize that resource development had to accommodate other stakeholders, and that doing so might be a little more expensive for the resource developer but less costly to society as a whole. I was influenced in my thinking on these issues by my friend Maurice Strong, who in 1972 had spearheaded the UN's landmark Stockholm conference on the environment. Rachel Carson's book *Silent Spring*, which I had read not long after its 1962 publication, had also made an enduring impact.

When the Mackenzie Valley pipeline was proposed, Brooks told me there was no available data, environmental or social. I told him we had already seen the social cost of the Distant Early Warning Line in the Northwest Territories and of the Canol pipeline across Yukon (outsiders coming in, raping women, supplying alcohol, and causing major social disruption were among the ill effects).

As an executive assistant, I didn't have the capacity to move policy at this level. Once I was a deputy minister, I was entitled to try. My area of responsibility, however, extended only to the pipeline's impact on the physical conditions; the social environment of the North fell under the jurisdiction of the Department of Indian Affairs and Northern Development (DIAND).

My counterpart at DIAND was Basil Robinson, also a British Columbian, though he hadn't lived in the province for decades. Robinson and I talked. I found he had a strong social conscience and wanted to change the culture in Ottawa when it came to dealing with the conditions facing the northern Indigenous Peoples. When the application for a pipeline was made, I told Robinson that there would inevitably be an impact on those northern communities and the people living there should be consulted. Robinson and I discussed the possibility of a commission to conduct consultations with the people. We agreed the project should not receive any go-ahead before a study had been completed and the idea of a pipeline had been accepted by people in the North. I proposed the study take the form of a royal commission.

We jointly took the idea to cabinet, and it was approved. Like the approval of Petro-Canada, this decision might not have come naturally to Trudeau's centre-right cabinet, but it was another way of keeping the NDP onside during the minority government period. Michael Pitfield played an important role in pushing the recommendation of a royal commission through.

Then the prime minister asked me who I thought should serve as royal commissioner. I recommended Tom Berger, a young judge in British Columbia who had served briefly as leader of the provincial NDP. I knew him from UBC law school, where he was one year behind me. He had also represented Frank Calder in his effort on behalf of the Nisga'a people in northern British Columbia to have their Aboriginal title to their lands in the Nass River Valley recognized. (The case went to the Supreme Court of Canada, and although Calder ultimately lost, narrowly, the court recognized for the first time that Aboriginal title existed in Canadian law.) I knew Berger would not only take the side of the people in the communities but also write an analytically strong report that would be unassailable. And that is exactly what he did. In the meantime, the appointment of the royal commission on 21 March 1974 took the issue off the table. We were postponing the plans and ambitions of Imperial Oil, the most powerful oil company in Canada. There had been strenuous arguments, via lobbying and telexes to the Prime Minister's Office (PMO), opposing the royal commission.

Throughout this period, I never thought of myself as an engineer of change. While I was part of the evolution of law toward requiring that environmental and social factors be taken into account in resource development, I wasn't conscious of that at the time. It would be presumptuous of me to claim such prescience. Everything I did was in response to a specific challenge, in response to an emerging need, and as the result of my own sensitivity to what I had previously seen and learned.

Between Petro-Canada, the Berger Royal Commission, and our policies to prevent oil companies from raking in windfall profits at the expense of Canadian consumers as prices rose, I developed a negative reputation in the oil industry as someone who couldn't be "brought around." I think those who saw me in this way were particularly disappointed because I was originally from Alberta and a resources lawyer. My client was the national interest, and that was my guiding star.

During my assignment as deputy minister of EMR, relatively little of my time was spent on issues of specific interest to British Columbia, though of course the province's coal, hydroelectric power, and oil and gas in the Peace River area all figured in our comprehensive energy study.

One British Columbia file I did spend time on was the placing of a moratorium on exploration for oil and gas off the west coast. Before my time, the federal government had issued permits to Shell and Chevron, among other oil companies, for offshore exploration between Vancouver Island and Haida Gwaii, and east and west of Haida Gwaii. Geological and seismic work was done. The geology proved to be extremely complex. Most of those structures were almost vertical rather than horizontal, but potential existed.

After the 1969 Santa Barbara oil spill from production off the California coast, alarm was raised in British Columbia about the potential for similar environmental damage from drilling and production. In 1972, cabinet instructed me to put a moratorium on exploration. It was the combined result of pressure from environmentalists, led in the House of Commons by David Anderson, a Vancouver Island Liberal MP and later minister of the environment, who were concerned about possible spills; First Nations concerns; and a jurisdictional fight over offshore rights with the government of British Columbia, which claimed it held the rights. The moratorium was essentially an order-in-council freezing the rights of the companies that held permits and suspending drilling requirements and lease payments.

The *Exxon Valdez* oil spill off the coast of Alaska in 1989 effectively confirmed public support for that moratorium and ended pressures from provincial government and industry sources to restart exploration.

My work as deputy minister put me in regular contact with Prime Minister Trudeau. Before the oil crisis, we didn't meet one-on-one; rather, I would see him when I would accompany my minister to cabinet to present memoranda on EMR proposals and/or reports, or occasionally at social events at 24 Sussex. Once energy became a central preoccupation of the government, however, I saw him frequently.

My relationship with Michael Pitfield grew increasingly close and co-operative during this same period. Pitfield was very much a part of advising me on the mood of cabinet ministers and senior officials, which helped a great deal in terms of EMR submissions to cabinet and the development of government policy during the energy crisis. I had many, many discussions with him before I posed my recommendations to my minister for cabinet discussion.

As deputy minister of EMR, I was not in the loop with respect to the drafting of the budget the government presented in the spring of 1974, other than having made my recommendations, as every deputy minister does, for what we wanted to see with respect to our department. I only saw the budget when it became public, and I certainly was surprised that it was so confrontational with the NDP. Was the government deliberately trying to engineer its defeat, because it calculated the timing was good for an election? Some suggested that was the case, but I was not in a position to know. And if Pitfield knew, he wasn't telling me.

In May 1974, the government was defeated in the House of Commons on a budget vote, and an election was called. The legislation to create Petro-Canada died on the Order Paper.

From 1972 to the 1974 election, the post of principal secretary to the prime minister – the chief of staff and principal political adviser – had been held by Martin O'Connell. He had previously been a Toronto-area MP and had served as minister of labour, but had lost his seat in the 1972 election. O'Connell resigned to run for Parliament again (and went on to be re-elected). Thus, there was a vacancy that needed to be filled quickly. It was the view of the brain trust around Trudeau, which at that time included Jim Coutts, Keith Davey, Marc Lalonde, and some others, that it would make for a very good image if a prominent deputy minister who had played a significant policy role during the energy crisis received that appointment. It would show the confidence of the public service in Pierre Trudeau and his re-election. Or at least that's what I was told, though I wasn't quite sure I followed the logic.

I pointed out that making me principal secretary would not go over well in Alberta, because I was anything but popular there, after all the controversies about energy policy. "Alberta doesn't matter," Davey said. He said the Liberals were not going to win anything in Alberta anyway, what mattered was Ontario. He told me the business community there knew very well that I had helped preserve the Ontario economy by advising a policy of gradually raising oil prices during the oil crisis instead of one big jump. He also noted that I had excellent relations with key people in the Quebec public service, which I did, and in the premier's office.[3]

For me, the clincher was Trudeau telling me, "We've worked well together" in dealing with the 1973 oil crisis. He added that if the Progressive Conservatives won, they would throw me out very quickly, and I would have to go back to Vancouver because there would be no role for me in Ottawa under a Conservative government.

Going back to Vancouver did not seem like such a bad thing for me personally. My plan had been to spend five years in Ottawa, and at that point I had been there for four. As well, a return to Vancouver would have meant more opportunity to see my daughters. By then Sheila and I had separated; she and the girls had moved back to Vancouver in 1972. My long hours and intense career focus were at odds with her expectations for the marriage and our family life. My work and its challenges had essentially left Sheila to raise our three daughters alone. Neither of us could overcome the disappointments.

Nevertheless, I told the prime minister that I was honoured to be asked and I would do my very best.

5 Chief of Staff to the Prime Minister

BY THE TIME I BECAME PRINCIPAL SECRETARY, a position now more commonly called chief of staff, Pierre Trudeau knew me very well and we were comfortable with one another in a work setting. Early in my tenure, I took it upon myself to write a speech for him, even though he had his own speechwriters. I thought I was a pretty good speechwriter. I had written speeches for ministers, and they had been pleased. After Trudeau read my speech, he curled it into a ball and threw it into the wastepaper basket. "Not very good, Jack," were his exact words. I didn't get the sense he was particularly uncomfortable with my speech but he wanted to say, in effect, *Don't presume to try to help me where no need is evident. You have enough to do without going outside your job description.* I remember the incident well because it fascinated me in terms of his setting the personal space between us.

As principal secretary, my role during the election campaign was to stay in Ottawa and support the prime minister in his capacity as leader of the government. Although the PMO didn't get significantly involved in the campaign, it did have a political role, and I was the link between the PMO and the national campaign committee. It should be noted that some PMO staff took full-time leave to work on the campaign.

Keith Davey and Jim Coutts, a highly effective team, were running the campaign. My connections with both men dated back to my years in Ottawa with Art Laing. At the time, Davey was national director of the Liberal Party. Coutts, a native Albertan, had been a member of the Pearson PMO while still in his mid-twenties. His title was appointments secretary, but that did not describe adequately the significant role he played of adviser and companion during Pearson's political travels. Coutts would be my successor as principal secretary.

The election held on 8 July 1974 was an enormous triumph. The Liberals were returned with a majority government, thanks mostly to strong support in Quebec and Ontario. Predictably, we were shut out in Alberta.

There was, of course, a sense of relief among the cabinet and caucus that the government had survived; however, there was also an attitude that, after the exhausting, stressful, all-hands-on-deck years of minority government, everyone deserved a break, and now that we had four years, we could relax and pace ourselves. I argued it was time to take charge, to attack problems with alacrity, to show that we were rewarding the confidence of the people, but it was difficult to mobilize the government.

Another challenge was the sense in the cabinet and caucus that Trudeau and his team in the PMO had been remote, and the loss in 1972 of the majority had been largely due to Trudeau's insensitivity to the tactical side of politics and to relationships. The prevailing feeling was that he had been governing too high up in the clouds. The 1972–74 minority government period had required considerably more communication. It was a terrific learning process for Trudeau and PMO staff about the kind of stability that relationships in cabinet and caucus gave to a government and the importance of information and broad-based sensitivity MPs could provide about what was happening in the electorate. During that minority period, the team developed a critical discipline, and Trudeau began to focus on day-to-day political and caucus issues. Nevertheless, concern arose among ministers that they had not been properly consulted about policy, and that things were run by an inner cabal of half a dozen ministers the prime minister would bring into his office for chats. Pearson had done the same when he led his minority governments. As an executive assistant, I had watched this from the outside: Laing hadn't been one of those invited ministers.

So, a sensitivity existed. After the election, it became more pronounced. The complaint in the caucus and in the cabinet was that there was insufficient access to the prime minister, even after the majority government came in. The attitude was that they understood in a minority government the prime minister can't consult widely because he had to make decisions quickly, but by now it should be different.

In response, I set up a process of consultation with each member of the cabinet to establish a much better communication system with ministers. To do that job, I hired as assistant principal secretary Michael Kirby, whom I had met at federal-provincial events of various kinds while he was working as principal assistant to Nova Scotia premier Gerald Regan. I had been quite impressed with Kirby's intelligence – he had a PhD in mathematics – and his attitude toward public service. He was keen to come to Ottawa. I assigned him to interview every cabinet minister about what their aspirations were for the government as a whole and for their portfolio in particular. He prepared a report for me, which Pitfield and I reviewed. Then we sent the prime minister a confidential appraisal of the aspirations of his cabinet.

To address the similar feelings among the caucus, I insisted that on a Friday (the easiest parliamentary day of the week), about twice a month, Trudeau bring for lunch eight members of caucus – six MPs and two senators – and the principal secretary. He lunched with the whole caucus in the four years. At first, he stubbornly resisted the idea. He didn't say it, but he gave me the sense he thought it was a waste of his time. Where did the reluctance come from? Many interpreted it as arrogance, but I think it really came from the introverted side of his personality.

I was present at those lunches, although political staff did not attend national caucus in those days. Things have since changed, but in my day, the idea that there would be anyone but a member of the two houses in a caucus meeting would be considered not only strange but also utterly anathema.

At the time I hired Kirby, the only person in the PMO with a policy capacity was Ivan Head, who handled foreign policy issues. There was no domestic equivalent; the PMO staff were dealing more with day-to-day operational issues. Joyce Fairbairn, from Lethbridge, Alberta, who had first come to Ottawa as a reporter, served as legislative assistant, which among other things meant she briefed Trudeau on what questions were likely to be asked in question period, and she helped manage relations with caucus. Pierre O'Neil, a Quebec journalist with a particularly keen eye for Quebec politics and politicians, was the press secretary. Colin Kenny managed the travel arrangements. There were also people responsible for handling appointments and correspondence, and there were regional desks, which dealt with the party and other regional issues. The British Columbia desk was run by Paul Manning, who had a considerable provincial political network. The regional desks functioned to keep us attuned to the political conditions in the provinces but did not play any significant role in federal-provincial relations. That was more the PCO's domain than the PMO's. Apart from Kirby and myself, there was no one in the PMO who had any in-depth experience in federal-provincial relations. The PCO had professionals who dialogued with their counterparts in provincial governments.

First thing every morning, I would bring together the key officials for half an hour, before I saw Trudeau, so that I had a comprehensive view of what was going on in the PMO. Trudeau would typically arrive just before 9:00 a.m. At about 9:15, he and I would have a meeting, along with the clerk of the Privy Council (at first Gordon Robertson, later Michael Pitfield) and often O'Neil, to go over the agenda for the day, taking into account issues that had emerged overnight. It was a tactical session: what we expected to happen and how to respond. Especially after Pitfield joined us, these meetings mostly took place in French. I had no issue with that. My strong belief was that the federal government should operate bilingually; however, the reality was, as a westerner of my generation, I was less than fluent in the language, though my comprehension was good. My own interventions were made in English. I continued to take French lessons.

Ivan Head would meet separately with Trudeau on foreign affairs, along with the deputy minister of external affairs, as the department was then known. And then Head would brief me. Although in principle I was also responsible for foreign affairs, Head, who had been in place before I arrived, was virtually autonomous. I was impressed with his intellectual capacity. He was not popular with the external affairs people, however, because they didn't like feeding their advice through him. He had himself been a foreign service officer earlier in his career.

After the 1974 election, Trudeau's principal concerns were Quebec nationalism and the constitutional reform process. And they were the main topic of a discussion he and I had at 24 Sussex not long after the vote.

Three years earlier, the Victoria Charter had ended in failure when it was rejected by Quebec premier Robert Bourassa. Bourassa was always hard to pin down on the subject of federalism-nationalism. He reminded me and many others of a weathervane, changing direction with the wind. I had attended the Victoria Conference and had seen the process first-hand.

Also present at 24 Sussex the day of our meeting was Gordon Robertson, clerk of the Privy Council. Originally from Saskatchewan, Robertson had won a Rhodes Scholarship to Oxford University, but by then he had been in Ottawa for quite some time. I had known Robertson, who had played a large role in my returning to Ottawa as a deputy minister, since my days with Art Laing. In fact, when I began my post with Laing, Robertson was just ending a ten-year assignment as deputy minister of our department, northern affairs and national resources, a position that also made him commissioner of the Northwest Territories. Within two or three months, Prime Minister Pearson appointed him clerk of the Privy Council and secretary to the cabinet. I saw him frequently in his role as chair of the public service team negotiating the conclusion of the Columbia River Treaty.

We sat in the garden, and had an exchange of views. Trudeau's are well known. Robertson had a very different interpretation of Canada. While he agreed with Trudeau that Quebec and the constitution should be priority policy areas for the government, he was much softer on Quebec nationalism than Trudeau was; and he felt that the prime minister should accommodate more than challenge it.

I gave the Canadian vision as expressed in western Canada: Quebec was not the only province that had its own identity and jurisdictional claims. I said, "You have to keep that factor in mind as you are dealing with the Quebec issue because it will stoke resentment if a province is treated differently from all the other provinces in terms of their constitutional entitlement." That was my warning at the time. Trudeau said, "Yes, I understand."

In British Columbia, there was very little sympathy for Quebec nationalism and even less in Alberta. The argument was that all provinces should be treated equally. And for British Columbia and Alberta, dealing with economic issues was a much higher priority than debating constitutional ones. But the governments of those two provinces were not shy to use Quebec's claims to their own advantage and to argue that whatever deal Ottawa might have made with Quebec with respect to certain programs and policies should also apply to them.

While I felt it was my duty to convey that western perspective, in fact, my own views were well aligned with Trudeau's. I have always believed that Canada needed strong central powers to prevent aggressive regionalism, a view shaped by having watched British Columbia premiers W.A.C. Bennett and Dave Barrett in action and the Alberta government's behaviour during the energy crisis.

As for my thinking about Quebec and the bilingual nature of Canada, this had evolved considerably since my early days in Alberta, when our history lessons were based on the British Imperial perspective, and it did not occur to anyone that there might be any reason to learn the French language, at least not for the purposes of communicating with Quebecers. The period I had spent in Ottawa in the early 1960s as executive assistant to Art Laing was one of momentous change in Quebec: the Quiet Revolution was in full swing. There were tremendous debates about Quebec among the executive assistants, and it was the Quebec assistants to other ministers who provided my education. These colleagues, though federalist, were very assertive in their Quebec nationalism, in their expression of the need for more aggressive recruitment of francophones into the federal government, and in the use of the French language there.

My work with Laing had also brought me into contact with Quebec, when we had clashed with that province regarding its attempt to assert jurisdiction over Inuit people without their consent. Then, during my time as deputy minister of EMR, I had to always be aware of issues and sensitivities involving Quebec. The October Crisis took place during that period. No one who was in Ottawa at the time could forget those days. Soldiers were guarding federal buildings and, in the wake of the kidnappings, the homes of many MPs and senior officials as well. I was offered the chance to have heavily armed soldiers posted at my house. I declined. I didn't want to draw attention to myself and where my family and I lived, nor did I want my wife and children to feel under threat. I doubted that the Front de libération du Québec (FLQ) had ever heard of me, a western deputy minister who had little profile in Quebec.

All to say that I came to my time at the PMO with a substantial awareness of the issues involving Quebec's place in Confederation. But this was Trudeau's issue, and I don't think that anything I said had much influence on decisions he made in this area.

One area where I did have some clout was cabinet representation from British Columbia. There, I was very much in the play.

We had won eight seats in British Columbia. When the time came to form the cabinet after the election, Trudeau did not want to reappoint Ron Basford, who was generally perceived as the strongest of the group. Basford had previously served as Trudeau's minister of consumer and corporate affairs, and then of urban affairs, where among other things he helped turn Granville Island from a down-at-the-heels industrial area to the busy food market and vital centre for arts and culture that it is today. Trudeau didn't believe Basford had performed well and found working with him to be uncomfortable. Trudeau told me he found Basford argumentative and unco-operative. So, his reluctance was partly a personality issue. The prime minister said he would rather appoint someone else, though he didn't say who.

I insisted that Basford be included in the new cabinet, arguing that failure to include the prominent Vancouver MP would be a terrible blow to the Liberal Party in British Columbia. It would cause tremendous discord and a loss of focus. Trudeau said, "All right, we'll make him national revenue minister."

My next challenge was to convince Basford to accept that portfolio. When I told him of his proposed new post, he said he wasn't going to take it and that he planned to resign. He felt he was being demoted, which he was. He had been hoping to have been made justice minister. I told Basford what the prime minister's attitude was toward him, and he was shocked. He had been unaware that he was perceived as negative and aggressive. I asked him to take the portfolio for the sake of the Liberal Party in British Columbia, that by doing so he would be maintaining his leadership role in the party. I told him that I would share with Trudeau his aspiration to be justice minister, but that meanwhile, in the offered portfolio, he would have a chance to prove himself anew to the prime minister. Basford agreed. And he changed his approach from a constant internal critic of cabinet business to become a co-operative and supportive colleague. He became justice minister a couple of years later. As it turned out, I did him a service, but I don't think he saw it that way at the time. He ultimately acknowledged his appreciation of me much later, at an event I held at Granville Island market to honour his contribution to that project.

I also strongly recommended to the prime minister that Ray Perrault be brought into the cabinet as the Leader of the Government in the Senate so British Columbia would at least have two ministers. Trudeau was not enthusiastic about Perrault either but accepted that Ray was the other Liberal personality in British Columbia and had an important network. Basford and Perrault were quite complementary, though they did not especially have a comfortable relationship: Perrault was the sunshine face of the party in British Columbia and Basford was the harder-edged, more ambitious one.

Margaret Trudeau had played a significant role in the 1974 election, charming Canadians and highlighting her husband's gentler side. Affable and genuine, she became enormously popular in her own right and started receiving considerable volumes of mail, including invitations.

She was inundated by correspondence with no capacity to respond to it. Margaret herself was hoping to have some help. Certainly, it didn't make sense to me to dump it all in a wastepaper basket. Her communications with Canadians through correspondence and public presentations were valuable opportunities to build on a positive image for Trudeau and the government. We couldn't tell Canadians who were writing to the prime minister's wife that they were wasting their time. It would have seemed like insincerity on Margaret's part, which would not have been fair. The images of the prime minister and the government were also at stake. As well, my earlier association with her father, James Sinclair, who along with Nathan Nemetz had recruited me into the Liberal Party in the 1950s, probably would have at least subconsciously left me positively disposed to providing her with support.

I told the prime minister we had to assist Margaret. Of course, in Canada there is no official First Lady as there is in the United States. And at that time, prime ministers' wives were considered private citizens who were not deserving of any privileges.

He said, "The media will go after us if we spend a penny on Margaret, they'll come after us with everything they've got." At the time, the media hostility to Trudeau, particularly after the 1974 election, was fierce. Many in the media had thought we would lose the election and were disappointed that they were wrong. Keith Davey and Jim Coutts had also raised political concerns, given the attitudes of the day and that Margaret had no official position in the government.

I argued vigorously that times had changed and Margaret was being made into a public figure by all the people who were asking her to attend their events. I argued that we would have a good answer to any media attacks: Canadians who wrote to the prime minister's wife deserved the courtesy of a reply. I asked the prime minister to let me set up an office in what was then known as the Langevin Block, which he wasn't willing to do. (After attention was drawn to Hector Langevin's involvement in residential school policy, it was in 2017 renamed the Office of the Prime Minister and Privy Council building.) But he agreed that I could appoint an assistant, someone who was already a member of the PMO. I asked Marie-Hélène Fox, who had been an adviser on Quebec issues, if she would assist Margaret with correspondence but told her the work would have to be done at 24 Sussex. Fox was bilingual and thoroughly schooled in politics and political issues. Although she herself was still quite young, I felt she had the personal maturity and the political background and awareness to help Margaret, who at that time was still only in her mid-twenties. Fox personally wrote the French-language responses; someone else was assigned from the PMO letter-writing unit to assist with English letters. Fox was more than just an administrative support. She became an adviser more broadly.

Not long after, Fox joined me in recommending to the prime minister that Margaret be granted a proper office. Facilities were lacking at 24 Sussex, and Fox found that running back and forth between the prime ministerial residence and her own office was an impediment to her efficiency. We had several unused offices in the Langevin Block. I suggested Margaret could use one of the spare offices when she needed to work with Fox, but said we wouldn't call it Margaret's office. That worked out quite nicely.

Because Fox continued to be a member of my staff, she would participate in the daily staff meetings. The whole staff would brief each other, and then I would meet for another few minutes with anybody who had a particular issue they wanted to discuss privately. I had quite a few interactions with Fox as what we called "the Margaret situation" evolved over the following months and things became increasingly uncomfortable for Fox. But I didn't report to the prime minister on a daily basis, only when there was something that emerged of significance. I didn't consider myself required to be a reporting channel on Margaret. I did what I could to support her. And in terms of my relationship with her, it was always friendly but kept at a professional distance.

In September 1974, Margaret Trudeau checked into the Royal Victoria Hospital in Montreal for psychiatric care. She spent about ten days in hospital dealing with what was reported at the time to be "severe emotional stress." Many years later, she was diagnosed with bipolar disorder, and would go on to become an advocate for people living with mental illness. At the time, I knew nothing of her difficulties in this regard.

Later that fall, Margaret went to Japan on a private visit to christen a ship, which gave rise to questions in the House of Commons about whether accepting the trip was appropriate. (But some of the critics seemed to have a double standard: was Margaret a private citizen or was she not?) Margaret also appeared on the *W5* television program to talk about her life. In November, there were press reports that she was planning to become a freelance photographer, which she denied. It was obvious to those close to the situation that she was publicly chafing under the constraints of being the wife of a prime minister.

I didn't spend much time with Margaret myself, and the prime minister didn't talk to me about her. I had to learn what was going on between them from others and in the media. On 22 November 1974, there was an incident in the House of Commons that took me totally by surprise. During a debate concerning conflict-of-interest regulations for cabinet ministers, a Conservative MP from Alberta, Harvie Andre, made a general reference to the possibility of divorce. Whether or not it was meant as a personal jab, the prime minister took it as concerning his own marital situation, and he reacted furiously. Trudeau was said to have called Andre a son of a bitch three times, though the words were not audible to the Speaker or to those in the Press Gallery. Trudeau also said that he would repeat the words to Andre's face if he were to step outside the House. Amid a major uproar in the Commons, Trudeau gathered his papers and stormed out.

"So, what was that about?" I asked Trudeau.

He told me to talk to Michael Pitfield, who filled me in. That's when I found out there was a problem with the Trudeaus' marriage. Pitfield was a confidant of the prime minister's in every respect: personal, policy, and political. I had not picked up on the situation. Pitfield had more or less been protecting Trudeau throughout that time.

Michael Pitfield and Trudeau were very much on the same wavelength in terms of national policy objectives. They shared a common history as two Montrealers, one from the French-Canadian elite and the other from the English-Canadian business elite. They were both perfectly bilingual and had a great respect for one another's intellect and integrity. While both had come from backgrounds of economic privilege, they had not joined their families' pursuits in the private sector but instead had chosen to make their mark in the world of ideas, public policy, and public service. They also held similar perspectives on Quebec. Pitfield felt, like Trudeau, that Quebec sovereignty had to be challenged, that accommodation would become appeasement. Both also believed that Quebec's best interests as a majority-francophone society were best served by remaining a part of Canada, that English Canada served to protect Quebec from absorption by the United States and becoming anglicized.

One of the stories that circulated, which the Conservatives started but the media megaphoned, was that Trudeau was a closet homosexual and his partner was Pitfield. Nothing was more ludicrous. I broke up laughing when I first heard that rumour. Trudeau's interest was in women, and he was the randiest guy. So far as I know, he was faithful to Margaret during their marriage, but before and afterward he was very active.

As for Pitfield, he had married Nancy Snow in 1971. While Trudeau and Pitfield were close, there was nothing sexual about their relationship. How such a story gained currency, I have no idea. Perhaps it was fuelled by Trudeau's long bachelorhood and his role in the legalization of homosexuality, when he was justice minister. At the time, homophobia was prevalent and accusing someone of homosexuality was deemed a slur. To attack Trudeau in this way was so ridiculous, in terms of being an *ad personam* argument, an expression of prejudice, and missing the target, that I couldn't believe a serious person in the media could give it credibility. Still, the story lingered.

In late fall, the prime minister announced Pitfield's appointment as clerk of the Privy Council, effective at the beginning of 1975. The strong differences Trudeau had with Gordon Robertson concerning approaches to Quebec and federalism had become untenable, given the importance that Trudeau placed on these issues. Robertson became secretary to the cabinet for federal-provincial relations.

In those days, the PMO had nothing to do with the prime minister's management of the public service, so I had no role in that decision. I wasn't even asked for my opinion. I was merely informed of the appointment by the prime minister and Robertson.

Pitfield was the person I most shared issues, priorities, and policies with – he was my closest colleague and friend. Although I held Robertson in high esteem, of course I welcomed Pitfield's appointment. Afterward, our interactions only increased.

The distraction of the prime minister's marital problems further slowed the pace of government, a pace that had already been slowed in the wake of the 1974 election, when much of the government had decided it deserved a breather. The disintegration of Trudeau's relationship with his wife (they formally split a few years later) had a profound impact on him. He wasn't as focused as he should have been on government, in my opinion. Naturally, his marriage was commanding his attention and Margaret's behaviour was hard to ignore. And his young sons were a consideration. He became much more the caregiver. Of course, the PMO continued to function, but it meant the prime minister wasn't available for meetings as frequently; he was using much more personal time.

Even so, Trudeau never abandoned the routine of showing up at the office at about 9:00 a.m., having read everything the night before no matter what was going on in his personal life, and then attending the morning meeting to review the business of the day. He never lost sight of what was going on, and he applied himself to decisions about priorities, but there were distinct family distractions: he had to turn to his children, he had to be home by a certain time, he had to turn to the issues of Margaret.

Trudeau swam regularly for exercise, usually at the Chateau Laurier. But when he went, his security detail had to clear everyone else out of the pool, which was not good public relations. He asked that a pool be built at 24 Sussex. It would be a government asset and available for future prime ministers to use.

Perhaps I was being a little paranoid, but I advised him that the media and opposition would leap on this if a single dollar of government money were spent on such a project. It's the same attitude that has seen 24 Sussex fall into its current uninhabitable state: no money can be spent because it looks as if money is spent for an individual's benefit and not the benefit of the Crown itself.

Keith Davey particularly was on Trudeau's side, as was Jim Coutts, but I disagreed. In my view, the only way to undertake the project was if benefactors would contribute the money to the Crown so that no public money would be spent. My stance caused a short period of some discomfort between Trudeau and me, because he thought it was nonsense. He thought the government should just pay for the pool. I was focused on what it would cost politically: he'd just won an election and now it would look as if he was proposing to spend a lot of money on himself. I've always had a strong sense of the politics of public policy, and I just didn't want to put the prime minister, in the early months of his new government, on the defensive, however ignorant the attack was in terms of public policy. Davey said, "In that case, there are a lot of friends of the prime minister's out there, and I'll take on the fundraising for the pool." I responded, "I'm not touching it as principal secretary. It would look like people were buying influence. I don't want to know, and the prime minister isn't to be told. If money is contributed anonymously, then there will be griping, but it won't have any staying power." So, the donations were anonymous. Not to Davey, but the prime minister didn't know where the money came from. He didn't know, and I still don't know. But there was indeed a lot of complaining about the pool.

Another initiative I took to address concerns that Trudeau was isolated from on-the-ground realities was to appoint a council of economic advisers to the prime minister. The idea was to have a direct connection to advice from the private sector and the academic community. I thought this would have political value as well as be useful for its own sake. We appointed a half dozen prominent members, including Albert Breton of Montreal, Carl Beigie of Toronto, and John Helliwell of Vancouver. Trudeau saw the political and policy value in reaching out in this way and personally attended two of the meetings. It demonstrated to the economic and business communities that he was concerned with and personally attentive to their issues.

This initiative did not go over well with the finance department. The deputy minister, Simon Reisman, was livid, and he lit a fire under his minister, John Turner, who was already becoming disaffected with Trudeau over other issues. Reisman believed that finance – or more likely he, himself – had a monopoly on economic advice to the federal government. This was one of a number of differences over policy that Reisman and I had over the years.

Trudeau then told me that he was under a lot of pressure from Turner. I did not want the council to be the cause of Turner resigning. So, we disbanded the council. I remember journalist Clive Baxter coming to see me and arguing that I should keep it, but I didn't talk to him about the pressure from Turner. I just said, "Well, you know, it's useful, but time is precious …" He said, "I don't understand." He was the only member of the press who asked me anything about the decision to disband the council.

Turner resigned as finance minister later in 1975, after I had left the PMO.

In the spring of 1975, I became the subject of a series of attacks in the press, led by *Vancouver Sun* columnist Allan Fotheringham. It was a total hatchet job, in violation of any ethical standards of journalism, and its real target was not so much me as the prime minister.

Not long before the columns appeared, I recall walking through the Hotel Vancouver and seeing Fotheringham seated in the lounge with my former business partners Morris Menzies and Merv Davis. With them was Alvin Hamilton, a Progressive Conservative MP who had been a cabinet minister under Diefenbaker. I recall being surprised but had no thought the gathering might have anything to do with me. Morris had a twin brother, Merrill, who was Hamilton's adviser on economic and political policy. My thought was the gathering had something to do with that relationship. Davis also was a Conservative. I waved and kept walking. I learned later that it was at this meeting that my former partners made allegations about me to Fotheringham.

In retrospect, I'm assuming that Morris and Merrill had been chatting, and that Merrill saw an opportunity to hurt the prime minister politically. Fotheringham, who disdained Trudeau, evidently was happy to do his part. One of their claims was that I shared in responsibility for their lease of a corporate jet, a claim with no foundation. Morris Menzies had served notice of a legal action about this, though it was never pursued (he had no case, legally or morally), so it had looked to me that by going to Fotheringham, he might have been trying to pressure me to settle the claim. More broadly, I believe my former business partners were resentful of my success in Ottawa. Never mind that I had done my best to save Brameda from their overspending just when global markets declined and then had avoided bankruptcy, saved part of the investment for outside shareholders, and persuaded Teck to acquire the company.

Fotheringham's first attack was published on 3 May 1975. It began, "An embarrassment within Prime Minister Trudeau's own office is about to explode," and what followed was a litany of falsehoods, innuendo, and personal insults, the whole with a strong undertone of anti-Semitism. (I have never been quick to blame anti-Semitism when things didn't go my way, but what else to make of a column that deemed it necessary to point out my legal name is Jacob and that also portrayed me as some kind of clever shyster who was enriching myself at the expense of others, a classic anti-Semitic trope.) The column ended with a multi-part question that Fotheringham said Conservative MP Elmer MacKay was planning to put on the Order Paper in Parliament the following week.

The *Vancouver Sun* offered me the chance to write a rebuttal, a wise choice on their part because I was seriously considering a libel suit. In my piece, published on 10 May, I rebutted the numerous false allegations (though I followed my lawyer's advice to refrain from comment on the airplane allegation because of the legal action under way). More difficult to address were the character-assassinating insinuations, which left me with a feeling of helplessness.

When I took the Fotheringham story to the prime minister, he said, "At least they're not calling you a homosexual." Trudeau himself did not have a prejudicial view of homosexuality, but in the culture of those times, labelling people homosexual was worse than accusing them of improper business dealings. He added, "They're using you to get at me, Jack, don't worry about it."

However, Fotheringham's attacks did damage my reputation in British Columbia for a time, including within the Liberal Party in the province. Once such allegations appear in print, they taint public perception, and then one gets labelled "controversial," even if the controversy has been manufactured.

MacKay never did put those questions Fotheringham had alluded to on the Order Paper. House of Commons clerks found their innuendo-laden wording problematic, and he was asked to revise them. Eventually MacKay did ask a series of questions about me, but they were largely different. There was no dirt to be found, but that did not stop the Conservatives from trying.

Much was also made of a letter I had written earlier that year to some of my former business associates informing them of my disputing a reassessment by tax authorities concerning taxes owing on the sale of some shares, and that my lawyer believed my chances of success were good. They would have been in similar situations, and my intention was to assist them by offering to provide more information about the matter, as well as suggesting that they contact my lawyer to be briefed by him. The letter was on my personal stationery, which simply said J. Austin QC, and I had sent it out using personal envelopes and with my own postage. The fact that I had provided my work address and office phone number – the PMO switchboard, which was the contact point not only for the prime minister but also senior PMO officials – as my contact information was used to suggest I was somehow improperly associating my office with a personal tax dispute. Note that it was not the revenue department that I was writing to. The other fact to note, which was misunderstood at the time, was that I worked very long hours and was rarely home except to sleep, so providing my home phone number would not have been helpful to anyone who actually wanted to reach me. This was in the days before telephone answering machines, let alone cellphones. Still, in retrospect, providing the PMO phone number and my East Block office address was a mistake, though hardly the hanging offence it was made out to be.

The bill to create Petro-Canada passed in July 1975. The prime minister had agreed that if he were re-elected, he would reintroduce the bill, and he did. He kept his undertaking to David Lewis in the face of considerable resistance from his own cabinet, though Lewis now had no leverage at all. Trudeau was fastidious in completing his undertakings. If he said he was going to do something, he did it, unless there was a good reason not to as a result of changed circumstances.

When I had accepted the appointment as principal secretary, I had told the prime minister that my hope was to become chair and CEO of Petro-Canada once it came into being, to make the policy into a reality. And he had agreed.

My term as principal secretary had always been meant to be short. The five years that I had originally planned to stay in Ottawa were almost up. Keith Davey and Jim Coutts had made it clear from the outset that Coutts would at some time be interested in the post. Coutts hadn't wanted to take it in the spring of 1974 as he wanted to be free to play an entirely political role in the election campaign, which he did.

Don Macdonald, still minister of EMR, was getting lobbied hard by the Alberta oil patch and their bankers in Toronto. He himself was right-of-centre on economic policy. Pressure on him to scupper Petro-Canada was high. Once it became clear Trudeau was going ahead, the focal point moved from opposing Petro-Canada to opposing me being any senior officer. Macdonald opposed my appointment. The political attacks on me by Fotheringham and by Progressive Conservatives in the House of Commons added another hurdle.

In August 1975, I was in Quebec City studying French, accompanied by my daughter Shari, when I received a call from the prime minister. He urgently needed to talk to me about Petro-Canada and my situation. Shari and I drove back to Ottawa. When we spoke, Trudeau said that if I still wanted the appointment to Petro-Canada with all the pressure against me, he would keep his undertaking to me, but he wanted to ensure I knew what I would be getting into. It was clear he was asking me to release him from his commitment. Despite my deep disappointment at the turn of events, I told him it was more important to me that Pet-ro-Canada become a reality than I serve as its chair. I assured him I would find other things to do.

Trudeau asked me who I thought the first chair should be. I suggested Maurice Strong, who had spent his early career in the oil industry in Calgary and had extensive high-level experience in business and in Ottawa. He was running the United Nations Development Programme from Nairobi when I contacted him. This was an ideal background for becoming chair of Canada's national oil company, in both domestic and international terms. Most significant was that he was a believer in the concept of a state oil company for Canada and excited about the chal-lenge of making it work. He knew that the resistance in the industry and financial markets was a major factor to overcome.

Strong became Petro-Canada's first chair, and brought Joel Bell and John Ralston Saul onto the executive team to organize the company. Bell was a lawyer with a business degree who had done policy research work in Ottawa. Saul, who went on to be a well-known essayist and public intellectual, was at that time an emerging writer with a PhD seeking an introduction to the business world and more knowledge of western Canada, whom Strong had identified as a promising talent.

I was asked to find a president and CEO from the oil industry in Canada and tried to persuade Arne Nielsen, president of Mobil Oil Canada, to take the role. I was not successful, so Strong at first filled those roles too. In mid-1976, Bill Hopper became president and CEO, while Strong stayed on as chair at that point. Hopper later took over as chair as well. By this time, Hopper had shed the negative view of state enterprise he had held when he had worked as a consultant for me during the drafting of *An Energy Policy for Canada*.

Then Trudeau asked whether I would like to be ambassador to Japan, based on my long history with that country and the many contacts I had established there.

At that time, Japan was *the* Asian country I specialized in; China was still in the throes of the Cultural Revolution and its economic ascendance was yet to come. My involvement with Japan dated back to my days in the BC mining industry, and during my time in the PMO, I had advocated building a stronger relationship with Japan, of course to gain access to their markets for Canadian resources, but of equal importance, to provide an incentive for scholarship in deepening Canadian insight into Japanese history and culture as a basis for people-to-people understanding and building trust. This was one area where my views did in fact align with those of the British Columbia and Alberta governments, which recognized Japan's economic importance to Canadians.

I thanked the prime minister for the offer and told him I would think about it.

As much as I would have loved the post, personal considerations precluded my accepting it, and I relayed my decision to Michael Pitfield. I told him my plan was to go back to British Columbia. What I didn't tell him was that, although I was earning a good salary in Ottawa, I was relatively broke because of the debts I had incurred as a result of my Brameda experience. Although ambassadors are well paid, living in Japan would have been expensive. If I had become chair of Petro-Canada, I would have earned a large salary comparable to those in the private sector. If that was not to be, I needed to re-establish myself in the practice of law in order to pay off debts and get myself back on my feet financially. As well, given my separation from Sheila, I would have been unable to bring our teenage daughters with me to Japan, so there was also a family concern.

Upon hearing of my intention to return to British Columbia, Pitfield said, "I wonder whether you would be interested in the Senate." The death earlier that year of my mentor Art Laing had left one BC seat vacant. Taken aback, I said, "The Senate? Why would I be interested in the Senate?" I was forty-three years old and scarcely knew what a senator was, but like most people, I perceived the Senate as a place for those nearing the end of their careers.

And Pitfield answered, "The prime minister has a vacancy to fill in British Columbia and says he needs somebody in the caucus who really knows the province and who is respected there." When I reminded him about the Fotheringham columns, he said, "Nobody takes that seriously." Maybe not in Ottawa, but in fact they did have an impact on people's opinions in British Columbia. As a personal friend, Pitfield argued that my joining the Senate would help me re-establish myself in Vancouver in the face of the Fotheringham-Conservative campaign against me, whose real purpose, of course, was to embarrass the prime minister.

I said, "Would the prime minister appoint me?" He replied, "Absolutely." He indicated the prime minister didn't feel he had strong representation in British Columbia. Pitfield suggested that I write the prime minister a letter of application telling him what I would bring to the role. (Years later, I would be the one persuading Pitfield to agree to join the Senate.)

I accepted the idea of becoming a senator and staying in public life because as a senator I would be able to both serve in Ottawa and practise law part-time in Vancouver. I took Pitfield's point that it would help me re-establish myself in law in Vancouver. I feared the attacks on my character would make it harder to earn a living there and support my family. Who would want a law partner who was continually under attack in the media? The Senate post would give me a base for managing my career.

So, I followed up on Pitfield's suggestion and found myself appointed to the Senate. The hostility toward me didn't matter in the slightest to Trudeau. Actually, in my view, he had a kind of a piquant attitude in making the appointment, as if to say, *To hell with you guys, Jack is my guy.* I don't know that was one of his motives – he never said anything to me of the kind – but knowing him, I believe it.

As it turned out, Fotheringham's efforts to dislodge me only served to provide me with a far more challenging and intellectually rewarding career than I might have had otherwise.

6 The Evolving Senate

THE SENATE I JOINED did not have a great reputation, despite the important role it played and the many talented, accomplished, and hard-working people there. It was widely derided as a sinecure for patronage appointees named by successive governments, its members stereotyped as doddering old has-beens. Indeed, the Senate was largely composed of people who had been very significant political players in their day, but whose time for political impact was eroding, or over.

Disdain for senators was also part of the culture of the House of Commons and the cabinet. The elected people always carried a resentment, which surfaced now and then, toward senators who were not elected, yet had the same legislative powers as the elected members. For the NDP, this extended to rejecting the body's very legitimacy because of its unelected nature. No NDP members would accept appointments to it.

Of course, it is true that the Senate was not set up on a democratic principle, if democratic means elected. It was created as a counterweight to the popularly elected House of Commons and to ensure that the legislative structure could not be easily changed. The House of Commons was to express the principle of direct democracy and the Senate indirect democracy, "democracy slow," based on selection of its members by a prime minister who held the confidence of the democratically elected MPs in the House of Commons. These appointees would be citizens representing propertied interests, hence the stipulation that they be property owners. Another way in which the Senate was to act as a counterweight to the House of Commons was by protecting regional interests – also viewed as minority interests. In the negotiations leading up to Confederation, the Senate was a major topic of discussion. The focus was on ensuring that Quebec would be able to protect its identity and interests vis-à-vis the English-majority provinces and the Maritime provinces would be able to hold their own in relation to Central Canada.

As Prime Minister John A. Macdonald described the Senate, echoing words used in the United States decades earlier, the chamber is "a saucer in which to let the passions cool." Macdonald also more famously called it a place for "sober second thought." (This inspired the name of our Senate softball team, the Sober Second Thoughts, but I digress …)

The Senate's key constitutional function – to provide oversight of the executive at a time when this role was fulfilled by the courts to a much lesser extent than is the case now – has been insufficiently appreciated. Oversight could not be expected to come from the Commons, where in times of majority government the executive normally has a disciplined group of supporters always seeking re-election, who are not bound to be objective or critical of government measures. The Senate has served to remind the cabinet that its power is not absolute, even if by convention the Senate's power is subordinate to that of the Commons. One of the first principles inculcated in new senators is the Salisbury Convention, developed in the House of Lords, by which the House of Commons has primacy in its legislative authority, but in turn, the upper chamber serves as a review chamber and can decline to enact legislation in certain circumstances: when the government is seeking to pass legislation that had not been part of its program in the election, legislation that could not ever be removed or repealed, or legislation that would make fundamental changes that did not have popular approval. This was one of the basic reasons for the initial Senate refusal to approve Prime Minister Brian Mulroney's so-called free trade agreement with the United States. (I refer to it as so-called because of its lack of an effective mechanism for dispute resolution.) Progressive Conservatives had not included the project in their 1984 election platform, so they did not have public approval. In addition, the passage of that legislation would permanently change Canada's relationship to the United States. Thus, the Senate forced the Mulroney government into the 1988 federal election to seek a specific mandate, which it then received. Afterward, the Senate approved the legislation.

An even more dramatic example of the Senate's exercise of its review function came on 31 January 1991, when it defeated Bill C-43, the Mulroney government's abortion bill, on third reading. In the previous election, no mandate had been sought to recriminalize abortion after the Supreme Court decision striking down the previous abortion law. Justice minister Kim Campbell had introduced a bill to amend the Criminal Code to make abortions illegal, except when a doctor determined that the mother's health, including psychological health, was threatened. The national debate was fierce. The proposed new law left people on both sides dissatisfied: it was too restrictive for some and too permissive for others. The Conservatives used their majority in the House to pass the bill there. The debate in the Senate was also fierce and did not divide purely on party lines; party discipline was not enforced and senators were free to vote according to their conscience.

My own position was against the legislation, for being too restrictive. When a day or two's notice was given that the vote on third reading was to take place, I was in Vancouver, sick with a heavy cold. I almost didn't go to Ottawa. I assumed wrongly that the government, which had a small majority in the Senate and the potential support of a few of the Roman Catholic Liberals, would be able to pass it, and I felt sick enough that I leaned toward staying home. But the pressure on me from my wife Natalie and many others was that my vote should be on the record. So, I went, and I voted against the legislation. As it turned out, the result was a tie, which meant the bill to make abortion illegal in Canada was defeated. While a couple of Liberals voted with the government, seven Conservatives voted with the opposition. The episode was a key illustration of the reserve power of the Senate to check the power of the executive, and a near political mistake on my part. I had thought my vote wouldn't matter. We have had no legislation on abortion since that time, although the issue remains a running sore in the Conservative Party to this day.

On more typical issues, how senators balanced their partisanship and their constitutional responsibility varied greatly. Among my Liberal colleagues, for example, there were highly partisan senators who took their cue from the national caucus: when the Liberals were in power, they would support whatever legislation the government of the day seemed to want. There were other senators who felt strongly that the constitutional role of the Senate was to hold the executive under review, ensure that the public was heard with respect to legislation, and conduct independent policy studies that the government might not find convenient.

These were separate poles, but it was not unusual for a senator's attitude to evolve with the passage of time. The newest of senators, including myself once upon a time, begin as partisans. There is largely a sense of appreciation and commitment to the prime minister who appointed you. As time goes by, a sense of the constitutional responsibility begins to assert itself. As prime ministers changed, senators felt freer to range into policy interests of their own. And there was nothing a government could do if it lost the support of one of its senators. The whole purpose of the Senate as initially designed and constituted was that the senators would be in effect a political judiciary. They were independent of the government and they were there to exercise their best judgment on behalf of the people of Canada.

The first time I entered the Senate chamber – not counting earlier visits to the galleries – was on 5 November 1975, for my swearing in. The custom is to have two senators sponsor you and escort you in, and you are expected to show some reluctance to assume this awesome responsibility. I had chosen as my sponsors Ray Perrault and George Van Roggen, two fellow British Columbians, and they put up a ceremonial effort at pushing me forward. I then stood before the Speaker and took my oath of office. Next, my two sponsors escorted me to my assigned seat, as was the practice. Not surprisingly, mine was in the back row and about as far away from the Speaker as you could get, the least prestigious real estate.

I was a very interesting new appointee to a lot of the senators, being viewed by them as close to the prime minister. I had a prominent record in Ottawa by that time and was also coming out of the Fotheringham controversy, so the Progressive Conservatives were all charged up and ready to try to find something to annoy the government side with.

In joining the Senate, I also joined the national Liberal caucus. This was the group of Liberal members of the House of Commons and of the Senate who met every Wednesday with the prime minister and cabinet members to discuss the issues of the day. When I walked in for the first time, I received a warm welcome. I already knew most of the MPs and certainly most of the cabinet, so I had a good number of friends. But there were people who had their reservations. One person who went out of his way to be supportive was Alastair Gillespie. He was minister of EMR at that time and very familiar with my work in that department. He came over to me and shook my hand, which did not go unnoticed, particularly by the Ontario Liberals. Sen. Keith Davey was very supportive as well, commenting on the importance of the appointment for Liberal representation in British Columbia. My standing with Liberal MPs and senators in the national caucus was critical to my image as a power player, somebody with elevated significance in the hierarchy of the Liberal Party.

A third introduction took place back in British Columbia, where it was important to re-establish myself. The prime minister had received a few letters from Vancouver Liberals criticizing my appointment. He showed them to me, saying, "You're nearly as unpopular as I am." Ron Basford, the leading BC cabinet minister, was very negative. I think he saw me as a rival. Meanwhile, Fotheringham continued to take pot shots; in one of his opinion columns in the *Vancouver Sun*, he simply said that he disliked me and brussels sprouts. Ray Perrault and the BC Liberal executive held a reception for me in the late fall of 1975, coinciding with a visit to Vancouver by the prime minister. Trudeau was the principal speaker, although his remarks about me were brief: he simply said in passing that he was very pleased to have me in caucus to represent British Columbia. This was his style. He never laid it on for anybody.

So those were the three most important bases that I had to attend to: the Senate, the national Liberal caucus, and the party in British Columbia. Everything progressed from there.

On 8 December 1975, I made my first speech in the Senate. In it, I set out my expectations for myself:

My earliest words to my new colleagues in this chamber must be words of commitment. First, to serve the collective interest of all Canadians with every effort and ability I have. Second, to defend and to further the well-being of our Confederation and to speak and act against every tendency in our country to irrational regionalism; to speak and act against the insecurities that give rise to separatist feeling amongst us; and to speak and act against attitudes of alienation and disaffection in Canadian society wherever they appear. Third, within the context of a strong and progressive federalism, to advance the real interest of my own province of British Columbia in every way I can fairly do. Fourth, to defend the individual rights of Canadians, however unpopular, and to assert the individual responsibilities of Canadians, however unpopular. Fifth, to support policies that will promote a healthy economy and a fair sharing of the benefits of Canadian patrimony to all. Sixth, while at all times defending the sovereign rights and interests of Canadians in the world community, yet to remain mindful that we are but one family in the global village and we have both a moral duty and a self-interest to further the well-being of all mankind.

When I joined, Eugene Forsey was one of the iconic members and somebody who really interested me. Pierre Trudeau had remarked, shortly after I was appointed, that the Newfoundland-born, British-educated CCF intellectual was one of the most distinguished people he'd appointed to the Senate – he didn't say the same about me! – and that I should get to know him. Trudeau hated making Senate appointments. He always had in mind the John A. Macdonald dictum that in appointing a senator he earned nineteen enemies and one ingrate. But this 1970 appointment was the one Trudeau really loved making. Given the NDP's stance on the Senate, Trudeau had told him that he could be appointed as an independent, but Forsey had decided to join the Senate as a Liberal, in order to be part of a caucus. He had told Trudeau not to count on him behaving as a partisan Liberal, however.

I did reach out to Forsey. We lunched a few times in the fifth-floor cafeteria. I was eager to learn about his experiences in Britain and something about his left-wing political culture. Any time he spoke in the Senate, I showed up. As a constitutional expert, Forsey was especially conscious of the Senate's constitutional role. He understood, unlike more ideologically rigid NDP supporters, that the Senate existed in our constitution and that to reject participation would be to give up a means of exerting substantial influence on government policy. I've always thought the NDP's position in refusing to have representatives sit in the Senate was a significant political mistake.

When I joined the Senate, the Liberals had been in power for twelve years and had a strong majority there. But the Progressive Conservatives in the upper chamber were active and contentious in their opposition to government measures. They were led by Jacques Flynn, a Quebecer who by then had been leader of the Opposition in the Senate for several years, after serving as an MP and member of the Diefenbaker cabinet. He was a political pro and very smart about Senate rules and procedures. My impression of the Conservatives, and it did not change for some time, was that they were interested in political opposition much more than in policy. Years later, however, I developed excellent working relationships with some of my Progressive Conservative colleagues, notably Duff Roblin (a former Manitoba premier) and Lowell Murray, both of whom became leaders of their party in the Senate.

Carl Goldenberg, from Montreal, was another leading senator of the day. He didn't take much interest in me, but he did more or less tell me that it would be good if I didn't have much to say for two or three years. I took it as a warning that I shouldn't be a brash young person, that there were older and somewhat wiser people there and I would get along better if I hid my light under a bushel for a period of time. In hindsight, perhaps he was also trying to avoid having me become a lightning rod for partisan attacks from the Conservatives, given the political climate.

David Croll, from Toronto, also was a very strong presence in the Senate at that time. Croll, who was first elected to the House of Commons in 1945, had accepted an appointment to the Senate ten years later, after it became clear that Prime Minister Louis St-Laurent was not going to appoint him to the cabinet. This, despite the fact that as a former mayor of Windsor and former Ontario cabinet minister, he was amply qualified, and between 1945 and 1950 he was also the only Liberal elected in Toronto. St-Laurent was under pressure not to appoint him and deferred to the prevalent anti-Semitic attitudes of the day. So instead of being the first Jewish cabinet minister (that honour would go to someone else from

Windsor, Herb Gray, appointed by Pierre Trudeau in 1969), Croll had become the country's first Jewish senator. I took time to learn about his career, and I was quite an admirer from afar. With his landmark study on poverty in Canada, he had staked out leadership on social policy. It had been published a few years before my arrival but was still a major topic of discussion, and his advocacy continued on, including in the national caucus. Aside from the study's intrinsic value, for me it also pointed the way to the policy work that could be done in the Senate. We talked in caucus, and sometimes he invited me to his office; to him, I must have been just a kid.

At the same time that Goldenberg and Croll were cautioning me not to come on too strong, I was encouraged by others in the Senate and on the government team in the House to take significant positions in caucus. This group, consisting basically of unquestioning supporters of the prime minister, saw me as one of the people sent by him to reinforce those in the Senate who were advocates of government policy. So, there was a sort of encouragement by one group to be very activist, and at the same time, others telling me the Senate had its own culture, and I should sit back, absorb it, and not make myself a target.

There was a strong, dominant male culture in the Senate in 1975, as there was in pretty much all parts of society at that time. Not quite half a century after the landmark Persons Case opened the way for women to be appointed to the upper chamber, only 6 of the Senate's then 102 seats were occupied by women. One important addition in 1978 was Florence Bird. She made a significant impression on me and a number of others for her deep understanding of Canada's historic discrimination against the rise of women in political and policy roles. Her work as chair of the Royal Commission on the Status of Women in the late 1960s created an inflection point in Canadian attitudes.

Similarly, there was a lack of ethnic diversity. Almost all the senators were of Anglo-Celtic and/or French-Canadian background. The diversity was provided by three Jews (I was the fourth), one Indigenous person, and three members of other backgrounds (Arab, Icelandic, and Dutch).

Even if Canada was a less demographically diverse place in 1975 than it is now, that composition did not at all reflect what this country looked like at that time.

Over the years, however, there has been enormous change. By the time I left the Senate in March 2007, considerable progress had been made. By then, the Senate had 105 seats. There were thirty-one women; a half dozen each of Indigenous people (First Nations, Inuit, and Métis were all represented) and racialized minorities (Black, Chinese, and South Asian); and an additional fifteen senators of various other backgrounds, including members of the Ukrainian, Italian, and Greek communities.

In my view, one factor that helped bring about that change was Pierre Trudeau's policy of multiculturalism. It helped bring about attitudinal change; it opened the door to seeing Canada as a much more diverse society, one in which it was possible to be fully Canadian without whitewashing one's heritage or fully assimilating into the dominant English or French cultures. The definition of a Canadian and the notion of what a Canadian looked like evolved in fundamental ways. The concept of the Canadian mosaic, as opposed to the US melting pot, took hold.

As well, it had been obvious to everyone as the years progressed, and not just to Liberals, that cultural and racialized minorities were important political constituencies in the country, and ensuring they had a role in governance was essential. A handful of members of minorities had succeeded in winning election to the House of Commons, but that was a much harder test. When electoral success was not forthcoming, prime ministers could ensure communities' representation in government by appointing people from those communities to the Senate to give them a voice in the legislative and policy systems of governance. And the extent to which these senators could indeed be representatives of their communities – their community networks and approval – was often critical to determining who exactly was appointed, for Liberal and Conservative governments alike. Of course, most of the people they named were also loyal party supporters. Not all members of minority communities appointed to the Senate were seen as having a representative function, however. The circumstances and purposes of my own appointment did not fit that mould.

As for women, along with the societal changes that brought them more actively into the business world and governance in Canada, there was a

strong emphasis on appointing prominent and successful women to the
Senate. Among my Liberal colleagues who made substantial contributions
to public policy in the Senate were former *Montreal Gazette* editor Joan
Fraser; Catherine Callbeck, a former premier of Prince Edward Island;
Anne Cools, a social reformer from Toronto; Lillian Dyck, with an accomplished background in academia, from Saskatchewan; Mobina Jaffer,
a British Columbia lawyer who was the first Muslim senator and first
senator of South Asian descent; Lorna Marsden of Toronto, a strong voice
in social policy issues who left the Senate to become president of Wilfrid
Laurier University and later York University; Céline Hervieux-Payette,
a former Quebec MP and a fellow minister in the Trudeau cabinet; and
among my closest friends from PMO days, Joyce Fairbairn, who brought
an understanding of tactical politics beyond most. When I served as government leader in the Senate, I asked Rose-Marie Losier-Cool of New
Brunswick to be the Liberal whip, the first woman to hold that role.

So, the changes in my time were remarkable and desirable. And even
the oldest senators gave way to the understanding that the Senate had a
much stronger foundation in public approval as a result of representing the
country's diversity. The greater the diversity in the appointments,
the stronger the support for the Senate, as minority communities recognized the value of the upper chamber as a conduit for participation in the
country's governance and for putting forward their concerns. Such a role
was entirely in keeping with the Senate's original function as a protector
of demographic minority interests as well as of regional ones, even if the
minorities the Fathers of Confederation had in mind were francophones
and Roman Catholics.

When Michael Pitfield first raised the issue of my going to the Senate,
we had discussed the upper chamber and what I could do there. His view
was that the Senate was lacking in small *l* liberal public policy initiatives.

There had been the landmark Croll study, and Sen. Herb Sparrow
would go on to publish a major study in 1984 on soil erosion in New
Brunswick, which was one of the most widely reported Senate studies
of its day. But by and large the Senate just moved along in a comfortable

way. That was Pitfield's view, at least, when I agreed to become a senator. He was far more a student of the Senate than almost anybody else I knew, and much of my early appraisal of the Senate's performance and potential came from that briefing with him. During my earlier years in Ottawa, I had rarely had occasion to think much about the Senate. I told Pitfield that making the Senate into a major centre for policy development was a rather big task for one senator to take on. While senators might not overtly declare themselves resistant to conducting policy studies, I suspected there was an attitude among most of the Conservatives, and probably more than half the Liberals, that such work would be a waste of effort. The feeling I anticipated –and found, once I became a senator – was that any studies the Senate might do would be left by the government to gather dust on a shelf – the same fate that royal commission reports are alleged to receive.

I didn't think one senator could make a difference, and certainly not in my early years. I told Pitfield the prime minister should appoint senators with backgrounds in social policy, Indigenous affairs, environment, and regional economic development. I also said that when he was ready to leave the PCO, I would very much like for him to join me as a senator to help push the Senate in the direction of more systematic activity on social policy. I registered my point, and then I made the same suggestion to Michael Kirby. He had an especially strong social policy bent and strong small l liberal and large L Liberal policy attitude, and he was playing a key role in government at that time. Kirby responded that it was an attractive idea, but who knew what the future would hold.

It took close to a decade, but both Pitfield and Kirby did go on to become members of the Senate, with Pitfield sitting as an independent. And they both became very active. As it turned out, Pitfield's highest-profile contribution in the Senate was not in the area of social policy but rather his leadership of a major study on the establishment of an intelligence agency that would be hived off from the RCMP. This led to the creation of the Canadian Security Intelligence Service. Kirby, as chair of the Standing Senate Committee on Social Affairs, Science and Technology, in 2001–02 produced a multi-volume study titled *The Health of Canadians: The Federal Role*, which had a major impact on health policy thinking in Canada and led to that committee intervening in a major health controversy, the Chaoulli case,[1] to make the representation that a part of the social contract for health care required timely care. This was also the first time the Senate was an intervenor in a court case. In 2006, Kirby and his committee also produced a landmark report on mental health titled *Out of the Shadows at Last: Transforming Mental Health, Mental Illness and Addiction Services in Canada.*

Another person who joined our little community, in 1984, was Lorna Marsden, former Liberal national policy chair and a staunch feminist. There were others, including Colin Kenny, who had been in the PMO when I was principal secretary. He was more right-wing than the rest of our informal group, particularly fiscally, but he was very supportive of many things the old team was trying to accomplish. In all, there were half a dozen of us, including Joyce Fairbairn. We knew the government game and how legislation worked, we had networks in the bureaucracy, and we could get things done.

Our aim was to step ahead of the government policy of the day, look down the road, and lay out a pathway.

Over my thirty-one years in the Senate, the staffing/research support available to us increased, in keeping with the greater expectations that were placed upon senators, in terms of participation in policy-making and oversight of legislation.

In its earliest days, if you were appointed to the Senate, you were a person of some means, and you looked after your own expenses. As more was expected from senators to represent and deal with broader issues of public policy, the arguments came back that greater resources were needed. For the Senate and senators to be accorded greater resources, the concurrence of the House of Commons was needed; budgets and spending need to be approved by both houses. And it took a long time for the Commons to agree to increase Senate funding. The House of Commons restrained Senate development for many decades out of a sense that senators were not deserving and possibly even a sense of rivalry. However, the senators at various times had points of leverage over the executive, and the executive in turn had points of leverage over the Commons.

Gradually, as we came into the late twentieth century, and the senators were playing a larger role in legislative review, policy development, and politics, the resources expanded to allow senators to hire policy and research staff in order to become more effective. When Michael Pitfield and I were in the Senate together, we hired, at his suggestion, Tim Barber, and we each paid half of his salary. It took both of our research budgets to hire one well-qualified person.

However, when I started in 1975, I was given a secretary and an office, and that was it. The secretaries mostly did not have a research capacity. They essentially handled communications: answering the phone, typing correspondence and memos, and communicating with other senators' offices and with others in the political process. As far as research was concerned, any senator or MP could ask the parliamentary library for help, and I did that many times before I had my own assistants, sometimes afterward. And I didn't have an office in Vancouver; senators don't have constituency offices.

The concept of what was considered ethically acceptable evolved considerably during my time in the Senate.

Originally, the Senate was seen as a citizens' chamber, and the citizens who sat there were not expected to give up their occupations. If anything, the thinking was that citizens had various interests and it was desirable that these be represented in the Senate. However, it was deemed important that these interests be disclosed and transparent.

It is difficult to imagine today that someone could sit simultaneously on the board of a major bank and on the Senate banking committee. When Sen. Salter Hayden chaired that committee for decades while serving on the board of the Bank of Nova Scotia for at least some of that period, this was not generally considered problematic, and perhaps even seen as a pertinent qualification. In 1985, when I accepted an appointment to take on the Bank of British Columbia's small international operation, I withdrew from the banking committee, and all other committees, for the year I served. This was not only to avoid any conflicts but also because of the time commitment involved. My attendance in the Senate declined that year, but the experience gave me a chance to learn banking, which would enhance my Senate contribution when I later returned to the banking committee. Attitudes continued to evolve. By the late 1990s, the then chair of the banking committee, Michael Kirby, introduced a practice of voluntary disclosure of outside interests for committee members, and by then, simultaneously sitting on a bank board was not something that would have been regarded favourably.

Another case that illustrates how attitudes changed over the years is that of Andrew Thompson. From 1964 to 1966, he had been the Liberal leader in Ontario and a popular person in the Liberal Party. He was appointed to the Senate in 1967 by Prime Minister Lester B. Pearson. In 1997, his very poor attendance record in the Senate over many previous years became a public scandal after it was exposed in the *Ottawa Citizen*. Thompson had been living in Mexico for several years, due to health reasons, he said. Under the Senate's rules, to continue to collect a salary and earn his pension he needed only to show up once every two sessions. If he had done that in 1930, nobody would have cared, and in 1960, not many would have cared. But by 1997, this was a matter of public outrage, part of which was directed at the Senate itself for not having done anything about the situation until it came to public notice. Once it did, however, Thompson was turfed out of the Liberal caucus and then stripped of his office and other privileges. A couple of months later, he resigned. As a result of the public shaming, the Senate reformed its rules about attendance. Still, the episode only heightened public cynicism about the Senate and its occupants, despite the many of us who were working diligently and in the public interest.

A typical work week during my early Senate years looked like this:

I would use Monday to fly to Ottawa from Vancouver. That was pretty well an all-day trip because of the time change. I'd catch a morning flight and would get to Ottawa around 4:30 or 5:00 p.m., and then would go to the office to prepare for the next day. Then I would get a bite to eat somewhere, head to the studio apartment I had rented on Slater Street, watch the TV news, and go to bed.

Tuesday, Wednesday, and Thursday were my working days in Ottawa. I would be in my office by 8:00 or 8:30 a.m., read two or three newspapers and the parliamentary library news digests, and then go through the folios my secretary would have prepared the previous afternoon. These were big books that had pages with pockets to hold memos, letters for signature, and other items requiring my attention. On Tuesday mornings there would often be committee sittings, and then a Senate caucus meeting over lunch. On Wednesday mornings, the national Liberal caucus would meet, and there often were committee meetings in the latter part of the afternoon. I was usually on two committees at any given time and served on a great variety of committees over the years. At 2:00 p.m., the Senate would sit. I generally was a good attender. My days were full, occupied by meetings big and small, phone calls, correspondence, and doing my homework on policy matters. Dinnertime was with other senators or MPs or visitors or nobody, and then it was back to my apartment to read something that I felt I should read, like *Maclean's, Foreign Affairs,* or the *Economist.*

The Senate did not usually sit on Fridays. I would try to get home to Vancouver on Thursday nights. I was affiliated with Allan Ainsworth's law firm, and on Fridays I would go in to look after whatever I was looking after. It was very much a part-time practice, until I eventually left it to join the cabinet. Ainsworth was a remarkable colleague and friend, and I always enjoyed his company. In addition to being a Rhodes Scholar and brilliant lawyer, he was a talented amateur actor, a master of accents and mannerisms, who could change personalities on a dime. He also happened to be an active Progressive Conservative. I don't know whether he ever got any grief from his fellow Conservatives for taking a Liberal senator into his firm.

In July 1976, a news report in the *Vancouver Sun* on the performance of BC senators described me as having been a "hyperactive" member of the Senate and, somewhat backhandedly, as "a pleasant surprise."

Commuting across the country was energy-costing, and of course on every flight I knew people, and people wanted to talk to me. I was somebody who represented Ottawa in British Columbia as well as British Columbia in Ottawa. I normally took the non-stops, and on every flight going to Ottawa, there were business people or academic people or union people. Everybody on the plane had access to me. On the trip back to Vancouver, I would try to sleep, but that didn't usually work out, because there were MPS and other senators on the same flights doing similar time travel, and they wanted to talk. So did other British Columbians returning from the capital and people from elsewhere headed to Vancouver. And because I was quite open to building relationships, taking on information, and learning about attitudes, most of those flights were a different form of working.

One person with whom I would often chat on these flights was John Fraser, who had been one year ahead of me at UBC law school. He had been active in the university's Conservative club and had tried to attract my interest. In the ensuing years, we continued to cross paths from time to time. In 1972, he ran as the Progressive Conservative candidate in Vancouver South, defeating my friend Gordon Gibson Jr, the Liberal candidate. Fraser went on to become environment minister in the Joe Clark government and, later, fisheries minister in the Mulroney cabinet. Subsequently, he served as Speaker of the House of Commons. In many ways we saw ourselves as opposite numbers, Conservative and Liberal, in representing British Columbia in Ottawa.

At one point, in 1982, I gave a speech on Liberalism in Canada, and it was the subject of columns by Bruce Hutchison and Jamie Lamb, both in the *Vancouver Sun*. Lamb encouraged Fraser to give his own speech on Canadian Conservatism, and Fraser did. In a subsequent column, Hutchison called our speeches "a polite, though wounding, duel," and observed, "It is encouraging to learn that even in the British Columbia of the popular caricature two men of opposite philosophies can think straight, despite the chaos of our times."[2] When we found ourselves on the same plane, Fraser and I would make a point of sitting together. After we had both left our political roles in Ottawa, we became members of the Vancouver Round Table, a public policy discussion group, and continued our good-natured political jousting in that setting.

People often asked me how I managed the commute for so long, given the three-hour time difference. My stock response was that I kept myself on Winnipeg time, a short-hand way of saying that I was as constant as possible in terms of real time, on a schedule that was a compromise between the Eastern and Pacific Time Zones.

Of course, this work schedule meant I was less available to my family and out of touch with my normal social world. My world became one of relationships through business and professional and political interests. It changed my relationships, my time, and my focus. It meant I had to work harder on being available in quality time to my family and personal friends, because the quantity time was in short supply.

Commuting across the country was a constant reminder of my role as a representative of British Columbia in Ottawa and a representative of Ottawa in British Columbia. I was far from alone in my awareness of my regional responsibilities. Most senators had a consciousness of and commitment to the importance of regional interests – and protecting them. Not surprisingly, this sense was particularly strong among senators from the Atlantic provinces, and even stronger in Quebec. While there was a high level of partisanship normally, when it came to regional interests or certain ideas of federalism, regional solidarity often trumped partisan solidarity. This was much less true with respect to Ontario senators – Liberal and Conservative – who saw themselves as largely members of a national Senate caucus. They tended to leave provincial politics to the provincial politicians and were more likely to act on the basis of what they saw as the national interest, though what that was could differ along partisan lines. In my own case, I was somewhere in the middle, advocating for British Columbia but also weighing national interests against regional ones.

There is a distinction between representing a regional interest and representing a provincial government. At various points, there were proposals to give the provinces a role in appointing senators. My view has been that there should be no such role. We have a system set out in the British North America Act in which you have a federal government with designated powers and the reserve power, and the provinces with designated powers. I believe the Fathers of Confederation were right in establishing the national Parliament as paramount in Canada. Only in the national Parliament can the interests of Canadians everywhere be addressed, negotiated, and assured, not in a community of communities and not in a league of provinces. The provinces should not be able to prevent the federal government from pursuing national policies, but that is exactly what could happen if they were given such leverage. Canada would not work well if that were the case.

So, I became quite adversarial when Prime Minister Pierre Trudeau in 1978 introduced a paper titled *A Time for Action: Toward the Renewal of the Canadian Federation*, quickly followed by Bill C-60. Never enacted, it would have created a House of the Federation that would have replaced the Senate, composed of fifty-nine members appointed by the Commons and fifty-nine by the provincial legislatures. I wasn't adversarial in a public way, but I made my case with the Liberal caucus, Michael Pitfield, and others.

I don't know what influences brought about that bill, given that it seemed to run counter to Trudeau's strong federalism, but Quebec was always uppermost in his thinking – and this was about halfway between the Parti Québécois's election to power and the first referendum on Quebec independence – so it must have been intended to appeal to the Quebec government or the Quebec public. In the context of a Parti Québécois government, however, allowing provinces to appoint people to the Senate would have been a poisoned chalice. It would have put people in the chamber who would have been opposed to almost every federal measure relating to national unity or constitutional change. In any case, the proposal went nowhere. The cabinet referred the matter to the Supreme Court of Canada, which ruled in 1979 that the federal government did not have the constitutional power to make any such fundamental changes to the Senate unilaterally.

During the period that I was in the Senate, there was a periodic clamour for "Senate reform," but the constitutional constraint on unilateral federal action, as well as differing views among the provinces, prevented any changes that would have required a constitutional amendment, for example, in the method of selecting senators, the number of senators from different provinces, and their powers.

It is beyond my scope here to provide a comprehensive history of Senate reform efforts. Suffice it to say there were several, including Alberta's calls for a "Triple-E" Senate (equal, elected, effective), the House of the Federation proposal, efforts to insert Senate reform into the constitutional deal that ultimately led to patriation, provisions that were part of the failed Meech Lake and Charlottetown processes, and an effort by Prime Minister Stephen Harper with Bill S-4 to limit senators' terms to eight years. Ultimately, they all failed.

Eventually even Harper, who had come to power promising Senate reform, gave up. Like every other prime minister before him, he eventually came to understand that the old system worked best for him politically, and it was effective in recruiting community leaders to the Conservative Party.

During my earlier years in the upper chamber, I was a proponent of moving to an elected Senate. What I proposed was filling new vacancies by holding an election with a preferential ballot, where voters ranked their preferences, and unless someone got 50 per cent on the first ballot, the ballots cast for the last-place candidate would be distributed to the voters' second-choice candidates, and so forth, so the winner would be somebody with a strong mandate. My thinking at the time was that regardless of the constitutional responsibility of an appointed senator, unless senators were elected, they would still face the dominant political attitude in the Commons that the person appointed has no mandate to oppose the person elected.

I suppose I was looking for something that would raise the credibility of senators in the governance system and credibility with the public more broadly. The problem was that each individual senator then would have been elected by the entire province, except in Quebec, where senators represent specific regions. (Senators from other provinces may carry a local designation – mine was Vancouver South – but that is merely honorary; in fact, they represent the provinces as a whole.) So, if a senator were elected province-wide, he or she would have a larger mandate than any MP or even the premier, because this person would have been chosen by the entire province's electorate.

I amended my view as a result of recognizing that electing senators in this way would essentially distort the authority of other elected people in Canada. It also didn't work in a province the size of Ontario. And there was the question of whether the way the political constituencies were distributed in large provinces would result in an imbalance over time of people supporting the same party. I moved away from my own concept. I hadn't thought it through.

Reaching almost back to the time the Senate was created, there has been dissatisfaction with its performance, the system of appointment, and the early subjugation of the Senate to the executive's power, which was largely based on the appointment power being reserved to the prime minister. This restlessness was also fed by periodic scandals involving certain senators' use or misuse of public funds. From time to time, prime ministers sought to give the Senate a better image by appointing people in whom voters had shown trust. One of them was Arthur Meighen, a former prime minister. Others included former Alberta premier Ernest Manning and two former premiers of New Brunswick, Louis Robichaud and Richard Hatfield. After he was voted out of office, former BC premier W.A.C. Bennett was very keen to join this prominent political group, but no vacancy opened in sufficient time before his seventy-fifth birthday.

There was also restlessness in western Canada and the Maritimes about the dominance of the Senate by Central Canada, which had 50 per cent of the senators until Newfoundland joined Confederation in 1949. Until then, the seats were allocated equally among the regions as they were defined: 24 seats for the west, 24 for Ontario, 24 for Quebec, and 24 for the Maritimes. The original idea was that some of the other Atlantic provinces would give up senators in favour of Newfoundland in order to keep the regional balance at 24, but that was rejected outright, not only by Newfoundland but also by the three Maritime provinces. And so the federal government had to give way and persuade Ontario and Quebec and western Canada to agree to add another 6 seats for Newfoundland. Much later, each of the northern territories was accorded a senator, bringing the total to the 105 we have now.

As the economic importance and demographic weight of the western provinces grew, their number of seats in the Senate was seen increasingly as unfair, and I believe this contributed to a rejection of the national process by people in western Canada. Why should Nova Scotia and New

Brunswick, whose respective populations were under one million, have 10 Senate seats each, while British Columbia, with about five million people, has only 6? Comparing British Columbia and the four Atlantic provinces together is even more telling: British Columbia, with double their population and in many ways its own distinct region, has only one-fifth of the number of seats they do. Some might argue that the Senate, unlike the House of Commons, was not designed on representation-by-population lines but rather to give compensatory weight to the smaller provinces. There is some truth to this. If we look at the Senate's constitutional history, however, we see that population was one of the governing principles.

Throughout my time in the Senate, I was an energetic advocate for greater British Columbian, and western, representation in the upper chamber. Similar calls were made by many other British Columbians, including by Premier Bill Bennett in the constitutional negotiations leading up to patriation.

In 2006, Progressive Conservative Ontario senator Lowell Murray and I co-sponsored a resolution in the Senate to increase British Columbia's Senate representation from six to twelve and Alberta's from six to ten, and to provide Saskatchewan and Manitoba each with one more senator. We thought this was modest but would recognize the equity principle. It was an attempt to initiate a constitutional amendment, and we were hoping that the proposal would be discussed at a federal-provincial meeting. The initial reception in the Senate was favourable. But the person who put the blocks to it was a fellow British Columbian, Pat Carney, a Conservative who had held three portfolios in the Mulroney cabinet from 1984 to 1988. Her position was that she wouldn't support a resolution that didn't give British Columbia twenty-four senators, the same as Quebec and Ontario had. Well, that was the breach of the dam. Instead of other people looking selfish in terms of their provinces' interests, this allowed the Quebec and Atlantic senators to say that will never happen, not twenty-four, and some of them went on to say – especially the Quebec senators – that preserving the present balance was essential to the stability of Confederation. It was a most interesting debate.

I'm sure we would have never got there anyway. Five provinces would have opposed the change. We were making a point, and it was terrific that Lowell Murray was willing to take a national perspective on the issue. It was very important that I have a Conservative co-sponsor (or in Murray's case, Progressive Conservative). I admired him for his vision and willingness to compromise, although he knew, too, that it wouldn't ever happen, so the political cost to him wasn't very high; nor was it to me. But there was a demand from western Canada, and I wanted to support it. To this day, British Columbia only has six senators, but I did what I could.

During the 1980–81 constitutional process, I had the honour of serving on the special joint committee on the Constitution of Canada. It was a profoundly moving experience. As much as I had been a lifetime student of Canada, I found I still had a lot to learn, even though no one had to convince me of the value of the Charter of Rights and Freedoms. I listened to witnesses from many communities and walks of life. They told the committee, as they spoke in favour of the Charter, about their disappointments with the treatment they had received in Canada, but also their optimistic belief that our democratic society would satisfy their needs in a fair and equitable way. They made a profound impact on how committee members understood the nature of this country and the need to eliminate political blockages that had delayed the evolution of a more just society. Canadians across the country closely followed the televised hearings.

There almost wasn't a joint committee. Originally, the people in the Commons did not believe that senators should have such a prominent role. I and other senators in national caucus argued that if the Senate were excluded from the process, the resulting bill could face slow going in the Senate, as senators would want to study it carefully, but if Liberal and Conservative senators were on a joint committee, they would be reporting to their caucuses and would be representing the views of their caucuses. There was a bit of a skirmish in the national caucus at the time, but it was resolved by Prime Minister Trudeau. Trudeau always called the shots.

The hearings focused on the Charter, as well as on the constitutional entrenchment of Aboriginal rights. (I will have more to say about the battle for section 35 in chapter 12.)

Governments will always resist the role of the Senate as an oversight chamber. They will bring to bear the cabinet, the parliamentary secretary, and members of the House of Commons to persuade, cajole, or demand compliance. This is still true to some extent even in today's mainly non-partisan Senate, but it was more the case in my day, when there could be clashes in national caucus and regional caucus, and sometimes in open meetings of committees, though mostly, pressure was exerted in the privacy of personal relationships and collegiality. For the most part, such efforts were focused on ensuring the passage of legislation. It was rare, over the years, for prime ministers to interfere with the inner workings of the Senate itself, beyond exercising their prerogative to appoint the Leader of the Government in the Senate, who would serve in cabinet.

One major exception was Jean Chrétien, who had no compunction about interfering in the naming of Senate committee chairmen, as I can attest from personal experience. In 1999, it was time to name a new chair of the Senate banking committee. I was the senior Liberal senator on the committee by length of service and active participation, so the Liberals on the committee recommended to Leader of the Government in the Senate Joyce Fairbairn that I become chair. Fairbairn was very supportive, but Chrétien blocked it, pointing out that I had supported Paul Martin's leadership bid against him, and he preferred to name Montreal senator Leo Kolber, who was a former director of the Toronto-Dominion Bank. I later learned that Kolber, whom I had known for a long time and considered a close friend, had gone to Chrétien and lobbied for the job. Kolber had been an important fundraiser for Chrétien, while Chrétien owed me nothing.

In addition to my personal disappointment, I also felt it was inappropriate, constitutionally, for any prime minister to interfere in the internal organization of the Senate, whose function is to review the powers of the executive. But Chrétien had no problem trying to direct Senate business through his Senate leaders. Fairbairn, with whom I had worked in the PMO, was sympathetic to me but powerless in this instance. I wasn't upset with her; I understood exactly what had happened.

I was, however, that same year made chair of the Senate rules committee, a position I kept until 2002, when Sharon Carstairs, who by then had replaced Fairbairn, removed me, explaining that as a Martin Liberal I did not deserve to be a committee chair.

In December 2003, Paul Martin Jr became prime minister after succeeding Jean Chrétien as Liberal Party leader, and he appointed me to the cabinet as Leader of the Government in the Senate. When a new cabinet was named after the 28 June 2004 election, which returned the Liberals with a minority government, political responsibility for British Columbia was added to my official duties. At my recommendation, Martin appointed as deputy government leader Sen. Bill Rompkey, a former MP from Labrador who had served as a minister in the Chrétien government. He and I got along famously.

I had already come to admire Paul Martin as a man of fiscal prudence, a strong social conscience and tremendous internal personal balance. Working with him in cabinet only increased my esteem. Martin and I went back a long way. I had first met him in 1966, when he was an executive at Power Corp. in Montreal, and I was working as a lawyer representing the Brenda group. I had negotiated and concluded a contract for Power Corp. to invest in the Brenda Mine project. Martin had participated in the evaluation. On that trip, on the day I learned that Power Corp. would be turning its contract over to Noranda, Martin, seeking to distract me from my disappointment, invited me to attend an Alouettes game with him, which I did. This really was our first chance to chat.

We next met when I was BC campaign chair during his father's leadership run in 1968. Paul Martin Sr had impressed me when we had worked together during my early years in Ottawa, not only because of his considerable wisdom and political abilities, but because he had always been very kind to me. Paul Jr was very active on behalf of his father, and we had several discussions as the process was under way. It was no surprise to me when Paul Jr later developed an interest in running for Parliament; by then, I was in the Senate. We had conversations about the political process. He became an MP in 1988.

When he ran unsuccessfully against Jean Chrétien for the leadership of the Liberal Party in 1990, I had supported him. It was a bitter contest, and relations between their respective supporters remained strained from then on. Chrétien named Martin to the finance portfolio in 1993, where he proved to be a major asset to the government and to the country. He left that role in 2002. In the early 2000s, a team had come together to promote his leadership of the Liberal Party when Chrétien, who already was losing party and public support for a variety of reasons, decided to step down. I indicated that I would be a supporter when a leadership convention was held. In November 2003, Paul Jr won the leadership, beating Sheila Copps by a substantial margin.

I served as a member of the Martin transition team, along with Mike Robinson, the head of Earnscliffe Strategies, a major consulting firm based in Ottawa; Arthur Kroeger, former deputy minister and Carleton University chancellor; Francis Fox, a former cabinet minister; Peter Nicholson, an economist; Tim Murphy, a Toronto lawyer who became Martin's chief of staff; Scott Reid, who became communications adviser; Michele Cadario, a communications adviser; Thérèse Horvath, Martin's long-serving executive secretary; and key members David Herle, the campaign manager, and Terrie O'Leary, long-time Martin policy assistant. So, when I was appointed to the cabinet as Leader of the Government in the Senate, it did not come as a surprise, though I had not received any assurance I would be given the post. Having at that point served in the Senate for twenty-eight years, I understood the institution and its workings and had valuable relationships with my colleagues. My appointment was well received there.[3] The other British Columbians in that first Martin cabinet were MPs David Anderson and Stephen Owen. In the second Martin cabinet, Owen and I were joined by David Emerson, Ujjal Dosanjh, and Raymond Chan.

In this period, I really had four main focuses as a minister: federal-BC relations; Asia, especially China; a positive evolution of the government's relationships with Indigenous Peoples (more on those subjects in subsequent chapters); and, of course, on the Senate itself. I was very much in the cabinet's policy inner circle. However, given that members of the House of Commons have an inherent bias against the Senate, there were ministers who thought I had too significant a role in the Martin government.

The job of government leader was challenging, because it involved reconciling two divergent roles: as a member of the cabinet, the job was to ensure the passage of the government's legislation through the Senate, but as a member of the Senate, my role was to ensure that the chamber could perform its oversight function effectively. I had to represent each side to the other. When I served in that position, I carried with me the mental image of a rider standing with one foot on the back of one horse and the other foot on the back of a second horse. The clear task was to keep them running side by side, or else!

The plan to create a Senate ethics officer along with an ethics commissioner to oversee the House of Commons brought that challenge into stark relief. A bill had first been introduced a few months before Chrétien's resignation. Several senators on the Liberal side and on the Conservative side united in opposition, not to the idea of ethics legislation but to the government imposing an ethics officer on the Senate. Those senators saw the issue as affecting the status of the Senate as a legislative chamber independent from the government. They believed that the Senate should choose its ethics officer and should make that appointment without government interference.

The Martin government inherited the issue, which became a major challenge for me, as the cabinet insisted that the proper authority of the Senate ethics officer must stem from an order-in-council, meaning from a cabinet decision, nominally endorsed by the Governor General. Some tempers grew short in both the House of Commons and the Senate. My timeline to resolve the issue was also short, given that the Martin cabinet wanted ethics legislation to pass prior to calling an election, which was contemplated for the summer of 2004. In addition, Prime Minister Martin had publicly declared the divestment of all his business interests. It was important for him that there be an ethics officer for the House of Commons to oversee his situation.

It took a lot of time, patience, and dialogue, but I was able to negotiate an understanding between the government and the Senate by which the government would appoint as ethics officer for the Senate only such person as chosen by the Senate itself. Initially, there were objections that the undertaking I gave in the Senate on behalf of the government would not be binding on future governments, but I successfully argued that my undertaking as a minister of the government would set a precedent from which future governments would be unlikely to depart. So far, the precedent has stood.

This bill was probably the most challenging during my time as government leader, but the job was never easy. Moving the government's legislation successfully through the Senate required enormous amounts of discussion and negotiation with my own caucus and with the Conservative leader, depending on the legislation. Once we had a minority in the House, after the June 2004 election, difficulties compounded as the Opposition tried to cause as much trouble in the Senate as it possibly could. There were also Liberals with grievances, particularly the Chrétien Liberals, a majority of the Senate Liberal caucus, who were upset with Martin's failure to win a majority. So, it was a rocky ship in my day, but I feel that I was highly successful in managing through some very difficult times.

Among my most supportive but also most critical colleagues both on the rules committee when I chaired it and with respect to the Senate ethics bill, were Richard Kroft of Winnipeg, Jerry Grafstein of Toronto, and Serge Joyal of Montreal. All three were trained as lawyers and used those skills to challenge me about every comma and every period. Frankly, I enjoyed being held to the standards to which they pushed me. Particularly unforgettable is their vigorous advocacy on behalf of Senate independence, and, in particular, in favour of having a separate Senate ethics officer.

Critical to my ability to navigate through the challenges of Senate operations was my chief of staff, Len Kuchar. A lawyer, Kuchar had served as chief of staff for an array of previous Liberal leaders in the Senate, in government and in Opposition, all the way back to Allan MacEachen as Opposition leader in 1985. And even before that, as a student, Kuchar had worked as a parliamentary messenger. This long experience had left him with an unsurpassed understanding of the rules, the procedural tricks the Opposition could play, the likely outcome of rulings by the Senate Speaker, and the interface with the House of Commons and its rules and procedures.

By the time I was appointed Leader of the Government in the Senate, Kuchar had moved to a policy role in the ministry of health. I prevailed on Joyce Fairbairn, one of the leaders for whom he had worked, to persuade him to return to the Senate. In turn, Kuchar recruited a team of highly capable staff members. And I continued to employ as my secretary Sheila McCann, who had been with me for many years and was always loyal and supportive. Kuchar and I became friends and my admiration for his professionalism has no limits.

Serving as leader was a great way to end my Senate career. When Harper formed his government in 2006, I declined to continue as Leader of the Opposition in the Senate, partly because I was about a year away from the end of my term, and partly because I didn't see any value in creating a new Opposition culture for the Liberal senators when I couldn't continue. The Senate Liberal caucus then appointed Albertan Dan Hays as the Leader of the Opposition, on my recommendation. He had previously served as Senate speaker and was a master of the rules of the Senate. He was succeeded by Jim Cowan of Nova Scotia, a colleague appointed by Paul Martin.

My last major political act as a senator was to support Bob Rae's unsuccessful bid for the Liberal leadership in December 2006. As I write this, he is serving as Canadian ambassador to the United Nations, and doing an outstanding job.

Even as Senate reform was blocked by external constitutional and political factors, I had pointed out to my fellow senators that there was much we could do within our own powers to enhance our status, performance, and relevance. I also warned that if we failed to address Senate reform from within, then the institution risked becoming irrelevant. "The priority study for the Senate is the Senate itself. How can we better represent the regions of Canada, our minorities and the national interest? How best can we include Canadians in our work and be seen to be open and responsive?" I asked my fellow senators on 24 October 2002.

I had also pointed out that during my time as chair of the Standing Committee on Rules, Procedures and the Rights of Parliament, I had advanced many proposals aimed at accomplishing these goals, including that the Senate sit in a different region of Canada once every session; the election of committee chairs by secret ballot; the review of government spending by all Senate committees; and a new system for deciding both the priority to be given to new policy studies and the funds to be allocated for such studies. I had also proposed the creation of a Senate citizen's commission, which would allow a committee of the Senate to add to its members, for policy study purposes, people with specific expertise; these extra members would participate in fact-finding and analysis but not in the final drafting of recommendations nor in considering legislation.

I made a series of other proposals in a private letter to Prime Minister Paul Martin in May 2004, while I was serving as Leader of the Government in the Senate. Recognizing the constitutional stalemate, these focused on changes to the Senate appointment process that would have been within the prime minister's own existing powers and, I argued, could have met responsible expectations for change. I suggested that as a matter of policy, he could state future appointments would be made in such a way as to include representatives of Indigenous Peoples from each of the country's five constitutional regions, that is, at least five Indigenous senators, or just under twice their proportion of the Canadian population. I suggested he declare establishing gender parity would be a consideration in future appointments to the Senate, so that the imbalance would never be greater than 60 per cent to 40 per cent.

I advocated the establishment of a Senate Eligibility Committee, whose members would be selected by the chief justice of the Supreme Court of Canada, the clerk of the Privy Council, and the secretary to the Governor General. They would choose ten persons from among the members of the Companions and/or Officers of the Order of Canada. Unanimity for their choices of individual members as well as the chair of the Senators Eligibility Committee would be required. The prime minister would advise the Senate Eligibility Committee of certain general criteria for persons to be elevated to the Senate. Criteria could centre on relevant public experience, such as demonstrated leadership on behalf of minority communities; national or regional political experience; and leadership in professional, labour, business, or academic life. The Senate Eligibility Committee would be empowered to receive recommendations from the prime minister, leaders of recognized parties in Parliament, and from the premiers with regard to their respective province or territory, and then based on the eligibility criteria that had been provided by the prime minister, the committee members would advise the prime minister concerning eligibility of those whose names had been submitted. The prime minister would select from this list persons to be elevated to the Senate.

In my letter, I also drew the prime minister's attention to the need to ensure a functioning Opposition in the Senate. At that time, there were only twenty-five Conservative senators.

Martin responded that my proposals were very much worth discussing, but given the upcoming election, the Senate was a low priority. If we were re-elected with a majority, I should bring it back to the agenda then. I don't know what would have happened with my proposals had we won a majority. Martin never indicated to me whether he was for them or against them.

Prime Minister Justin Trudeau has brought about significant changes to the Senate. In early 2014, while in Opposition, he threw the Liberal senators out of caucus. I don't know his reasons, but the decision came in the wake of various scandals, particularly regarding some senators appointed by Harper. Some commentators at the time suggested that in the run-up to the 2015 election, he wanted to distance himself from the Senate. Removing the Liberal senators from the national caucus was nothing I ever recommended or would recommend, because the chamber works on the parliamentary principle of adversarial debate; the whole culture of the chamber requires a certain level of partisanship in order for the debate to be full and contested.

After Justin Trudeau took office, he made major changes to the way in which senators are appointed. Of course, that included not appointing any senators as Liberals. While the prime minister retains appointment power, there is a non-partisan committee that advises on Senate appointments, a simpler version of what I had advocated in my letter to Paul Martin a decade previously.

Justin Trudeau's changes have created a positive shift in how Canadians view the Senate and changed the tone of how the institution is presented in the media.

Other developments have emerged. For example, in the three years following the announcement of the new appointment system, one-quarter of government bills were successfully amended by the Senate – a significant difference from the previous government. That's not to say that senators used to be passive; there was just as vigorous a debate over legislation in my day, but it was done behind closed doors. Senators' influence on legislation was exerted in caucus meetings or in ministers' offices. Now, those discussions are out in the open and accessible to Canadians in public debates, including through live broadcasts and subsequent transcripts of proceedings. This air of transparency allows Canadians to engage with the parliamentary process and see how, even if a proposed Senate amendment is ultimately rejected by the government, the issue was raised and thoroughly examined.

Although this openness has highlighted the Senate's role as a legislative body focused on the thoughtful review of legislation and ensuring the consideration of issues of public concern before new laws are adopted, the fact that there is now a non-partisan majority in the Senate has created a host of new challenges. One is that the government can no longer count on the Senate to pass its legislation in a timely fashion. In the previous era, though negotiations took place within the privacy of the party caucus, once the differences were settled, a government majority in the Senate could move forward with resolve. Ensuring that legislation is passed today requires greater effort in terms of achieving the agreement of a sufficient number of independent senators. Another challenge is that the Senate may amend legislation in ways unacceptable to the government, leading to stalemate. Individual senators each wield greater clout because their support cannot be taken for granted; they are now the "loose fish" referred to by Sir John A. Macdonald, describing

MPS without party affiliation. Trudeau must have understood that he was giving up some legislative control.

Another set of challenges is for the Senate itself, for an independent upper chamber to articulate to Canadians, in a public way, how it plans to manage the examination of legislation and its rules for both open debate and coming to final decisions. For example, how does the new Senate handle the development of new caucuses within the independent structure? What would the rules be for their representation on the Senate's all-important committee system? How should debate be structured in an independent Senate so that it is efficiently pursued but does not impinge on the rights of members to speak? In the previous system the party caucuses assigned certain senators to participate in debates. Who determines speakers in an independent Senate, when coherence, regional interest, time discipline are no longer under the control of its leadership?

These questions were more easily dealt with under the old partisan system. The two groups in the Senate were governed by a top-down approach. Senate party caucuses were used to debate and conclude assignments whose implementation was managed by party whips. In the new, more independent Senate, that will no longer work.

How exactly these and many other operational questions get answered is up to the Senate and individual senators to decide. For transparency and dependability, new practices need to be written into the Senate rules. Without such codification, Canadians could begin to think the Senate is letting itself roam free from the responsibilities of how the work of Parliament gets done. These changes must also be guided by first principles. At the outset, senators will have to ask themselves how to develop processes that best support the constitutional roles and legislative responsibilities of the appointed chamber.

The new, independent Senate is a grand experiment, but it's an experiment that is retrievable or amendable by this prime minister or his successors. It's the result of a policy change, and not a constitutional one. Perhaps the next Conservative or even Liberal prime minister will want to reassess the policies of the Justin Trudeau government with respect to the Senate and particularly seek to recapture greater control over its processes. In my own view, the ideal Senate would be roughly divided into thirds: government, opposition, and independents, providing the conditions for adversarial debate while avoiding excessive partisanship. The independent senators would hold the balance of power.

But no future government should make further changes to the Senate without first ensuring a public assessment of how the upper chamber has functioned under the current arrangement. It's essential that any public debate about the Senate's future be conducted from a place of objectivity, insight, and analysis. It is not too early for senators, officialdom, academics, and the public to begin that process.

7 The Expo 86 Backstory

EVEN BEFORE I BECAME A SENATOR, I had seen how members of the Senate could advance the policy interests of their respective provinces.[1] I was soon to find out what a senator who also is a member of cabinet – and the regional political minister – could accomplish.

The 18 February 1980 election, which returned the Pierre Trudeau government to power, had left British Columbia without any Liberal representation in the House of Commons. In the previous year's election, won by Joe Clark's Progressive Conservatives, Art Phillips had been the sole Liberal elected from British Columbia, from the riding of Vancouver Centre. Phillips had been one of the most successful mayors of Vancouver, highly regarded for his progressive development policies. After the Clark government's defeat, Phillips ran again, but unfortunately for the Liberal cause, he was defeated by Conservative Pat Carney.

In fact, there was no Liberal representation west of Manitoba, even though the party had won a majority. Trudeau turned to the Senate to appoint ministers to represent the three westernmost provinces. His first cabinet included one BC minister, Ray Perrault, who had already been in the cabinet as Leader of the Government in the Senate. Perrault continued to serve in that capacity, to which was added political responsibility for British Columbia. Senators H.A. "Bud" Olson of Alberta and Hazen Argue of Saskatchewan were also appointed.

I had been disappointed, frankly, at not having been included. There had been a number of people in the cabinet and caucus who had thought I could be a strong policy representative for British Columbia. However, people in the PMO conveyed to me that Trudeau had decided to stick with Perrault, at least for a while. They saw him as a good constituency politician and someone who was warmly received inside the Liberal Party in British Columbia, and that was certainly the case. I put disappointment aside and continued with my Senate activities, including serving on the committee on the constitution. I also continued with my law practice, all the while educating myself on provincial and national events and issues, and building a deeper knowledge of how the economy worked, which interested me a great deal.

In September 1981, I was at home in Vancouver when I received a call from the PMO saying there was to be a mini cabinet shuffle the next day. If I could take an overnight flight to get myself to Ottawa by the next morning, I would be named to the cabinet as a minister of state. In effect, I would be a junior minister to John Munro, the minister for the Department of Indian Affairs and Northern Development. An instant decision was required. Was I coming?

I was taken completely by surprise.

I said, "Well, of course I'm coming."

After I hung up, I told Natalie about the call. I explained to her that it was an opportunity of a lifetime to make a contribution for British Columbia, for federalism, and on policy issues that were significant to me. I told her I was asked for an immediate answer and had said yes. She was in shock, upset that I was forced to make a decision with such important implications for our life together without being able first to consult her. At that point, we had been married for three years. Our marriage nearly ended there; however, she came to accept the decision, which dramatically changed our lifestyle and priorities. I am sure this was not the first time that politics and political ambition strained a marriage.

The next morning, I showed up at Rideau Hall in Ottawa for my swearing in. It was a relatively small shuffle, and the ceremony was conducted in an expeditious fashion. Because I was new to the cabinet, I was sworn in as a privy councillor as well as a minister of state. I wore a kippah that I had brought from Vancouver and swore my oath on a Tanach[2] provided by the PCO. I became the fourth Jew to serve in the federal cabinet, after Herb Gray, Barney Danson, and Bob Kaplan, all from Ontario. Trudeau had appointed all of us. (Clearly, his youthful flirtation with anti-Semitism was a thing of the distant past.) By the time I joined the cabinet, Danson was no longer in federal politics; however, Gray and Kaplan were still cabinet members.

After the ceremony, Trudeau addressed the press, as did some of the ministers. I recall speaking briefly about the reasons for my appointment and about what my objectives were. These included enlarging the federal presence in British Columbia, serving as a backup to other ministers, and bringing to Ottawa a greater sensitivity to BC attitudes and issues. I don't recall anyone having had any questions for me.

When I later got to talk to Trudeau about the cabinet appointment and his reasons, he told me it was clear the Liberal Party needed stronger BC representation, and Perrault couldn't handle it alone. He felt that I had a contribution to make in dealing with the provincial government and a number of the most important stakeholders in the province, including organized labour, the business community, Indigenous communities, among many other sectors. The basic division of labour was to have me deal with the policy issues and leave Perrault to deal with the party's organizational issues in British Columbia and on maintaining his extensive networks of contacts there, as well as his responsibilities as Leader of the Government in the Senate.

Back in British Columbia, the reaction to my appointment was total shock. My reputation still hadn't entirely recovered from *Vancouver Sun* columnist Allan Fotheringham's attacks. Meanwhile, the media were sensationalizing the role I had played in creating a uranium cartel while I was deputy minister of EMR.

Perrault was very supportive and went to work to assure people that he and I would be a good team. We had been long-term friends. I had supported him when he sought the provincial Liberal leadership, and he had supported my campaign in Kingsway in 1965. He and I had maintained a good working relationship. There was no conflict between us; in fact, he seemed delighted to have a teammate who could carry some of the load.

Among those surprised at my appointment almost certainly was John Munro, who I am sure was not given much notice that he was about to get a junior minister. It was never Trudeau's habit to consult and inform ahead of time concerning cabinet appointments, basically because he didn't want arguments and representations. (In my view, that's the right way to make appointments: if you've decided to make them, you make them.)

However, it was not a huge surprise to insiders in Ottawa that my first cabinet assignment involved Indigenous affairs. Inside the caucus and in discussions with my colleagues, I had become a significant voice on behalf of the welfare and rights of Indigenous Peoples. When I had served as a deputy minister, I had instigated the creation of the Berger Commission. I believed that before any northern pipeline could be built, first an understanding of the impacts of such a development on the people who lived in those regions, as well as on the environment, was essential. More recently, I had been a strong advocate for the inclusion of section 35 in the constitution (more about that in chapter 12).

During my first meeting with Munro, he said, "Listen, this is a very big department, I've got more than enough to handle, why don't you take over British Columbia? Keep me informed, but I'll take your lead where I can on what we should be doing there." It was a generous offer – it's hardly usual for a senior minister to voluntarily give up part of his portfolio to the junior minister – but I didn't think this was the right way to proceed. I didn't want to be put forward as a sort of minister for BC Indigenous affairs, because I thought it would make me a target both for those who wanted something from the department and for those who opposed giving resources to the department, at a time when part of my role was supposed to be building networks of Liberal support in British Columbia. I told Munro it would be better for him to be seen as the one making the decisions, as he was the minister and also not from British Columbia, which gave him some protection. He agreed with that view but invited me to take a special interest in British Columbia and to advise him as to what should be done there, which I gladly agreed to do.

Munro included me in all his briefings with the deputy minister, Paul Tellier, one of the youngest deputy ministers of the time, who had an impressive intellect and the energy for program development and operations to go with it. It was no surprise that he went on to an illustrious career, becoming clerk of the Privy Council under Prime Minister Brian Mulroney and then a prominent businessman in Quebec. I found him welcoming and an interesting person with whom to work and discuss the issues of his department.

The background I gained during this period was invaluable. I learned a great deal about how the federal government was dealing with First Nations issues, who the First Nations leaders were in British Columbia, and what positions they were taking on the various conflicts of the day. So, I was able to be in touch with many of those leaders, and some of them became good friends.

I worked with Munro for about seven months, until I was made minister responsible for Expo 86. During that period, I also set about building relationships with people in the business community and other sectors in Vancouver, which became very useful when I went on to have a larger portfolio.

At Prime Minister Trudeau's direction, from the beginning, I also joined Ray Perrault in acting as British Columbia political minister, though formally that title remained Perrault's.

At the time I joined the cabinet, the issue at the top of Premier Bill Bennett's federal-provincial priority list was Ridley Island. That was the port facility in Prince Rupert, a small coastal city 750 kilometres northwest of Vancouver. The province was seeking the construction of a coal terminal there to enable the shipment to steel manufacturers in Asia of high-quality metallurgical coal that would be mined in the Tumbler Ridge area of northeastern British Columbia. That route was considered more efficient and cost-effective than shipping the coal south to Vancouver. Ports are a federal responsibility, and the one at Ridley Island was a federal Crown corporation.

Part of Bennett's interest in developing northeast coal was political. The provincial ridings in the northeast coal area were incredibly important to the Bennett majority. As well, his economic development minister, Don Phillips, who represented South Peace River (as the riding was then called), was from that region. But that was far from the whole story. Like his father Premier W.A.C. Bennett before him, Bill Bennett believed that British Columbia had to be developed in full; there had to be economic activity in all parts of the province and not just in Vancouver, Victoria, and Kelowna. The BC government was also looking for ways of building long-term capacity in the province's economy while costs were apparently low and there was hope that, if you built the capacity others would come and make it profitable and make further investments.

I was very familiar with northeast coal from my Brameda days, when my partners and I had had an interest in two properties in the Sukunka coal block, as northeast coal was also known. It was a large area, and others were active in exploration and development there as well. As a result of having been caught in the commodity downturn of 1969–70, we had sold Brameda to Teck, which had acquired these interests along with our other assets. By the time I was in the cabinet, I had absolutely no personal financial interest in the outcome of the project. All my stock was long gone.

The federal government, myself included, was highly skeptical of the economics of the Ridley Island coal terminal project, and we relayed our concerns to the province. I showed them the econometric studies on the project that indicated there would be no profit to the province but rather losses for years. My advice to Bennett was not to proceed. The province, through its railway company BC Rail, would have to build a very expensive spur line to link the coal area to the existing rail lines through northern British Columbia to Prince Rupert. The federal government would have to upgrade the tracks on the Canadian National line (CN was then a federal Crown corporation) that would be used to bring the coal the rest of the way to port, because a higher grade of track would be needed to bear the weight of the heavy coal cars.

We knew the governments wouldn't get the money back in charges or taxes for a very long time, if ever. That would require higher coal prices and higher taxes on the mining companies. Still, the companies had to get their operations going, so what they required, and received, were major tax breaks. As the old quip goes: a long-term investment is an investment that you don't get back for a very long term!

Nonetheless, on 30 October 1981, Perrault, myself, and two other federal ministers announced that Ottawa had agreed to spend $230 million to build a coal facility at the port, $175 million for the CN track improvements, $100 million for equipment, and another $4 million to build road access to the terminal. Just over a month later, the final hurdle was cleared when we reached a deal on coal handling charges with the mining companies involved. Ron Basford, the former federal cabinet minister who by then was in charge of northeast coal development for the British Columbia government, and not especially friendly to me, acknowledged to a reporter, "I give him full marks. He got it done."[3]

Why did the federal government agree to put money into a project it didn't really believe in? While we went into it with our eyes open, knowing the cost to the federal taxpayer in the so-called short run, the view was that making Prince Rupert a more prominent port, building a larger technical capacity there, would be a major economic investment for that community, which basically had only fishing to sustain it. While there had been pulp and lumber operations, these were marginal. For Prince Rupert, the project was another try at building a permanent economy. For decades, there had been a sense in the community that its day had not quite come. When the city was founded in 1910, there had been tremendous excitement about its future as a gateway to Asian ports. Charles Hays had chosen the site, on Kaien Island, as the western terminus of his Grand Trunk Pacific Railway, and he had had big plans to further develop the city. He died in the sinking of the *Titanic*, and it has often been said that the city's hopes died with him. The rail line was completed, however, and later taken over by CN. Other development plans fell by the wayside. I remember Art Laing had a line about Prince Rupert. He was a big fan of the city, and as a cabinet minister was always trying to find ways to help. But he would say many felt that "Prince Rupert has a great future – and always will have."

My success on the Ridley Island port deal earned me credibility with the provincial government in Victoria. But an even bigger challenge awaited, one whose ultimate success led to even more dramatic improvements in the relationship between the BC and federal governments.

Long before I had come on the scene, the BC government had begun making plans to hold a world's fair in Vancouver in 1986, marking the hundredth anniversary of the city's founding. The building of a transcontinental railway had been a condition of British Columbia's entry into Confederation in 1871, and 1886 was when the first train had arrived, so the fair was to have a transportation theme. Initially, it was to be called

Transpo 86. At the province's request, the federal government in 1980 had secured approval for the fair from the Paris-based Bureau International des Expositions (BIE), and had committed to providing a commissioner general for the fair and to carrying out the usual federal responsibilities for things like diplomatic support and customs formalities. By the summer of 1981, Ottawa had also committed, in a broad way, to providing a host nation pavilion. Premier Bennett had undertaken, in a letter to the prime minister, responsibility for the fair's administration and financial viability, including responsibility for any operating deficit. The federal government estimated its costs at $100 million. As well, there was a commitment of $60 million, tied to the fair being held, for the light rail transit project that became Vancouver's SkyTrain, for which the credit goes to Ray Perrault. Although Perrault had tried to get more funding for Expo, Trudeau had turned down the request. The prime minister didn't see why he should do fed-bashing British Columbia any favours.

By September 1981, when I joined the cabinet, it was a tough time in Canada: We were in a severe recession and interest rates were around 20 per cent. British Columbia's economic situation was particularly grievous. The Bennett government was having second thoughts about going ahead with what by then was called Expo 86. The NDP opposition was blasting Bennett and his Social Credit government for planning to hold a party while the province had more urgent preoccupations. The province asked the federal government to commit to sharing responsibility for the fair's deficit and was threatening to cancel the event if Ottawa refused – and presumably would blame Ottawa and engage in another round of fed-bashing. Meanwhile, Vancouver, under Mayor Mike Harcourt (later himself an NDP premier), remained aloof, not wanting the city to get saddled with a deficit. The experience of Montreal's 1976 Olympics, which ran up massive deficits, was fresh in everyone's minds.

On 21 December 1981, Bennett announced the province's plan to build a trade and convention centre on Pier B-C[4] was dead for the foreseeable future because of escalating cost projections. The pier was federal property that had been leased to the province. Pier B-C was the old CPR ship terminal; it had been a major centre in the early life of Vancouver.

A week later, Perrault and I went to see Bennett in Victoria, to get a better sense of what exactly the province was proposing in terms of enhanced federal help for Expo. I told the premier if he wanted to keep fed-bashing that was his political calculation to make, but it wouldn't help me do anything for the province. He said, "Let's look at what you're prepared to do."

I truly believed that Expo 86 was important to the BC economy and restoring our economic confidence. And I could see it was dead without a significant federal role. Agreeing to share the deficit would have amounted to writing the province a blank cheque, obviously a non-starter. In my discussions with Bennett, he had offered to share the operation fifty-fifty, but I told him that would never work. It would have to be one or the other, and the federal government had no interest in running the fair. The province either ran it or it didn't happen, I told him, and he accepted that.

Perrault and I had been accompanied by Sen. Bud Olson, who, like me, had been appointed to cabinet to provide western representation. He was the economic development minister as well as the chair of the cabinet committee on economic development. We had sought his help not only for those reasons but also because he was a former Social Credit MP who had become a Liberal in 1967. We thought as someone on the right wing of the Liberal Party he might be of assistance in building bridges with British Columbia's Social Credit government. Olson ultimately played a key role in the negotiations with the province and closing the deal. He was a very sensible man.[5] As a side note, western Canada being the small place that it is, I will mention a personal connection: in the 1957 federal election, Olson had beaten Natalie's father, Harry Veiner, the long-time mayor of Medicine Hat, who had been running as a Liberal.

Perrault and I made a pitch to the economic development committee of cabinet to give us enhanced authority to negotiate a bigger contribution so that Expo 86 could take place. The matter was discussed in the winter of 1982, but it was turned down fairly quickly. Although Olson was chair of the committee, and as a fellow westerner he was sympathetic to our request, he had to respect the consensus of the committee members. There were different ministers with different arguments but basically the eastern ministers saw little value in investing in a province that had no elected Liberal members and a tradition of fed-bashing. They also doubted British Columbia had the capacity to carry out a world exposition and felt there was little political support to be gained in the province from associating with the Bennett government.

However, as I recount in greater detail in this book's introduction, I saw no value in being a minister for British Columbia if the province was not recognized as a critical and valuable part of Canada, and if the federal government was not prepared to assist provinces suffering serious economic problems, as British Columbia most certainly was. I appealed the economic development committee's decision to the cabinet's P&P, the inner cabinet, and there, I argued vociferously that our support was essential, both on political and economic grounds. I also was able to make my case directly to the prime minister, who, much to the shock of the other ministers, ultimately called the decision in British Columbia's favour.

This allowed the negotiations with British Columbia to proceed, and by 1 April 1982, we were able to announce to an invited crowd of more than 1,000 people at the Hotel Vancouver that the federal government had committed $134 million to building a convention centre and cruise ship facility at Pier B-C, which would serve as the Canadian pavilion for the fair. We had been able to bring in federal economic development funding available for the convention centre as well as leverage the National Harbours Board's pre-existing interest in the cruise ship facility to access funding it had available for that project. This was above and beyond the $60 million contribution for the SkyTrain, which had been handed over to the province a month earlier. The hotel and offices would be added to the project later. Perrault, Olson, and I, along with Bennett and several of his cabinet ministers, spoke at the event. The federal and provincial governments had each sent out invitations. There was no co-ordination, so some people received two, which at least one newspaper columnist joked was a status symbol.

While Bennett and his team hogged the spotlight that day, years later, Bennett credited me publicly with having been "instrumental" in making Expo possible. By the provincial election of 1983, Bennett was speaking on the campaign trail about how the relationship between British Columbia and Ottawa had improved, and as a result he was getting things from Ottawa. For once, a BC premier wasn't running against the federal government, promising to do a better job of beating up on Ottawa.

Not long after the big announcement, I received an official letter from the prime minister informing me that I was now a minister of state for Expo 86, in addition to my other duties. Trudeau's approval had been conditional on my taking responsibility for the project. Normally, it would have fallen to the Department of Public Works. The minister at the time was Roméo LeBlanc, whom I had known for many years and with whom I had a good relationship. However, he had been opposed to the federal government playing a significant role in Expo 86 because, he said, his department did not have sufficient lead time or capacity to design and build the host pavilion.

So, Trudeau had said to me, "What are you going to do about that?" I told him that with his approval, I would create a private construction company, hire people locally in Vancouver from the private sector to run it, and the budget would be managed by Treasury Board to ensure there would be no question about how the dollars were used. Treasury Board wanted to put someone on the project full-time, based in the office in Vancouver, and I welcomed the idea.

Thus was born Canada Harbour Place Corporation. I found the name awkward, I had wanted to simply call it Canada Place Corp.; however, the public servants deemed that too generic. To run the corporation, I hired Vancouver-based Ken Bream, a Harvard MBA and highly experienced builder with Cadillac Fairview whose projects had included the Eaton Centre in Toronto. He was appointed president and CEO, and in turn hired his senior staff. In June, at the same time as we announced Bream's appointment, we announced that the project on Pier B-C would be called Canada Place, in order to maintain recognition of the federal role in the project.

We also appointed a board with a social and political cross-section of prominent British Columbians, including business, labour, and Indigenous leaders. The first chair was Robert Rogers, who accepted the position after retiring from a long career in the forest industry, most notably at the helm of Crown Zellerbach. The following year, however, he had to withdraw when he was appointed lieutenant-governor of British Columbia. He was replaced by Ian Barclay, another senior forestry executive. I was very happy to have the public support of Rogers and Barclay for our work, and it swung a lot of the business community behind the project.

While many members were Liberals, it was far from a Liberal patronage board. Obviously, the labour leaders were NDP supporters, as I believe the Indigenous leaders were. Among the others was a high-profile Progressive Conservative, Gowan Guest, who was a lawyer in Vancouver. In the late 1950s, Guest had been an executive assistant to Prime Minister John Diefenbaker. He and I had developed a pleasant relationship over the years. We weren't close friends, but we talked about politics, rarely agreeing on anything. When I was forming the board and asked him to join, he agreed, as a matter of public service. He was among those removed from the board after the Conservatives came to power in 1984. They told him he had made the political mistake of his life by agreeing to do anything for the Liberals. I was disappointed, even upset, for him.

I also was able to nominate a representative to the board of the provincial Crown corporation, and that was Keith Mitchell, a Vancouver lawyer from an established Liberal family who had himself long been active with the party. We had known each other since he had worked as an assistant to Art Laing in the late 1960s, after I had left Ottawa. Over the years, we worked together on Liberal Party matters, and he was always an important adviser to me on political issues in British Columbia.

Bream got going, and by October 1982 or so, he was recommending a project advanced by Zeidler Architecture, the firm responsible for the Eaton Centre in Toronto. Public Works reviewed the project and approved it. There was no public tender because there was no time. I don't recall there having been any complaint from the architectural world. I think there was general recognition that we were coming to the table very late to build a host pavilion.

We wanted to include a hotel and offices in the design – otherwise, it would have looked terrible – but there would be no more money from Ottawa for the capital project. To finance this plan, we would have to find other sources of funding. So, with Bream's financial capacities and those of some of the board members, we decided to invite bids for a nine-ty-nine-year lease for the air rights over the project – the right to use the space immediately above the site – and that's how Tokyu Corporation of Japan eventually won the right to build the hotel, which became the Pan Pacific. Their $30.1 million bid was by far the highest, about double the closest Canadian competitor. It made the project what it is today.

In December 1982, at an event held at the Hotel Vancouver, we un-veiled a maquette of Canada Place. This was Vancouverites' first look at the now-iconic building, which evokes a ship, complete with Teflon sails. The prime minister was present, and he was very pleased with the design. Trudeau's brother Charles was an architect, and Pierre Trudeau himself took a keen interest in architecture, which had become more widely known when he purchased as his private residence Cormier House in Montreal, an Art Deco building designated historic. On one visit to Vancouver, Trudeau asked me whether I knew the Marine Build-ing. Of course I did. (It's a landmark in downtown Vancouver.) He said, "Could you get me a conducted tour? I understand it's the finest example of Art Deco in western Canada." A tour was arranged.

In March 1983, I had the privilege of serving as minister in attendance to Her Majesty Queen Elizabeth II during a visit to British Columbia. When a reigning monarch visits Canada, the government appoints a cabinet minister to be with her or him at all times. The protocol is if there is anything the queen requires, she conveys this to her minister, a member of her Privy Council.

I was present when Queen Elizabeth and Prince Philip arrived in Vic-toria's Inner Harbour aboard the royal yacht *Britannia* on the morning of 8 March 1983 and then spoke on behalf of the federal government at the welcome ceremony on the legislature lawn. There were boos when I mentioned Trudeau's name, and again when I said a few words in French. I hosted a luncheon banquet at the Empress Hotel, at which the queen, next to whom I was seated, attempted small talk about dogs and horses, subjects about which I know next to nothing. We ended up chatting in-stead about British history.

In Vancouver the next day, the *Britannia* docked at Pier B-C. At 10:00 a.m. the queen and the prime minister attended a ceremony on the pier to inaugurate the construction of the Canadian pavilion. Trudeau and I made presentations. Queen Elizabeth pushed a button that allowed the first bit of concrete to be poured. After a busy day of various engagements, the queen hosted a dinner on the *Britannia*. Trudeau was present, as was Governor General Edward "Ed" Schreyer, along with about fifty or so prominent British Columbians, including Premier Bill Bennett, former premier Dave Barrett, Vancouver mayor Mike Harcourt, BC Court of Appeal chief justice Nathan Nemetz (my former law partner), and Sen. Ray Perrault. What made the biggest impression on me were the massive Persian carpets on the floors throughout the boat; they were remarkable.

The following year, I was honoured to serve the same function during the visit of King Juan Carlos and Queen Sofia of Spain. They came to British Columbia to unveil a commemorative plaque recalling the history of Spanish exploration on the BC coast in the eighteenth century and their trading post on Vancouver Island, where they had commercial relations with the Nuu-chah-nulth people.

In 2005, Natalie and I travelled to Saskatchewan to perform the same role when Queen Elizabeth and Prince Philip visited that province. We were in a minority government and Ralph Goodale, the Saskatchewan minister who normally might have performed that role, could not leave Ottawa at that time. As a senator, I was more expendable.

New Orleans was planning a BIE-approved world's fair for 1984. As minister responsible for Expo 86, it was also my job to oversee the negotiation of Canada's agreement to participate there. The Americans were very keen for Canada to come – partly because of the Acadian connection, but also because of Canada's importance as a North American neighbour – and we had earlier indicated in principle that we would attend.

After negotiations were well under way, I was scheduled to go to New Orleans to seal the deal. I was to meet with Sen. Russell Long of Louisiana, a prime mover behind the fair. By then a senior member of the US Senate, Long was also the son of the famous former Louisiana governor and senator Huey Long. Then, I learned from Canadian officials that the head of the US House of Representatives Budget Committee had cancelled a $1 million planning budget for US participation in Expo 86. So, I cancelled my trip to New Orleans.

A day or two later, Senator Long called. He wanted to know why I had cancelled. I said, "Well Senator, your side has cancelled the budget to attend Expo 86. How do you expect me to explain to my colleagues why we would be planning to go to Expo 84, when the United States is signalling that it's not interested in coming to our Expo 86?" He answered, "I understand what you're saying, just leave it with me." A couple of days later, he phoned to say the budget had been restored for Expo 86. I thanked him and asked how he had managed such quick action. He said he had just phoned congressman so and so, explained the situation to him, and the congressman had replied, "Senator Long, if I'd known you were involved in this, I never would have cancelled it."

Once we had negotiated and signed the agreements, the Americans wanted a celebration in New Orleans and some press statements made there. So, I led a group to New Orleans, and on 25 July 1983, I officially announced Canada's participation in the fair. Senator Long was at the airport to greet me, along with a Cajun band and dancers, and so on. Of course, this was all for his own political benefit. I and the small group that accompanied me were essentially props in his exercise. He had a dinner for me, with maybe forty people, at a hotel. We spoke of the importance of Canada-US relations, and I advertised Expo 86. The governor honoured me with the title of Admiral of the Louisiana State Navy. I still have the certificate.

After the dinner, Senator Long and I returned to my hotel and chatted for an hour, mostly about Canada-US relations. Then I went to bed early. In the morning, my staff and I boarded our government aircraft to return to Ottawa. They all looked exhausted, and when I asked them about that, they confessed they had partied all night in the French Quarter. They all fell asleep as soon as the plane took off. I had no one to talk to on the trip back to Ottawa.

Following the tender and acceptance of Tokyu Corporation's bid for the air rights to build the hotel at Canada Place, company officials came to Vancouver for more detailed negotiations. When the agreement was ready, the Tokyu side wanted to sign it in Japan because they wanted the controlling shareholder, Noboru Gotoh, to host the ceremony. As well, I believe, they also wanted us to understand who they were and what their position was in Japan. And so, in August 1983, Natalie and I, along with Ken and Leslie Bream, travelled to Japan. In my legal and mining career I had dealt with several Japanese companies and visited Japan on a number of occasions, but this visit provided the most remarkable insight into the culture of aristocratic Japan and left an enduring impression.

Gotoh had taken over and expanded the company his father had originally developed, which had played a key role in building the street railway systems for the city of Tokyo. A decade or so after the Second World War he branched out into the hotel business in Asia under the Pan Pacific brand. Their bid to come to Vancouver was their first move into continental North America, and thus a significant one for the company. We met at Gotoh's palatial residence in the suburbs of Tokyo, where he hosted a dinner for the four of us in his private restaurant. I don't mean dining room, it was organized more like a small and traditional Japanese restaurant, and we sat at a bar. After dinner, he took us to visit his private museum, which had one of the most exquisite collections anywhere of Japanese, Chinese, and Korean artifacts.

Tokyu Corporation carried out their obligations to the full and built a beautiful facility. The Pan Pacific at Canada Place became the number one hotel in Vancouver and remained so for a long period of time.

While I was in Japan that August, Ray Perrault was dropped from the cabinet, to my surprise. I was sad for him, and disappointed to see British Columbia lose a valuable minister.

To be successful, Expo 86 needed the United States, the Soviet Union, and China. With the Louisiana matter sorted out, the Americans were on board. As for the Soviet Union, arrangements for its participation had been made before I entered the picture.

China was going to be more complicated. That country had not attended a BIE exposition since the 1920s, long before the Communists took power. The Canadian commissioner general for Expo 86, Patrick Reid, who was also the overall commissioner general for the fair, was working hard to persuade China to come. But that country had several concerns it expected to have addressed before it would agree: Would it be treated as one of the major nations? Where would its pavilion be located? What would it be allowed to do? How could China afford it? What would the political image be?

By 1983, China had moved away from the philosophy of Mao Zedong toward that of Deng Xiaoping, which emphasized economic growth, economic investment, and international trade. The thinking was that China had to be much stronger economically in order to be a country secure from interference, secure from invasion, and secure as an active player in the global governance system. Expo 86 fit perfectly with China's desire to tell the story of a modernizing, economically growing China.

For political reasons, the Chinese wanted a cabinet minister to come to negotiate with them, something few other countries required. China sees everything as a political issue, and they wanted to be accorded a higher level of invitation. So, I went with Reid to China in the late fall of 1983, and we discussed with the Chinese officials the issues of concern to them. Perhaps their biggest concern was what location they would have. Once I told them that their pavilion would be in a quadrangle with the American and Soviet pavilions (the fourth side was open to False Creek), that took the issue off the table. That was just where they wanted to be, with the so-called great powers. Even back then, they were sensitive to being seen and respected as an important country. Even then they saw themselves as a rising great power.

After a week of discussions, documents being drafted, and so on – there were a couple of officials with us to do that work – we had an agreement in principle, and the Chinese offered a banquet to celebrate what they saw as an important step in joining the world commercial and trading system. I was seated at the head table for the event. To my left was an empty chair. We had started to eat, we'd made our speeches, and the chair remained empty. I inquired and was told we might have a guest. I was not told who.

And then Premier Zhao Ziyang arrived, his presence a signal of how important this new decision was for China. He was the fourth-ranking leader in the country's ruling hierarchy. He brought a calligraphy with him, which he himself had written, saying, as I recall it, "Celebrating a partnership with the nations of the world." That calligraphy would be on display in their pavilion at Expo 86.

While I was in Beijing finishing with the Expo negotiations, I learned that Prime Minister Pierre Trudeau was arriving on his peace mission. This was a key part of the final months of his prime ministership, all structured by Ivan Head. Trudeau travelled to China, the Soviet Union, the United States, European capitals, among other places. I think he was realistic about his chances of advancing world peace, but what he wanted to do was at least raise the profile of nuclear disarmament on the international agenda.

Zhao gave a dinner for Trudeau, to which I was invited. Trudeau sat on Zhao's right, I sat on his left. On my left was the Chinese minister of forests, who wanted to talk to the minister from British Columbia about co-operation and marketing in the Canadian forest industry. I admit I didn't dwell very much on that conversation, because my right ear was tuned to the discussion, in English, between Zhao and Trudeau, as translated by Zhao's interpreter. It was a tour de force of global relations.

In January 1984, Zhao visited Vancouver as part of a North American tour. I hosted a state dinner in his honour at the Hotel Vancouver on 22 January, attended by about 850 people. At the head table were former Conservative prime minister Joe Clark, sitting Social Credit premier Bill Bennett, former NDP premier Dave Barrett, and Mayor Mike Harcourt, along with my former cabinet colleague Ray Perrault. Writing in the *Vancouver Sun* on 25 January 1984, columnist Marjorie Nichols was struck by the politically inclusive nature of the event. She described the guest list as "heavily larded with Liberals, to be sure, but it was nonetheless one of this century's truly non-partisan gatherings. There were New Democrats, including Dave Barrett and several NDP MPs, rubbing elbows with provincial Socreds and federal Conservatives and a whole busload of heavies from the BC Federation of Labour, as well as a huge contingent from Vancouver's Chinese community." After remarking on the absence of fist fights at the bar, her article continued, "Credit for the evening must be accorded to the host, BC Senator Jack Austin, who also did something that has never been done publicly in this province in living memory. In his pro forma toast to the visiting premier, Sen. Austin managed to say something nice about Bill Bennett, Mike Harcourt, and Joe Clark, all of whom were seated at the head table."

In my address to the banquet, which of course was an address to Premier Zhao, I noted the relationship that had been established between Canada and China in the exchange of diplomatic relations in October 1970, and I recalled an old Chinese saying, "You cannot see the flowers from horseback," in assuring Zhao that China should look forward to a very close and co-operative relationship for many years. The saying essentially means that it's important to take the time to get to know one another better. I also mentioned the agreement that had been entered into in 1983 between the United Kingdom and China regarding Hong Kong – the fifty-year, one country, two systems agreement – noting there were many Canadians living in Hong Kong, and Canada was very pleased that China had come to such an arrangement.

In response, Premier Zhao said Canada was a country that China looked forward to working with co-operatively, that Canada had a lot to teach China, and Canadians were welcome to invest in China

A few days later, at a lunch hosted by Expo 86, Premier Zhao officially announced China's participation. At the head table with Zhao and I were Premier Bennett, Patrick Reid, the Chinese foreign minister, BC tourism minister Claude Richmond, and Expo 86 chair Jim Pattison,[6] a leading member of the BC business community, whom Bennett had put in charge of making the fair happen.

Of course, Zhao represented a completely different approach from that of today's president Xi Jinping. Until 1989 and Tiananmen Square, China had been following the Deng Xiaoping philosophy of economic growth and global co-operation. China was joining international institutions and becoming a part of the global governance system. Zhao was a proponent of this approach. In 1989, Zhao was deposed because of his opposition to his government's harsh response to the Tiananmen protests. He lived out the rest of his life under house arrest.

Expo 86 construction continued, on time and on budget. Once construction was under way, the project was less demanding of my time. It was still a significant responsibility, but I had great confidence in Ken Bream. We talked frequently about was going on, the issues, the problems he was encountering. For example, there were problems with the footings, and additional money was required to make sure the piles were stable. There were all sorts of problems, as there are with just about any construction project.

But as the structure rose, and people actually saw how large and dramatic it was, it changed the tone in British Columbia. The griping and the anti-federal noise declined quite dramatically. For people in the Lower Mainland especially, the project became an impressive symbol of the federal presence.

The federal government changed with the September 1984 election, which was won by Brian Mulroney's Progressive Conservatives. They thus inherited the project, and instantly saw the advantage of claiming all credit. Mulroney handed responsibility to his minister of transport, Don Mazankowski, who was essentially the chief operating officer of the Mulroney government. They quickly put several of their own people onto the Canada Harbour Place board.

In early 1986, before Expo opened that spring, Mazankowski hosted at the Pan Pacific Hotel a private dinner for all the commissioners general from the various countries. He invited me to that event. At the dinner, he asked me to stand and introduced me as the man who initiated and began the development of Canada Place and who helped create the project in the first place. It was the one and only acknowledgment I received from the Conservatives, but a very nice one. However, it was made at a private event; no such recognition would be forthcoming publicly.

When Expo 86 started, I wasn't invited to any of the official openings, not of Canada Place nor of Expo itself. I got something of an apology from the British Columbia government, but was told it was a federal-provincial event, and they couldn't invite me because the Conservatives didn't want any Liberals there.

Expo 86 proved to be wildly successful, attracting 22 million visits and providing an important economic boost to British Columbia. The federal contribution ended up being closer to $275 million, including operating costs. British Columbia did run a deficit, which it addressed by initiating a lottery. Canada Place, which brought Vancouver's citizens access to the downtown harbourfront for the first time, stands as a lasting legacy.

During the fair, Pierre Trudeau, by then in retirement, came to Vancouver to see it. Keith Mitchell and I took him around, particularly to the Canada Pavilion, to show him what we had done. When we were standing at the edge of the prow, a young man approached us – he'd recognized Trudeau – and said, "Prime Minister, thank you so much for this great project." After he had walked away, Trudeau turned to me and said, "Did you put him up to that?" I said, "Absolutely not, that's just serendipity." I am not sure Trudeau believed me.

In 1955–56, the year after I graduated from UBC law school, I returned as a lecturer. I was younger than many of my students.

Taking my LLM at Harvard in 1956–57 was a fabulous experience that opened many doors. I spent long hours at my assigned study desk.

Members of the federal and BC Columbia River Treaty negotiating teams attend
a meeting in Ottawa, circa late 1963. From left: MP Jack Davis; federal cabinet
ministers Arthur Laing and Paul Martin Sr; senior federal public servants
Gordon Robertson, Ed Ritchie, Gordon McNabb, and J.F. Parkinson; and me.
Among those representing the BC government were cabinet ministers
Ray Williston (third from right) and Bob Bonner (second from right).

On our way to the Soviet Arctic in 1965, we stopped in Copenhagen to learn more about the administration of Greenland. From left: Graham Rowley, secretary to the Advisory Committee on Northern Development; me; then MP John Turner; northern affairs and national resources minister Arthur Laing; a host official; deputy minister E.A. Côté; and a host official. Harry Rosenberg, a hydro engineer in our department and the other member of our delegation, took the photo.

In Irkutsk to visit a hydroelectric station, we were treated to a "light lunch" at the Baikal Limnological Institute on 31 May 1965. From left: MP John Turner; deputy minister E.A. Côté; the head of the Limnological Institute (name unavailable); northern affairs and national resources minister Arthur Laing; Soviet interpreter Vladimir Novoseltsev; and Canadian Press reporter John Best. (Jack Austin photo)

A staged campaign photo from my 1965 run in Vancouver Kingsway.

I had the good fortune to be part of the first official Canadian mission to China after the opening of relations in 1970. On the Great Wall of China on 5 July 1971, are me; mission leader and industry minister Jean-Luc Pépin; his wife Mary; and a Canadian affiliated with the embassy in Beijing. (John Burns photo)

As principal secretary to Prime Minister Pierre Trudeau, my office was in Room 201 of Parliament's East Block, at one time the office of Canada's first prime minister, Sir John A. Macdonald. I'm seen here in June 1975. (Edie Austin photo)

When a deal to patriate the constitution was announced on 5 November 1981, the entrenchment of Aboriginal rights had been sacrificed in the final deal-making, to my profound disappointment. I'm directly behind Prime Minister Pierre Trudeau and finance minister Allan MacEachen. At right: Quebec premier René Lévesque. (Fred Chartrand/Canadian Press)

Queen Elizabeth and Prince Philip on a visit to Vancouver in March 1983. Here, as federal minister responsible for Expo 86, I show the royal couple a maquette of Canada Place, which served as the Canadian pavilion for Expo and is now a convention centre. (Nick Didlick/Canadian Press)

At an event during the March 1983 royal visit, Prime Minister Pierre Trudeau; me; Queen Elizabeth; Canada Harbour Place president and CEO Ken Bream; Canada Harbour Place chair Bob Rogers (later lieutenant-governor of BC); Prince Philip; and my wife, Natalie Veiner Freeman, all seem quite amused.

Toyku Corporation of Japan purchased the air rights over part of the Canada Place site in order to build the Pan Pacific Hotel. We signed the deal in Vancouver on 14 October 1983. Front: Tokyu managing director Isao Ishiyama and me. Back, from left: Tokyu's general manager for overseas development Makoto Yuki; Herb Grueter, a senior consultant to Toyku; Hideo Matsuo, executive managing director of Tokyu; Toshito Shiota, executive general manager of international affairs, Toyku; and Ken Bream, president and CEO of Canada Harbour Place.

Chinese premier Zhao Ziyang speaks at a banquet I hosted in his honour during his visit to Vancouver in January 1984. My wife, Natalie Veiner Freeman, is to his right.

"VISIT OF THE RT. HON. PIERRE ELLIOTT TRUDEAU
TO EXPO 86, MAY 31st, 1986, ACCOMPANIED BY
JIMMY PATTISON, CHAIRMAN OF EXPO 86, SENATOR
JACK AUSTIN, FORMER FEDERAL MINISTER FOR
EXPO 86 AND KEITH MITCHELL, A DIRECTOR FOR
EXPO 86 CORPORATION."

Jim Pattison, a leading member of the BC business community who was
appointed chair of Expo 86 by the BC government, gave me this photo and note
as a memento of our work together. The photo was taken when Prime Minister
Pierre Trudeau visited Expo in 1986. From left: Pattison, Trudeau, me, and Keith
Mitchell, a Vancouver lawyer who was the federal appointee to the Expo board.

In 1987, I embarked on the first of a series of international trips with Pierre Trudeau, beginning with the Silk Road route from Pakistan into China. Here we are in Xinjiang province. (Natalie Veiner Freeman photo)

Our 1987 trip included a cruise along the Yangtze River, prior to construction of the Three Gorges Dam. (Natalie Veiner Freeman photo)

Meeting Nelson Mandela at the offices of the ANC in Johannesburg was the highlight of our 1992 trip to South Africa. From left: Canadian ambassador Christopher Westdal, Nelson Mandela, Pierre Trudeau, ANC official Walter Sisulu, me, and Natalie. (Photo courtesy of Natalie Veiner Freeman)

The Team Canada mission to China in November 1994 was a resounding success. I'm at the lectern, at left, emceeing as Prime Minister Jean Chrétien and several premiers and territorial leaders participate in a discussion. (K.K. Wong photo)

Prime Minister Paul Martin stands before his cabinet before we are sworn in at a ceremony at Rideau Hall in Ottawa on 20 July 2004. I'm in the front row, at left. (Tom Hanson/Canadian Press)

Prime Minister Paul Martin, me, cabinet colleagues David Emerson and
Belinda Stronach listen to the opening statement of elder William Commanda
read by Claudette Commanda in Ottawa on 31 May 2005. The meeting,
between federal cabinet ministers and the leaders of five national Indigenous
organizations, formalized an Indigenous role in federal policy-making and was
part of the process that led to the Kelowna Accord. (Jean Levac, *Ottawa Citizen*;
republished with the express permission of *Ottawa Citizen*, a division of Postmedia
Network Inc.)

I was delighted to welcome Chinese president Hu Jintao to a banquet we held in his honour at the Pan Pacific Hotel during his visit to Vancouver, 16 September 2005.

In 2007, after my retirement from the Senate, Natalie and I travelled to China, where I was honoured with a dinner at the Great Hall of the People to mark my contribution to Canada-China relations. Natalie and I flank Sheng Huaren, vice-chairman of the standing committee of the National People's Congress. Among those who attended were Maurice Strong (front row, third from left); Lu Congmin (front, second from left); former Chinese ambassador to Canada Mei Ping (middle row, second from the left); Victor Yang (middle row, behind my right shoulder); Canadian ambassador to China Robert Wright (front row, fourth from left); my sister-in-law Shirley Fitterman (middle of back row); Herb Fitterman (back row, second from right); Ron Stern (back row, third from right); and Janet Stern (behind Sheng Huaren).

During my 2007 visit, I met with Sheng Huaren in the Hong Kong Room of the Great Hall of the People. My friend Wei Shao, seated behind me, a Vancouver lawyer who was a guest at the dinner, was kind enough to step in as interpreter.

Since retiring from the Senate, I've remained active. This screenshot shows me participating in a July 2020 online discussion on Canada-China-US relations, sponsored by Simon Fraser University's Jack Austin Centre for Asia Pacific Business Studies.

8 One Minister, Many Files

MY ROLE IN MAKING EXPO 86 a reality may have been my proudest accomplishment in the Trudeau cabinet, but it was far from my only file. In January 1982, when I was in the thick of trying to secure the federal contribution to Expo, I was given responsibility for the Canada Development Corporation (CDC). This was a holding company with billions of dollars in assets, formally headquartered in Vancouver but in fact run from Toronto, in which the federal government held a 48 per cent interest. The other 52 per cent of the shares were to be held by private Canadian investors. This was an experiment in the private sector managing, in accordance with private sector norms, a mixture of government assets that were in the commercial sector and other private assets. CDC had been created by the federal government in 1971 as a means of promoting domestic control of the Canadian economy.[1] At the time, there was a great deal of concern about foreign ownership of Canadian resources and businesses. CDC's philosophical underpinnings trace back to the late 1950s and the Royal Commission on Canada's Economic Prospects, led by Walter Gordon.

Although I had had no involvement with CDC in its first decade, I had followed its progress. When you are in government, you pay attention to many issues outside your own area of responsibility because they affect the government as a whole, and what affects the government as a whole affects the parts of the government. As well, my experience with the uranium industry crisis of the 1960s and early 1970s and with issues relating to the creation of Petro-Canada in the early 1970s had led me to take a greater interest in national economic development policy and the respective roles of government and business. For Canada, how to manage creative investment by Canadians in both existing and emerging business sectors has always been a crucial question. Once I was in the Senate, and therefore without operating responsibilities, I spent a lot of time thinking about issues of industrial policy and about whether Canadian business should, or could, be an instrument of national policy as well as a producer of wealth for its shareholders and management.

Although historically Canada had been a net importer of foreign capital, and therefore its business assets were owned significantly by foreign investors, the major infrastructure developments were backed by the federal government and, to a lesser extent, by provinces. The development of a national railway system, air transport, and national broadcasting are obvious examples. The state took the risks where business investors feared to tread. And so it should be, because the investments were for the development of the nation as a whole and their commercial value was not entirely to be calculated according to the standards of business risk and return to the investor. For example, in the early part of the twentieth century, various railway systems failed as general business declined and investors fled. When these were vital to dependent communities and local economies, the federal government was forced to step in and become the owner of last resort; hence, the creation of the Canadian National Railway.

Aware of this history, creative thinkers in Canada began to imagine business models where new enterprise could be encouraged through the investment of government capital and private capital together and managed by business leaders rather than by government employees. Many examples emerged, not least the CDC, which was designed to take federal government capital and invest it in Canadian business development. Government would be the initial shareholder, and as private sector managers succeeded in growing the business investment, Canadian private investors would be permitted to buy equity shares so that in time the result would be a public Canadian company owned by Canadian investors as majority shareholders. The company would be run by private sector management and the majority of the directors would also be from the private sector business community. The sought-after policy result would be Canadian ownership, new business development, and an increase in both employment and the net worth of Canadian investors. Unfortunately, things didn't work out as intended. Experience showed it was hard to reconcile the government's accountability to the public and the private sector's responsibility to shareholders.

In 1981, Ottawa backed down from naming Maurice Strong chair of CDC after protests from the financial community about "government interference." Strong was accepted as a director, however, along with Joel Bell, to represent the government interest. There were disputes between CDC's CEO, Tony Hampson, and Strong – a major policy difference between the private directors and the government about how to manage the company – and consequently Strong and Bell were pretty well sidelined. I had had talks at the time with both Strong and Bell about their experiences. As well, Michael Pitfield was very much in the loop on what was taking place, and I heard a certain amount from him. So, I came to my new role with a fair amount of background knowledge.

There were strong pressures from the Canadian financial community to eliminate any government role in CDC. Hampson had been selected as president and CEO partly because he had impressed as a senior official in the finance ministry, and it was thought he would be able to balance the responsibilities to government and private investors. However, Hampson by this time wanted to market the company as a purely investor-owned entity. As for the Progressive Conservatives, they had never liked CDC in the first place and wanted very much to see it all moved into the private sector. Liberal opinion was more divided; while some favoured privatization, there was major resistance to having these Canadian government-owned assets privatized as part of a corporation that did not operate with government ownership and public interest as a core theme. There had also been a public controversy involving the commercial way in which the CDC was operating Connaught Laboratories, acquired in 1972. Connaught Laboratories had been created to give Canadians a secure domestic source of vaccines, in terms of quality and quantity. In 1989, the Mulroney government would approve the sale of Connaught Laboratories to a predecessor of Sanofi Pasteur, a pharmaceutical company based in France, on the theory that a larger manufacturing base would bring down product prices. National security of supply was given no thought, something that would come back to haunt Canada during the COVID-19 pandemic, when this country had to scramble for access to foreign-manufactured vaccines. The divestment decision was purely commercial. There couldn't be a better illustration of the dichotomy between public interest and the narrower principles of business management.

At the beginning of the 1980s, CDC became the subject of considerable media attention, and there were a lot of distracting questions in the House of Commons. Eventually, the PCO and other departments had concluded the government's involvement in CDC was becoming a negative and aggravating experience, joint management of Crown assets was a failure, and something had to be done about it. For the Liberal caucus, the bottom line was that we had to solve the problem somehow. Although finance minister Allan MacEachen was the minister responsible, he did not have time to deal with the situation. The prime minister asked me to take it on, "as the only businessman in the cabinet" (though in fact there were one or two others). My assignment was to resolve the problem and make it disappear as a public issue.

I phoned Tony Hampson, and we began a series of meetings. He explained that the situation wasn't working and what he wanted to do was privatize the Crown assets. I told him that wasn't an option – these had been bought with public money and had been entrusted to CDC to manage – but the government was prepared to take the public assets back and let CDC become a purely private corporation with its other acquired assets.

The question was, how do we accomplish this? During this period, I was consulting others, including Maurice Strong and Joel Bell. Bell suggested I hire Jim Baillie, a senior corporate lawyer in Toronto. He fit the bill as someone who had a prominent voice in the business community. With him, I looked at options for the repatriation of the Crown assets. One possibility we considered was an act of Parliament, but that would have been debated endlessly and taken too long. It would also have exacerbated the controversy that the prime minister was trying to sideline.

We came up with the idea CDC would incorporate a wholly owned subsidiary under the Canada Business Corporations Act. CDC would transfer the Crown assets to the subsidiary, called the Canada Development Investment Corporation (then known as CDIC, now called CDEV), and then gift its shares in the subsidiary to the Crown. This is how we regained control of those assets, which were essentially liabilities, even if we called them assets. CDIC also would hold the government's shares of CDC until market conditions improved and they could be sold at a fair price. I persuaded the cabinet of the merits of this idea, which was regarded as an excellent way to maintain the concept of managing Crown assets in a commercial-sector operational style. Declaring the CDC idea a failure had been hard on some people in the cabinet who thought it could have been an excellent example of co-operation between the private sector and the public sector. Nevertheless, the CDC controversy was effectively ended.

By the fall of 1982, I had begun my role as the minister responsible for CDIC, and as such, its formal shareholder. To the CDC shares were added other companies already publicly owned, including Canadair, De Havilland, Teleglobe, and Eldorado Nuclear. Later the government acquired Fishery Products International to prevent an economic failure in Newfoundland. The government's shareholding in Massey Ferguson was also included.

To run CDIC, we named Maurice Strong as chair (a role for which he did not receive any compensation beyond that paid to all directors) and Joel Bell as president. They moved to Vancouver, which we had designated as the headquarters for CDIC in order to enhance the presence of the federal government in British Columbia. The choice of Vancouver raised hackles in the East, but I defended the decision, arguing, among other things, that British Columbia deserved to have at least one federal agency or Crown corporation headquartered there. Eventually, however, I had to accept that it wasn't practical in terms of the mission of CDIC, because all the action was back east, given the locations of the company's major assets.

Strong and I had first met in 1964, when he was a senior executive with Power Corp. and I was executive assistant to Art Laing. He had come to see me concerning a subsidiary company's successful bid to construct a hotel in Banff National Park. We ended up discussing broader topics, and I was impressed by his grasp of national and international issues. We went on to develop a close and lifelong friendship of mutual interests and shared activities. We had similar perspectives on many issues, including on government's economic role and the environment, although I was more skeptical than he was of the utility of the United Nations.

To many, Strong was an enigma, perhaps because his career had so many facets. As a high school dropout, he had left his small community in Manitoba and gone out into the world. In his formative years, he worked as a fur trader in the Canadian North, an intern at the United

Nations in New York, and an oil executive in Alberta. He developed not only his remarkable entrepreneurial, organizational, and networking talents but also an early awareness of the cost of destructive environmental processes. Over the course of his career, he moved between public and business pursuits, and between Canada and the wider world. In 1966, at the request of external affairs minister Paul Martin Sr, Strong left the presidency of Power Corp. to organize the creation of the Canadian International Development Agency (CIDA), the federal government's vehicle for delivering foreign aid. In 1968 he became its first leader, pioneering collaboration with similar organizations in other countries.

Strong had a lifelong fascination with and attraction to the United Nations. He went from CIDA to become the principal organizer of the landmark UN Conference on the Environment, held in Stockholm in 1972, at which the nations of the world identified the condition of the environment as a collective global challenge and responsibility. That conference paved the way for his creation of the United Nations Environment Programme, based in Nairobi. It was the first UN organization to have its headquarters based in the global South. He was the program's first executive director. (In 1992, he would serve as UN secretary general of the landmark Earth Summit in Rio de Janeiro.)

He returned to Canada in 1976 at my request to take on the role of chair of Petro-Canada, staying for two to three years before leaving to lead another Crown corporation, the International Development Research Centre in Ottawa. His focus on North-South issues was enduring and stemmed in part from his belief that poverty was a threat to global stability.

Over the years, Strong developed a remarkable array of international contacts. In our chats, he would mention remarks made to him by world leaders, from Indira Gandhi, to Henry Kissinger, to the king of Bhutan. He wasn't dropping names so much as conveying insights. Strong and his wife, Hanne, were among the very few non-family members present in 1978 when Natalie and I were married in a small ceremony at our home in Vancouver. In 1981, we accompanied them to Bhutan, a journey that was unforgettable not only because it offered insights into a fascinating country that at that time was largely closed to the outside world but also because of the time the four of us were able to spend together.

With responsibility for CDIC, I was now saddled with major corporate issues, and being a corporate lawyer was extremely helpful. My experience of running an operating mining company also proved an advantage. And so, I began to evaluate these assets in order to understand where things actually stood and how to bring them back into commercial performance.

The underlying premise of both CDC and CDIC was that the companies they held should be managed to commercial success and then they could be privatized, bringing an appropriate return to the Canadian taxpayer. Generally, the companies had been acquired because they were in trouble and there were important reasons not to let them go under, such as avoiding job losses, preserving important technologies, and retaining high-level management; however, there was no policy reason that they should be run by the government indefinitely. I had urged the creation of Petro-Canada because I believed it could serve as an important policy instrument, but that did not mean I believed government should be widely involved in the private sector.

The biggest problem we had on our hands, as it turned out, was Canadair, an aircraft manufacturing company based in Montreal that the federal government had owned since 1976. We had thought we knew its financial situation. What we didn't know, among other things, was that the company's management had not been transparent about the fact that they had been selling their Challenger executive jets at immense discounts. As well, they had orders on their books that were less solid than they appeared. The company, which had looked to be nearly profitable, in fact was in a substantial loss position.

Although I was given complete control over how to deal with these issues, without interference from anyone in the political system, it was clearly government policy that Canadair was not going to be shut down. It was an important part of Canada's industrial competence. After consulting business advisers, including Baillie and Bell, it was obvious the only real choice was to write off $1 billion of its net loss of $1.4 billion, write down the assets, ask Parliament for another $240 million to keep Canadair afloat, and find new leadership for the company.

The $1 billion writeoff caused quite a shock in Parliament and across the country when it was announced in the spring of 1983, and understandably so. It was called the biggest writeoff in Canadian business history. We effectively had no choice if we wanted to keep Canadair going and establish the company on a viable commercial path. I was transparent about the problems when I appeared before a parliamentary committee: I explained that the Challenger had cost more and taken longer to develop than was expected due to a series of technical and commercial problems, and "Identification of the financial difficulties was seriously impeded by the excessive optimism of Canadair itself," as I rather politely put it. We replaced Canadair's leadership, but left the board mostly intact. One board member, a BC businessman named Sean Sullivan, became my principal analyst. I give him a lot of credit. He dug deep into Canadair and was the most diligent of directors.

At De Havilland, an aircraft manufacturer in Toronto, there also was a serious problem. De Havilland was losing considerable amounts of money, though the company's situation was less dire than that of Canadair. I appointed as chair Barney Danson, by then retired from politics, and made other changes to the board of directors. Then I left it to them to advise me on whether changes would be needed in the company's management.

De Havilland had a history of manufacturing excellent products, including the Beaver, Twin Otter, and Caribou, designed to serve in rugged Canadian conditions. A few years earlier, the company had started producing the Dash 7, a four-engine short takeoff and landing (STOL) aircraft, which was a quality engineered plane but was not so commercially successful. The company also was developing the Dash 8, a twin-engine turbo prop that would be relatively economical to operate, but needed more funding to proceed with the project. The business case for the Dash 8 indicated the aircraft would fill a need in the market and many potential buyers were interested.

There was a major debate in cabinet about whether the government should keep putting money into the Dash 8 or just have me sell De Havilland with the products it had and at the loss it was taking. The biggest asset De Havilland had was the Downsview Airport in northern Toronto, an absolutely fabulous piece of real estate that was very attractive to a number of possible bidders. I advocated keeping the company and funding the Dash 8. Finance minister Marc Lalonde went along, although I am sure his advisers had serious concerns about the government taking this commercial risk. So, the cabinet approved the money, with the support of the Ontario ministers and the acquiescence of Quebec ministers, who'd taken a lot of blows over Canadair from their Ontario counterparts during cabinet discussions about keeping Canadair going. The Dash 8 proved popular and went on to considerable success.

A few years later, the Mulroney government sold off Canadair to Bombardier and De Havilland to Boeing, but the sales of those companies most likely would have taken place in any event had the Liberals been returned in 1984. I'm sure the Turner government would have pursued the Trudeau government's policy of finding private sector buyers for them.

Not all CDIC's holdings presented such major challenges, but all brought responsibilities. Eldorado and Teleglobe were much less complicated, and Massey Ferguson and Fishery Products International moderately so. I was extremely hands-on concerning all these issues, even while I was overseeing the federal contribution to Expo 86.

The more successful I was at handling various assignments, the more assignments I received. On 10 September 1982, after I had been in cabinet for a year and still had my hands full with Expo 86 and the creation of CDIC, I was given an enormous promotion: the addition of the social development portfolio to my other responsibilities. With that role came a seat on cabinet's powerful P&P, which gave me a much higher profile within cabinet, in caucus, and across the country. As well, I was officially made the political minister for British Columbia.

When I became minister of state for social development, succeeding Jean Chrétien, I became ultimately responsible for some $31 billion in federal spending annually, or about 42 per cent of the budget. As I explained to reporters at the time, most of that was not discretionary. The vast majority of it was either transferred to the provinces under existing statutory programs and agreements, or to individual Canadians for things like unemployment insurance and family allowances. My principal responsibility as minister was to chair the cabinet's social development committee, whose members were the ministers responsible for communications, employment and immigration, environment, Indian affairs and northern development, labour, national health and welfare, veterans affairs, justice, Canada Mortgage and Housing Corporation, Secretary of State, Solicitor General, and the Office of the Coordinator of the Status of Women. What we collectively had discretion over, subject to oversight from P&P and the prime minister, was about $5 billion for new and non-statutory federal programs that fell within these areas, including how to allocate that spending among those policy areas. A different set of ministers were grouped in the economic development committee of cabinet, whose chair at that time was Donald Johnston, successor to Bud Olson. Every minister, no matter how junior, was a member of at least one of those committees. Ministers retained responsibility for running their respective departments. Our committees decided how to spend the global amounts – or spending envelopes – we had been given. My committee had two envelopes: one for social affairs and the other for justice and legal affairs.

This particular system of cabinet decision-making had been introduced by the Trudeau government in 1980. Colloquially known as the envelope system, its more formal title was the Policy and Expenditure Management System.[2] The envelope system was a response to cabinet ministers' concerns, developed in the first part of the Trudeau era, that government policy was being made by a tight little group of experts in the PMO, and cabinet was largely a discussion group, there merely to add advice and implement the decisions made by the prime minister. These concerns I had addressed as principal secretary. The objective was to create a system of meaningful cabinet leadership in developing policy and in integrating it with the important political considerations of regions, minorities, and economic interests. Pitfield, as clerk of the Privy Council and secretary to the cabinet, led the PCO's response, assisted among others by Michael Kirby, who after leaving the PMO had joined the PCO.

The operating purpose of each of the envelope committees was for the policy designs and objectives of each department to be placed for discussion before all the ministers of each committee and evaluated in terms of the policy designs and objectives of every other ministry. That way, all ministers were fully exposed to the broad ranges of policy – either social policy or economic policy – and understood where their portfolios and responsibilities stood with respect to those of their colleagues. The departments and their deputy ministers and other officers were now to be made into full-fledged policy advisers to the government and not simply people to carry out decisions in which they had not participated. Plans were brought bottom-up from the departments, rather than top-down from the PMO. The PMO and PCO were essentially removed from initiation and given the role of evaluation and integration.

In practical terms, the way things worked was that if a minister on the committee wanted a cabinet decision with respect to policy or legislation, or with respect to disputes over administration or policy development, he or she would prepare a document with a specific format called a Memorandum to Cabinet. It would be submitted to the PCO and PMO, each would vet it and provide briefing notes to the prime minister, who would review the Memorandum to Cabinet and decide on its ongoing process. If it was in my envelope, it would come to my committee, along with the prime minister's comments as to whether it should move forward or with what amendments. Then my deputy minister would provide me with the background issues, options, possible objections of other ministers, and so on. I had no discretion at that point to decide whether to put it on the agenda or not, but I did have the latitude to decide what priority to accord any given item.

If we had too many urgent items to deal with in our regular meetings, then extra ones could be added, though this was difficult to do because ministers' schedules were already full. With the agreement of the committee, we would add meetings in late afternoon or over dinner. Many items were time consuming, partly because most items also had spending requests, but the amount of money in our envelope was fixed.

Of course, the budget envelopes came down from the top: the minister of finance, with the approval of the prime minister and the associated acceptance of the Treasury Board minister, would hand my committee a budget of a given amount, and that would be what we would have available to spend for the coming budget year. So, the system had the added benefit of constraining ministers' demands for additional funding. And rather than lobby the finance minister or PMO, they would have to make their case to their colleagues for a bigger share of what was in the envelope.

Effectively, the social development committee was preparing budgets for each of the departments covered by the committee. There were two kinds of spending. Statutory spending was what we had to spend by law on programs already approved by Parliament. The committee held a continuing performance review to evaluate whether the money was being well spent, and the committee could always recommend changes in statutory provisions. That was most of our budget. But that still left a substantial sum available for new programs. Among the possible new programs we debated were basic income policies and pharmacare. We discussed such big-concept issues so that everybody would realize what the opportunities and constraints were. The process was for each committee to send its decisions to P&P. There I would present my committee's decisions on spending priorities and policy initiatives, and then things would be hotly debated. Johnston would do likewise. Separately, the PCO and the PMO would provide their advice. In cases where P&P was deadlocked, the minister of finance, who in this period was Marc Lalonde, would provide his advice to the prime minister, who would make the final decision.

I thought the envelope system was brilliant. For me, there was the added interest of having seen the concept in development – Michael Pitfield had discussed it with me in the late 1970s – and then he ended up being told by the prime minister to make it work. However, the system had its adversaries in the bureaucracy and in the party. Although I thought it should be the permanent system for Canadian cabinet governance, some very senior bureaucrats opposed it. They thought it was too inclusive, too time consuming, too cumbersome, and it had moved power away from them, particularly to the Privy Council, where my deputy minister was based, and made him, in effect, senior to all the other deputies.

John Turner was very much opposed to the envelope system because he thought it diminished the role of the prime minister. He abolished it when he became prime minister in 1984, after returning to politics and winning the Liberal leadership in the wake of Trudeau's retirement. He went back to the previous system, one in which the minister of finance also played a much more dominant role in adjudicating the priorities, always with the permission of the prime minister. Turner had been a political force of his own when he was minister of finance. So, the envelope system ended with Turner. No one ever brought it back.

One of the principal policy issues that was debated in the social development committee during my time as chair was what became the Canada Health Act, championed by health minister Monique Bégin. The act was one of the Trudeau government's great accomplishments for its defence of Canada's medicare system. At stake were whether the single-payer model would be maintained or whether extra billing and user fees would be allowed; these were being introduced in certain provinces. We insisted on the principle that Canadians deserved health care on the basis of need and not on the basis of ability to pay. When the matter was before our committee, we vigorously debated questions of the philosophy, impact on the medical profession, and impact on financial arrangements with respect to the provinces, foreshadowing the public debates when the bill was introduced. At that time, we believed that the provinces, because of the federal transfer payments, would have the fiscal ability to provide timely care.[3]

Another major issue during that period was the *Report of the Federal Cultural Policy Review Committee*, published in November 1982. It was the fruit of a federally commissioned national consultation process on culture and broadcasting policy that had been led by composer Louis Applebaum and writer Jacques Hébert, and contained 101 recommendations. Perhaps the most controversial was that CBC Television relinquish all production activities outside news and acquire programs from independent producers to better reflect Canada's diversity. The Applebaum-Hébert report had been the first such review of cultural policy since the landmark Massey Commission report in 1951, which among other things had led to the creation of the Canada Council.

When the prime minister asked me to chair the newly formed cabinet subcommittee on culture and broadcasting that would review the report, I pointed out I knew very little about these issues. And he replied that was exactly why he was asking me. He said he wanted someone with no preconceived notions, no axe to grind, and no connections in that field, who would come at things in a neutral way. Once I began educating myself and started holding a series of meetings to hear from an array of significant people in the cultural sector, I found the topics fascinating. More than that, I found the ferocity of the advocates in this area amazing. The passion, the commitment, the deep reservoirs of belief in their causes were impressive, as they made the case for federal financial resources for their particular interests and concerns.

It did not take me long to see the wisdom of setting up a cabinet subcommittee to hive off this entire topic from the general business of the social development committee. I did my job of channelling the pressures from the industry advocates that followed the report. I took those pressures off the system, gave everybody a fair hearing, and in the process, learned a lot about that industry.

Eventually, we made our recommendations for government legislation and spending to the social development committee and from there to P&P. We advocated implementing several of the report's recommendations, including the one concerning CBC Television production, for example. There were some extremely tricky issues in that alone; the hold that unions had on CBC production by means of their collective agreements was remarkable. We also wanted the National Film Board to become more involved in production financing.

Although I was fascinated by this experience, cultural policy was not a continuing focus.

Looking back, I can see today that I was sometimes too cautious.

In 1983, just after the patriation of the constitution and the adoption of the Charter of Rights and Freedoms, the Canadian mission in London advised our federal government that a Magna Carta was about to go up for sale in England by a family that had owned it for generations. The Magna Carta's historic significance is that it was the first to set out limitations on the rights of the Crown – it is the foundation for due process in our legal system. There are several versions of this document in existence. This one was the Edward I version of 1297. It was said to be in very good condition. The asking price was the equivalent of about Can$500,000, and my team at social development wondered whether the cabinet would be interested in purchasing it.

I had talks with the Treasury Board. They weren't keen to pay anything for it. I had talked to Trudeau. He didn't think it was relevant, but he was prepared to be convinced if English Canadians thought it was important to have a Magna Carta alongside the Canadian Charter. Trudeau wasn't especially interested in early British constitutional history, but he told me to go look at it.

I arrived in London with two historians from what is now called Canadian Heritage. Once we got there, I was told there had been other offers and the price had risen to $750,000. Once I learned of the price increase, I made the decision not to follow through with plans to travel north to see it; I did not think I could sell it back in Ottawa at the increased cost. I explained my reasoning to the two historians who had accompanied me. They were extremely disappointed. However, I did not even want to see the document as I was afraid that if I did, that would only increase pressure on me, from the vendors as well as the historians, to follow through with the purchase. In any case, the decision would not have been mine alone. I would have had to persuade cabinet. As it turned out, that Magna Carta was sold to Texas millionaire Ross Perot for $1.5 million, according to press reports. Perot is probably best known for his 1992 presidential campaign, as a third-party candidate.

Even today, I remain highly ambivalent about my decision. It would have been fitting to be able to display the Magna Carta alongside our own constitution, to teach Canadians about the struggle for rights, even though these were aristocratic rights, not public rights; still, it was a step in the limitation of the Crown's authority. I was concerned at the time that it could be a divisive issue between anglophone and francophone members of cabinet, and that the media would have accused us of wasting taxpayers' money.

In retrospect, I should have pressed on and tried to persuade the government to buy it. Apart from everything else, if Canada had wanted to sell it today, it could have made a considerable profit. When Perot's foundation sold the Magna Carta in 2007, to another American, it went for US $21.3 million.

As minister of social development, I had excellent bureaucratic support. Michael Pitfield had assigned to me some of the best of the brightest civil servants of the day. My deputy minister was Gordon Smith, who had come from external affairs, but during a stint in the PCO he had been among the architects of the envelope system. He also served as clerk of the social development committee of cabinet. I interacted with Smith virtually every day and met with him and his assistant deputy ministers a few times a month. One of them was Michael Sabia, principal draughtsman of an important speech I gave, who went on to a distinguished career that has included leading the Caisse de dépôt et placement du Québec, the province's pension fund manager, and serving as federal deputy minister of finance.

While advocacy for certain policy issues was coming from various ministries, part of my department's job was to assess these requests in terms of the total government framework. The department was also looking at social development issues that were not necessarily being sponsored by departments, like guaranteed annual income or pharmacare. There was also outreach to the provinces in the social development field, and there was liaison with the provinces, who were receiving federal transfers. The department also performed assessments of value for money in all programs, which were not necessarily being done by the constituent departments, including how provinces were performing with respect to the objectives for which the money was granted. There was also a minor international component because Canada was involved in UN programs in social development.

I also had an excellent personal political staff, led in Ottawa by Pauline Sauvé, who had had previous experience as a Liberal staffer on Parliament Hill. Not being fluent in French myself, I knew I needed a French-speaking chief of staff who could guide and represent me in communications with francophone players in the bureaucracy and in political offices.

I was also fortunate to have an excellent staff in Vancouver (please see the Acknowledgments). They won accolades for their work in helping various municipalities, Indigenous communities, organizations, and companies tap into funding available under an array of federal programs. We worked hard to ensure that British Columbia got its fair share of federal funding. One major coup was wrangling $4.5 million from the Treasury Board as a federal contribution toward architect Arthur Erickson's transformation of the former courthouse in the heart of downtown Vancouver into a new home for the Vancouver Art Gallery.

Sometimes I managed to get British Columbia more than its fair share. In June 1983, the federal government announced contracts to build navy frigates would be awarded to companies in Quebec and New Brunswick. British Columbia did not get the contracts, and frankly, we did not deserve them; we weren't competitive. But I had made the case that as a matter of economic fairness, British Columbia was entitled to two of the six frigates. I held up the decision, arguing and arguing. And I went to finance minister Marc Lalonde, who basically said, to hell with you. But in the end, I did manage to negotiate a rather substantial consolation prize: more than $250 million for shipbuilding in British Columbia, which was announced at the same time as the winners of the frigate contracts were named. A few months later, I announced that contracts had been given to five BC shipyards for the constructions of two icebreakers, two coast guard vessels, and fisheries and hydrographic vessels, as well as refits of some navy ships. These were less complex ships than the frigates but, as I pointed out at the time, would have a higher labour content. Hundreds of new jobs were created during a difficult economic period in the province.

Another maritime issue about which I lobbied hard in Ottawa on behalf of British Columbia concerned the administration of ports. In 1983, the National Harbours Board was replaced by the Canada Ports Corporation, which in turn was allowing certain larger ports to be managed locally rather than by civil servants in Ottawa. Vancouver was among the cities granted this status. Prince Rupert also had a strong case for such autonomy. The minister of transport had approved it, I believed in it, as did British Columbians generally, not least the people in

Prince Rupert.[4] Still, the bureaucracy was fighting it, right down to the
last minute. Was I taking their jobs? Would some of them have to move
to Prince Rupert? In September 1983, when I became aware of an effort to
block approval, I contacted the appropriate ministerial colleagues. Prince
Rupert's case prevailed.

During this period, I played a role in the naming of the Sinclair Centre in
downtown Vancouver. Born in Scotland and raised in British Columbia,
James Sinclair had been a Rhodes Scholar and had served in the Royal
Canadian Air Force during the Second World War. He became a prominent political figure in British Columbia, sitting as a member of Parliament from 1940 to 1958, and was fisheries minister from 1952 to 1957. To a
later generation, he would be best known as Margaret Trudeau's father.

The federal government had rebuilt and connected four derelict heritage buildings in the block surrounded by Hastings, Howe, Cordova, and
Granville Streets. Public works minister Roméo LeBlanc had kept me
informed as the project went to tender and progressed. The plan was to
attract commercial interest in the building as well as locate some federal
offices there, such as the passport office. Eventually, LeBlanc asked me,
as the BC political minister, whether I had any ideas about a name. I suggested naming the complex for James Sinclair. LeBlanc said, "You have
to clear that with the prime minister." LeBlanc of course was well aware
that Sinclair was Trudeau's former father-in-law.

I went to the prime minister, and he asked me why I had chosen Sinclair. I explained that, in addition to the important contributions Sinclair
had made as a federal cabinet minister, he had been a political mentor
to me in my very early days as a Liberal. After his defeat in 1958, he had
started a Liberal businessmen's club, meant for young people, as part of
an effort to rebuild the Liberal Party. Nathan Nemetz had mentioned the
club to me. When I saw Sinclair at events, he was always very encouraging to me. He promoted my interest in going to Ottawa, but I hadn't
taken that idea seriously. Trudeau told me that he wouldn't stand in my
way but wanted it made clear that this wasn't his idea.

And so, on 14 November 1983, we held the naming ceremony at the site. It was an emotionally charged event. Construction of the project was not yet finished, but Sinclair by then was very ill, and we did not want to wait much longer. He came in walking slowly, with a cane. He had lost a great deal of weight and looked quite frail. When he got up to talk, thirty years rolled off him; the Sinclair of old delivered a blockbuster speech. He died a few months later.

The fisheries portfolio that Sinclair held is, of course, one that deals with a crucial policy area for British Columbia. And it is an area to which I devoted attention as the federal political minister for the province.

By the early 1980s, the British Columbia commercial salmon fishery was beset by an array of problems aptly described by resource economist Peter Pearse and his commission in their landmark 1982 study *Turning the Tide: A New Policy for Canada's Pacific Fisheries*. In a nutshell, the issue was overfishing of a diminishing resource. Part of the problem the Pearse report identified was the failure of an earlier federal policy that had sought to limit overfishing. This was the Davis Plan of 1968, named for Jack Davis, the fisheries minister at that time, who, as a British Columbian, gave the West Coast fishery the attention it deserved.[5] The issue was that because nobody owned the fish it was an open resource, and each vessel had an incentive to catch as many fish as possible. Historically, licences had been introduced as a revenue measure to fund the government's building of public docks and ports, but not originally as a means of limiting the number of vessels. By Davis's tenure, the salmon stock was declining and at the same time, prices were declining due to competition from American fishermen elsewhere on the coast, plus Russian and Japanese vessels, so the fishery was becoming uneconomic.

Davis decided in 1968 to control the entry of new players into the fishery, to prevent expansion, and later reduce the number of boats, with a buy-back program initiated in 1971, which I had heard a lot about when I was a deputy minister. Davis's argument was that there was a profitable fishery for a limited number of fishers. The plan was quite complicated, but there was a big loophole: while the plan controlled the number of boats, it did not effectively control their size or capacity to fish. The result was bigger boats with more sophisticated equipment. As the Pearse report notes, after observing that the number of salmon boats had declined, "The plan has clearly failed in its main purpose, which was to control and reduce excessive fishing capacity. Investment in fishing power continued as the value of the catch increased, and the capacity of the fleet, already excessive when the program began, doubled or perhaps trebled."[6] The Pearse report became essentially a checklist for policy objectives and negotiation with all the stakeholders.

Recognizing the problems in industry, one issue I took on in 1982 was this West Coast salmon fishing problem, encouraging the fisheries department to try one more time to deal with the challenges. I wasn't in any way pressing the department to do anything it wasn't already doing in terms of policy development. Rather, I was urging department members to complete their work so we could get it on the cabinet agenda.

I had a very pleasant working relationship with the fisheries minister, Pierre De Bané, a long-time MP from Quebec who later became a colleague in the Senate. I always found him easy to talk to. De Bané wasn't a hands-on minister; he just listened to his department, which was doing good work. It produced a number of very important papers on the fishing industry and on the objectives for policy, which continued to be the reduction of the fleet's catching capacity while allowing an equitable return for those who remained in the fishery, without destroying the resource. The policy was not just to maintain the resource, but to rebuild the stock.

My principal role was to support De Bané in the cabinet process for getting approval of the policies the department wanted to introduce. On 18 June 1984, De Bané tabled the Pacific Fisheries Restructuring Act in the House of Commons. To summarize the legislation: The first priority was stock rebuilding. The second was moving to individual fishing allocations so each boat would get its own quota and couldn't overfish that quota; this was designed both to provide an economic return to the boat and also spread that economic return over a series of licences rather than have the bigger boats catching more fish. A buy-back program would continue, and we had received authorization from cabinet to fund it to the tune of $100 million over a period of time. There was to be enhanced Indigenous participation and further development of the BC sports fishery. And there was a program for fishing community adjustment and economic development.

However, time was running out on the Trudeau government. Pierre Trudeau had announced a few months previously that he would be stepping down, and a Liberal leadership convention had just selected John Turner to replace him. The parliamentary session was about to end, and the expectation was that a new election would soon be called.

I had hoped – in vain, as it turned out – that because the Pacific coast salmon fishery's issues were so well known, we could debate and pass the bill quickly. A bill introduced earlier by De Bané on the Atlantic fishery had passed in one day. Pearse himself backed passage of the bill, and it had the general support of the BC government, although I wasn't sure whether it was great support short of real help, or their position was just, "It's your problem but we won't get in your way." The provincial government's fishing jurisdiction was freshwater, so it was indeed our issue. Moreover, they saw no reason to get drawn into the controversies between the federal government and the fishing community. And controversies there were. There was tremendous opposition by a number of interests, among them the big players in the commercial industry.

So, the bill died on the Order Paper, and instead of a comprehensive reconstruction of the West Coast fishing industry, attempted by Davis, recommended by Pearse, and further attempted by De Bané and myself, changes were made incrementally, with day-to-day decisions by the public service and by ministers of fisheries, as particular problems became acute. Licences were bought back now and then when they were available, policies were introduced to help protect the owners of fishing vessels from the most severe consequences of bankruptcy, and so it went.

It was not until the Harper government in 2009 appointed Bruce Cohen, a judge in British Columbia, to report on the decline of sockeye salmon in the Fraser River that there was a return to a more comprehensive approach. Cohen undertook an enormous study, including broad consultations, and delivered his report in 2012, making seventy-five recommendations, mostly about protecting the wild salmon fishery, many of which have been implemented by the Harper and Justin

Trudeau governments. It is a profound disappointment that despite these measures, sustainability has not been achieved. Wild salmon and other fish have continued to decline.

I had supported John Turner in the 1984 leadership race because I had thought he was more likely to be successful in electing MPs in western Canada than either of his two main challengers, Jean Chrétien and Donald Johnston.

Turner and I both had attended UBC. I didn't know him there, but I had certainly heard about him. He had graduated not long before I arrived, and "Chick" Turner's reputation as a star athlete and Rhodes Scholar still loomed large on campus. We met in Ottawa in the early 1960s, when I was Art Laing's executive assistant and he was his parliamentary secretary and then had travelled together with Laing to the Soviet Union in 1965 (as recounted in chapter 2) as well as to Yukon, accompanying the Soviet delegation on their return visit. A decade later, when I was principal secretary to Trudeau, then finance minister Turner had objected vehemently to my having created a council of economic advisers for the PMO, forcing me to disband it. So, there had been bumps, but we still had a good working relationship.

I was among those whom Turner had called in for a chat after his stormy resignation from the Trudeau cabinet in September 1975, about a month after my appointment to the Senate. I had gone over to his office and heard Turner's version of his important final meeting with Trudeau. I had also been among those who heard Trudeau give his version of that same meeting, I was struck by how little the accounts had in common. Turner then went off to Toronto to work in the private sector. Occasionally, when I was in the city, we would meet and chat over lunch at Winston's, where he had a permanent table. This was before I joined the cabinet. We were simply maintaining contact without any particular agenda. Turner would tell me about his work as a lawyer and would offer a critical perspective on what Trudeau and the government were doing.

Once Turner won the Liberal Party leadership, Trudeau warned me that Turner was not going to keep me, or the other western senators, in the cabinet. This Turner had made clear to Trudeau in their discussions about the transition.

When Turner was forming his cabinet, he invited me to his suite at the Chateau Laurier. I walked over wondering what I would hear from him, given what I had heard from Trudeau and a couple of others. He chatted with me generally about what he was thinking for ten minutes or so and then said, "Jack, I want to thank you for your service to the party, I'm not continuing you in the cabinet, but I hope you will support me in the caucus and help my government get elected." In response, I acknowledged my disappointment but wished him well.

I didn't take the decision personally. I understood that he wanted to make a clean break with the Trudeau era. He was a different person with a different agenda, and his supporters wanted to make a political culture change. Keeping me on when I was such a prominent Trudeau supporter – and had been so prominent in British Columbia at a time when Turner himself was planning to run for a seat in the province – would not have been the correct political move for Turner. Frankly, I felt he'd made a serious mistake, but his decision was consistent with the philosophy he had adopted.

As it turned out, of course, I wouldn't have been in the cabinet much longer in any case. The 4 September 1984 election was a landslide victory for Brian Mulroney's Progressive Conservatives. Turner won in Vancouver Quadra, giving the Liberals one seat in British Columbia.

I had given everything I had to being a successful minister. But now it was time to gear down and focus on other things.

9 My Introduction to China

WHILE CAMPAIGNING FOR THE LEADERSHIP of the Liberal Party in March 1968, Pierre Trudeau had said that if he became prime minister, he would offer to exchange diplomatic representatives with China without preconditions. It was his belief that China should be engaged in a positive way and brought back into the global community. He made it clear, however, that Canada would still expect to maintain relations with Taiwan.[1]

China had some twenty years earlier "closed its door" to the world, as the Chinese put it, when the Communists came to power. Behind that closed door, Mao Zedong and his government set about making radical changes at enormous human cost. The period is complex, but Mao and the leadership used the first twenty years to change the structure and culture of Chinese society and the economy. And for most of that period, little in the way of detailed information was available to the outside world. Nor did much of the outside world really care.

Trudeau, who had visited China in 1949, as the Communist revolution was under way, and then again in 1960, had a strong sense of the future importance of China to the global community and a belief that the global community, particularly the developed world, had to signal to a Communist China that it would be treated as a respected and equal member. China had to be persuaded to open its door to the world and to be a friend to all nations, not a hostile presence. Trudeau believed China as an outlier would be very destructive, as it was in the early 1960s, when it tried to foment a communist revolution in Indonesia, for example.

By 1969, with the country still in the throes of the Cultural Revolution, China was ready to "open the door" on its own terms to a world that had forced open the door in the colonial period. There were various motivations. Probably the biggest political objective was to supplant Taiwan in the international sphere and reclaim China's seat in international organizations, including the United Nations. As well, Mao Zedong and Zhou Enlai had come to the conclusion that China could not grow its economy internally; it had to be done in an international marketplace. Although China did not have a lot in those days to export, the country needed to export what it could in order to earn foreign exchange to buy oil, other commodities, and industrial products from the world community that would help them build their industrial capacity. A third objective was military: money was needed to buy arms from the Soviet Union and other countries. China has always believed its borders were not secure.

China had chosen Canada to test the developed world on the terms of its entry into the global system. It was a good choice, as Canada clearly sought China's entry. Indeed, Trudeau had sent messages that Canada would be supportive. Perhaps Canada was also chosen as a signal to the United States. It helped that Canada had played no role in the historic repression of China. It helped that the first successful leader in the overthrow of the Qing dynasty, Dr Sun Yat-sen, had visited Vancouver and had raised money from the Chinese community, without interference from Canadian authorities, to support his revolution, which began in 1911. It helped that Dr Norman Bethune, a Canadian surgeon who died in 1939 in the service of the Communist Party, was praised by Chairman Mao as a selfless friend of China and his work and example were taught to generations of Chinese. It helped that in 1960 Canada sold millions of bushels of wheat to China on deferred payment so that China could offset the consequences of a serious famine. As well, Canadian Christian missionaries had had a presence in China, and Mandarin-speaking sons of these missionaries were working in the Canadian foreign service as key experts on China. They would be among our first diplomatic representatives there.

All this was the foundation for a negotiation that led to the exchange, on 13 October 1970, of mutual diplomatic recognition. At that time, I was deputy minister of EMR, and while I was not a member of the negotiating team, I sat on the Interdepartmental Committee on External Relations (ICER), a committee of deputy ministers headed by the deputy minister of external affairs, Ed Ritchie. ICER played an advisory role in the negotiations and was kept informed as to the progress. As a British Columbian,

I was already well aware of the importance of Asia, but my focus had been on Japan, then Asia's leading economy. The ICER assignment marked the beginning of an interest – no, a fascination – with China and its people.

One of the main difficulties in the negotiations related to the status of Taiwan. At first, China sought agreement that Taiwan was a part of China and should be under Chinese sovereignty. The United States and all western European countries rejected this approach. With the importance of the goal in front of them, the Canadian and Chinese negotiators agreed on a compromise, that Canada would "take note" of China's claim without expressly agreeing or disagreeing with it. There were many difficulties, with some days of disappointment and others of excitement. The best day of all was not that of the formal exchange, but the day we knew that both governments had come to agreement. There was no Maotai in Ottawa that day, but we found other drinks to help us celebrate.

Among those deserving credit was Mitchell Sharp. As secretary of state for external affairs, he had administrative and political responsibility for the conduct of the negotiations and their successful outcome. During a long career as a public servant and then in politics, Sharp had made many major contributions and was well regarded in cabinet, caucus, the public service, and by the business community. I held him in the highest regard. Sharp was steadfast in his support of Trudeau's policy of engagement with China.

What were our expectations when we exchanged diplomatic relations fifty years ago? Frankly, I never saw in ICER or cabinet committee discussion in the 1970s, or in talks with Pierre Trudeau on our private 1987 trip to China an expectation that China would adopt Western values in its political system. Nor at that time did we anticipate China's incredible rate of economic growth and the problems that would ensue. What we hoped was that China would join the world system of trade, financial governance, and international institutions and play a constructive role. I believe it did so for many years. However, as China grew so quickly in stature, it came up against American policies to contain it. The United States changed the rules of the International Monetary Fund, the World Bank, and World Trade Organization to exclude China's pro rata voting entitlement. These developments were taken into account in China's responses, which moved to create structures and programs outside the US-dominated international system. This in turn encouraged those in China who sought the power of Chinese nationalism to enhance the Leninist system and their own role.

I don't believe those of us who sought engagement were naïve about China. Given China's history of political authoritarianism – Imperial, Nationalist, or Communist – along with a history of food insecurity, internal wars, and invasion and occupation by international powers, their perspective on governance was bound to differ. We understood that. We sought engagement to prevent China from continuing to disturb the international system by fomenting insurrection in developing countries, prevent it from joining the Soviet orbit, and support those in China who sought economic modernization as the way forward. This modernization could only come with access to international markets, and particularly the "golden" market of the United States. We believed that growing prosperity in China would create a more open society and confirm in China the value of international engagement. However, the Tiananmen conflict of 1989 turned China's history from the relatively liberal policies of Deng Xiaoping, Hu Yaobang, and Zhao Ziyang to the more controlling policies of Li Peng and Xi Jinping.

In June 1971, Canada sent its first official delegation to China under the leadership of industry minister Jean-Luc Pépin. I had the good fortune to be one of the six deputy ministers included in the twenty-four-person group, which also included business representatives. My assignment was to open the technical relationship in mining and oil and gas between the government of Canada and appropriate departments in China.

We arrived in China by train from Hong Kong, then a British colony. There was no through train. We were obliged to walk across the border with our luggage, and then get on another train on the Chinese side. At that time, Shenzhen was a fishing village that you could see as the train headed out. (By 2021, it was a metropolis of 12.5 million people.) We rode in comfortable luxury cars from another era, complete with fancy antimacassars.[2] On the table, there was fruit I didn't recognize. It was my first introduction to starfruit and to fresh lychee. And the fresh lychee on ice were absolutely delicious.

We disembarked at Guangzhou (which we then called Canton), and were brought to the airport, where a Vickers Viscount was waiting to take us to Beijing. We could see it was used for freight normally: they had installed a few seats for us, and there were also three or four ordinary chairs, which were not bolted in. We first flew to Hangzhou, where we stopped for lunch. We saw nothing but the airport. There was a buffet of cold and hot foods laid out on a big table in a tent. There were also tables for us to sit at and eat. The food was all brand new to me. It was nothing similar to what was served in Vancouver's Chinatown in those days, which was a sort of a Westernized Cantonese. We were there just long enough to eat, and then boarded the plane to continue another couple of hours to Beijing, where we were met at the airport by Premier Zhou Enlai himself.

Zhou was our official host. The deepest impression remains of this brilliant man, an immense figure in Chinese history. I value my memory of the three days in which I sat and listened to the discussions between Zhou and Pépin in the ballroom of the Beijing Hotel. Zhou was well briefed on international affairs and talked comfortably about global politics, economics, and business. And while he used an interpreter for the formal meetings, Zhou was competent in both French and English and used those languages in casual conversation. He had spent time in Europe before the Second World War, and during the war had been Mao's delegate to the Americans in Chongqing.

Beijing in June 1971 was unforgettable. We stayed at the Beijing Hotel in top-floor rooms with a view of the roofs of the Forbidden City. The streets were crammed with bicycles and men and women dressed in almost identical clothing. There was little electricity for light, and clearly none for heat. The government offices were sparsely lit. Although it was June, the cavernous buildings still held the winter's chill; even senior officials still wore long underwear, which could be seen overlapping the tops of their socks and at their wrists. It was an experience to be of Western appearance, with none others to be found except our delegation and a small team who had just opened our embassy in temporary quarters.

People would surround me on the street and touch me, to see whether I was real. That China does not exist today, not even close.

One of our visits was to Peking University, where we met with party officials who informed us about the importance of the Cultural Revolution, then under way. They brought in a professor, who had a PhD from the University of Toronto and whom they upheld as an example of a bad person. They accused him of having marked his students harshly. When Pépin asked what the professor's field was, he was told nuclear physics. Pépin remarked, "You must have a lot of nuclear physicists to be able to treat one as badly as this." There was silence. Then our hosts all got up and left. There were no diplomatic consequences. Our hosts pretended it didn't happen.

The concluding banquet was our introduction to the Chinese custom of the host moving to every table to toast his guests. At my table, we had been introduced to Guizhou Maotai, and after two small glasses, I had had enough. I watched with amazement as Premier Zhou went from table to table, drinking a glass, each one poured from a Maotai bottle. This was only a few years after my trip to the Soviet Union with Art Laing, and I whispered to the Chinese foreign affairs official next to me, "He could drink the whole Russian government under the table." He whispered back, "Don't tell anyone, but it's water."

It was a remarkable visit. While the times were difficult, the restrained energy of the Chinese people was apparent. Napoleon once said about China that it was a sleeping giant and suggested that when it awoke, it would shake the world. Even then, I believe I saw Napoleon's sleeping giant beginning to rise, and I knew that rise would change the world and its ways, even in my lifetime. I came away with a profound belief that in one way or another, China would be significant, either as a hostile outlier not accepting the global norms of international behaviour and seeking to set up a different global society, or as a member of the existing system even if playing on their own terms. Though there would be downsides – unfair trade practices, intellectual property theft, China's record on human rights – we believed engagement was essential and that the benefits of China as a member of the world order would greatly outweigh the alternative.

It was evident to me that Canada had to play a key role in the rise of China, both in the interest of global order and in the interest of Canada. The Americans were also changing their stance on China. Henry Kissinger's secret diplomatic mission occurred not long after our departure. It paved the way for US president Richard Nixon's momentous visit the following year. For me, this trip marked the beginning of a lifetime of working to advance relations between our two countries, balancing the economic goal of growing trade and investment against the emerging challenge of how to manage our differences over human rights and authoritarian governance.

I would return to China many times.

In October 1973, Prime Minister Pierre Trudeau travelled to China for his first official visit there. He had suggested I accompany him, and I was on the original draft list to go. But by that time, we were in the midst of the first OPEC oil crisis, and as deputy minister of EMR, I had other priorities.

During the 1970s, Canada was slowly building a diplomatic presence in China, selling wheat and a few other products, and China was going through domestic transitions from Mao to Deng Xiaoping. An important milestone in China's opening its door came in 1978, with the adoption of the policy of "socialism with Chinese characteristics," which meant allowing some market forces to operate in order to spur economic growth while maintaining the Communist Party's political control.

My first trip back to China occurred in November 1983, when, as the federal minister for Expo 86 in Vancouver, I went to negotiate that country's participation. This was not the impoverished, highly regimented country I had visited a dozen years earlier. The Cultural Revolution was in the past. People were more economically secure. They were also more relaxed. Though the officials I met were still cautious, there was much greater willingness to have an open discussion, and they displayed a high degree of curiosity about Western things. Several of those we talked to had already travelled to Europe or America once or twice. (In 1971, even senior civil servants had not asked questions about Western society; it had been dangerous to open the subject or show any interest.) On the streets, there were more cars than there had been, but bicycles still predominated. There were more hotels, though in Beijing we stayed in the same one as we had on my earlier visit. The food served was of far higher quality because of the availability of better ingredients.

My wife, Natalie, and Shirley Fitterman, who is not only Natalie's sister but also her best friend, accompanied me, of course at their own expense. Shirley is not especially fond of Chinese food, so she brought some of her own supplies in her luggage, including two jars of peanut butter. She would eat it in her room. At one of the events at the Canadian mission, Shirley mentioned her peanut butter, which elicited enormous interest. One of the women at the mission absolutely begged her for whatever she had left when she was leaving Beijing. So, when we left, Shirley gave up a jar. It was a taste of home for someone who hadn't seen peanut butter in months, if not years. In those days, the mission was very isolated, and Western food and goods were not readily available.

By 1983, foreigners were already less of a novelty in Beijing, but Shanghai was a different story. There, when we were walking down the main road, Nanjing Lu, near the Peace Hotel where we were staying, we were mobbed by curious Shanghai residents. Our escorts had to push people away to make space for us to continue. Shanghai was still a city that had been largely closed off to foreign travel and was just being opened up at that time.

Located on the Bund, a group of European-style buildings in the old foreign quarter, the Peace had once been the Cathay, a famous hotel in the pre-communist period when the city was a major centre for Western expatriates. It had been built by the Sassoons, a Jewish family originally from Iraq. Across the street, the Kadoories, another Jewish family from Iraq, built the Majestic Hotel. These became centres for Western life in Shanghai, and staying at the Peace we gleaned a sense of what things had been like in those days. Both, of course, were taken over by the Communists in 1949. At the Cathay, the famous jazz bar remained intact, and some of the pre-war players, much aged, came back to entertain.

Although my main business had been in Beijing, the stop in Shanghai for a couple of days was part of the official visit. Our hosts were the mayor and city council. At that time, under Zhao Ziyang and Hu Yaobang, China was opening to the West, so the country needed visible demonstrations of the fact that Westerners were acceptable. Our visit served as an assurance to Shanghai officials that their city was now on the party's recommended travel list for highly important Western dignitaries. Shanghai had been snubbed by Mao's Communist Party because it was seen as having been, under the Kuomintang, the cesspool of the Western pollution of Chinese society.

From Shanghai, we flew to Guangzhou, in Guangdong province, and stopped for a day or two. It was the way to leave China at that time, and from there, we took the train to Hong Kong. Guangdong was almost like a different country. It was very poor. People were allowed to have very small, informal businesses, and there were lots of these set up on the sidewalks, underneath the overhangs of low-rise apartment buildings. These were built over the sidewalks so that when people threw their slops out the window, they would land in the gutter and not on passers-by. Today Guangzhou is one of China's most progressive cities, wealthy and industrious. It is a true southern capital and the centre of the "Cantonese" people. They are Han, like more than 90 per cent of the Chinese population, but speak a language different from the Mandarin of Beijing and show a streak of independence from the northerners. A Canadian has no trouble understanding this.

In the 1970s, Asia was not a priority for Canada's external affairs department, by any means. At the time, prevailing perception was that China wasn't important, India was a pain in the neck (it conducted a "peaceful nuclear explosion" using a CANDU nuclear reactor Canada had sold it, causing international tensions), and there was a small but sophisticated Japan section that did its own thing. The department had really only been focused on Asia when it was part of the tripartite commission created to supervise the implementation of the Geneva peace accord in Indochina (1954–73).

By 1979, Tom Delworth, a career diplomat who was then director general of the Asian and Pacific affairs bureau and had served as ambassador to Indonesia, was advocating for the development in Canada of a research capacity on Asia. At the time, Canadians knew relatively little about the countries there, and had relatively few interactions and connections with them, apart from Japan. Creating such a research capacity was not something that could be done within the external affairs department. The idea was to set up an independent foundation where publicly available research could be concentrated on Asian issues for the benefit and knowledge of Canadians. It could also do consulting work for the private business sector. The Clark government had shown some interest but was defeated before it was able to move forward.

There was also interest in some parts of the business sector in the initiative actually proceeding. Business circles are small, and as it turned out it was a former law partner of mine, John Bruk, who went on to play an instrumental role. As the president of Cyprus Anvil Mining and a leading exporter of mineral concentrates to Asia, he had heard of the idea and supported it. Bruk was a Conservative. And he was a supporter of Erik Nielsen, the Conservative MP for Yukon, which was where Cyprus was doing its mining. He came to me looking for help from the Liberal government on this file. That meant he came to someone with a natural affinity to support initiatives that built a focus on Asia Pacific, as it supported not only my public policy interests but also, of course, the interests of British Columbia, Canada's face on the Pacific.

A comprehensive report had to be written and submitted to the government outlining the purposes, organization, and structure of the foundation. My wife, Natalie, then a professional journalist and business writer, volunteered to prepare a draft. She and Bruk worked together on the project and submitted the necessary document to the department. Neither of them charged or were paid for their work.

There was a lot of resistance in Ottawa to the federal government sponsoring an independent foundation. There were no precedents – resistance number one. Number two, Asia Pacific "isn't that important." Number three, we didn't have the money to contribute to this endeavour. And number four, who would run it? Delworth and his small group faced a lot of opposition within his own department. I took up the advocacy at the cabinet level, helping to move it through the political process by using my relationships in the PCO and PMO. Allan MacEachen, who had become external affairs minister in 1982, wasn't enthusiastic, and there were major players in that department who didn't believe in it. Through all this, Delworth was consistent in trying to move the concept forward. We shared an understanding that the foundation should be about the totality of relationships with Asia, and not focus too narrowly only on promoting business. If Canadians were to do business with Asia, developing a broader understanding of Asians' cultures and outlook was essential.

It was helpful, however, that Bruk was able to show that Canadian business was interested in Asia and the creation of the foundation. This was encouraging to Trudeau, who was receptive to the idea but always weighing how this stood in the balance of so many other issues and opportunities. Gradually, Trudeau came to support the project. His terms were that the business community and the provinces match the federal contribution, in other words, one-third, one-third, and one-third. Trudeau told me that if I assured him personally of the feasibility, he would support the foundation, but he didn't want it to be a federal initiative by itself. It needed a bigger constituency if it was going to be successful, and I agreed with him. For my part, I insisted that the foundation be headquartered in Vancouver.

Legislation to create the Asia Pacific Foundation of Canada was introduced and quickly passed, with all-party support, in June 1984, in the House of Commons and in the Senate. The Liberals' loss of the September 1984 election left it up to the Mulroney government to follow through. The fact that Bruk was a Conservative proved helpful in getting the foundation off the ground. Bruk became the first chair. Ray Anderson, a long-time Canadian trade official and diplomat who had been our high commissioner to Australia, took on the presidency.

In the early days, external affairs exercised a great deal of influence. The foundation had a board of directors, and a small number of them were appointed by the minister, including the chair, but the board elected the president and also replaced itself in tranches of one-third every three years. A director's term was nine years. Although the foundation in theory had a great deal of independence, in reality, the money largely came from the federal government. Some provinces contributed, in particular British Columbia, Ontario, and Quebec. The business community almost entirely failed to do anything, though it had the benefit of the foundation's work and the individual directors from business were a blue-ribbon group.

The foundation set about its work, sponsoring research, holding conferences, and, more broadly, advancing Canadian awareness not only of Japan and China but also Indonesia and the Philippines among other Asian nations. Based on Natalie's work on the report to create the foundation, she was retained as one of the foundation's first senior employees and played an instrumental role in getting the foundation up and running. Because of my position in cabinet, she did not accept any salary until the Mulroney government took office. She served as a senior policy adviser and director of public affairs and stayed with the foundation until 1988.

Another early employee was Colin Hansen, who was brought in as a junior administrative assistant and went on to become vice-president. He spent several years at the foundation and developed a fascination with public policy and political life in the provincial sphere. He was elected to the BC legislature as a provincial Liberal in 1996 and served in cabinet posts, including finance, health, economic development, and minister responsible for Asia Pacific Initiative, in the Gordon Campbell government. His experience at the foundation gave him a solid grounding in the facts and challenges of Asia, which was helpful later, when engaging the support of the BC provincial government in developing policies regarding Asia and China.

In late 1984, with the Liberals newly in Opposition, Edgar Kaiser Jr asked me to become the president of the international division of the Bank of British Columbia. Although the division also had a London office, most of its focus was on Asia, more particularly Hong Kong, where the bank had a deposit-taking subsidiary. Kaiser knew that I had some familiarity with that part of the world and was very keen to bring me on board.

An American who had become a Canadian citizen, Kaiser was a grandson of Henry Kaiser, a major US business figure in construction, health care, the automobile industry, and shipbuilding. He had moved to British Columbia to run his family's coal properties in the southeastern part of the province. I had originally been introduced to Kaiser while I was serving in the Trudeau cabinet. I had made it my business to develop contacts with the important economic figures in the province. At that point, Kaiser was already a very big name in British Columbia. Making the introduction were Jack Poole and Bob Lee, key BC business figures in their own right, both active in real estate development. Poole was a major commercial property developer in Vancouver and Toronto, but is best known for having been a leading player in bringing the 2010 Olympics to Vancouver.

As for Lee, I had first met him when we were students at UBC; it was only later that he became a good friend. He had built a successful real estate business, Prospero, in particular by serving clients from Hong Kong and Taiwan seeking to buy property in Vancouver. When I was in the Trudeau cabinet, I had Lee appointed to the Vancouver Port Authority. When I had proposed the appointment to him, he had said, "Why? I don't know anything about shipping." But I explained that his real estate expertise was needed on that board. The port had some of the best real estate in the city of Vancouver, but as I made clear to Lee, they didn't know how to get value from the real estate they owned that was not needed for port purposes. The board was very happy to have him. Later, Lee was instrumental in creating a major new residential housing development at UBC that brought the university more than $1 billion. He went on to serve as the university's chancellor. Lee was known for his strong sense of ethics, public spiritedness, and philanthropic generosity. Many in the community have benefited.

Kaiser had become chair and CEO of the Bank of British Columbia in September 1984, charged with getting the bank back on its feet after it landed in financial trouble as a result of the 1980–81 recession. In June 1984, I had appointed Kaiser to the Canadair board, but he did not stay long, leaving around the time he accepted the Bank of British Columbia post. While in the Trudeau cabinet, I had had no involvement with the Bank of British Columbia's issues; that was a matter for the Department of Finance.

When Kaiser made me the job offer, I hesitated, because at first, I wasn't sure whether it would take me away too often from my Senate duties in Ottawa. I told Kaiser I would look into whether it was possible. Still, I was feeling keenly that I'd been in Ottawa since 1970, without a chance to live in the rest of the world and catch up to the realities of my own province. When I had been in the cabinet, I was very connected to British Columbia in the sense of administering to requests and dealing with communities and constituencies. Even then, I was not fully living in the province, I was just back on weekends. My main focus was in Ottawa. I wanted a chance to base myself in Vancouver and be viewed in British Columbia as a British Columbian, not just representing Ottawa in British Columbia. I wanted a chance to be in Vancouver during the week, being seen and approached, and listening to people, catching up on the evolving social and political scene. What I was looking for was, in effect, a sabbatical.

I talked with Allan MacEachen, who was by then the leader of the Liberal Opposition in the Senate, to make my case. I noted that the Liberals had a big majority in the Senate. The legal requirement was to attend at least once in every two sessions. I told MacEachen that I would keep up my Senate attendance well beyond that. He agreed that so long as I attended at least a few times a month, I could accept Kaiser's offer to get the background and experience, but only for a year. And that was my arrangement with Kaiser: I would work for the bank for a year, and from there we would see what would happen.

I was in Ottawa for a few days a month when the Senate was sitting, and I did my constituency work, my policy work, and my BC caucus work. I did not take on any Senate committee assignments, which was not a problem, given the surplus of Liberals looking to fill a limited number of Opposition committee seats.

Working for the bank taught me a great deal about the economy of British Columbia and my deputy, Henry Bow, helped me understand banking operations. I also learned a great deal about Hong Kong, at that time still under British colonial administration. While British colonial rule was a top-down authoritarian system, Hong Kong's legal system was independent and essential to the growth and stability of business. The business community came to understand and rely on the British system of justice and fairness. My year with the bank also gave me insight into the Canadian relationship with Hong Kong, including the ties resulting from Canada's wartime sacrifices there, as well as Hong Kong's more recent history and what was then the imminent end in 1997 to Britain's lease on the colony.

Perhaps most of all, I had the opportunity to meet and do business with many members of Hong Kong's Chinese business elite, some of whom became good friends. My Harvard law degree and contacts, as well as my background as a former Canadian cabinet minister, facilitated introductions. Among my closest friends were Michael Y.L. Kan and his wife Morgiana (Morgie). I had met Kan through James Wolfensohn, who knew him when they were at Harvard Business School. I also knew Wolfensohn from my days at Harvard. He had a career as a prominent investment banker and served as head of the World Bank. When I took the Bank of BC post, Wolfensohn helped connect me with Kan and a few others in Hong Kong.

Pedigree in Hong Kong was incredibly important in business terms, as I discovered. In Chinese business culture, it has always been important to find out who you're dealing with. Things are not transactional in the North American way, where everything is objective and it's all about the deal; people don't care who they're dealing with, because they believe the lawyers will make sure their legal rights are guaranteed in the contract. In Hong Kong, people lost face if they dealt with the wrong people. The personal credentials of the people they were dealing with and their backgrounds had a significance in Hong Kong and in Asia generally. I brought my knowledge of Japanese business culture; it was also of advantage to tell them how much time I'd spent in Japan and the companies I'd dealt with there.

I was very active through the year. We were trying to establish a high-quality reputation in Hong Kong, in some ways competing with the two other Canadian banks that had significant operations there, the Canadian Imperial Bank of Commerce and the Royal Bank. I also did a modest amount of business in Taiwan. Essentially, I was in the business of lending money. The loans were secured by properties in Hong Kong. I focused primarily on the Chinese entrepreneurs in Hong Kong and any Canadians who would do business with us. The fact that the Bank of British Columbia had originally been sponsored by the province gave it important credentials. In China, government's involvement in a business entity makes a business highly credible and reliable.

Among the bank's clients were people in Hong Kong who were interested in making investments in China. Of course, these loans were always secured by assets in Hong Kong or Canada or the United States, not in China itself. One of my clients was Robert Ho. That's a common name. There was another Robert Ho in my life many years later – a descendant of a major Hong Kong business family who created a foundation to develop knowledge of Chinese Buddhism around the world, and he was a major philanthropist in Vancouver – but this Robert Ho was the owner of a very substantial business called Fairmont Shipping, which owned a number of freighters that crossed the Pacific.

As a patriotic Chinese, Robert Ho wanted to help China, then still a very poor county, develop its air transportation system. The only foreign planes that China had in those days were second-hand British propeller planes and a few aircraft the Russians had provided. They had almost nothing in the way of an air transport system in 1985. Ho knew of my background as a cabinet minister with responsibility for Canadair and De Havilland. And he was familiar with the Dash 7, a short takeoff and landing aircraft, and thought it would be a very good airplane for China, which outside the major centres had small and somewhat primitive airstrips. Ho introduced me to his contracts at the Civil Aviation Administration of China (caac), China's sole aircraft purchaser at that time. At my request, De Havilland brought an aircraft to China as a demonstrator, and the Shanghai branch of caac initially bought three Dash 7s from De Havilland, basically at De Havilland's cost, as the opening of a relationship. Fairmont, under Robert Ho, guaranteed the Bank of British Columbia's financing of the transaction. The bank made only a small amount on the loan, minimal compensation for the time I had spent on it, which included several trips to China. De Havilland went on to sell more planes to China.

Things went well for the first eight months or so, but by the latter part of 1985, the Bank of British Columbia was running into trouble, for reasons that had nothing to do with me. The bank was starting to have liquidity problems as a result of a loss of confidence in western regional banks after two Alberta banks collapsed. And Kaiser himself did not have the confidence of Canadian regulators, who had been concerned about a loan guarantee he had made earlier that year to T. Boone Pickens, an American entrepreneur. Pickens was making a takeover attempt of a company in the United States called Unocal. Kaiser had risked a rather large amount of the bank's capital. In fact, the bank made money on the deal; still, it was a problematic move. Kaiser ran the bank more like a personal business than a bank, though not in any fraudulent way.

As a result of the bank's liquidity problems, I was cut off from further lending and further buying. For the months of November and December 1985, I had very little to do, although I had the embarrassing job of apologizing to newly developed major business contacts in Hong Kong that I couldn't do further work. I explained that the bank certainly would honour its obligations and could clear cheques and so on, but I couldn't do further lending or provide other financial services.

I overcame the damage to my personal reputation through my continuing presence in Hong Kong. Once people understood that it wasn't me but the bank that was failing with the regulators, the problem went away for me personally. In any case, it was time for me to return full-time to my Senate duties. My year was up. It had become apparent that continuing with the bank would not have been tenable. My role there not only took time away from my work in the Senate, but it also curbed my ability to be effective there. As an officer of the bank, I could not speak on any subject of political significance without running the risk of adverse client reaction for the bank. So, I resigned.

In April 1986, as the result of an intervention from Stanley Hartt, then deputy minister of finance, Kaiser was replaced as president and CEO of the bank, though he continued as chair. Kaiser had not wanted to play by Ottawa's rules. He tried to involve me, asking me to make representations in Ottawa on his behalf; however, I refused to become involved.

At the end of December 1986, a year after I had left the bank to focus more fully on my Senate duties, the bank was bought by the Hongkong and Shanghai Bank (HSBC), long and well established in Hong Kong, which inherited its assets and obligations. This worked out well for HSBC, which thus gained a presence in Canada.

During my rounds of introducing myself in Hong Kong, I had met Edward Woo, a Hong Kong lawyer; Peter Eng, a former academic; and K.K. Wong, an engineer with a PhD from Queen's University. They were

Hong Kong property developers, well-known and well-regarded people. Eng and Wong were brothers-in-law, married to sisters. A few years before I met them, they had founded the University of East Asia.³ It was located in Macao, then a Portuguese colony, about forty-five minutes by hovercraft from Hong Kong. The British colonial authorities had limited university education dramatically in order not to create a class of Hong Kong Chinese that might have the education to challenge their governance. Nonetheless, there was a burgeoning business and economic success story in Hong Kong, and the children of successful businesspeople wanted university educations. Some could afford to study in Britain, the United States, or Canada, but many could not.

Macao had no institution of higher learning, which gave the three founders the opening in 1981 to apply to the Portuguese government for a permit to create a private university. They received it and proceeded to build a campus. The university had no problem attracting students. Most were from Hong Kong, but others came from places like Singapore, Indonesia, and Malaysia, which have large ethnic-Chinese populations. Courses were offered in Mandarin, Cantonese, Portuguese, and English. The offerings were primarily in the liberal arts and business. To head the board of governors, the three founders recruited Lord Asa Briggs, a prominent member of Britain's educational establishment. The three founders had put in significant capital and were hoping to recoup it by building upscale houses and apartment buildings close to the university. It was a business model analogous to the way some developers build houses at golf courses.

Shortly after I met the three founders, they invited me to see their campus. I was trying to do business with them for the Bank of British Columbia, so of course I went. And I was quite impressed. Later, as I was leaving the bank, they invited me to join their board. I accepted. As a result, I gained significant insight into the attitudes of the Chinese communities of Hong Kong and Macao toward the colonial administrations of the time, and I learned a great deal about the social life and business life of Hong Kong in particular.

I served on the board from late 1985 to 1989. At a session in the early fall of 1986, the founders discussed with me how to raise the profile of the university, first, with the business leaders in Hong Kong where they were hoping for financial support; second, with the Portuguese authorities in Macau; and third, with Chinese officials in the education ministry in Beijing and Guangzhou. It was hoped to lead to a stronger image of official approval and support, which in turn would be attractive to students and their parents. At that discussion, I said we should aim high. I proposed approaching Henry Kissinger as probably the most famous foreign name known in China and throughout East Asia, because of his role as US secretary of state under President Richard Nixon in opening up US relations with China. I noted that Kissinger charged high fees for his appearances. The founders said they were prepared to pay what he asked.

In my role as the deputy minister of EMR, I had met Kissinger during talks in Washington during the 1973–74 energy crisis. I was involved in meetings with him again in 1974 and 1975, when I was principal secretary to Prime Minister Pierre Trudeau. And I had teased Kissinger that I had made it to China before he did.

So, Kissinger knew who I was when I called for an appointment to see him at his office in New York, where he had established a private consulting business. When we met, I explained to him what the University of East Asia was and the offer of an honorary degree. He agreed to attend at the campus in Macau, receive an honorary degree, and deliver an address. He also agreed to speak to business leaders at a private dinner arranged by the founders in Hong Kong for the preceding evening. Kissinger was fabulous in both presentations, at the university on 5 March and at the dinner in Hong Kong the previous night. In short, his visit was a major success for the university and for its founders.

Later the same year, we awarded an honorary degree to Pierre Trudeau, which I also arranged, again to raise the university's profile. At that time there were some 100,000 or more people in Hong Kong holding Canadian passports. I had advised the founders and the board that I would be accompanying Trudeau on a private visit to Pakistan and China that would have us in Hong Kong in early October 1987. This would afford an opportunity to bring him to the university. Trudeau, of course, had also been a very big player in the opening of Western relations with China. After that plan was made, the board of governors then decided to award me an honorary doctorate at the same time. I received the news when I was in London, on my way to Islamabad. I neither asked for it, nor expected it. It was the decision they made to thank me for the service to the university in bringing Kissinger and Trudeau.

Trudeau didn't speak at the award ceremony, which took place on 6 October 1987; he had agreed to accept the degree if I spoke rather than himself. He did, however, review the speech I wrote, and made some valuable comments. My remarks focused mainly on China's emergence as an increasingly significant player in the world economy – and it was clear even then that this would be on its own terms[4] – as well as on the history of Canada-China relations and on our growing ties. I suggested the two countries co-operate in bringing about the creation of a Pacific Organization for Economic Co-operation and Development, along the lines of the Paris-based OECD. "Its purpose would be to institutionalize objective economic and social fact-gathering about the Pacific, to provide a forum for informal and consultative meetings between governments on regional issues and from time to time, to issue reports and studies on matters as agreed by its governing council. It would have an administrative apparatus, preferably neither large nor bureaucratic, which by itself would provide valuable working experience for its members and over time develop a group of leaders with a Pacific esprit de corps." My aspiration for such an Asia Pacific community and its function might at some future time, probably distant, be realized if the United States and China were to become members of the Comprehensive and Progressive Agreement for Trans-Pacific Partnership. That grouping is the leading sign of commitment as of now among many members of the Asia Pacific nations to work collaboratively in creating a community of interests.

Trudeau did speak for some thirty minutes at a private dinner held in Hong Kong. He answered questions, mostly about his view of Hong Kong's importance and role, and the significance of the 1984 agreement between China and the United Kingdom for the recovery by China of its sovereignty over Hong Kong in 1997, subject to a fifty-year transition period. The guests were some of the most prominent political and business people in the then colony. Also attending were a few businessmen who had moved to Canada and who had flown in specially from Vancouver or Toronto for what was considered a big insider event. It was a huge success for the university, though Trudeau, whose focus was on the big picture and the sweep of history, was perhaps more enigmatic, more philosophical than the Hong Kong business community expected. They had been hoping for more of a ground-level discussion of practical business and immigration issues. For both Kissinger and Trudeau, the university's auditorium, which held about 3,000 people, was packed.

One of the unanticipated consequences of our having raised the profile of the University of East Asia was that the Portuguese authorities decided they wanted to take control of the university, which was a private institution. Their explanation was that they wanted to perpetuate the recollection of Portugal in Macao and China, to preserve the 400-year history of Portuguese rule in Macao, which was to come to an end in 1999. They expropriated the university, negotiating a settlement with the founders that included having the Portuguese name their own rector and change the university's name to the University of Macao.

The university's last rector before the takeover was a Canadian, Paul Lin, a native of British Columbia who had founded the Centre for East Asian Studies at McGill University and who had lived in China from 1949 to 1964, working as an editor and translator. He explained to me that he had never been a Communist but had gone as a Chinese nationalist who wanted to be part of the rise of the new China after the Communist revolution.

I was on the university's board until the transaction was completed. Little did I know that my involvement with China was just beginning.

10 Building the Canada-China Relationship

IN THE LATE 1980S, economic liberalization was in progress under Deng Xiaoping, who famously declared that it did not matter whether a cat was black or white so long as it caught mice. His pragmatic policy was to release the energies of the Chinese people in a constructive way, so they could bring about the modernization of China. This included opening up education and opportunities for study in the Western world, because the Western world had the technologies.

Along with economic liberalization, there were signs things were loosening up politically. A wider variety of comments were permitted. People were posting their messages on walls, with some challenging political comments. There was a freer internal debate than China had seen under Mao, or has seen since the June 1989 events at Tiananmen Square in Beijing.

In April 1989, the sudden death of former party general secretary Hu Yaobang from a heart attack sparked a protest movement led by students, but eventually workers joined. Hu had been near the very top of the leadership of the Communist Party and was associated with the more liberal wing. In the following weeks, the protests gathered momentum. There were demands for greater political freedoms – and a statue-of-liberty-like figure called the Goddess of Democracy was erected – as well as criticism of corruption. And there was indeed corruption in Chinese society. As Deng said, when you open the window, you get fresh air but you also get mosquitoes and flies. This was one of his aphorisms, telling the Chinese people there are costs to rapid modernization, including costs in human behaviour.

By mid-May, many thousands were gathered in Tiananmen Square in central Beijing, among them hunger strikers. Within the country's leadership, there were divisions about how to respond. Zhao Ziyang, by then the party's general secretary, served as a leading voice for moderation and peaceful engagement; however, those advocating a hard-line response, including martial law, won out.

On 19 May Zhao went to students in Tiananmen Square to tell them they had gone too far and were courting disaster. They ignored him. He was reported to have cried, knowing what was coming. On the night of 3–4 June, the disaster became real, as troops that had been brought in from the countryside, and had probably been told stories that weren't true about who these people were and what they were doing, brutally crushed the protesters. The Chinese government decided it had to demonstrate across the country the party's authority. Hundreds, if not thousands, of people were killed. As for Zhao, he was deposed and spent the rest of his life essentially under house arrest, secretly writing a memoir of his time in the party.

I had been following events closely from Vancouver. Of course, I was deeply unhappy and disappointed with the way China's leaders decided to demonstrate their authority and the permanence of the Communist Party. But I also felt that what had happened had been inevitable: the students had been overreaching in demanding democracy, in effect demanding the removal of the Communist Party from power.

As for Zhao, whom I had hosted at a state dinner during his visit to Vancouver in January 1984, I admired his courage and historical perspective. I've always seen him as one of the great leaders of China in this period. I tried, two or three times after 1989, to send him messages, but Chinese officials wouldn't accept them.

The Tiananmen events of June 1989 created a setback in China's global relationships. Canada, while maintaining formal diplomatic ties, withdrew from a number of program arrangements and suspended ministerial visits. I agreed with the Mulroney government's reaction at that time, expressing disapproval of the harshness of the action, without breaking off relations. Canada maintained Trudeau's belief that come what may, China was a major player in the global system, and Canada had to have a relationship with China.

Business between Canada and China came to a virtual halt as a result of Tiananmen. When I went back to China in the fall of 1992, things were still very quiet. I had been in Hong Kong for business reasons so decided to go to Beijing to assess the situation through appointments with business contacts.[1]

During my visit, I was staying at the China World Hotel, the newest Western-style hotel in Beijing at that time. I just happened to see on the hotel notice board that the Canada-China Trade Council was having its annual general meeting there. I went to check it out. Not much was happening at the meeting, but I registered and joined the trade council, originally founded in 1978 by Paul Desmarais Sr, the chair and CEO of Power Corp. in Montreal.

Among the three or four dozen people in attendance was André Desmarais. I didn't know him, though I had met his father, Paul Desmarais Sr, when I was principal secretary to Prime Minister Trudeau. At the meeting, André and I chatted. He called me in early 1993 to invite me to an annual general meeting in Vancouver. The organization needed a new president, and he asked whether I would be interested. I attended the meeting and was elected president. Earl Drake, who had been Canada's ambassador to China during the events of 1989, became vice-president of the council and my most valued friend and partner in building the new Canada-China relationship. In this period, we changed the group's name to the Canada China Business Council (CCBC) to reflect the much wider scope of its activities.

At the same time, André Desmarais succeeded his father as chair of the council. We had a series of discussions about how to recruit more members and have the council become more active. I set about developing business plans with different scenarios. It was a challenging time for CCBC, as the international trade group in external affairs was withdrawing its modest core funding, and Tiananmen Square was still fresh in the public consciousness. André Desmarais was absolutely first rate in his support of my efforts as president. He presided at all board meetings and was present at every function in China. The endowment he put together for the organization, with contributions from his own company, Power Corp., as well as nine other partners, provided a solid financial base.

In the fall of 1993, the Liberals were returned to power under the leadership of Jean Chrétien. André, married to Chrétien's daughter, France, had certainly told his father-in-law about CCBC and the role it could play in attracting major Canadian business corporations to focus on China. Chrétien was also in touch with Paul Desmarais Sr to obtain his views. A few weeks after he became prime minister, Chrétien pulled me aside at a caucus meeting and said, "Jack, Paul tells me you're now the president of the Canada China Business Council, and I want to rebuild the commercial relationship with China, and so I'm telling you, come up with your best ideas." I asked for one commitment, that he attend the CCBC AGM once a year, alternately in China and in Canada. He gave and kept that commitment, attending from 1994 to 2001.

The CCBC board in 1994 was composed of considerable China experience and talent. Those supporting André Desmarais and myself included Peter Kruyt, vice-president of Power Corp.; James Kelleher, Mulroney's trade minister; Neil Tait of the Bank of Montreal; and former ambassador Earl Drake. Other directors represented companies that had aspirations for significant business relations with China.

Early in our planning, I understood that if Canada was to rise on the Chinese radar, we needed to make a significant impact because we were not the most important country on their horizon. At that point, I had come to believe that what the Chinese Communist Party leadership most sought was its revalidation and acceptance in the industrialized world in order to assure their own population that the events at Tiananmen would not hinder China's economic development aspirations. For his part, Prime Minister Chrétien had made a strategic decision that Canada had an opportunity to situate itself as a leader in fostering revalidation, positioning Canada to gain preference in the Chinese market. There was more at stake than Canada's economic self-interest, however. In Chrétien's view, isolating China for much longer would be a major error that would negatively impact international security, political stability, and growth. In this, I was in complete agreement with him.

The key to my strategy for rebuilding the Canada-China commercial relationship was to use the annual general meeting and business policy conference of CCBC as the focal point for the prime minister's visit to China in 1994. CCBC would control all aspects of the business activities, including attendance, sponsorships, organization of the hotel, functions, and the banquet for business leaders. For CCBC, this AGM and those that followed were a major source of revenue, as we charged business attendees for our services. In return, through our contacts with our Chinese counterpart organization, the China Council for the Promotion of International Trade, we facilitated introductions to potential Chinese clients and suppliers.

By 1994 Canadians, especially business leaders, were attracted by the size of China's population, its development needs for goods and services, including financial services, and an interest in the country's culture and history. Whether they were ready for business or not, they wanted to take a look. There could be no better way than to join a business delegation organized by CCBC and led by the prime minister of Canada. Top-drawer treatment by the Chinese would be guaranteed. When CCBC tested the interest of the business community, success seemed assured.

Early in our planning, we adopted the name Team Canada for our trade mission and conference. I am told the credit for the name goes to then trade minister Roy MacLaren, but I was the one responsible for the development of the concept and its execution. The Team Canada mission descended on Beijing in November 1994, led by Prime Minister Jean Chrétien, nine of the ten provincial premiers, and the two territorial leaders. Accompanying them were about 400 business leaders, who each paid their own way. Jacques Parizeau, the sovereigntist premier of Quebec, did not join us; he evidently had decided that a Canadian mission wasn't for him. He got such hell from the Quebec business community that his successor, Lucien Bouchard, was aboard for the next official Team Canada mission to Asia (South Korea, the Philippines, and Thailand) in 1997 and the next official one to China in February 2001. After our tremendous success in 1994,[2] the federal government used the Team Canada brand for several similar trips to other countries.

The premiers were not part of the original plan, which was to have Chrétien and some federal ministers lead a business delegation. But I happened to have a conversation with BC premier Mike Harcourt. Natalie and I have been long-standing social friends with Harcourt and his wife,

Becky, though not political friends, given our different affiliations. (Harcourt is NDP.) We rarely quarrelled about politics; we just stayed away from the subject. After a doubles tennis game with our wives, Harcourt told me he had heard rumours about Chrétien going to China and asked what was up. At the time, he was chair of the council of premiers and territorial leaders. I filled him in. When he asked why we hadn't invited the premiers, I replied that inviting them was a fantastic idea. He took up my suggestion to call Chrétien. And Chrétien, to whom I had given a heads up about the call, said the more the merrier.

We had a phenomenal visit, with some $2.6 billion worth of firm contracts signed. It put us at the top of the list of Western countries working with China. Despite the fact that Chinese officials never initially signalled to us at what level their leadership would respond, the final results were quite amazing. Premier Li Peng came to validate our efforts at a major networking event in the banquet room of the Great Hall of the People. We were the first foreign group to use the facility after the Great Hall instituted a policy of renting it out to generate revenue. In order to extend the network and allow the Canadian attendees to enhance their relationships, we had included for each Canadian businessperson two extra banquet tickets so they could invite their Chinese business contacts. Some expressed concern about whether their contacts would attend, given that the relationships were mostly new and they did not know their counterparts very well. I assured them this was not likely to be a problem. For most of the Chinese who were invited, this would be their first opportunity to be inside the Great Hall and see the Chinese leadership in person. They would be there.

Li Peng was the *bête noire* of the Western press and public opinion after Tiananmen, as he was seen as the principal actor in the decision to use force. That perception had made him reticent about attending and speaking to the AGM banquet in the Great Hall. Vice-Premier Zhu Rongji had been delegated to receive us. Just before the banquet was to start, I was told Premier Li would attend to make some welcoming remarks, but he would not stay. The Chinese were concerned about how the Canadians would react to his presence. The reaction proved friendly and welcoming. He stayed and enjoyed himself in this reinforcement from a foreign group. Chinese ambassador Zhang Yijun, seated next to me at the prime minister's table, gave me a fine compliment, saying, "Jack, you are a mover and a shaker."

Even more important to the Chinese leadership was the return visit of Premier Li Peng to Canada in 1995, which followed his disappointing tour to Europe earlier that year. The warm welcome from the Canadian government and business leaders provided him with validation when news reports about the visit went back to China. All foreign policy is based on domestic imperatives, and in order to be effective, it's important to understand the domestic situations of the countries with which we are engaging.

We also understood that visible co-operation between the Canadian government and our companies seeking to do business in China increased the confidence of Chinese business people. Those active in China at the time all knew a story that goes something like this: A Canadian business leader, in a discussion with a prospective Chinese customer or supplier, had highly negative things to say about the Canadian government's domestic policies. After receiving no follow-up from the Chinese contact, he or she would inquire of the Chinese ambassador, who would say, "Well, frankly, the Chinese could never do business with a private company that couldn't get along with its own government." This was not so much a problem with Quebecers, for they had developed a holistic view of the roles of government and business quite different from the dichotomous perspective of the English-Canadian business community at that time.

After our great success in 1994, we at CCBC were left by Canadian trade officials to do our own thing. Chrétien returned to China in 1996 and 1998 to speak at our CCBC AGMs. His presence attracted his Chinese counterparts, in turn signalling to the Chinese business community how important and acceptable doing business with Canadians was. In Beijing in 1998, Premier Zhu Rongji told the audience that Canada was China's best friend. We branded those trips as Team Canada missions as well, although external affairs did not.

On the alternate years, we held our AGMs in Canada. These included banquets attended by Prime Minister Chrétien and senior Chinese leaders. In 1995, Premier Li Peng attended the meeting in Montreal; in 1997 President Jiang Zemin attended in Toronto; and in 1999 Premier Zhu Rongji attended in Toronto.

On both the 1994 and 1996 visits, there were announcements related to a deal under way to sell two CANDU heavy water nuclear reactors to China. These were for generating electricity, to help reduce China's dependence on highly polluting coal. In 1996, Premier Li Peng attended to make the announcement jointly with Prime Minister Chrétien. It was startling to see them with their arms around one another. Chinese sources indicated to me that Premier Li overcame considerable internal opposition to heavy water reactors in order to make this happen. The reactors were built at Qinshan, which is between Shanghai and Hangzhou, and have successfully operated since coming on line in 2000.

I marvelled at how times had changed since a quarter century earlier, when as deputy minister of EMR, I had been part of efforts to market the CANDU reactor for power generation. At a nuclear energy conference in Japan, I had been approached by a prominent Hong Kong businessman, Lawrence Kadoorie, who was interested in buying a CANDU for the power utility he owned there, China Light and Power. Kadoorie told me he was trying to reduce his company's dependence on oil; this was before the energy crisis, so he showed a lot of foresight. There was no place in Hong Kong to put such a power plant; however, Kadoorie had negotiated a site just over the border, in China, at Daya Bay. At that time, China was still fomenting much trouble in Asian countries, and the cabinet was not prepared to put a CANDU in either China or Hong Kong. A French company later built a nuclear reactor on the site.

I remained president of CCBC until 2000, when I became deputy chair. I stayed on the board and remained active. I gave up my executive role at the request of André Desmarais because I was a Paul Martin supporter, and Chrétien had become uncomfortable with that association. At the time, supporters of Martin were pressing Chrétien to resign. I wasn't active or any kind of organizer, but I was, correctly, identified with the Martin group. When Chrétien asked and I said I was committed to support Martin at the next leadership contest, he didn't take that well. So, I understood when I was asked to step down, and I wasn't angry. Political choices have a cost.

As a result, I had no operating role in the last Team Canada mission, in 2001, to Beijing. Once I was gone, the people who succeeded me were happy to have the department organize the trip, although it was still a

CCBC AGM, and they were using the same formats I had designed. I attended as an ordinary delegate, and I found myself assigned to a seat at the back of the government airplane, with the reporters and photographers, while the prime minister, premiers, and their entourages were in the upper deck, and the business executives sat in the front. During the flight, Chrétien came to the back of the plane to visit with the media people and saw me sitting with them. He expressed surprise and invited me to take a seat with the business executives. I told him I appreciated his offer, but I was well settled and enjoying listening to the reporters' banter.

Of course, I resigned from CCBC in 2003, when I joined the Martin cabinet.

At the 2,000-person CCBC banquet in Toronto in 1997, I was seated at the head table next to Prime Minister Chrétien, along with President Jiang Zemin and his ambassador, Zha Peixin. An interpreter sat behind us. At one point, Jiang said to Chrétien, "Why don't we organize a formal agreement between the National People's Congress and the Parliament of Canada, where the parliamentarians can get to know one another and get to know one another's countries, something similar to your agreement with the Congress of the United States?" Chrétien turned to me and said, "Well, Jack will organize it."

I called a meeting of the other political parties, to let them know the government was proposing such a parliamentary organization be created, while making clear it was understood this was the prerogative of Parliament, not the executive. The agreement of the other parties did not come easily. There were a lot of negative feelings, partly based on Tiananmen, partly based on sympathy for Tibet, partly based on a general reticence about China being communist. There was also no precedent for a parliamentary association with a country that was not a democracy. With such countries, there were only "friendship associations." Parliamentary associations were a more senior category, involving formal bilateral agreements. The argument I made was that China was too important not to try to develop relationships and a deeper understanding by parliamentarians of Chinese ideology, viewpoints, policies, and people. NDP MP Bill Blaikie objected to calling the group a parliamentary association, arguing the National People's Congress was merely a rubber stamp, not a parliament. I pointed out it was a legislature, it passed laws. We agreed to call the new group the Canada-China Legislative Association.

Because Canada's Parliament is bicameral, we had two Canadian co-chairs, initially myself from the Senate and Reg Alcock from the House of Commons, later Joe Volpe. Of course, there was also a Chinese co-chair, initially Jiang Xinxiong, and later Lu Congmin. They both had held ministerial rank in the Chinese government and later were senior officials in the National People's Congress.

In November 1998, our group of eleven Canadian parliamentarians travelled to China for a week-long visit and our first meetings with our Chinese counterparts. It was also timed to coincide with the CCBC AGM in Beijing. By that time, Li Peng was no longer premier but was the chair of the National People's Congress. He received us in his office at the Great Hall, and then we had working meetings with our equivalents in the legislative association.

People have denigrated these sorts of missions as junkets, but in our case, it was far from that. Many of our earliest discussions involved comparisons of the roles of the legislators. On that first trip, however, we also discussed such topics as the rule of law, the development of civil society, human rights, respect for minorities, and environmental protection. These discussions were genuine and meaningful. At the start of official meetings, our counterparts were obliged to give us the party line, and they did. Once that was out of the way, the discussions were useful exchanges, although there were lines we didn't cross, like bringing up the events at Tiananmen or mentioning the brutality of the Cultural Revolution. Some of the most valuable exchanges were in more informal settings, as when having a bite to eat or travelling on a bus or walking to a temple. We would chat in a very comfortable way. It was an open era, by Chinese standards. Some of the Chinese legislators spoke English fluently; however, none of the Canadians spoke Mandarin. We would bring our own translators from Ottawa, who were present to facilitate informal discussions as well as the more formal ones. We did not need to rely on those the Chinese government provided. The exchanges continued more or less annually, alternating between Canada and China. There were additional meetings among the co-chairs.

We were building trust and knowledge on both sides. China's exponential economic growth was always fascinating to us – its economy was doubling every seven years – and we had many questions about the implications for Chinese government policy-making. We also discussed how we might be able to encourage more Chinese tourism to Canada, how this country might become a "preferred destination." The Chinese, for their part, wanted to know more about Canadian social policy, pension plans, health plans, and the role of the private sector. They also wanted to have us explain our attitude to state-owned enterprises in Canada: what we call "Crown corporations."

In this period, between my parliamentary and CCBC roles, advancing the Canada-China relationship – in the political world and the business world – was a big part of my public policy work. Of course, I was not involved in the formal bilateral diplomatic relationship between the two countries. Still, I had countless meetings with Chinese ambassadors in Ottawa, and visiting high officials, vice-premiers, and premiers. It was a very active and comprehensive engagement on my part.

I remained co-chair of the Canada-China Legislative Association until I rejoined the cabinet in December 2003, which meant I had to give up all other activities. My successor was Sen. Joe Day from New Brunswick, who continued a high level of activity and engagement. Senator Day also took over from me the role of chair of the Canada-Mongolia Friendship Association, which I had initiated. His visits to Mongolia assisted Canadian mining interests there.

Within the context of my cabinet role, I continued to have a strong focus on China and also remained keen to advance Canada's relationships with Asia more broadly. This was also a priority for Prime Minister Paul Martin, who was not unfamiliar with China, dating back to the time he owned Canada Steamship Lines, which served Chinese ports.

The Martin period was a high point in Canada-China relations. Not more than a couple of days before Martin took office, while Chrétien was still prime minister, Canada had received a visit from Chinese premier Wen Jiabao. I sat in on a discussion chaired by Jean Chrétien – Paul Martin was also there –about the further development of the Canada-China relationship. Wen also met separately with Martin. There was a gala dinner, at which Wen gave an upbeat speech about Canada-China relations. Several accords were signed for co-operation in different areas. China also had, only two years previous, joined the World Trade Organization, something we had strongly supported, and the impact on our trading relations had yet to be determined. It was a positive period in the relationship, and Canada had a lot to look forward to.

In January 2005, Prime Minister Paul Martin made an important visit to Asia, first travelling to Thailand and Sri Lanka in the wake of the devastating tsunami that had hit about three weeks earlier, and then India, Japan, and China. Martin was not originally interested in including Japan, but I had insisted, in part to signal to the Japanese that they had not been forgotten despite Canada's strong focus on China, and also to give a boost to the Woodstock, Ontario, bid to be the site of a new assembly plant that Toyota was planning to build in North America. Some US sites were also in contention. Industry minister David Emerson, also in favour of including Japan for that reason, joined in my advocacy.

I had told the prime minister and his staff that if he would go, I could set up a meeting with the Keidanren, Japan's senior business council. The meeting was set, thanks to Kazuko Komatsu, a Vancouver businesswoman (owner of Pacific Western Brewing) who was the daughter of a prominent Japanese samurai family and had strong connections in that country. I had come to know her through my relations with various Japanese business people in Vancouver and involvement in the Thursday Club, a discussion group about Japan. Of course, Martin also met with the Japanese prime minister, Junichiro Koizumi. Martin, Emerson, and I met with the top team of Toyota executives to make our representations. Our efforts paid off, and Canada won the bid. Komatsu later told me that the fact that the prime minister had gone to Japan and had meetings with the prime minister and the Keidanren had made a marked difference to the decision-making; the business differences were very minor, but the Canadians' attitude and willingness to work hard to accommodate the Japanese investment had tipped the balance. There was also $55 million in federal support, which was repayable, and $70 million of support from Ontario. To keep these figures in perspective, it was an $800 million investment that created thousands of jobs, directly and indirectly. The plant continues to operate.

From Japan, we went to China and met with President Hu Jintao and Premier Wen Jiabao. The discussions touched on a range of subjects: trade and investment, human rights, consular relations, and transportation. It was a good visit, but what received the most publicity was the behaviour of Conservative MP Jason Kenney, later a Harper federal cabinet minister and, even later, premier of Alberta. Martin had decided to follow an old parliamentary practice of bringing an official Opposition observer on all official trips. The Opposition designated Jason Kenney. He was known to be pro-Taiwan and very anti-communist. Martin was reminded of this but decided to accept him. We were in a minority government position at that time, so he had his political reasons. As it happened, Zhao Ziyang had died a few days before our arrival in Beijing. He was the former premier who had been under house arrest since the events of Tiananmen in 1989. Kenney, with a group of journalists and TV cameras in tow, went to Zhao's home to try to pay, he said, his condolences to the family. He got as close as he could, and then he publicly denounced the Chinese government's treatment of Zhao, and by implication, the events at Tiananmen. This grandstanding was a huge breach both in diplomatic terms (interfering in a domestic matter) and politically (interfering in Canada's relations with a foreign country on an official visit). It was also an absolutely asinine thing to do, so far as I was concerned. Afterward, Kenney did not rejoin our group. He had immediately gone to the airport and left China. We only learned of the incident when we heard from Canada that CTV was running the tape on its national news.

Martin apologized to the Chinese leadership for this behaviour. Although it was an embarrassment, it did not set us back. The Chinese saw past it. As for Kenney, while his stunt may have scored him some political points at home by appearing to be standing up for human rights in China, it did not change anything in that country. I have never seen a case where lecturing the Chinese publicly on human rights has yielded any positive result.

Prime Minister Martin invited Hu Jintao, who was general secretary of the Communist Party in addition to being president, to make a return visit to Canada. Hu arrived in Ottawa that September, along with a delegation of advisers, for two days of discussions headed by Martin. In the formal session, Hu Jintao proposed to Martin – and all this was prearranged, nothing was by surprise – that we establish a relationship at the highest level China offered any country, which was called a "strategic partnership." This was the political equivalent of most-favoured nation status in a trading relationship, and Canada was not the only country to receive this offer. What it meant in more concrete terms was to be defined by a joint committee led by Canada's deputy minister of foreign affairs and China's vice minister of foreign relations. The objective of the committee would be to expand activities in the bilateral relationship in trade, investment, education, and people-to-people relations, but also to build the potential for co-operation on issues in multilateral organizations such as the UN, World Bank, and World Trade Organization.

Although Martin accepted the invitation to further develop the concept, there was no formal agreement. And nothing came to fruition, as our government was defeated in an election five months later by Stephen Harper's Conservatives, who held a very different attitude toward China.

Other topics discussed with Hu included, of course, the trade relationship. The Chinese economy was expanding at a rapid rate, and Canada wanted to take advantage of all export opportunities in agriculture, manufacturing, and resources. The Chinese were very good customers for us in those sectors. We also discussed the development of people-to-people relations, including in the education and tourism sectors. They also expressed interest in the oil sands and would go on to make a major investment in the Harper period. New bilateral agreements were signed to expand co-operation in the fields of transportation, railways, nuclear energy, food safety, plant and animal health, and reproductive technologies.

During President Hu's stop in Ottawa, I was invited by the Chinese delegation to have a separate discussion with him. Most of the discussion related to the interparliamentary role and, in particular, the possibility of exchanging parliamentary interns, putting some Canadian students and young professors on the staff of the National People's Congress and having Chinese counterparts come and study the Canadian parliamentary session for several months. I described how we already had a similar program with the US Congress. They didn't say yes or no, they just said it was a very interesting idea.

Earlier, I had asked Chinese ambassador Lu Shumin whether they could schedule President Hu through Vancouver on his way back to China. I was hoping to hold a dinner for him. I had noted the large Chinese Canadian community there – significant in terms of the overall bridge relationship because of their language capability and cultural understanding of the two societies – but obviously, there were political reasons as well, to demonstrate that the government and I were able to further economic, trade, and political dimensions of our relationship. The stopover was arranged, and we held the dinner at the Pan Pacific Hotel. Industry minister David Emerson was co-host. There were about 120 people from business, academia, and the community who were interacting with China at all levels. The extremely successful event validated the importance of Vancouver's Chinese community and made clear to the broader Vancouver community that I was playing a significant role in the relationship with China.

The Asia Pacific Foundation of Canada, which I had helped create in 1984, found itself with less and less funding. The Mulroney government had amended the funding scheme. In place of creating a permanent endowment, it decided to fund the foundation through annual transfers from the operating budget of the Department of External Affairs (renamed in the early '90s the Department of Foreign Affairs and International Trade), CIDA, and other ministerial budgets. This made the foundation increasingly dependent on the policies and programs of contributing departments and inevitably created conflicts about direction and administration. As a result, the private sector quickly lost interest in supporting what to them was simply another government program, however worthy. The provinces also backed away from the foundation because they did not see it as entirely independent or as a policy partnership. The mood in the public service and among some people at the political level was that the foundation was not a success, was not doing anything important, and should be wound up. Once I was appointed to the Paul Martin cabinet in 2003, I was in a position to take action. I was determined not to let the foundation be closed.

The Trudeau government had planned that, instead of the foundation being operated by annual grants from the department, there would be a $50 million endowment set up so it would have a permanent income that would be its primary source of financial stability and planning. However, by the time the 1984 election brought the Conservatives to power, that had not occurred. In fact, the 1983 report signed by businessman John Bruk advocating creation of the foundation and providing a blueprint, had called for a $100 million endowment.

In 2004, I asked for a meeting with Ralph Goodale, then finance minister, with whom I had had a relationship for decades. He is one of the finest people in public life I've ever worked with: straightforward, honest, and thoughtful. I took him through a short history of the Asia Pacific Foundation, which he said he had never heard of. When it was created, Goodale had been in Saskatchewan, involved in provincial politics. He agreed to the endowment of $50 million if the prime minister were to support it. I also spoke with the president of the Treasury Board at the time, Reg Alcock, who had co-chaired the Canada-China Legislative Association with me. And of course I spoke to Prime Minister Martin about it, as well as with the other BC cabinet ministers and an array of MPs (including members of opposition parties). The general consensus was in favour of the endowment. Eventually, the details were sorted out, the cabinet approved it, and the announcement was made in late 2005. I took control of the foundation for the purpose of its restructuring to bring in new people, with the endowment as leverage.

I recruited a high-profile new chair, John McArthur, who had been helpful to me when I was working on creating Petro-Canada. By then, he had retired as dean of the Harvard Business School. Originally from Burnaby, British Columbia, he had maintained his Canadian citizenship and had a major international profile. His acceptance of the role bolstered the credibility of the foundation in many quarters, and he set about putting the organization on a stronger course.

From 1999 to 2005, John Wiebe led the foundation as president. Wiebe took a strong interest in environmental issues in the Asia Pacific. He was a founder of the GLOBE Foundation and its annual global sustainable business conference held in Vancouver at Canada Place.

In 2005, the Asia Pacific Foundation of Canada named a new president and CEO, Yuen Pau Woo, who had been the organization's director of policy. For the first three years, we appointed a co-CEO, Paul Evans, a professor of Asian studies at UBC who took a leave of absence from his academic post. Evans's appointment was in response to strong criticism from university people that the foundation had no academic credentials and was too business-oriented. The combination was very effective in giving the organization a new start. After three years, Evans returned to UBC and Woo continued on successfully, until 2014. A couple of years later, he was appointed as an independent senator by Prime Minister Justin Trudeau.

Taking over in 2014 as the foundation's president and CEO was Stewart Beck, a career public servant. He had retired as Canada's high commissioner to India and had previously served as consul general in Shanghai, where I first met him. Today, the foundation continues to play a vital role in increasing Canadian awareness of the Asia Pacific region and its opportunities, peoples and cultures, and through its counterpart organizations in Asia also enhances awareness of Canada in the region.

By the time I joined the Martin cabinet in December 2003, North American trade with China was growing exponentially, but British Columbia's ports, railways, and roads were not keeping pace. Despite the inherent geographical advantages held by Vancouver, and especially Prince Rupert, when it came to ocean travel time to China – those routes were two to four days faster than their competitors in getting goods to railhead for transport to the central US markets – opportunities were being lost to other North American ports.

Shortly after my appointment, I visited Premier Gordon Campbell for a discussion about British Columbia's policy priorities. Enhancement of West Coast transportation infrastructure was high on his list. Campbell's deputy, Ken Dobell, an engineer with a straight-shooter attitude, had previously been city manager of Vancouver when Campbell was mayor. Dobell presented the province's economic case to me, and it was undeniable.

Just as I had collaborated with the Bennett government in advancing Expo 86, I collaborated with the Campbell government to advance what came to be known as the Pacific Gateway Strategy. But as difficult as it was to persuade the Trudeau government to support Expo 86, I found only a gentle push was needed to bring the Martin government onside. The reason was obvious. The great race of the North American Pacific coast ports to handle the explosion of trade with Asia, and principally China, was on. All those ports in Canada, the United States, and Mexico were failing to keep pace with the hundreds of billions of dollars being invested in China, and elsewhere in Asia, in port and transportation infrastructure. The supply chain was being stretched to the limit.

When I reported to Prime Minister Martin that British Columbia's priority was to increase transportation capacity to meet this demand, he expressed immediate support and suggested the matter soon be brought to cabinet. Given his own background in the shipping industry, he understood the issues as well as anybody. When I approached transport minister Jean Lapierre about the issue, he told me his department was looking at it; he had already heard from Dobell. Before long, Lapierre also was satisfied a strong case had been made for a major investment that would bring a rapid and sizable return to the Canadian economy; he assured me he would support me in a pitch to cabinet. In a cabinet meeting held in Winnipeg in August 2005, I led off the discussion, Lapierre supported it, as did industry minister David Emerson, a fellow British Columbian. When Martin called the decision, there was no opposition whatever.

The Pacific Gateway Strategy was introduced in the House of Commons in October 2005 as Bill C-68. Its initial focus was on much-needed infrastructure improvements to the ports of Vancouver and Prince Rupert, but it was much more than an infrastructure megaproject. Within the overall federal funding commitment of $591 million over five years was $35 million to support a new Pacific Gateway Council, which would be an advisory body of knowledgeable Canadians mandated to deepen ties with Asia, build public support and consensus on an evolving Asia strategy among private and public stakeholders, and advise government on how to advance the Pacific Gateway Strategy. It had been important to me that Pacific Gateway be not only a transportation policy but also a more holistic attempt to better position Canada for the rise of Asia at the dawn of what many expected to be the Pacific century. While some Canadians saw the Pacific Ocean as simply Canada's western boundary, British Columbians have long understood it to be a pathway to and from Asia. I was looking for the council to raise awareness in Ottawa, and in Central Canada in particular, about the importance of what was taking place in Asia.

Unfortunately, the Martin government fell before we were able to pass the legislation. However, under David Emerson, who became the Conservative minister of international trade after crossing the floor following the January 2006 election, the new government re-announced the policy, but without the council. They reduced it back to a transportation policy and removed the relationship factor.

I had been absolutely blown away – totally shocked – by Emerson's decision to join the Harper cabinet, only three weeks after he had, during the campaign, launched a particularly virulent attack on Harper. Emerson's constituents in the traditionally NDP-leaning riding of Vancouver Kingsway[3] were far from happy that their MP had joined the Conservatives.

During the Martin government, I had found Emerson a very enjoyable colleague. The former CEO of Canfor, he had an impressive resume including a PhD in economics, and he was very much on the leading edge of what was taking place in the globalization of commerce and investment. We had worked together very effectively as a team. I found particularly valuable the insight he provided into the world of global supply chains.

After he made the jump, he was labelled an opportunist, but I think it was more that he never really had any interest in the political work or party politics. He had gone to Ottawa because he had certain policy priorities. John Reynolds, a former BC Conservative MP who by that time was a Harper political operative, spoke to Emerson and, in spite of his earlier highly critical remarks about Harper, invited him to continue as industry minister in the Harper cabinet and continue to work for British Columbia there. Emerson accepted, and continued with much of the Gateway policy we had initiated.

Stephen Harper's Conservatives came to power holding a very different attitude toward China. As proactive as we were in developing the relationship, they went in the opposite direction and almost discontinued the dialogue. The Harper Conservatives held a general view that China could never be a co-operative colleague in the international system, it was basically an adversary, and the contradictions in the value systems of the two countries – particularly China's shortcomings on human rights and the rule of law – made good relations impossible. China's behaviour concerning Tibet was a critical issue. More broadly, there was a belief that the Communist system threatened the moral and Christian values of Canadian society. The Canadian foreign minister did not receive the Chinese ambassador for an unusually long period, and ministers did not attend Chinese events. When the summer Olympics were held in Beijing in 2008, Harper was the only significant foreign leader who did not attend the opening ceremony. The Chinese took notice.

I was deeply disappointed with the Harper policies toward China. I saw a lifetime of work in building the Pierre Trudeau strategy of engagement being thrown out. The Mulroney government had carried on with engagement, too, as had the Chrétien and Martin governments. We had worked on building a positive relationship that would serve us well when dealing with the most stressful issues. Building trust is at the core of managing even the most difficult relationships.

In 2009, however, the Harper government did another 180-degree turn, and decided to improve relations with China. The policy became known as "cold politics, warm economics." I first heard the phrase from Paul Evans at UBC. The explanation given for it has always been pressure from the business community, and particularly from western agricultural and oil and gas interests to whom Harper was quite sensitive. In December 2009, Harper visited China, where he was chided by Premier Wen Jiabao for having taken so long to visit a friend. The Chinese were pragmatic, and they were happy to see the Harper government was opening relations, wanting a better trade and business relationship. On that trip, they announced Canada would be granted approved destination status for Chinese tourists, a lucrative boost for the Canadian tourism industry.

That had been an objective the Martin government had been close to achieving, but then we were defeated, and when the Harper government at first turned hostile to China, the Chinese had parked it. To promote improved Canada-China relations, the Chinese also lent two panda bears to select Canadian zoos.

In March 2007, I turned seventy-five, the mandatory Senate retirement age. After I left Parliament, Lu Congmin, vice-chair of the international committee and now deputy secretary general of the National People's Congress, with whom I had worked previously on the Canada-China Legislative Association, advised me that if I was able to come to China in 2007, the leadership of the National People's Congress would like to honour my service to the Canada-China relationship with a formal banquet at the Great Hall of the People. It was not an offer to be turned down.

That fall, I travelled to China with Natalie, along with Natalie's sister Shirley and Shirley's husband Herb Fitterman, and Ron and Janet Stern, among the closest friends of Natalie and myself.[4] Prior to the dinner, there was a formal meeting in the classic Chinese format, also in the Great Hall. My opposite number was the vice-chair of the National People's Congress standing committee, Sheng Huaren, a very powerful official in China. Attending the banquet were almost all the Chinese members of the National People's Congress who had been part of any delegation to Canada or in China as hosts, and of course the Canadian ambassador Robert Wright, along with three or four people from the embassy. Maurice Strong, who was then living in Beijing as a business consultant, made a point of attending, as did a former law partner of mine, Victor Yang, based in Hong Kong, with whom I had worked to obtain a representative law firm licence in China for our firm.

Ron Stern, who practised law in Vancouver in his early years, now heads Stern Partners, a private equity firm based in Vancouver. The firm holds a wide-ranging group of businesses, in manufacturing, distribution, retailing, and services, among them the Winnipeg Free Press newspaper. At this point, I had just accepted Stern's invitation to become senior adviser – international, at the firm. It has proven to be a place of compatibility, where I have shared my views on all manner of matters: business, political, and economic, and on the performance and personalities of various political leaders, ancient to modern. Stern has made a deep and positive impression on his colleagues in the Vancouver business community. I have worked with many Canadian business leaders over the years. He stands out in that group not only for his interpersonal skills and his analytical business capacities, but because he sees the world in a very broad perspective, deeply interested in social policy, international relations, and governance, and has a record of being of assistance to BC Indigenous communities. Over the years, we have had extensive conversations in these areas and on the challenges to liberal democracy. Unknown to most, he is a quiet and significant philanthropist. I remain with Stern Partners to this day.

After the banquet, we took the opportunity to do some travelling, including to Guilin, Tibet, and Xi'an. In Tibet, we visited the Potala Palace, two significant monasteries, and an orphanage where the children were blind. Herb, who was a prominent ophthalmologist in Vancouver, had a lot of questions for the staff there. He said he hoped to be able to come back with equipment to see what he might be able to do for the children. As it turned out, his health declined and a trip back was not possible.

This time, Shirley did not bring any peanut butter, nor would the Canadian embassy staff have taken any interest if she had. In 1983, you couldn't get Western food in China, but by 2007, you had all the Western food you wanted in the most modern hotels in the world. In those twenty-four years, China had gone through three or four centuries' worth of change.

Retiring from the Senate did not mean retiring. Some fifty years after I had last taught at UBC, I returned.

In the course of my previous work on China, I had met frequently with Professor Pitman Potter, a Chinese legal systems, human rights, and trade specialist at UBC. He was also at that time director of UBC's Institute of Asian Research, and when I left the Senate, he asked me to join the faculty of the institute as an honorary professor and senior fellow. I assumed the unpaid position in 2008. The arrangement was that I received an office and was expected to give lectures to the faculty and students on China once in the fall and once in the spring, and to sit in on seminars to offer my input as a "practitioner." In other words, what they sought from me was to share what I had learned from the operating experience of dealing with the Chinese through issues spanning government policy, diplomacy, business, and cultural affairs. Part of my participation was to attend many sessions with visiting scholars and government officials from China. These were frequent over the course of many years.

Among my key colleagues have been professors Paul Evans, Yves Tiberghien, Tim Cheek, and Brian Job. This team of four have gone out of their way to include me as a fifth member down through the years. My relationship with them has been invaluable not only on an academic level but also on a personal one. We have shared many insights and debated many possible strategies about how to further the Canada-China relationship.

From Paul Evans, I received an introduction to the "Fairbank culture" at Harvard University. Evans wrote his doctoral thesis on John Fairbank, a Harvard professor who, during an especially difficult period in US-China relations in the immediate post–Second World War era, was the go-to person on Chinese history, political behaviour, and associated culture. Fairbank focused on understanding the immense differences of worldviews between Chinese and Western societies and the importance of understanding China on its own terms. I found a remarkable commonality with the ideas of Fairbank, and therefore with Paul Evans. Evans's 2014 book *Engaging China: Myth, Aspiration, and Strategy in Canadian Policy from Trudeau to Harper* is the definitive work on the topic.[5]

Yves Tiberghien is an expert on the political economy in the Asia Pacific region. His insight into economic and business issues, as well as the general socio-political picture, is unrivalled. He has two major focuses: China and Japan.

Tim Cheek is, to digress, a cheeky Australian, a professor of political science at UBC since 2002. His work has included a major study on Mao Zedong. His knowledge of political and social life in China during the Mao years and to the present day is inexhaustible.

In Brian Job I found an astute scholar on security issues in the Asia Pacific. I wished that when I had been a member of the Canadian cabinet, I had had some of the insights he provided me with. In 1997, he had been one of the initiators, along with Paul Evans (then at York University), and Professor David Dewitt (also at York University), of the organization of the Canadian Consortium on Asia Pacific Security. Once I was at UBC, he recruited me to participate.

I cannot believe that a more competent expertise on China specifically, and the Asia Pacific in general, exists at any university in Canada. Over the years I hosted a breakfast club at the White Spot on West Broadway in Vancouver, where the conversations on Asia Pacific policy were among the most compelling of my post-Senate life. What we developed in those years was a major relationship between China and UBC. With the approval of then UBC president Stephen Toope and his executive committee, we created a UBC China Council to monitor relations between UBC and Chinese universities, government agencies, and foundations, and to advise the university's president and executive with respect to whatever proposals were presented and how UBC should react. The council was formally established in 2013, and I was and remain the co-chair. It meets three or four times a year and as required. The council's role remains advisory and internal to the university. At UBC, there wasn't a top-down management of the China relationship. Each faculty managed its relationship as it saw fit. What the council did was to allow the sharing of knowledge about significant issues and recommend initiatives of various kinds.

Toope already had had a keen interest in the university's links with China. On one of his earlier trips there, during a visit with senior officials in charge of higher education in the central committee of the party, the officials had expressed curiosity about the fact that UBC's relationships with Chinese universities were all at the faculty level, where, say, UBC's forestry faculty would work with its counterpart at a Chinese institution. They wondered why the university as a whole had never entered into an agreement with a Chinese university, and whether UBC had a policy of only engaging at the faculty level. And Toope, as I recall him telling me, replied there was no such policy; it was just that in our system, relationships came up from the bottom and were not normally dictated from the top down.

The Chinese officials expressed an interest in UBC developing relationships with universities in Chongqing, because the area was more remote and had fewer international connections. Situated in the southwest part of the country, it is one of only four cities in China that also has provincial status. In August 2013, Toope led a mission to Chongqing, in which I also participated, resulting in the signature of a major academic co-operation agreement with the Chongqing government. That the deal was with the government and not directly with the universities was important: this meant the arrangements did not depend on the balance sheets of the Chongqing universities but were guaranteed by Chongqing itself.

This marked a high point of UBC interest in furthering co-operation in various study areas with Chinese universities. Other Western universities also were active in building relationships with Chinese universities, with some setting up branches on Chinese university campuses, though Canadian universities were more cautious. It was an era of openness in China in the field of education and apparent willingness to accept some of the Western standards of academic freedom.

During this golden period, I also tried, unsuccessfully, to organize a president's advisory council on China at UBC. I felt the university would benefit enormously from such a body, which would be composed of a slight majority of Canadians along with people in key policy roles in different parts of the world, who would provide a perspective different from that in North America. I noted that once these prominent people learned how deep and how significant UBC's expertise on Asia was, and particularly on China, they would be essentially communicators of that expertise and make UBC far better known in their respective countries. There were discussions, and I drafted a constitution and plans for it; however, the initiative was never approved. Although the idea had been enthusiastically received by the UBC China Council, the president and his executive committee were very cautious about broadening the scope of UBC's China profile.

In China, things were beginning to change, although it would be a few years before the full impact would be felt. In the last year or so of the Hu Jintao period, 2012, there were debates inside the Chinese Communist Party about corruption and the party's loss of control. There were concerns about the impact of so many Chinese being educated in Western systems, as well as access by people in China to Western media. That debate matured inside the party in relation to the choice of a successor to Hu Jintao. Xi Jinping was leading a faction that wanted the party to reassert its discipline throughout Chinese society, and there were other factions with other views. The question was an internal one: how do you preserve the party's social and political control in China while maintaining the pace of economic growth? There must have been an amazing internal struggle, the details of which are far from well known in Western society.

In the summer of 2013, an unknown faction within the party leaked an internal memo called Document Number Nine. It was the Xi Jinping doctrine for Chinese relations with Western societies, especially as it affected the domestic system. This was our first real notice of serious changes under way, and it hit our view of co-operation and prospects of open, co-operative dialogue like a cold rainstorm. Among other things, the document expressed suspicion of academic co-operation and exchanges. The Chinese had begun questioning where they were going in their relationships with the West and reassessing the extent to which they wanted to work within a Western value system. By then, Xi Jinping was both general secretary of the Communist Party of China and the country's president. And, while it was never confirmed that Document Number Nine was official policy – the Chinese tried to say it was a discussion document and of no consequence – we took note of it and wondered how important it would be to the central policy-making of the Xi Jinping era.

We continued building the university's relationships with China and connections with Chinese policy leaders. One such initiative of the UBC China Council was to request that the university award an honorary doctorate to Justin Yifu Lin, a professor of economics at Peking University, who had served as chief economist at the World Bank. The UBC Senate approved the award, on Toope's recommendation, in expeditious fashion and it was conferred in 2014. I myself had received an honorary doctorate from the university in 2011.

Meanwhile, we were continuing to ask questions about Document Number Nine, as to whether it was a draft or something more serious. We learned it was quite serious, but its impact was felt gradually, like the frog in the warming pot. There was no sharp imposition of change. However, the party was gradually convincing academics and others in

China that they had to pay attention, that party discipline and the resistance to Western values was critical to the control of China by the party, which was in their view critical to China's economic and political rise. By about 2015, Western universities were beginning to see a less open dialogue with colleagues in China, and it appeared that the party was exercising more control over relationships at the academic level.

UBC remains Canada's Asia Pacific educational gateway. Its essential requirement is to maintain the Western culture of academic independence: the search for truth in the social sciences and the most objective scientific and technological development. That is its polar star. The use by authoritarian political leaders of facts – real or otherwise – primarily for political purposes, particularly for societal control, is conceptually in conflict with the university's mission. Along with all Western universities, keeping its values intact while being open to engagement with universities in societies that do not share its values is a day-to-day challenge.

In 2007, Simon Fraser University (SFU) and the Asia Pacific Foundation honoured me with the announcement that they were planning to create a Jack Austin Chair of Asian Economies in SFU's economics department. This came as a total surprise. Subsequently, for various operational reasons, it was decided instead to create the Jack Austin Centre for Asia Pacific Business Studies in SFU's Beedie School of Business, an initiative spearheaded by the school's then dean, Daniel Shapiro. I was thoroughly pleased with the more applied focus on Asian business practices and the learning opportunity for Canadian students. I have served as a council member of the centre and continue to participate regularly in its seminars and webinars. Based on the current endowment, the business school has been awarding fellowships for PhD and master's program studies. During the COVID-19 pandemic, it has used Zoom to hold a series of conferences, called the Canada-China Economic Forum, which are focusing on business practices and the commercial standards and other transactional issues in the bilateral business relationship. The centre is led by its co-directors, Professor Daniel Shapiro and Professor Jing Li.

Western business remains insufficiently familiar with and aware of Chinese business practices, both domestic and international. The centre seeks to raise that standard of knowledge in order to develop a larger competence by Canadian investors in accessing the vast China market. It should be noted, however, that the focus of the Jack Austin Centre is not only on China but also the Indo-Pacific, where each country has its own norms of practice and behaviour in the business setting. During his presidency of SFU, Andrew Petter was a dedicated leader for engagement internationally and particularly in the Asia Pacific. His encouragement for those of us working to develop the centre made a difference.

In May 2011, SFU honoured me with the President's Distinguished Community Leadership Award at an annual event recognizing individuals for their contribution to the welfare of British Columbia. In June 2017, SFU awarded me an honorary doctorate.

I became involved with a third British Columbia university, Royal Roads, located in the suburbs of Victoria. Shortly after I left the Senate and returned to Vancouver, I had been contacted by the university's president, Allan Cahoon, to ask whether I would be interested in serving as a member of his advisory council. We had a discussion, and what interested me in particular was that Royal Roads had a few years earlier established an MBA program in China, taught in Mandarin, and delivered in several cities. The language of instruction and the fact that students could study in their home country made it relatively affordable and accessible, and thus very popular. I accepted Cahoon's invitation.

Cahoon was interested in promoting the university's brand in China, and wondered whether it would be possible to attract the support of an important Chinese official. I didn't think any serving officials would be interested; however, I suggested we contact Fan Gang. Then a young and emerging personality in Chinese economic research and studies, he spoke fluent English, and we had first met while I was involved with CCBC. He was a professor of economics at the graduate school of the Chinese Academy of Social Sciences and director of the China Reform Foundation's National Economic Research Institute. When I spoke with him during a visit to Beijing, I explained our program and asked whether he would speak periodically to our students in China, adding that we would be grateful for his support for our program. He agreed. In 2011, Royal Roads awarded him an honorary doctorate. He continues to be a leading figure in Chinese economic policy. In 2016, the university also honoured me with an honorary doctorate.

When Justin Trudeau led the Liberals to victory in the 2015 election, I was very optimistic, and I believe the Chinese were optimistic, that he would be able to take Canada into a new and positive era in relations between the two countries.

There was talk of reaching a trade agreement with China. But it turned out that the ideas of the Canadian and Chinese governments about what that agreement might look like were far apart. While the Chinese were envisaging something akin to the free trade deal Canada had with the United States and Mexico, Canada was looking for a model progressive agreement that would include labour standards, environmental standards, promotion of gender equality, and so on, and not merely as aspirational side letters, but in the heart of the agreement. It was a case of Canada aiming to export into a trade negotiation with the Chinese the height of Canadian domestic aspirations. The Chinese, for their part, were just looking to deal with classic trade issues like tariffs, quotas, and dispute settlement. Canada missed the opportunity by asking for too much. The Chinese saw this as overreach, a foreign country (and a mid-size one at that) telling them how to manage labour standards or forcing an environmental agenda they were not prepared to adopt.

I was quite disappointed, but I didn't think there was anything irreparable about it. I saw it as an inexperienced new government in Canada wanting to make a point globally that it was progressive. Canada was asserting that these new factors had to be recognized globally as the responsibilities of a nation state.

The election of Donald Trump as US president in 2016 meant that Canada's ability to get China's attention was reduced to almost zero. Global attention on China's relations with the West became focused on

Trump's China policies. Nevertheless, talks continued at the diplomatic level about a possible trade agreement, and CCBC was holding meetings with Canadian business leaders about what they would like to see in such an agreement; officials continued to do groundwork. If Trump was one barrier to progress, Canada's arrest of Huawei executive Meng Wanzhou in December 2018 at the request of the United States, and China's arrest of Canadians Michael Kovrig and Michael Spavor and its curbing of certain Canadian agricultural exports in response, became the ultimate barriers. China considers everything political and does not believe in the independence of the Canadian judicial system, which was hearing the US extradition request. The incident, which ended in September 2021 when the United States dropped its proceedings against Meng, giving Canada no further reason to hold her, and China's simultaneous release of "the Two Michaels" had a severe impact on Canada-China relations.

The Justin Trudeau government was right not to cave to the pressure from China to release Meng. No sovereign democracy can refrain from enforcing its own laws in order to satisfy a foreign power. Canada must defend its Western values and rule of law or be forever condemned to the no-principle, hard-politics pressures of international life. In that case we are a weak power indeed with no political leverage in almost any situation. It is only when we call on other Western powers on the basis of values, democracy, and the rule of law that they may respond as they are put in the position of defending themselves and their values as well.

In October 2020, we marked the fiftieth anniversary of the opening of relations between Canada and China. Both the Meng and Two Michaels issue and the COVID-19 pandemic put a damper on what otherwise would have been more extensive festivities. As I write these lines, we are certainly a long way from the time in 1998 when Premier Zhu Rongji called Canada "China's best friend."

The CCBC celebrated the anniversary at its AGM in Beijing. I followed the event online from my home in Vancouver and was extremely grateful to be honoured with a lifetime achievement award for my service to Canada-China relations over the last fifty years. I found that recognition especially meaningful coming from CCBC, which itself deserves high recognition from the Canadian community for its exceptional role in promoting bilateral connections in economic relations, trade, services, and multi-faceted person-to-person relations. The challenges ahead for CCBC are probably greater than they have ever been, but looking at the record, I am confident CCBC will remain a leader by building on what has gone before.

Understandably, Canadian public opinion is highly critical of China's behaviour; however, we must try to maintain our communication with China and the Chinese people at the highest level possible, and at all levels. I agree with former Australian prime minister Kevin Rudd, who speaks of "constructive realism." By this I understand him to mean, co-operate on issues we have in common; engage on issues that are difficult but where each side accepts the value of engagement; work to build trust to address other issues that each side believes are core to their interests and cannot be challenged.

I should also mention here five more people who have each played an important part in my understanding of China's place in the world: Joseph Caron, who has had the distinction of serving as Canada's ambassador to China, Japan, and India, a unique hat trick that has provided him with an incredibly broad perspective on Asia; Donald Campbell, a former deputy minister of foreign affairs, who also served as ambassador to Japan and South Korea, and more recently has been chair of the Canadian National Committee for Pacific Economic Cooperation; Albert Cheng, a Canadian who at one time served as a member of the Hong Kong legislative council and has given me deep insights into Hong Kong's people and its issues; Mei Ping, who served as Chinese ambassador to Canada from 1998 to 2005, and with whom I had many exchanges on virtually every significant issue in the Canada-China bilateral relationship when it was strong and positive; and B. Michael Frolic, a professor at York University, whose lifetime work has been the study of political communism, first in the Soviet Union and then in China where he was a young student, later a member of the Canadian diplomatic mission. I was privileged to be interviewed by him for his new book *Canada and China: A Fifty-Year Journey*. It will undoubtedly set a new standard for understanding the historical context of what has taken place.

Engagement with China remains essential to Canadian interests. A failure to engage will not affect Chinese domestic policies and behaviours of deep concern to Canadians. China is a permanent reality in the global system. So is Canada. Our governance systems are vastly different. So are our history and culture. We see the role and status of the individual in our respective societies in starkly different ways. Neither country is likely to change fundamentally. Certainly, Canada is not in a position to impose its human rights standards on China, as much as many Canadians might like to do so. We are not in a position to remake China in our image. The best we can do, and have done, is to keep open the dialogue on human rights, encourage the development of the Chinese legal system, let them study our system, and use our relationship to quietly achieve the resolution of certain cases where possible.

Taking the long perspective, the Xi Jinping era will pass and the next generation of leaders in China may take a different approach to their national interests. It is best for us to keep the dialogue as non-confrontational as possible. This will help make it possible for future Chinese leaders to engage the world on more constructive terms.

Whatever the more immediate future holds, however, Canada's relationship with China will inevitably take into account the state of the US-China relationship. As a neighbour of the United States, which is our number one trading partner, Canada is caught in the rip tide of the disputes between that country and China. And those disputes are only likely to increase as China's rise brings about a new and difficult emerging reality for the United States. The Pacific Ocean has been American "property" since 1945, but now China, which has developed its "blue water" capacity, is challenging the rights and claims of its southeast Asian neighbours in the South China Sea, where vast seabed resources are expected to be found and where the fisheries must be recognized and treated as a sustainable food source critical to the well-being of all. China has made clear that it no longer accepts the United States as the sole international rules-maker. Nor does it accept the United States as the major power in the East Asia region. The growth of Chinese military power is designed to rival and exceed that of the United States in the South China and East China Seas.

China also has made clear that its rivalry is technological as well, and it is seeking to be superior in every way in all the electronic technologies, including artificial intelligence, 5G systems, robotics, and so on. This was made plain by the 2015 release of the Made in China 2025 plan, which leverages state power to boost the country's capacities to develop technology and render China more self-sufficient in the manufacturing of technologically sophisticated products, including for transportation and communications.

In these battles for dominance, Canada can be little more than an onlooker. But it would be foolish to think we are a neutral one. While our relations with China are a matter of high importance, and that country is a critical market for Canadian exports, the geopolitical reality, as well as the economic and cultural ones, means that Canada is entirely within the US sphere of influence – no ifs, ands, or buts. Our values, political practices, human relations, cultural convictions, legal systems, and behavioural practices are, when viewed internationally, virtually identical to those of the United States. In economic and business terms, we have been fortunate to build our standard of living in an important way on the growth of the US economy. With a population of only 38 million spread in a thin line across more than 5,000 kilometres, we cannot support ourselves at our desired standard of living solely on our domestic market. We would need upward of 100 million people in Canada to achieve that balance; therefore, we are trade dependent as are few other nations. And we are also militarily dependent on the United States for our defence.

That does not mean Canada needs to automatically copy US policy with regard to China, any more than it did back in 1970, when we led the way in opening relations with China, and the United States followed. While Canada by itself cannot be a significant player in the China-world relationship, I believe Canada should promote a coalition of middle powers to be composed of such players as Germany, France, Australia, Japan, and others, who seek to determine common policies. Middle-power co-operation may not be a satisfactory substitute for a rules-based international system, but while that system declines as a result not only of Chinese but also American exceptionalism and the use of trade as a political weapon, it is the best option we have – for now.

From the beginning, one key objective of our engagement with China was to bring it into the international community rather than leave it as a hostile outlier. China accepted the rules of the World Trade Organization when it joined in 2001, although from time to time it absolutely ignored them, implementing mercantilist policies contrary to WTO standards. What I saw in most of the Hu Jintao period was a China that was following the Deng Xiaoping maxim of "hide your light," and acting basically as a co-operating society within the global system. Now, the situation has changed.

No one said the Canada-China relationship would be easy, and it hasn't always been. Still, it is important to take the long view, and maintain both a sense of optimism and a sense of reality in the necessary future of a positive relationship between our two countries and our peoples.

11 The American Elephant and the Aztec Eagle

CANADA'S ECONOMIC RELATIONSHIP with the United States, one in which natural resources figure prominently, has been a central focus of my career. My master's thesis at Harvard Law School dealt with the law of Canada-US-Mexico international waterways, and I was able to put that background to use in my work on the Columbia River Treaty. When I was a young lawyer handling transactions in the resource sector, the extent of American dominance and the importance of US capital in developing the Canadian oil and gas and mining industries were eye-opening. During my time with Art Laing, we were confronted with American interest in possible Canadian exports of fresh water. Then, as deputy minister of EMR during the 1970s, I played a key role in Canada's responses to the oil crisis and the creation of a producers' arrangement for uranium, as well as the birth of Petro-Canada, all of which were intended to defend Canadian interests against the negative effects of US policies. The Americans had a long practice of treating Canadian oil production – and other resource production – as nothing but a surge tank, a reserve when they needed it but ignored otherwise, with no accountability to Canadian industries developed for and dependent on the US market. Later still, as the federal political minister for British Columbia in the early 1980s, I spoke out strongly, in cabinet and elsewhere, against unfair, protectionist tactics Americans were using to curb our softwood lumber exports.

Most of the time, it's not that Americans are particularly seeking to harm Canada. They are simply looking out for their own interests and, as a world power, are either unconcerned about or oblivious to the im-pact of their actions on others. They often forget about us. In any case, while virtually every Canadian government has understood that the

Canada-US relationship is its number one priority, for the Americans, domestic political considerations are always far more important than any bilateral relationship. Their steel, aluminum, and forest industries and certain other sectors are given favours that are not only antithetical to neighbourly relations but also can't be justified under bilateral and multilateral trade laws.

As Canadians well know, our country is dependent on the United States in many ways: economically, politically, and for defence. Our standard of living is dependent on their markets and our ability to export to them. Beginning with the Cold War, we have served as part of their defence shield, positioned as we are between the United States and Russia, and have joined with the United States as partners in the North American Aerospace Defense Command. We are protected by American defence strategies and capacities, and we have to take into account what the Americans think in almost any international policy initiative we take; however, as Prime Minister Chrétien's refusal to follow the Americans into Iraq demonstrated, this does not necessarily mean our actions are always in lockstep. If any recent example were needed of how Canada's foreign policy must be mindful of our relationship and obligations to the United States, the arrest at Vancouver airport in December 2018 of Huawei executive Meng Wanzhou, in fulfillment of an obligation to act on a US warrant, and the subsequent tensions and Chinese reprisals, provides a case in point. The incident showed how much of Canada's fate in its relationship with China is at the beck and call of the United States.

Canada benefited enormously from the multilateral organizations the United States created after the Second World War: the United Nations, the International Monetary Fund, the World Bank, and the trade body first known as the General Agreement on Tariffs and Trade, later the World Trade Organization. The US economy would enjoy the greatest benefits from the building of international trade and financial institutions, not just through exports of manufactured goods and technology, but far more significantly, financial services and the use of the US dollar as an international settlement currency. The International Monetary Fund and World Bank also financed US exports in the billions of dollars over the years. At the same time, US corporations were strengthened by means of domestic tax allowances and government and private investment in technologies. US tax laws provided corporations with an incentive to do business in foreign countries, allowing them to write off their foreign expenses against their US income, thereby lowering their taxes in the United States. This was the incentive for the substantial, even dominant, US investment in Canadian oil properties.

My focus of interest was always on finding ways for Canada not only to defend itself but also to advance in an evolving competitive global economic system. This need to assert Canada's own self-interest was a major factor in bringing me to the study and advocacy of a closer government-business interface in Canada.

Canada has a history of using state capital to build the national infrastructure needed to foster Canadian independence: land grants to the Canadian Pacific Railway, the federal government's amalgamation of various failing railways into publicly owned Canadian National Railway, CN's creation of Trans-Canada Air Lines (forerunner of Air Canada), and the creation of the CBC. Not to be forgotten was Canada's investment in the St Lawrence Seaway project, which created economic opportunities from Montreal to Thunder Bay. There are numerous other examples, including the Canadian Wheat Board, Eldorado Nuclear, and the CANDU nuclear reaction program of Atomic Energy of Canada, a Crown corporation. The specifics can vary, but the underlying government rationale is the same: either the activity or product is essential to our national competitiveness, or we need the technologies and the spinoffs from those technologies, or both. As a smaller economy, Canada also has needed to use state capital to ensure Canadian control of key parts of our private sector so that it aligns with Canadian interests, not foreign ones.

In some cases, as with Canadair, the need for government involvement was short-term, to operate a failing business considered a strategic player in the Canadian economy. CDIC, of which I oversaw the creation in 1982 and served as minister responsible, was essentially a collection of those activities. In other cases, such as the oil industry and the creation of Petro-Canada, injecting a longer-term Canadian equity presence into an industry almost entirely foreign owned and operated was needed, in order to gain knowledge about our own economic resources. The fact that our oil industry was primarily owned and controlled by US companies meant that nearly all the geological work was done by American corporations, as were the drilling, pipeline construction, and refining. The information was held privately in the United States and not shared with Canadian government authorities. American control of the industry also meant the development of Canadian resources had nothing to do with Canadian economic requirements, rather it had to do with the requirements of those individual corporations. Many of them were holding Canadian lands but not putting money into their development. It was more economic for them to develop other resources elsewhere that were cheaper to bring into production, which would give them a larger profit, while keeping Canadian resources in the ground as a further reserve. And there's a third category, in which the government does not take an ownership role but restricts foreign investors from participating in critical sectors, such as Canadian banking and the newspaper industry.

I believe Canadian political independence, such as it can be, requires Canada's control over its own economy, its own culture, and storytelling about the nature of Canada. Other reasons to avoid excessive US ownership in the Canadian economy are to prevent profits being exported back to the United States rather than being left in the Canadian economy, and the fact that Canadian subsidiaries of American companies, such as the Canadian branch auto industry, are not allowed to compete against the parent company in third markets.

Because of Petro-Canada and the creation of Uranium Canada, I became known as a strong economic nationalist. But I would not want anyone to think I am anti-American. I am not. I admire the United States in many, many ways. Being pro-Canadian is not being anti-American, any more than Americans are being anti-Canadian when they are looking out for their own country's interests. I always smile, however, when I think of the famous comment Robert Thompson, the Social Credit leader, made in the House of Commons in the early 1960s, "The Americans are our best friends, whether we like it or not." They are indeed our best friends, and we do like it, but not all the time.

As much as I have been an economic nationalist, I have also understood that Canada is part of a continental economy, and our economic interests lay in having fair access to the US market and the Mexican market.

In 1983, while I was a member of the Trudeau cabinet, we did a significant review of the possibility of a broad-based free trade agreement with the United States. Although there was a lot of discussion within Canada, nothing came of it. The cabinet concluded we could not get an agreement that would provide an objective dispute settlement process, because the US Congress would not agree to any foreign authority having a role in making decisions on US trade that would diminish the role of Congress and US sovereignty and control.

We turned to a second consideration, the negotiation of a few sectoral agreements that would have essentially replicated, for other industries, the highly successful Canada-US Auto Pact. When we approached the United States with that proposal, we found rejection of a sectoral approach, because there, too, the US Congress would not accept the idea of a non-US dispute settlement authority, even one equally composed of Americans and Canadians. By this time, we were also in the throes of the never-ending softwood lumber dispute, which marked its fortieth anniversary in 2022. US political decision-making has cost the BC economy a great deal of the value of its forest resources, and other provinces have been similarly affected.

The Mulroney government that succeeded us in 1984 went on to negotiate a comprehensive free trade agreement with the United States. This was a real breakthrough in many ways, and although I had reservations about certain aspects of the deal, in particular the lack of appropriate dispute settlement provisions, I felt it would advance Canadian economic development through freer access to the US market. Like Mulroney, I ultimately would have accepted what we were able to get, because I was quite aware of the US Congress's firm determination not to give up an iota of US sovereignty. Mulroney's ability to create a close personal relationship with President Reagan produced positive benefits for Canada in several sectors. Irish eyes were indeed smiling.

At the caucus meeting where Liberal leader John Turner announced his decision that the Liberals would oppose the free trade agreement

Mulroney had proposed, I said, thinking back to Wilfrid Laurier, I had thought I belonged to the free trade party. Since the 1911 election, in which free trade was the central issue, the Liberal and Conservative stances had flipped. But Turner needed a defining issue politically. In my view, our position had less to do with the merits of the deal than it did with that political necessity. Opposition parties oppose, so Turner argued against the deterioration of Canadian sovereignty; however, Canada was giving up no more sovereignty than the United States was.

Mulroney had a majority in the House of Commons, and it passed the necessary legislation to enact a free trade agreement. Turner asked the Liberal majority in the Senate to stall passage of the enabling legislation. The reasons offered were legitimate. In the 1984 election, Mulroney and the Progressive Conservatives had not introduced or run on a policy proposal for a free trade agreement with the United States. In addition, a free trade agreement, once entered into, would be politically irreversible for Canada. It was the Senate's role to ensure that Canadians were consulted on a major policy initiative, which would be a change in Canada's relationship with the United States for all time and have significant economic implications for our country. The Liberal majority in the Senate therefore stalled passage of the enabling legislation pending the results of the 1988 election, in which the issue went on to play a central role.

During that campaign, the Turner Liberals took a lead in polls, based on their defence of sovereignty. Many remember the Liberal ad with an eraser eliminating the boundary between Canada and the United States. Although I supported Turner during the campaign and made sufficient noises about the deficiencies of the deal to be kept on the team, I remained relatively quiet. The NDP opposed the trade pact, as did a majority of voters. In the end, however, the Mulroney Tories won the election with 43 per cent of the popular vote. Not long afterward, the Senate passed the legislation.

At the time of the debate on the free trade agreement, one of the leading opponents was an old acquaintance of mine, Mel Hurtig, an Edmonton-based publisher who, as a founding member of the Committee for an Independent Canada, was seen as a hard Canadian nationalist. When I had been a minister in the Trudeau government, Hurtig had proposed that the federal government finance a Canadian encyclopedia. I was one of his principal advocates in cabinet for this project, and we came through; however, by 1988, Hurtig and I had gone in opposite directions on Canadian nationalism. He publicly expressed the fear that Canada was going to end up as an economic colony of the United States, as he later outlined in his book *The Vanishing Country* (2002). Another acquaintance of mine, University of Toronto professor Stephen Clarkson, in his book *Uncle Sam and Us* (2002), argued that the question isn't whether Canada will survive, but what type of country we will become. I felt that Clarkson was focused on the right question.

Once the free trade agreement was in place, the Canadian public's fear of greater economic integration with the United States began to erode. By 2002, a poll by Michael Marzolini of Pollara found that 66 per cent of Canadians were urging the Chrétien government to develop even closer economic ties with the United States, and 87 per cent said Canada had to look beyond its borders to "improve economically."[1]

In the late 1980s, around the same time as the Canada-US free trade deal was in the ratification stage, I began to develop a strong interest in Mexico and the possibilities of a trilateral relationship. But the story of my involvement with Mexico does not start then. It begins a few years earlier, with Vancouver businessman and philanthropist Walter Koerner. Koerner and his brothers had operated a lumber business in Czechoslovakia but had left in 1938, one step ahead of the Nazis. They arrived in British Columbia the following year, and became important figures in the province's forest industry.

After I was appointed to the cabinet, Walter Koerner contacted me on behalf of UBC. The university hospital was seeking to acquire a $1.5 million nuclear magnetic resonance scanner (an MRI machine) and was looking for federal money to support its acquisition. I went to work in support of UBC's hospital development program. The machine was delivered in December 1982, flown in from Britain on a Canadian Forces Hercules. It was the first in North America big enough to scan the entire human body, according to a *Vancouver Sun* news report.

This was the beginning of what later became a social relationship. Koerner and I would meet from time to time at the Timber Club, a public restaurant at the Hotel Vancouver. He had a deep knowledge of British Columbia's business world, its relation to the US and European business communities, and key people. He was willing to share that knowledge with me, which proved useful in my service to British Columbia's economic interests in the various struggles for policy development and funding in the Ottawa process.

In about 1985 or 1986, Natalie and I invited Walter Koerner and his wife for dinner, and he responded that he would like to come, but had obligations to Hugh Keenleyside, who was in town. Of course, we invited Keenleyside too. Keenleyside had served as ambassador to Mexico in the 1940s, so we chatted about that country. He discussed the hostility that existed in Mexico toward the United States and the arrogance of Americans toward Mexico. I remember him saying we should look geopolitically at North America as an entity, and that Canada had an interest in viewing Mexico as a partner in dealing with the United States. He suggested I read *Distant Neighbors*, by Alan Riding, which I did. It was my first look at the US-Mexico relationship, at least since my much earlier work on rivers, when I had seen how poorly the United States treated Mexico with respect to the Colorado and the Rio Grande.

Mexico stayed in the back of my consciousness until Maurice Strong invited me to visit him at a huge property he had bought in southwestern Colorado, called the Baca, in the spring of 1988. I didn't realize at the time that his motives were more than social. Strong had become interested in the US-Canada-Mexico trilateral relationship and had joined with former Arizona governor Bruce Babbitt and former Mexican finance minister Jesús Silva Herzog in conceptualizing a new organization that would serve as a forum for the informal and open exchange of views among opinion leaders in the three North American nations. My visit coincided with a small meeting at nearby Colorado College, where those three, along with a few others, were considering how to proceed. Strong invited me along. Also at this meeting was John Wirth, the Stanford University provost and Latin American studies professor and historian who had first approached Strong and the others with the concept of a trilateral institute.

Afterward, Strong told me he was unable to stay with the project – he had too many other commitments – and asked me whether I could "take the Canadian assignment." I told him I was interested. Given that the Liberals were in Opposition, I was under less time pressure than usual. Over the following months, I had a series of discussions with Wirth about how to bring this organization into being. Another American, Susan Herter, who had served as chief of staff to US vice-president Nelson Rockefeller, also was working with Wirth. She played a key role in getting things off the ground, enlisting support from the government of New Mexico and setting up the headquarters in Santa Fe.

What emerged was the North American Institute (NAMI), and I became the Canadian co-convenor. We had our founding meeting in Santa Fe in December 1988. We went on to create quite an active organization. Over the next dozen years, a period when trilateral perspectives were made especially timely by the negotiation and then enactment of a North American Free Trade Agreement (NAFTA), NAMI held major conferences in various cities in all three countries, and many smaller meetings, on a wide range of topics. These included not only trade but also environmental co-operation, social policy, federalism, education, and relations with other countries.

One such conference I organized was titled Japan's Relations with North America: The New Pacific Interface, held in Vancouver in July 1990. I had wanted to be able to attract some senior Japanese, so it had been especially important to ensure that our speakers would be absolutely first rate. It was suggested to me that I invite Ken Courtis,[2] a Tokyo-based Canadian who at that time was vice-president of Deutsche Bank Capital Markets and the bank's senior economist for Asia. Courtis accepted and then became keenly interested in NAMI, so we were able to recruit him to come and speak to a number of subsequent meetings. After I became president of CCBC, I involved Courtis as a keynote speaker in the November 1994 first Team Canada mission. At least one of the senior business leaders said while the whole trip to China was phenomenal, the highlight was Courtis's presentation in Beijing. Over the years, and not least when I was involved with CCBC, Courtis became an invaluable source of information and insight on Asia for me, as he is for so many others.[3]

In all, NAMI held twenty-nine trilateral meetings. Another particularly memorable one for me was the November 1995 session in Toronto titled NAFTA's Relationship to the Caribbean and Central America: Informal and Formal Integration and the Question of Cuba. Our keynote presenter was former US Treasury secretary and former senator from Texas Lloyd Bentsen. His presentation, somewhat to the surprise but also delight of the Canadians and Mexicans in the audience, included criticism of US policy toward Cuba. Bentsen called for the removal of economic sanctions and the resumption of normal diplomatic relations between the United States and Cuba.

While I was active in NAMI, I saw many signs that the Mexican state was evolving toward a more effective democracy. The country had, since 1929, been governed by the Partido Revolucionario Institucional (PRI), or Institutional Revolutionary Party. The PRI was the most durable dictatorship in the Western hemisphere. It combined anticlericalism, nationalism, socialist ideals, and corruption, and its overarching concern was to defend Mexico against interference by the United States. (In the nineteenth century, Mexico had lost roughly half its territory to US expansionism.) The country's constitution limited the presidency to a single term of six years. The naming of the PRI presidential candidate – and thus the next president of Mexico – was an internal matter for the party. The PRI's loosening grip on power started becoming obvious in 1988, when its candidate for president, Carlos Salinas de Gortari, was declared the victor only after the election-tabulation computer system was said to have crashed, halting the count. Fraud was widely assumed (and later confirmed). This eroded public perceptions of the PRI's legitimacy and permanence. Ernesto Zedillo, elected in 1994, was the last PRI president. An economist, he was an excellent, honest leader, and he tried his best at reforms of various kinds. During this period, NAMI was a venue for raising issues about the struggle in Mexico for a more democratic and inclusive system, creating a forum for politicians, academics, and economic activists in each of these three countries to compare their governance experiences and to encourage dialogue and problem-solving.

To hold up the Canadian end of NAMI's academic work, I brought in Rod Dobell, a professor of public policy at the University of Victoria, with a PhD in economics from MIT. (He is also the older brother of Ken

Dobell, with whom I would later work closely when Ken was deputy minister to Premier Gordon Campbell.) Rod Dobell proved to be a tremendous contributor of academic papers on various policy issues.

My work for NAMI was supported by a number of Canadians. I was very grateful for the strong interest of Mitchell Sharp, formerly Canada's foreign minister; Tom Axworthy, a former principal secretary and chief of staff to Prime Minister Pierre Trudeau; Lorna Marsden, a Senate colleague; and Sen. Céline Hervieux-Payette, also a former cabinet colleague, who brought a valuable Quebec perspective to the discussions.

I believed that where interests, cultures, and traditions are so diverse, NAMI's form of consultative, informed discussion could be a useful supplement to official negotiations. We were in a position to influence the perceptions of officials and politicians but not carry the baggage of past policies or the weight of official commitments or diplomatic obligation. I remained involved throughout NAMI's active existence. I served in my personal capacity, with no formal connection to my work in the Senate. By the mid-1990s, however, my main focus was shifting back to Asia, with my assignment as president of CCBC. I asked Charles Kelly from Vancouver, who had been an active member, to run the Canadian part of the NAMI operation, organizing meetings and communications, as I needed to ease my way out. Kelly, a BC businessman, had served as executive assistant to federal urban affairs minister Barney Danson in the mid-1970s.

Over the years, my involvement with NAMI brought me into contact with some of the most prominent figures in Mexican government and policy circles; they became involved in the organization or attended our events. The go-to guy on the Mexican side of the organization became Jesús Reyes-Heroles, until his public responsibilities forced him to reduce his NAMI involvement. He was a consulting economist who served as Mexico's secretary of energy in the mid-1990s and Mexican ambassador to the United States from 1997 to 2000. He was succeeded as NAMI's Mexican coordinator by Emilio Carrillo, who headed one of the leading business law firms in Mexico. I had developed an excellent relationship with Carrillo when he served as Mexican ambassador to Canada in the late 1980s. Another was Jorge Castañeda, a professor and political adviser who in 2000 became Mexico's foreign minister under President Vicente

Fox. Andrés Rozental, who had been deputy minister of foreign relations, also was a key supporter.

NAMI's highest-profile event, held in Santa Fe, came in August 2000. It was attended by US secretary of state Madeleine Albright, Mexican foreign secretary Rosario Green, and Canadian foreign affairs minister Lloyd Axworthy, an early version at the foreign minister level of what Prime Minister Chrétien would later call the Three Amigos when he met in 2001 with US president George W. Bush and Mexican president Vicente Fox.

Then, on 20 June 2002, tragedy struck. NAMI founder John Wirth was in Toronto, delivering a lecture on Zebulon Pike to Friends of Fort York,[4] when he dropped dead of a heart aneurism. He was sixty-six. Like everyone else, I was stunned and deeply saddened by the news. After his death, NAMI lost its momentum. There were no more trilateral conferences, and over the next couple of years, its activities petered out. Wirth had been the organization's driving force.

The early years of my involvement in NAMI coincided with a discussion in Ottawa about whether to expand our free trade deal with the United States into a trilateral one with Mexico. The Mulroney government was in favour of the concept, but there was considerable opposition, in part because of concerns about having to compete with lower-paid Mexican labour, but also because of fears that Canada would find itself caught up in Mexico's problems with the United States.

In April 1991, Mexican president Carlos Salinas de Gortari visited Ottawa as part of a concerted effort to persuade the United States and Canada to join with Mexico in a trilateral free trade deal. Addressing a joint session of Parliament on 8 April, Salinas said, "I am convinced that such a treaty is unquestionably the best option for the parties involved. It is an opportunity for our three nations to create a major economic zone that while respecting our cultural differences will have the vitality to compete successfully with the European market and the Asian Pacific Rim." During his visit to Canada, which included stops in Montreal and Toronto, Salinas made a point of meeting with opponents of a trilateral deal, including with the labour movement, aiming to address their concerns. He took a similar approach in the United States. Salinas arrived at a moment when the Canadian decision was in doubt. I believe his visit and eloquent arguments tipped the balance.

I had been among the trilateralists from the beginning. Like Salinas, I saw North America as best able to compete globally if it acted as an economic unit. Another important impetus for Canada was that once its bilateral free trade deal with the United States was concluded, the United States and Mexico had begun looking at the possibility of a similar deal between their countries. Such a development would have positioned the United States as the only one of the three with preferential access to the other two markets – it would be the hub and Canada and Mexico the spokes – meaning that companies would have a greater incentive to locate their production in the United States. It would not be in Canada's interest to allow that to happen. I also argued a more prosperous Mexico would be a market for Canada, not only for the United States. And I believed, a bit too optimistically, that the United States would be less arbitrary in its trade relationships with Canada if it had to deal with Mexico at the same time. Of course, even combined, Canada and Mexico would continue to be outweighed by the United States.

I became known in Ottawa as someone who had an active interest in Mexico, at a time when there were not many on Parliament Hill who did. Around 1991, I was invited to join a Toronto-based group called the Canada-Mexico Business Retreat, headed by Conservative senator Trevor Eyton, a former president and CEO of Brascan. Tom d'Aquino, CEO of the Ottawa-based Business Council on National Issues also was a key participant. Among the members of his council were CEOs of large Canadian corporations that either had investments in Mexico or were considering them. Laurent Beaudoin of Bombardier, whose company already had operations in Mexico, was a Canadian leader in the retreat group. We met regularly with senior Mexican businesspeople, both in Canada and Mexico. As time went on, the NAFTA negotiations and the implementation issues under NAFTA were increasingly the backdrop for our meetings. As various issues arose, there were exchanges between the Canadian and Mexican business leaders. My involvement was purely on a volunteer basis. I attended the meetings – many of them in Mexico – at my own expense.

Participation in the Canada-Mexico Business Retreat meetings enhanced the work I was doing with NAMI, not only by providing wider insight but also by increasing my standing with the Mexicans who were active in the organization – a different group of people from the Mexican business figures active in the retreat – as well as with some business circles in Canada. It put me in an interesting echelon of issues and relationships for a period of time. At the retreat meetings, we shared insights with our Mexican counterparts, who had little experience with trade treaties. These insights in turn were shared with their contacts in the Mexican government. Evidently, the Mexican side found our input valuable. In 2000, President Ernesto Zedillo named Eyton, d'Aquino, and me to the Order of the Aztec Eagle, the country's highest honour given to foreigners. We received our medals from Ambassador Ezequiel Padilla at a ceremony at the Rideau Club in Ottawa in mid-November 2000. We were also invited to attend the inauguration of Zedillo's successor, Vicente Fox, in Mexico City. Two weeks later, I travelled to Mexico for the event, which took place on 1 December 2000. The election of Fox, of the business-oriented Partido Acción Nacional, or National Action Party, had broken PRI's seventy-one-year hold on power – a historic occasion. Canada's official representative was foreign affairs minister John Manley.

I was pleased that Fox went on to pay much more attention to Canada-Mexico relations than his predecessors had done. He visited Ottawa in April 2001 and October 2004, addressing Parliament on the latter visit, which marked the tenth anniversary of the NAFTA deal. In September 2005, President Fox made an official visit to Vancouver. Fox's one-day visit was busy. It started with a breakfast with the Vancouver Board of Trade, then meetings with Prime Minister Martin, a luncheon, and then a visit to UBC. He was accompanied by my old friend Ambassador Emilio Carrillo. I was delighted to see him again.

I had become involved in NAMI and in the Canada-Mexico Business Retreat with no personal business agenda whatsoever. But, as it often does, one thing led to another.

In Ottawa in the early 1980s, I had got to know Michael Phelps, a Manitoba lawyer who served as chief of staff to then energy minister Marc Lalonde. Phelps and I would discuss energy policy issues, including Lalonde's 1980 National Energy Program, which elicited intense objections in Alberta and became a major political controversy. Phelps and I had hit it off, and after he left Ottawa in 1982 and joined Westcoast Energy in Vancouver as a senior adviser to its president, we kept in touch. In 1987, Phelps was promoted to president and CEO of Westcoast Energy. Our conversations continued, and at a certain point in the early 1990s, he said I was giving him valuable insights for free and engaged me as a consultant.

Phelps was looking to leverage Westcoast's expertise in building and operating pipelines to get international consulting contracts, where they didn't have to put up a lot of cash but could earn income. This orientation led Phelps and his group to become interested in both Mexico and China, two countries with which I was by then very familiar.

In the mid-1990s, Mexico's state oil company, PEMEX, had decided to solicit foreign bids on a major contract, more than $1 billion, for tertiary recovery of oil in the Campeche oil field,[5] part of the Gulf of Mexico. This was much more than a consulting contract; it was a major investment and operating role. Westcoast was interested in making a bid and invited me to work on the project with them. The international business community was watching closely this international public tender to make sure that Mexico conducted the process according to international standards. Before submitting their bids specifying price and terms, all the prospective bidders were discussing with the Mexican authorities what they wanted, how they could do this or that, what the policy results would be, how the financing would work, and so on – all customary business practice.

Westcoast was interested in studying this project and learning about the industry in Mexico and how it operated. Mexico was interested not just in Westcoast's technical capacity, but in who these people were, what they had done previously, and how they had behaved elsewhere. In most of the world – and this certainly was my experience in Asia – trust and reputation are essential ingredients in business relationships. You need to know with whom you are dealing and have confidence they will deliver.

This is especially true in places where the court system cannot be relied upon. In the United States and Canada, by contrast, business is conducted at a faster pace and the courts serve as safeguards to protect contracts. Business, therefore, is more transactional.

Where I played a role was in introducing Westcoast executives to key Mexican players. The fact that I was a Canadian senator, had been a senior Canadian minister, had been deputy minister of EMR, and that my Mexican contacts had come to know me through my work at NAMI and involvement in the retreat group were important factors in the Mexican assessment of the people I was introducing to them. Phelps assembled an international consortium with four other companies, and they won the contract for what was called the Cantarell Nitrogen Project in 1997. It was an exciting project, and at that time was the largest foreign investment in the history of Mexico. The investment proved highly profitable for both Westcoast and Mexico, and it vindicated my belief that a Canadian relationship with Mexico would be of economic advantage to Canada.

Phelps and his crew were also interested in my background in China. We started travelling there – I was always accompanied by one or more of Westcoast's senior executives, particularly Graham Wilson, the chief financial officer, and Michael Stewart, head of business development operations – and talking to people at the China National Petroleum Corporation, the state-owned enterprise, about developing their gas fields in Sichuan and about a natural gas vehicle fleet. But the Chinese simply weren't ready. We also discussed assisting in pipelining, but they weren't ready for a foreign investor in that area, either.

The Chinese did eventually ask whether we might be able to help with an air pollution problem they were experiencing with a major steel manufacturer, Baosteel, operating in a suburb of Shanghai. It was discharging volatile gases from its blast furnaces. Westcoast could handle that easily with a co-generation plant. Such plants capture the gases, which are extremely hot and moving rapidly as they exit the blast furnace, and put them through turbines that create electrical energy. Negotiating that deal and building the plant was a very long process, but the short story is that Westcoast concluded the deal in 1997 and the plant – built "inside the fence," that is, right at the steel facility – went into operation in June 2000.

It was the first environmental project in the steel industry in China. It was a demonstration model and of course the Chinese copied it and used it many, many times elsewhere. Critical to the success of that project was a Vancouver consultant Westcoast hired, Dr David T. Fung, a chemical engineer who headed ACDEG International, a group of companies.

Combining Canadian nationalism and North American continentalism may sound paradoxical, but I believe I've been totally consistent in my approach. I am a nationalist in terms of the ownership of Canadian economic activity. I have always tried to be supportive of policies that built Canadian ownership of Canadian resources and promoted Canadian ownership to the extent that Canada had its own capital to finance its economic development. I regarded foreign companies operating in this country as focusing narrowly on their commercial interests, not seeing themselves as responsible players in building a Canadian society. For Canadian companies, to protect Canadian interests is ultimately in their business interest, whether they know it or not.

When it comes to trade, I am a continentalist. Our standard of living relies on our capacity to be a successful trading nation. As Art Laing used to say, the world does not owe Canada a living. Not only does enhanced access to US and Mexican markets provide greater business opportunities, but also it strengthens the ability of Canadian companies to compete in other international markets. One of the underlying objectives of my economic nationalism was to ensure that Canada had the capacity to play, and be treated fairly, within that continental league.

As a result of my work with NAMI and conversations with its US and Mexican members, it became clear to me that Mexico was far more important to Canada's long-term continental interests than many in Ottawa had believed, and our trade partnership should not only be with the United States but also should include Mexico. A more prosperous and democratic Mexico would be an important export market for Canada, whereas an impoverished Mexico, with only a small educated class, would not only be a human tragedy for Mexico, but become a more and more significant problem and focus for the United States, with a negative impact on Canada. With the trilateral trade relationship now in its third decade, Mexico still confronts major internal problems related to poverty, crime, and corruption, yet it has made enormous strides in modernizing its economy and has benefited from its outward-looking approach.

Some Canadians wondered why we should be concerned about Mexico, particularly when its lower labour costs meant it could build an auto manufacturing industry that could result in the export of Canadian jobs. Our Auto Pact, however, served to protect us to a significant extent. That said, one factor I did not take into account was the development of the maquiladora system by which a number of Canadian companies parked themselves in a virtually tax-free legal zone, usually in certain parts of northern Mexico, and exported their products under NAFTA back to the United States and Canada on a low- or no-tariff basis. A few Canadian companies took advantage of this opportunity to lower their labour costs to the disadvantage of Canadian workers. Many US companies did the same.

Still, on balance, I believe NAFTA was an enormous success for Canada, as well as for its partners. Evidence can be found both in economic statistics and in what happened when US president Donald Trump threatened to do away with the agreement after his election in 2016. For reasons of his own populist branding, and as a form of partisan disparaging of an important accomplishment of the Democratic Clinton administration, Trump had railed against NAFTA as detrimental to the United States. He called for its trashing, or at least a major renegotiation. To carry out his policies, he appointed as trade representative Robert Lighthizer, an experienced trade specialist with a US-first approach and a propensity to invoke protectionist measures. I believe that one underlying reason for the Trump administration's tough stance with regard to NAFTA is that it, and particularly Lighthizer, wanted to lay the foundation for American trade negotiations with Europe and China, to create the impression that a review was under way of all US trade relations, and that no one should take access to the US market for granted. As the Chinese saying goes, "You kill the chicken to frighten the monkeys." Canada and Mexico were the chickens. However, in the end, NAFTA proved too valuable to US interests to kill. For thirty-five or thirty-six US states, Canada is their most important export market. The "new" United States–Mexico–

Canada Agreement on trade, which came into force in 2020, ended up closely resembling NAFTA, even if the two agreements are not identical.

Over the years, the specific issues may have changed, but the fundamental geopolitical and economic realities have not. Defending Canadian sovereignty and nation-building from coast to coast to coast, while acknowledging and fostering the north-south economic ties also essential to our prosperity and well-being, has been a dual objective throughout my career. It remains a perennial challenge for Canada.

12 Recognition and Reconciliation

IT WAS DURING MY BOYHOOD IN CALGARY that I first became aware of the presence of First Nations, through my visits to the Calgary Stampede. While the annual event is best known for its chuckwagon races and bronco-riding contests, it also has been a venue where important First Nations communities from the Prairies have put on exhibitions that have demonstrated their presence and cultures. At the Stampede grounds, I saw people in animal-skin clothing, including chiefs in enormous headdresses of eagle feathers; there were blankets, beadwork, teepees, and other highlights of their ceremonial cultures. I watched as their dancers performed, particularly the famous chicken dance. The first impression I had was of peoples with very strong traditions and cultures of their own. I took an interest in them, partly because I belonged to a minority culture myself.

There were no Indigenous students at the public schools I attended. We learned about the buffalo and how they used to range, and about the construction of the Canadian Pacific Railway, which opened up the West to European settlement and remained the lifeblood of the settler community. What they didn't teach us was about how the railway development and farming by settlers disrupted First Nations communities – how they lived, their economic basis – and how the people were pushed onto reserves. Nor had I ever heard of the Indian Act. All that was unknown to me in my youth, and to others of my generation.

Later, when I was at law school in the early 1950s, our legal education reflected the prevailing attitudes and discrimination against Indigenous people. For example, under section 12 of the British Columbia Evidence Act as we then learned it, it was unlawful for any court or judge to receive evidence from an Indigenous person, an "uncivilized person destitute in the knowledge of God" who did not have a belief in eternal reward or punishment. I was also aware at that time of attempts by the Nisga'a and other First Nations to advocate for their rights, but under the law as it then was, First Nations people were barred access to the courts and could not pursue their rights there. The situation in those days was completely prejudicial to First Nations. British Columbia, and for that matter the rest of Canada, was a hotbed of negativity toward First Nations, as well as toward Chinese, other Asians, Blacks, Jews, and also, toward eastern and southern Europeans, like Ukrainians and Italians. British Imperial culture predominated. So, it's not surprising that given my own background, not being a member of that dominant community, I was interested in the dominant society's impact on other minority communities in Canada.

In the late 1950s, while I was working as a lawyer on the Craigmont mine, I made several visits to Merritt, a town in the Nicola Valley, 270 kilometres northeast of Vancouver. I had previously heard about the condition of Indigenous people there and elsewhere in the province, but I hadn't seen it for myself.

I was profoundly shocked by what I witnessed. Members of the nearby Coldwater First Nation lived in absolute poverty, their social organization destroyed. This was not the result of the mine. The pre-existing situation traced back to the effects of earlier settlement and the continuing colonialist policies. I saw First Nations men in a drunken stupor picked up by the RCMP off the streets of Merritt on Saturday nights, loaded into the backs of pickup trucks to be delivered back to their reserve. The white people in the community just laughed at their drunkenness. When I expressed shock, others involved in mining told me that was just how things were. The prevailing attitude was at best one of callous indifference, at worst active prejudice. What I saw in Merritt registered very deeply with me and was a significant factor motivating my later engagement on Indigenous issues.

A more uplifting experience came when I served as executive assistant to northern affairs and national resources minister Arthur Laing in 1963–65. While the Indian affairs department was responsible for matters concerning Indigenous people in the provinces, our department was responsible in the North. We travelled widely in Yukon and the Northwest Territories and met many Indigenous people. They had maintained their own structures, traditional economic activity, and community integrity. Laing saw my interest in Indigenous people and encouraged it. In the North, he went out of his way to arrange meetings with leaders like Elijah Smith in Yukon. Smith was a statesman, and a spokesman for his people, the Kwanlin Dün First Nation. He was also a bridge between two cultures.

In talking to Smith and others, I learned about and became sensitized to the devastating social cost that Indigenous communities had suffered during the construction of two military projects in the North. The Canol pipeline had been built by the Americans during the Second World War, with Canadian permission, to carry oil from Norman Wells to a refinery in Whitehorse; fuel was then shipped on to Alaska to be used for military purposes. Later, there was the construction of the Distant Early Warning Line, which had a significant impact on the Inuit and Dene. In both cases, the presence of large numbers of predominantly male, white workers resulted in attacks on women, abusive behaviours of many sorts toward the local people, environmental damage, and the destruction of traplines. The easy availability of alcohol was as toxic as could be imagined.

I became much more aware of the costs to Indigenous communities of non-Indigenous people's indifference to the effects of intrusions, whether for military purposes or resource development. I learned more of the history, for example, how a previous government had moved certain Inuit communities to the High Arctic, using them as pawns to buttress Canada's sovereignty in the Arctic, while remaining oblivious to the all too often fatal consequences of displacing people and then leaving them without the means to support themselves.

I also became aware that Indigenous children were being forcibly taken from their families and placed in residential schools managed by various Christian denominations, contracted by the federal government. This was occurring in the North as well as across the country. The prevailing view in Ottawa at the time was that these schools were necessary. The bureaucrats and the churches thought they had a "civilizing" mission, and the goal was to provide Indigenous people with the tools they needed to work in a wage economy. We heard objections to these schools from Indigenous people and sympathized; we could see the negative impacts on families, even if we did not realize the full scope of abuses committed there. As for what came to be known as the Sixties Scoop – the taking of Indigenous children out of their communities and sending them to be adopted by non-Indigenous families – this was also taking place in the North, but I had no awareness of it.

While Laing, as a minister, and even I as his executive assistant, could and did question the residential school policy with both political and bureaucratic officials, we had no hope whatsoever of effecting change. The prejudicial interests and attitudes were far too entrenched. In the North, what Laing and I tried to do was introduce policies of amelioration: more health care, doctors, nurses, electricity, airstrips, and other infrastructure.

Once I was deputy minister of EMR in the early 1970s, I had more of a chance to make a difference. It was the perspective and sensitivity I had developed with Art Laing and in my earlier years that led me to push, along with my counterpart at Indian affairs Basil Robinson, for the creation of the Mackenzie Valley Pipeline Inquiry, as I describe in an earlier chapter. My own department's jurisdiction was limited to the pipeline's impact on the physical conditions in the North, not on its people, but I felt very strongly about the necessity to consult northern communities.

The decision to consult Indigenous people and other residents of the North about what impact resource development would have on their lives – and to take their perspectives into account before any development occurred – was a first in Canada's political history. The CPR wasn't constructed by listening to Indigenous people, nor was the CN. Western settlement was not a subject of consultation, either. The inquiry commissioner, Tom Berger, travelled extensively in the North, holding hearings in communities there as well as in southern Canada.[1] It set a tremendous precedent. Once you've consulted, there's no going back. It set up an expectation of consultation and a sense in some of the First Nations communities – not just in the Northwest Territories – of a right to be consulted. The broader impacts were only dimly understood at the time, including by me, but I would draw a direct line from this experience to the inclusion of Indigenous people in the constitutional consultations that were to come a few years later. The inquiry hearings also helped raise awareness in southern Canada that the North was not just a treasure chest of resources waiting to be exploited, as it had been portrayed in the political discourse until that point, but the ancestral and permanent home of Indigenous Peoples.

Federal policy had been to encourage investment in northern resource exploration and development. It had promoted oil and gas research and exploration in the High Arctic – the government had a 45 per cent stake in Panarctic Oils Ltd – as part of a broader effort to develop an economic base in the Northwest Territories. The North was a significant cost to the federal treasury. Supporting the people in the North, however poorly it might have been done, took a lot of money. The traditional economy of hunting and fishing did not provide an economic base for the introduction of electric power and other tools of the Western economy. Mines were developed, particularly in Yukon, but also some in the Northwest Territories. The government policy was then to find economic activities in the North to bring in a wage economy and relieve the federal government of its financial responsibilities. So, part of my mandate as deputy minister of EMR was to try to set up viable conditions for resource development. At the same time, I felt it was important to do so in a way that took into account the issues of the people in the communities where that resource development might take place.

Berger's report was published in 1977, based on his extensive hearings across the North as well as in southern Canada and studies that had made it clear the construction of the pipeline would have been enormously destructive in many ways, including environmentally. As well, the economic case for the pipeline was far from proven. Berger recommended that no pipeline be built in Yukon and called for a ten-year moratorium on construction of the pipeline in the Mackenzie Valley in order, in the meantime, to address Indigenous land claims and develop solutions to social and political issues with First Nations communities. The takeaway was straightforward: you couldn't just come onto their lands and into their communities to do whatever you wanted, as had been the case. This was the first time in Canadian energy policy that there had been an analysis of the social, environmental, and physical costs of such a project. The government could see the political cost of approving the pipeline would be very high.

Overall, I was delighted with the report, which was articulate, respectful of Indigenous people, and compassionate. Some others were not. The oil and gas industry was disappointed they couldn't get on with the job in the old way, and my early support for the inquiry cost me all sorts of relationships in the sector. In my public comments, I took a measured approach. By that time, I was a senator and felt a need to show my understanding of the views of all stakeholders, including those who were disappointed. And those included not only the oil companies but also individuals in the North, including members of Indigenous communities, who had hoped construction of the pipeline would bring them jobs and other economic benefits.

One place where I did differ with Berger was over what I saw as his alignment with the most politically radical movements among Indigenous Peoples in the North, whom I perceived were trying to move toward territorial government based on ethnicity. I did not believe that having a whole series of small communities each proclaiming its own version of autonomous political authority would be any basis for a viable governance system. My own view at the time was that in the North, political evolution could be furthered by means of the territorial government. I understood the Indigenous view that the territorial legislators were essentially captives of a public service that represented the non-Indigenous community's interest. But I thought Indigenous people, who after all were a majority in the territory, could gain control, as more and more powers were devolved locally and less and less was run from Ottawa. I wanted to see the development of political institutions in the North and political leaders from the North and from the Indigenous communities that would be progressive and self-governing in the interests of all the communities and the nation as a whole. I saw the territorial government as one democratically elected by all the people who lived in the territory, with the usual powers of a provincial government, although it wouldn't have provincial constitutional standing.

It was obvious, even in my time, that the Northwest Territories was too vast for effective administration, the interests of the Inuit people in the northeast and along the Arctic coast were quite different from those of the First Nations in the southern and western parts of the territory, and the territory should be split. Sometimes, it can take decades for changes to happen. It doesn't mean the people in a previous generation weren't aware of the issues, it's just that the political circumstances for acting weren't appropriate.

In 1980–81, I served as the Liberal whip of the Special Joint Committee of the Senate and of the House of Commons on the Constitution of Canada. The committee's orders of reference were to consider and report on the *Proposed Resolution for a Joint Address to Her Majesty the Queen Respecting the Constitution of Canada*. This document, published by the government in October 1980, was essentially the draft constitution, including the Charter of Rights. Until patriation in 1982, Canada's constitution was an act of the British Parliament, and the power of amendment resided there.

Patriation and all that flowed from it was Prime Minister Pierre Trudeau's major policy initiative in his last electoral mandate, and he wanted frequent briefings about the committee's progress. I had a direct channel to him through Joyce Fairbairn of the PMO and ensured that he was aware of significant developments. The joint committee heard from Canadians across the land, including premiers, provincial ministers, academics, business and labour leaders, and Inuit, Métis, and First Nations leaders. The passage of the new constitution for Canada along with patriation of all constitutional rights was a monumental achievement by the federal government and the provinces, or most of them.

For me, the greatest achievement was section 35, giving clear constitutional recognition to the inherent rights of the Aboriginal peoples.[2] It was a moment of triumph for common sense and decency, and a great step forward toward reconciliation, which cannot occur in the absence of recognition of Indigenous rights.

It almost didn't happen.

The original draft introduced by the federal government in the fall of 1980 – the one referred to the joint committee for study – did not include entrenchment of Aboriginal rights. That draft simply had a provision, section 24, that any rights and freedoms that pertain to native peoples would not be abrogated by Charter rights, a sort of "without prejudice" clause. There had been some resistance from the Progressive Conservative Party, but also on the Liberal side, with respect to including First Nations status and issues in the constitutional process. Prime Minister Pierre Trudeau and justice minister Jean Chrétien were loath to entrench Aboriginal rights before they were defined, and there was also considerable opposition from the provinces on this issue.

My own position was strongly in favour of embedding some kind of constitutional entitlement and recognition. I made my views known in caucus, where there were countless discussions, and in conversations with the prime minister, with Chrétien, and with Chrétien's key adviser Eddie Goldenberg.

The joint committee received briefs and presentations from an array of prominent Indigenous leaders and representatives of Indigenous organizations who explained their perspectives eloquently and in some detail. They spoke of their painful history of dispossession and their continuing subjection to colonial rule and assimilationist policies. They expressed fear that patriation could infringe on their rights as nations to whom the Crown had an obligation, bringing further dispossession, and that equality provisions of the Charter could be turned against them to deprive them of their rights. They explained why the proposed section 24 fell far short of what was just and advocated strongly for a provision that would entrench Aboriginal rights in the constitution.

They made their case not only before the committee but also before the people of Canada. In a precedent-setting move, the joint committee's hearings were televised, and thousands of Canadians tuned in. People told us they saw us on television and commented on how they had been moved by certain presentations. Clips were also featured on newscasts.

When the joint committee first met in early November 1980, I had opposed televising the hearings. Television cameras had only been introduced into the House of Commons a few years earlier and were banned in the Senate. The introduction in the Commons had not been an unqualified success. My fear was that televising the proceedings would be a distraction and would prompt grandstanding by politicians and presenters of briefs. I felt the public could get a full account of the substance of the proceedings from the journalists who would be covering them, and in this way, the democratic process would be served.

Fortunately, I lost the argument. For the most part, we forgot about the television cameras as we rose to the historical moment. If the cameras had any effect, it was to improve our focus, as we knew the country's eyes were upon us. And, televising the proceedings played a key role in winning public support for the entrenchment of Aboriginal rights in the constitution. Viewers were moved by what they heard from the new generation of Indigenous leaders, people who knew how to argue their case articulately in Western terms and whose dedication to having Canadians understand their situation was immense. These presentations made a big impact not only on the public but also on members of our committee. Meanwhile, some Indigenous representatives had travelled to London, where they were lobbying the British Parliament, either against patriation entirely or to ensure their rights were protected. The concern was that the Crown was about to slough off its obligations to Indigenous Peoples. While this lobbying yielded no direct result, it did add momentum to putting Indigenous concerns on the public agenda.

On 30 January 1981, Chrétien appeared before the committee to propose an amendment that would entrench Aboriginal rights in the constitution, as well as define Aboriginal peoples as Indians, Métis, and Inuit. This was an advance for the Métis in particular, who until that point were lacking recognition. The two provisions were labelled section 34 (1) and (2). It was a momentous occasion. NDP MP Peter Ittinuar,[3] himself an Inuk, was given the honour of reading the English text and Liberal MP Warren Allmand of Montreal the French version.

For me, it was a profoundly important moment, and it was observed that as I spoke, there was emotion in my voice and there were tears in my eyes. "Mr Chairman," I said, "I too want to associate myself with the incredible accomplishment of Canada that we are seeing this afternoon in this committee, the coming together of the natives, the Aboriginal people, the Indians, the Inuit, the Métis, in a common policy, and the joining of that common policy of the government and of the Progressive Conservative Party and the New Democratic Party. I think it proves just how strong, how practical, how pragmatic, but particularly how just and equitable Canadians can be and are." I went on to recall the discriminatory provisions of the British Columbia Evidence Act that I had learned in law school, and added, "It is a long trip to take, and yet the Canadian society has been able to take that trip." In closing, I paid tribute to Chrétien for his delivery of the amendment.

The committee hearings wrapped up the following month, and the committee reported out to Parliament. Constitutional debates continued in Parliament and across the country. There was no agreement with the provinces on the proposed Charter, or for that matter, on the new constitution as a whole. The federal government therefore was proceeding unilaterally. Meanwhile, among Indigenous people, opinion was divided about section 34 as it then stood. The Inuit maintained their support, but many First Nations rejected the proposed wording as inadequate.

In three provinces, the courts were asked to rule on whether the federal government could proceed with patriation unilaterally. The results varied, and the matter went before the Supreme Court of Canada. It ruled in September 1981 that while the federal government had the legal right to proceed unilaterally, doing so would violate convention. The ruling, making credible the federal threat of unilateral repatriation, brought the provinces back to the table. At the same time, unilateral federal action was constrained by the spectre of public disapproval. Thus, the decision gave new impetus to an effort to reach a federal-provincial accord.

One was indeed reached, on 5 November 1981. But in the new text, the section entrenching Aboriginal rights was missing. With seven provinces opposing that provision, it had been sacrificed for the sake of reaching an accord on the Charter and patriation as a whole. All that remained was an agreement to hold another constitutional conference with Indigenous participation, something that seemed unlikely to result in entrenchment of Aboriginal rights, given that the proposal would run up against the same provincial objections, plus, at that point, a constitutional amendment would be needed.

While I fully understood the *realpolitik* of the situation, I was bitterly disappointed. Speaking in Calgary at an Alberta Liberal convention held a few days later, I said that Ottawa and the premiers had made a serious mistake by leaving Aboriginal rights out of the constitution and I grieved at what had been done. I repeated in the Senate on 10 November 1981, that "I grieve for the loss of the possibility of Aboriginal rights being established," and added that I hoped that the federal government would do whatever it could to ensure Aboriginal rights, at least in areas within its own power. By this point, I was a freshly minted cabinet minister. Behind the scenes I did what I could to get the provision restored. At the same time, many other voices were being raised, not least those of Indigenous people themselves.

In the face of considerable pressures, the negotiators returned to the table a couple of weeks later and restored section 34 (renumbered as section 35) with one change: the word "existing" was inserted to describe the rights that were being entrenched. The extent to which that word watered down the section was at that time a matter of some dispute, but it was necessary to make the section easier for the provinces to swallow. As I suggested at the time, and as later court decisions indicated, it did not in fact make much difference to the provision's meaning.

Speaking in the Senate on 3 December 1981, my cabinet colleague Ray Perrault generously stated the provision was restored "due in no small measure" to Indian affairs minister John Munro and myself. While I like to think I did my part, other forces were also in motion.

In my own remarks in the Senate four days later, on 7 December, I said that public opinion, which had expressed itself through opinion polls as favouring the Charter of Rights and section 35, "fell like a battering ram on the provinces, and they gave way." I said the removal of section 35 on Aboriginal rights and the removal of the definition of Aboriginal peoples had been "a nightmare disappointment, with the gravest political harm to Canada."

"Canada cannot be a caring, equitable and tolerant society and not address itself to the rights and problems of the Aboriginal peoples," I said. "That is why it is so important, not only to the Aboriginal people, but also to all Canadians, that the idea of their having rights be clearly established as part of their entitlement as Canadians – that is, to give them the status in our Constitution and amongst Canadian citizens of equality as a community with all the other communities of our country and to begin from that fair base what will no doubt be a difficult and painful negotiation to establish specific terms of agreement between them and the greater Canadian society. I am not frightened of that process or of the pain of it, because it represents over time the reconciliation of old and difficult grievances, and the alternative would be unthinkable …

"There will be the entitlement of the political process to negotiate with the political leadership of Canada, problem by problem, issue by issue, and place by place. It is a remedy that Canadians have suppressed."

After patriation, there was a series of conferences attended by Indigenous representatives, the prime minister, and the premiers. The first of those, which had been provided for in the constitution, took place in March 1983, in Ottawa. I was an observer at the dramatic two-day meeting, which resulted in constitutional amendments that provided for constitutional protection for land claims agreements, gender equality between Indigenous men and women (though removal of the Indian Act's blatant discrimination against women was yet to come), and further conferences.

This was the meeting where Bill Wilson, a prominent Indigenous leader from Vancouver Island, faced off against Pierre Trudeau. Wilson told him, "I have two children in Vancouver Island, both of whom for some misguided reason say they want to be a lawyer. Both of whom want to be the prime minister." The laughter in the room only increased when, after a pause, Wilson added, "Both of whom, prime minister, are women." Trudeau responded that he would stick around until they were ready. Wilson's daughters did, in fact, become lawyers. The video went viral thirty-two years later, when one of them, Jody Wilson-Raybould, was appointed justice minister by another prime minister Trudeau.

Beneath the edgy humour, Wilson was making an important point, in his blunt, highly personal style: that it should not be unthinkable for people of Indigenous background (and, for that matter, women) to aspire to the country's highest office. I was present for that exchange, sitting a row behind the prime minister, and I remember thinking that Wilson was a bit over-the-top. But I wholly agreed with his point.

Wilson himself was a lawyer, the second Indigenous person to graduate from UBC law school, a decade after his cousin Alfred Scow. Wilson and I would chat from time to time, and he would share with me his outrage and sense of frustration about how the federal government was handling Indigenous matters. His criticisms were never directed at me personally. Our conversations continued into the Mulroney period, during the Meech Lake and Charlottetown processes.

As a cabinet minister in the Trudeau government, I had many preoccupations; by early 1982 my priorities became Expo 86, and the CDC. Indigenous files were no longer a primary focus. Nevertheless, throughout my time as minister, I succeeded in facilitating federal funding for projects in First Nations communities in British Columbia, just as I did for other communities. Funding was secured for water and sewer systems and fire protection, for the benefit of the Aboriginal Friendship Centre in Vancouver, and for a community hall in Alkali Lake, to cite a few examples. I admired the Alkali Lake Band, now called Esk'etemc First Nation, for their successful battle against alcoholism.

When it came to securing funding for Indigenous initiatives, however, my proudest accomplishment during that period was my role in the creation of the Northern Native Fishing Corporation. My involvement started with a phone call from a member of the Nelson family, which owned British Columbia Packers. The fishing and fish processing company was trying to sell its fleet of gillnet fishing boats on the northern coast, along with their licences, because their operation was no longer economic. A group of First Nations was interested in buying the boats and licences to protect the jobs of the Indigenous fishers who had been renting them, and a price had been negotiated. As it turned out, the First Nations were represented by their law counsel Ron Stern, who some years later became a close friend. The problem was that the Indigenous groups did not have the money to make the purchase, so they were looking for federal funding. The goal was to create a sustainable economic base for those communities and for the Indigenous fishermen who would first rent, then buy the boats once they had saved enough for a down payment. In addition to his legal work for the First Nations, Stern was a staunch advocate on their behalf, pressing me to find the federal funds for the project.

I told both the Nelson family and Stern that I was interested, but we would have to be certain there was a business case for proceeding. Many questions had to be answered and safeguards put in place, as with any business deal. And, of course, I would also have to find the money. First, I went to John Munro to get his backing, which was forthcoming immediately, and then we jointly went to cabinet to lay out the plan, which was approved. We put in place an initial management team to oversee the project, headed by Jean Rivard. He was a Cree originally from Saskatchewan who had a strong business background and was executive director of the Native Brotherhood of British Columbia.

Things came together, and in August 1982, Treasury Board released the $11.7 million in funding for the project, allowing the company, owned by the Nisga'a, North Coast Tribal Council, and the Gitxsan Wet'suwet'en Tribal Council, to purchase about 250 boats and close to the same number of salmon licences. The licences were to remain the property of the Northern Native Fishing Corporation. According to press reports at the time, it was the largest Indigenous economic development project ever financed by the federal government. The company, based in Prince Rupert and still owned by the same First Nations, remains in operation.

While I had no further involvement with the Northern Native Fishing Corporation, that contribution helped establish my relationship with First Nations. About twenty years later, I went to bat in Ottawa for a First Nations organization that had come to me for help in acquiring funding so they could conduct a major study. They created the First Nation Panel on Fisheries, which produced a report in May 2004 titled *Our Place at the Table*. It was an excellent report, and set out Indigenous entitlement to equitable participation in the BC fishing industry. By the time it was published, I was in cabinet again and pressed for recognition of some of its claims.

The vast majority of the Indigenous Peoples of British Columbia have never ceded their rights to their lands. Historically, no treaties were signed between them and the Crown, with a small number of exceptions on Vancouver Island and in British Columbia's northeast. The province just asserted control over what it declared to be Crown lands, and left only small parcels as First Nations reserves.

In 1887, Nisga'a chiefs travelled by boat to Victoria from their homes in the Nass River area in the northwestern part of the province, in an effort to reclaim their lands. They were rebuffed. In 1913, they petitioned the British Privy Council, but got nowhere. Subsequently, efforts to launch land claims were made illegal under the federal Indian Act, until the law was changed in the 1950s. In 1967, Frank Calder and other Nisga'a chiefs launched a case against the government of British Columbia seeking recognition of their Aboriginal title to their lands. The case was finally decided by the Supreme Court of Canada in 1973, which narrowly found against Calder, on a technicality. In the process, however, it upheld the concept of Aboriginal title to land as having predated the arrival of Europeans (the issue in this case was whether it had since been extinguished). This led to a land claims process with the federal government that began in 1976.

The province joined the talks in 1990, culminating in a long negotiation process during the 1990s that led to the Nisga'a Final Agreement in 1998. Under that deal, Nisga'a title to 2,000 square kilometres of lands was recognized, and an agreement was reached on Nisga'a self-government, taking the Nisga'a out from under the Indian Act and paving the way for them to once again manage their own affairs. At the same time, however, the Criminal Code and other federal and provincial laws continued to apply in the territory, as well as the Canadian Charter of Rights and Freedoms. This was not a challenge to Canada's constitutional order, but consistent with it. And the rights of non-Indigenous residents would be protected. The key achievement of the treaty was to reconcile in today's world the Nisga'a people's culture and system of government, and the culture and system of the majority population.

I was not involved in the negotiations, though of course followed their progress with great interest. My contribution was to act as sponsor of the ratification legislation when it reached the Senate in late 1999, a role for which I had volunteered. I also spoke to our national caucus about the agreement. Whether we would support it was not at issue – this agreement was important to Prime Minister Chrétien – but there were a lot of questions. I explained its political significance in British Columbia generally, as well as what was at stake for the federal Liberal Party in the province. Explaining British Columbia to my non-British Columbian colleagues in Ottawa was a familiar role.

By the time the agreement was before Parliament, it had already been ratified by the Nisga'a and the British Columbia legislature. But Bill C-9, the enacting legislation, got a rough ride through the House of Commons. The Reform Party, then the official Opposition, had attempted to filibuster, introducing hundreds of amendments in an effort to obstruct the process. The Liberals, who not only had a majority but also the support of all the other parties, pushed it through.

The Reform Party was giving voice to fearmongering that was in play. Although specific concerns had been raised about the deal's constitutional status, the existence of overlapping claims by other First Nations, and whether the rights of non-Indigenous people would be protected – concerns to which we had full and satisfactory answers – these objections also seemed rooted in a lack of public acceptance, in some quarters, of the fact that Indigenous people did have rights. Public opinion in British Columbia had lagged behind the recognition of Indigenous rights by the courts and in the constitution, and there was still a very deep bias against the idea of Indigenous people having special entitlement, as well as a fear of their possible growing economic power and how they would use it. The dominant philosophy remained that Indigenous people should assimilate and be like everybody else, although there was considerable hypocrisy in this argument, given continuing discrimination against Indigenous people in the job market and elsewhere. One has to admire those within the British Columbia and federal governments who finally said yes, if the Nisga'a are willing to negotiate a final agreement, we will move forward on this chronic issue.

There were no senators representing the Reform Party, but I knew there would be more opposition to the agreement from Progressive Conservative members of the Senate than there had been from their colleagues in the House. Many MPs had First Nations communities in their ridings, and there was a reluctance to speak against an agreement that other First Nations generally applauded, even if they were not necessarily advocating the same for themselves. My chief opponent during second and third reading debates on the Nisga'a Final Agreement was Progressive Conservative senator Gerry St Germain of British Columbia, a former Mulroney cabinet minister.

In moving second reading of the bill in the Senate, on 16 December 1999, I described the Nisga'a Final Agreement's significance, calling it a milestone in the negotiation of modern treaties in this country. I noted the agreement, so long in the making, would at last provide certainty, and the lack thereof had proven very costly to the British Columbia economy. The agreement provided certainty not by extinguishing rights, but rather by agreeing to define them. I also remarked that the Nisga'a treaty clearly demonstrated the advantages of negotiating these issues rather than going to court.

After a debate, the bill passed second reading on 10 February 2000, and then went to the Standing Senate Committee on Aboriginal Peoples, of which I was a member. I had the honour of serving as chair while the bill was before the committee. Although I was already chair of the Standing Senate Committee on Privileges, Standing Rules and Orders, and chairing two committees was unusual, I had asked for the assignment. The Liberal caucus had agreed. There had been considerable concern that the bill might get tied up in committee by Conservative senators, and we wanted to ensure that did not happen.

Our committee heard from some thirty witnesses in more than twenty-five hours of meetings, giving full and fair opportunity to those who wished to speak to all sides of the issues. And then we reported out, allowing me to move third reading in the Senate on 30 March 2000 to begin the final debate. When I spoke that day, I addressed in some detail the concerns that had been raised in committee and continued to elaborate in responses to senators' questions over the course of the debate, which went on for several days. Senator St. Germain presented the argument that neighbouring Gitsxan and Gitanyow First Nations had competing claims, and that these should be settled before concluding the Nisga'a Final Agreement. I answered that the deal did not deprive them of recourse; they could still have the boundary adjusted through negotiation or litigation.

To those concerned that the treaty created a new order of government and was thus a constitutional amendment (meaning the constitutional ratification procedure would apply), I stated this was not the case: implicit in the Supreme Court's 1997 decision in the Delgamuukw case was that a right of collective governance was part of Aboriginal title; however, I noted that "if the court has another view on this issue, we will certainly hear about it, as the honourable senator says, and will have to accommodate it." At the time, a case was before the courts, launched by then BC Liberal Party leader – later premier – Gordon Campbell, challenging the agreement on this basis. Ultimately, he was unsuccessful. (I hasten to mention that the federal and BC Liberal parties are not related.) I noted that the Nisga'a treaty would have constitutional protection under section 35, and by bringing that section into being the federal government and the provinces had agreed to a limitation on their powers.

The bill passed third reading in the Senate on 13 April 2000, and received royal assent a few hours later from Governor General Adrienne Clarkson. With a few exceptions, the Progressive Conservatives either voted against it or abstained. They moved two last-minute motions attempting to stall passage, but these were defeated by the Liberal majority.

What a great day it was, the Senate gallery filled with Nisga'a leaders wearing their full ceremonial regalia, in their elaborate button blanket capes, mainly in red and black, and in headgear representing their clans: eagle, killer whale, raven, and so on. This startled some of my colleagues, whose ideas of First Nations dress were more informed by the feathered bonnets and buckskins seen in some other parts of the country. Among those present was Frank Calder, who had been first elected to the British Columbia legislature in 1949, even before he and other First Nations people had the right to vote, and whose court case more than a quarter century earlier had played an important role in his people's struggle for their rights. Also present, of course, was Nisga'a Tribal Council president Joseph Gosnell, who had led the Nisga'a through the last decade of negotiations, after the death of his older brother James, who had been instrumental at the earlier stages.

A month later, I went to Gitwinksihlkw, one of the Nisga'a communities, along with Indian affairs minister Robert Nault, for the celebration marking the treaty's coming into force and the inauguration of the Nisga'a Lisims government. NDP premier Ujjal Dosanjh, with whom I would later serve in cabinet after he entered federal politics, headed the British Columbia delegation. Dosanjh was elected as a Liberal in the 2004 election and served in the Paul Martin government as minister of health.

Many of us were of the belief that the Nisga'a Final Agreement would demonstrate the advantages of negotiation, as opposed to litigation, but other First Nations in the province and their organizations rejected the agreement as a model. It has, however, served the Nisga'a well.

As First Nations moved toward self-government, they focused on capacity-building. This meant not only expanding their own knowledge base but also working to remove legal obstacles to their progress and replace them with laws and institutions that would better allow them to advance their interests. In early 1999, several months before the Nisga'a Final Agreement reached Parliament, we passed the First Nations Land Management Act. It was a major step in transferring responsibility for economic management from Indian affairs to First Nations. In this case, what was transferred was the ability to manage lands for those First Nations that had decided to do so. For those opting in, the relevant sections of the Indian Act ceased to apply. Much of the impetus for the legislation came from the Musqueam First Nation in British Columbia, important land owners in Vancouver, who were one of the five in the province to initially opt in,[4] joined by another nine or so in the rest of the country. Dozens of others have since joined them.

Before reaching the Senate, the bill had sailed through the House of Commons without careful study; there hadn't been a lot of interest in it. In the Senate, a number of issues were raised. The biggest stumbling block was the expropriation provisions in the bill, which had been poorly drafted. This had been noted by some senators, and that had led to resistance to the whole of the legislation. At the time, non-Indigenous leaseholders on Musqueam lands, who had just seen a major rent hike after years of extremely low rates, were expressing fears that they would arbitrarily be subjected to expropriation. Although there had been no indication the Musqueam actually planned to do this, leaving the law as written could have had unintended consequences. For reconciliation to advance, it is essential that legitimate interests of non-Indigenous stakeholders be taken into account.

While I had been keen to see this legislation passed, as I supported its main provisions and it was of special interest to several British Columbia First Nations, my view as a legislator was that the bill did not contain a fair balance of powers. So, with the support of Indian affairs minister Jane Stewart and assistance from others, including the Indian Affairs office in Vancouver, I brokered agreement on amendments that would essentially bring the bill's expropriation powers into line with those in other expropriation legislation, while preserving the bill's substantive measures. I also was in communication with Musqueam leaders, as I wanted to be sure that First Nations could live with the amendments. These amendments were passed by the Senate committee studying the legislation, paving the way for the bill's passage in the Senate and then passage of the amended bill by the House of Commons.

Another important piece of legislation for First Nations that I helped through Parliament was the Westbank First Nation Self-Government Act of 2004. It took that First Nation out from under the Indian Act and left them to make their own policies and laws in a wide range of areas, in addition to the land management and taxation powers they already had. New powers concerned, for example, social policies, public works, and Okanagan language and culture. In those areas, they would no longer be hampered by federal bureaucracy but free to make their own decisions locally. By this time, I was Leader of the Government in the Senate, so I was responsible for managing the passage of all government legislation that made its way there. In Ottawa, I met with Westbank representatives, including Chief Robert Louie and his business adviser Tim Raybould about the legislation. I assured them there would be no difficulty; it would be handled expeditiously. Unlike the legislation to implement the Nisga'a Final Agreement, which had also involved a land claim, the Westbank bill made its way through the Senate – all three readings and a day in committee – in less than two weeks, with bipartisan support. By this time, we were in the run-up to an election, so it was important that the bill be passed before the end of the session. Otherwise, it would die on the Order Paper.

The process of how bills were prioritized and managed generally went something like this: once a bill was ready and approved by the cabinet committee on legislation, the government's House Leader in the Commons would decide, given all the other legislative priorities, where it fit, and the minister and his or her staff would consult with the opposition parties to see whether they had any problems with the legislation, in order to reach an agreement on how many days of debate would be allotted. Once a bill was scheduled on the Commons side, my staff would be informed by the House Leader's staff, and then similarly, I would schedule it for debate in the Senate based on where it fit into other priorities and after consulting with the opposition. This is what is known as the hidden wiring of Parliament.

The First Nations Fiscal and Statistical Management Act, which received royal assent in March 2005, was another important piece of legislation I helped see through the Senate, not an onerous task because it, too, had all-party support. Its purpose was to help First Nations build financial independence, which involved the capacity to monetize their land base and other resources, including through taxation, and manage their money so that they would have the resources to take care of their needs and realize their ambitions. The act created several capacity-building institutions, in particular, the First Nations Finance Authority, the First Nations Tax Commission, and the First Nations Financial Management Board.

The legislation was First Nations driven. Leading the effort was Manny Jules of the Tk'emlups te Secwepemc (formerly known as the Kamloops Band). Although his role was instrumental, he was not alone. The initiative was also backed by the First Nations organizations in British Columbia, including the First Nations Summit led by Grand Chief Ed John, a hereditary chief of the Tl'azt'en Nation and a graduate of UBC law school. As the British Columbia political minister, I joined them in pushing to ensure the legislation's passage.

During the Mulroney era, Jules had led the successful effort to amend the Indian Act to allow bands to levy property tax on reserve. He was an obvious first chair of the newly created First Nations Tax Commission, where he has worked to facilitate the development by First Nations of the capacities to use those powers effectively and equitably. Another British Columbian who has played an important role in economic capacity-building is Harold Calla, a chartered professional accountant who is a member of the Squamish nation. In 2005, when he was serving as director of finance for the Squamish nation, I had him appointed to the board of the Canada Mortgage and Housing Corporation to represent British Columbia. The Squamish are major real estate holders, and I thought it would be useful to help him – and through him the Squamish and other First Nations – expand their knowledge of the mortgage industry and how it works. I received a lot of credit at that time from First Nations people for the appointment. Later, Calla became executive chair of the First Nations Financial Management Board.

At the same time, First Nations–led initiatives to develop governmental capacity were under way, and the name of another British Columbian figures prominently here, too. Satsan (Herb George), a Wet'suwet'en hereditary chief, has led the Centre for First Nations Governance in promoting the development of governance structures based on First Nations laws, traditions, and culture, leveraging the Aboriginal rights already entrenched in the constitution and further recognized by the courts, and integrating Western practices where they wanted to. This, with a view to leaving the Indian Act behind.

The big picture is that for Canada as a whole, reconciliation includes creating space for First Nations ways of doing things, while First Nations peoples, too, are faced with the issues of how to reconcile their traditional cultures with Western social and political values and modern commerce. First Nations are making their choices about which aspects of Western society to adopt and which to reject. They are building their societies by maintaining the histories and cultures they hold valuable, and in some cases maintaining traditional governance structures, while also building up their economies.

In my private business activities – before I had to set them aside in order to rejoin the cabinet in 2003 – I also was respectful of First Nations interests and mindful of their rights. In 2001, a mining company of which I was president sold all its assets, and the board of directors and I decided to research wind power in British Columbia. We had in mind a project in co-operation with First Nations communities. The technical research we had done showed us that the Hecate Strait, which separates Haida Gwaii from the British Columbia mainland, was the only world-class wind resource in the province. Excited by this finding, we applied for and acquired provincial and federal licences, which continue to exist. The idea was to build offshore windmills close to Haida Gwaii.

I discussed our plans with Miles Richardson, a Haida leader whom I knew. He alerted me that the Haida Nation claimed jurisdiction over the strait. Richardson told me that I needed to talk to Guujaaw, who was then president of the Council of the Haida Nation. So, I made an appointment with Guujaaw, then flew into Sandspit, and we met at a coffee shop in Queen Charlotte City. I explained our project. Harnessing wind power would be a boon to the Haida, who are dependent on electricity generated by diesel, which is environmentally unfriendly and expensive. Guujaaw informed me the Haida did not recognize provincial or federal authority over the strait. I replied that in that case, I would also need a licence from the Haida.

The idea that they would issue a licence was not something they'd thought about, but he got back to me later and said yes, we will give you a licence, but you will have to let us know what you are looking for it to say. We went with a format that was basically a copy of our provincial licence, which authorized us to go ahead with the design and planning of the wind farm. His council approved it. By requesting a licence, we were recognizing their title.

We had named the company NaiKun, to honour the Haida. This was their term for Rose Spit, a geographic feature on the northeast corner of the northern island, that tradition had it was the place where the first people came out of the clam shell.[5] Frankly, it had not occurred to me to consult them about the name of the company, and I was told they were not entirely comfortable with my using it, as it was a sacred name. I apologized and asked whether they wanted us to change the name. They agreed to let it stand because part of the agreement was to give them a 50 per cent interest in the management company. Later, however, the name was changed to Oceanic Wind.

The company did a lot of work in 2002–03, but once I was appointed to the cabinet in December 2003, I had to resign from the company, and thus the project. I turned it over to people who had invested in it, in particular Mike Burns, who had previously worked for Premier Bill Bennett. Burns had been Bennett's principal negotiator on the agreement between the federal and provincial governments to set up the operating relationship for Expo 86.

While I no longer have any stake in this project, except as a small shareholder for nostalgic reasons, I'm confident that, given concerns about climate change and the need for decarbonization and reduction of greenhouse gas emissions, it eventually will see the light of day.

When Paul Martin became prime minister in December 2003, one of his most important objectives was to pursue a policy of reconciliation with Indigenous Peoples and to devolve greater management authority to them. Martin made his perspectives and intentions clear in his government's first Throne Speech, delivered on 2 February 2004: "Aboriginal Canadians have not fully shared in our nation's good fortune. While some progress has been made, the conditions in far too many Aboriginal communities can only be described as shameful. This offends our values. It is in our collective interest to turn the corner. And we must start now." The Throne Speech emphasized that the goal was "to see Aboriginal Canadians participating fully in national life, on the basis of historic rights and agreements – with greater economic self-reliance, a better quality of life."

As a tangible sign of Martin's commitment in this area, he not only created a cabinet committee on Aboriginal affairs – up until then, it had been lumped in with other policy areas – but also appointed himself chair, both for symbolic and control reasons. Martin appointed to this committee the ministers most active on social policy issues. I was categorized as one of those when it came to Indigenous affairs, and correctly so. Martin also recognized me as someone who had followed a consistent policy of reconciliation with Indigenous Peoples and had considerable experience in the area, including a long period of service on the Senate's Aboriginal affairs committee. I had the honour of serving as the alternate chair of the cabinet committee when Martin himself was unavailable, which was fairly often, given his many responsibilities.

The committee's time was almost entirely occupied with working toward what came to be known as the Kelowna Accord. This was a plan that aimed to close the gap in the quality of life between Indigenous people and other Canadians. In particular, its objectives were to significantly reduce poverty and bring advances in education, health, housing, and access to clean water for Indigenous people. Goals included eliminating the gap in high school graduation rates between Indigenous people and others, reducing infant mortality and youth suicides, and building more housing and infrastructure. If the First Nations Fiscal and Statistical Management Act was about financial capacity-building, Kelowna was about social and self-governmental capacity-building, given that the various Indigenous communities were to manage these programs, while being accountable to governments for how the money was spent and for achieving measurable results. It was to have been another step away from the Indian Act.

The cabinet committee was involved in overseeing the long consultative process that led to the accord: interactions with First Nations and the other Indigenous Peoples, assessing progress in coming to agreements, dealing with the provinces, and so on. Our communications with First Nations were not exclusively with the Assembly of First Nations, although its Grand Chief Phil Fontaine was highly involved. I came to know him well during this period and appreciated his positive contribution. We also were consulting the chiefs in various provinces. We understood that they had the real power, whereas the Assembly of First Nations was mainly an advocacy group.

We recruited many people for membership in committee studies: how to do housing, how to do education, how to do health, and so on. We asked them, How should we approach those things? Do you agree these are the areas? If these are the areas, what are your priorities? Our Indigenous partners accepted the approach very quickly. Another person with whom I worked closely during this period was Grand Chief Ed John of the British Columbia First Nations Summit. His leadership in the co-ordination of policy development among BC First Nations has strengthened their negotiating effectiveness.

The process leading to the Kelowna Accord was run full-time by a secretariat in the PCO, headed by John Watson. He had been brought to Ottawa from his post as director general of the Aboriginal affairs regional office in Vancouver. I had been in contact with Watson on many files over the years and knew him to be highly capable. His contribution to the work of the committee was outstanding.

Political impetus came from Martin, of course, but also his Indian affairs ministers, Andy Mitchell, who served for the first few months, and then Andy Scott, who was named to the post in the cabinet shuffle that followed the 2004 election. Scott was passionate about moving forward. He was able to get his administrative-minded department excited that reform was a real possibility, and the way to go was to allow First Nations more authority and provide more resources, rather than focusing steadily on constitutional issues. Another minister who made a major contribution to the process was Ethel Blondin-Andrew, herself a Sahtu Dene from the Northwest Territories, who was minister of state for children and youth.

The process culminated in a meeting in Kelowna held on 24–25 November 2005, which brought together the prime minister, all the premiers and territorial leaders, and several Indigenous leaders. The miracle was that there was an agreement not only among First Nations but also with the provinces. British Columbia premier Gordon Campbell had played the leading role in bringing the provinces all on board, having travelled the country to meet with his counterparts. Campbell had pivoted from being an adversary of First Nations aspirations in his opposition to the Nisga'a Final Agreement to a crucial ally a few years later. The $5.1 billion the federal government laid on the table, an amount to be spent over five years, also provided no small incentive for concluding an agreement.

As Martin said at the time, the Kelowna Accord was "an unprecedented step forward." If implemented, it would have brought enormous and tangible benefits to Indigenous people and become a significant advance in the process of reconciliation.

However, as the first ministers and Indigenous leaders met in Kelowna that Thursday and Friday, all were aware that a confidence vote was expected in the House of Commons the following Monday, and the minority government was about to be defeated. Because of that situation, I was not able to travel to Kelowna, a significant disappointment to me. But my own work on the accord was done, and it was my duty as Leader of the Government in the Senate to remain in Ottawa to lead the end-of-session scramble to see to the passage of legislation that otherwise would have died on the Order Paper. We passed about a dozen bills that day, including two of special interest to First Nations: the First Nations Commercial and Industrial Development Act and the First Nations Oil and Gas and Moneys Management Act.

The election that followed on 23 January 2006 brought to power the Conservative government of Stephen Harper. During the campaign, it had been clear that reconciliation was not among Conservative priorities. When Harper's government presented its first budget that spring, funding for investments in the welfare and future of Indigenous Peoples fell far short of what had been set out in the accord. Harper's failure to implement the Kelowna Accord dealt a real setback to the process of reconciliation. We had been hopeful at first that his appointment of Jim Prentice as Indian affairs minister was a sign his government would move forward. I had come to know Prentice some years earlier, before he had entered politics, when he had served on the Indian Claims Commission of Canada, a federal panel dealing with land claims. I knew him to have a progressive attitude. We would talk occasionally about the frustrations that First Nations experienced with the process of proving claims. The claims the commission dealt with concerned the restoration of lands that belonged to treaty-negotiated reserves but had been taken arbitrarily by settlers or by municipalities. The commission was there to recommend either the restoration of lands or compensation. It did not have the power to make decisions. Its recommendations were forwarded to the government for action. I remember discussing with Prentice how frustrating it was that the government would only agree to a handful of settlements a year, when dozens of claims were pending. I can only imagine Prentice was disappointed with his government's decision on the Kelowna Accord.

Certainly, it was a deep and bitter disappointment to me.

As for Martin, the Kelowna setback did not deter him from moving forward at a personal level. Since leaving politics, he has maintained a strong focus on Indigenous initiatives and has created a private foundation to continue this work.

Once my own parliamentary life was behind me and I was back in Vancouver, I continued my involvement with First Nations projects and people. At the same time, I maintained an active focus on China.

One project that brought those interests together was the initiative of the BC First Nations Summit to erect a totem pole in Beichuan, in China's Sichuan province. Beichuan had been the site of a devastating earthquake in 2008. The summit wanted to send a message of healing and recovery to the Qiang minority, upon whom the disaster had had a severe impact. The pole was erected at the new city of Beichuan in the fall of 2011 in the presence of Grand Chief Ed John, National Chief Shawn Atleo, Grand Chief Stewart Phillip, Joan Phillip, Dave Porter, Bob Chamberlin, and other leading members of First Nations from Canada and representatives from the Qiang minority. The year prior to the raising of the pole in Beichuan, Chinese president Hu Jintao stated, "I want to thank the Chief for the gift of the totem pole to the Qiang people. This is a symbolic and generous gesture which is very much appreciated. It helps to build understanding between our peoples." First Nations have shown they are important diplomats for developing constructive Canada-China relations.

Paul Blom had contacted me, on behalf of the BC First Nations Energy and Mining Council, about whether I could assist in finding federal support, particularly in transporting the pole to its destination in China. This support was obtained. Blom remains a key adviser to the leadership of the BC First Nations on public policy and business issues. Given my long-standing interest in relations with China, I was delighted to discover that Blom had spent time in Taiwan studying the language and culture, and has lived and worked in China for many years. He has taken on a directorship at CCBC and advocates for First Nations relations with China. This brought us to consider how we could help develop good business relations between Chinese investors in BC projects involving the First Nations. There were some early problems where Chinese investors believed that federal and/or provincial government approval was all they needed. Creating knowledge of the constitutional rights of First Nations and the need for their consent and participation was essential for good relations and successful outcomes.

In British Columbia and many other parts of Canada today, it is common practice at public meetings to begin with a land acknowledgement. This reminder that there were people who were here for millennia before the settlers arrived indicates a very welcome attitude toward reconciliation. Still under way, however, is the process of fully accepting Indigenous Peoples as equal participants in Canadian society and as communities with rights, needs and wants, identities and cultures.

The positive role of section 35 of the Constitution in helping to change public attitudes should not be underestimated. It moved reconciliation to the courts from the legislatures, a by-product of which was to increase public respect for the results of the process, given that the public tends to have greater respect for judges than for politicians. In the courts, Indigenous Peoples have been able to apply section 35 in a way that they would never have been allowed to leverage their direct relationship with a British Crown largely indifferent to their situation. Eventually, this encouraged negotiation rather than litigation; First Nations could negotiate on the basis of Supreme Court–recognized rights, as affirmed in various court decisions. Moving reconciliation to the courts was also beneficial from the government perspective: it was helpful for the political leadership that the public now understood it was not just acting in a discretionary way in its relationships toward Indigenous Peoples but had legal obligations to respect.

We have reached the stage where the courts have essentially laid out the legal framework. What has to be done now in Canadian society is for rational and pragmatic processes to guide the negotiations between the parties in specific instances of dispute. I see us moving now to negotiate place by place, issue by issue, the more permanent recognition of rights on all sides.

Various other factors softened public opinion and eroded old prejudices, bringing about a more generous attitude toward Indigenous issues and reconciliation. I believe the work of the Royal Commission on Aboriginal Peoples, headed by Georges Erasmus and René Dussault, which held hearings in the early 1990s and then issued a multi-volume report in 1996, had a significant impact, albeit not one that could be measured right away. Twenty years later, the Truth and Reconciliation Commission, chaired by Murray Sinclair, further sensitized Canadians to the experiences and continuing suffering of Indigenous people.

The growing political savvy and communications skills of Indigenous leaders also helped attitudes evolve, as did the economic and political successes of First Nations like the Musqueam, Squamish, Ktunaxa, Westbank, and Haida, to name a few of the British Columbia nations with which I am most familiar. The James Bay Cree and the Inuit of Nunavik are two other examples that come to mind.

I watched a strong tradition grow, from Art Laing to Paul Martin, to remediate the way in which Canada dealt with Indigenous people and Peoples. Has Canadian society truly abandoned the assimilationist attitudes of the past? Such attitudes undeniably can still be found, but they no longer are driving federal policy. Challenges will continue to be posed by local conflicts that occur as Indigenous communities, having had their right and entitlement acknowledged by the courts, seek to act on their rights and build their own economic capacities. Non-Indigenous neighbours or competitors can be hostile to these efforts when they see their own interests as negatively affected. For reconciliation to advance, it is important that Indigenous people exercise their rights in a spirit of fairness toward other members of the Canadian family. At the same time, it is important that non-Indigenous people express their concerns and advocate for their own interests from a place of respect and historical awareness.

Progress has been made in the recognition of the rights of Indigenous Peoples and toward reconciliation with Canada and other Canadians. I recognize that many problems remain unresolved, but I am optimistic that a better future awaits.

13 Travels with Pierre

PIERRE TRUDEAU had an insatiable appetite for travel. As a young man, he had backpacked through Eastern Europe, the Middle East, and Asia. As prime minister, he had the opportunity to travel widely for international meetings and state visits. Trudeau enjoyed seeing new locales and meeting people from different societies. His focus was always on what made a particular society tick. His conversations were never about the weather or any other small talk. Rather, they were about the challenges those societies faced and how these were managed. For Trudeau, travel had a serious purpose.

After his retirement from politics in 1984, travelling to new places was a priority. He set himself the objective of visiting every continent and sites of particular geographical or cultural importance. In 1986, he went to the Soviet Union for a journey on the Trans-Siberian Railway, accompanied by Sen. Leo Kolber, Kolber's wife, Sandra, and some others from Montreal.

In that period, I was visiting Montreal three or four times a year to see my daughter Edie, and I would arrange to see Trudeau whenever I was there. We would have lunch, or sometimes breakfast, at the Ritz-Carlton. Occasionally, we would instead meet in his office at the Heenan Blaikie law firm. We would discuss the political issues of the day and our own recent activities. We also would talk about our previous travels and the places we hoped to visit in the future. He took a particular interest in a trip Natalie and I had made to the remote Himalayan nation of Bhutan in July 1981 with Maurice Strong. At the time, the country was closed to most visitors. Strong and his wife, Hanne, had been invited there by the Bhutanese foreign minister because of his development work with the United Nations and were told they could bring one other couple with them. We had the opportunity to see a truly fascinating country and meet its young king, Jigme Singye Wangchuck, as well as visit India en route.

In one such discussion, Trudeau told me that he and the Kolbers were thinking of travelling along the land-based Silk Road route from Pakistan to China, and asked whether Natalie and I would be interested in joining them. I chatted with Leo Kolber and talked it over with Natalie. We were in. Both Trudeau and Kolber asked me to take on the organizational arrangements, partly because I had a reputation as a good organizer – once a chief of staff, always a chief of staff – and partly because I had many good connections in China.

Our Silk Road trip in the fall of 1987 was the first of four Natalie and I would take with Trudeau. Although Trudeau was by then a private citizen, he remained an international celebrity, and his name opened many doors. Travelling with him allowed us to meet prominent people and visit remote areas closed to ordinary tourists. Our accommodations ranged from luxurious to primitive. We visited steamy jungles and bone-dry deserts; we were received by national leaders in capital cities and by community leaders in remote villages. Wherever we went, whomever we talked to, the goal was to learn, experience something new. We had no particular political agenda. We deliberately kept a low profile, and our trips rarely resulted in press coverage.

Our travels also gave me a chance to deepen my understanding of the complex prime minister with whom I had worked and provided a few opportunities for some reflective conversations about past events. These trips put our relationship on a different level. As a deputy minister, as principal secretary, and a member of his cabinet, I had always addressed him as "prime minister," and he had called me "Jack." When we began travelling together, he invited me to call him "Pierre."

When I took on the organization of the Silk Road trip, I told Trudeau that I planned to use his name with the embassies of Pakistan and China in order to make arrangements. We would need the help and/or permission of both governments to travel through some of the remote border areas, where either security was an issue or tourists were prohibited, or both.

I noted that he would therefore be obliged to meet heads of government or other important people as part of the tour. At that time, Pakistan was led by a dictator, President Muhammad Zia-ul-Haq, who had come to power in a military coup a decade earlier. Trudeau told me to go ahead.

I told the Pakistani ambassador that Pierre Trudeau would like to visit his country to travel the Karakoram Highway. That was one of the traditional Silk Road routes on which traders travelled between China and Europe. I sought his recommendations and his government's assistance in the difficult areas we would be going through. I worked with the Chinese ambassador, Zhang Wenpu, with respect to the Chinese part of the route and suggested to him that when in Beijing we would like to meet with all the Chinese ambassadors to Canada in the Trudeau period.

On 21 September 1987, we arrived in Islamabad. There were six of us: Trudeau, Natalie and I, Sandra and Leo Kolber and their adult son Jonathan. Upon arrival, we were welcomed by senior Pakistani government officials, ushered into cars on the tarmac, and driven to our hotel. We were told Zia would be receiving us for a private dinner that evening at the presidential palace. As it turned out, the men in our group dined with Zia, while the women dined separately with his wife. After dinner, we enjoyed a traditional performance by soldiers on horseback on the lawn of the presidential palace. The president asked Trudeau if he could have a private conversation with him. He agreed, and it went on a little over an hour. I learned very little about what passed between them.

Zia found some value in hosting us, and he could not have been more hospitable. For obvious reasons, including the execution of Prime Minister Zulfikar Ali Bhutto after dubious legal proceedings, Zia did not have a great reputation in the West, so meeting with a well-known Western statesman was of interest to him. As well, we were going to be heading into contested territory, the former princely state of Jammu and Kashmir, and while Trudeau at this point was a private citizen and not in any way a representative of the Canadian government, the Pakistanis might have tried to suggest this was a Canadian endorsement of Pakistan's claim. The area has been the subject of an ongoing dispute – and a series of wars – between Pakistan and India since partition in 1947. The two countries are separated by a "Line of Control" that goes through the territory, but not an internationally recognized border.

I raised this history with Trudeau when I was organizing the trip, but he brushed off any concern that his presence in the area would be politically or legally problematic, given that he no longer held any government position.[1] I also briefed external affairs before we left. As it turned out, there was no overt attempt by Zia or the Pakistanis to claim any political recognition by virtue of Pierre's trip. As for us, while a trip to Pakistan at that time might not have been politically acceptable to many people in Western countries, we were not there to endorse Zia but to experience and learn about his country.

For our journey northward to the Chinese border, we were entrusted to a military engineering unit, led by a general. We travelled in army jeeps. They had offered to fly us by helicopter, but Pierre wanted to see things from the ground. We had allotted ourselves a few days to reach the border – the distance from Islamabad by road is about 750 kilometres – so did not need to rush, although our military escorts kept us on schedule. Arrangements had been made for the Chinese to pick us up at a specified time, and punctuality was essential. We were able to take in the spectacular scenery as well as the local sights and sounds, including a polo match using a sheep's head as a ball, in Gilgit, the capital of the Gilgit-Baltistan area. This hadn't been arranged for us, and we were the only foreigners present. It was just an ordinary market day.

One of the places we wanted to see was the Hunza Valley, which is famous not only for its apricots but also as the ancestral home of a substantial community of Ismaili Muslims, whose spiritual leader is the Aga Khan IV, a long-time friend of Trudeau. We went to see an agricultural station there. On our way north from the Hunza Valley, we received word that the road ahead was flooded and impassable. Heavy rains had triggered a rockslide, creating a dam behind which a newly formed lake stretched across the highway. The general offered to summon helicopters to take us across. Trudeau was adamant that he didn't want to travel by helicopter, and asked whether there was another option. We were told that the army engineers could build a raft to take our jeeps across. And that is what they did. By the time we got there, the raft was ready. It felt a bit precarious, but it did the job.

When we arrived at the opposite end of that lake, there was a van stuck there. Unbelievably, it was full of French-Canadian tourists, about a dozen of them, who had been visiting further north and were travelling back to Islamabad. Of course, they immediately recognized Pierre, and started calling his name. They were excited to see him and also thrilled at the prospect of crossing the lake on the raft that had been assembled for us. Pierre stopped to chat with them for about twenty minutes. I was occupied with discussing arrangements with our escorts, so didn't hear the conversation. But when we were on our way again, I asked him, "Were there any separatists there?" He replied, "No doubt, but they were all very polite."

Our last stop in Pakistan was a military outpost perhaps a kilometre or two from the border, where we stayed overnight. All I remember about the accommodations is that the beds were tiny (I am six feet tall and of medium build) and we slept in our clothes, as indeed we did most of the time on that part of the trip. As we were having breakfast, I was surprised to see the Chinese, with whom we would continue our journey, drive up in their jeeps. I had expected we would be meeting them right at the border. I asked the Pakistani general whether that was normal. He said it was perfectly normal, relations were good and the two sides met at the outpost all the time. (There was no station on the Chinese side.) The Chinese were military personnel, and they included a physician – to make sure that we were doing okay with the altitude, which was about 15,000 feet – and a translator.

When we set out that morning, I noticed Pierre was wearing a T-shirt that said K2. I asked him, "What's K2?" He replied, "You'll find out." I did. At 28,250 feet, K2 is the world's second-highest mountain, and we could see it in the distance when we crossed into China's Xinjiang province through the Khunjerab Pass. Once we were on the Chinese side, we were not on paved roads, just trails. At one point, we were on a mountain road that was barely wide enough for the jeeps, with a precipice on one side.

Our first overnight stop was in Tashkurgan, an oasis and ancient stop on the Silk Road route. The place where we stayed had no plumbing, and the outhouses had probably been there since Marco Polo's day. The men's outhouse was one great big shed with more than a dozen holes. There was no privacy. On the plus side, the local community had organized a welcome banquet for us, followed by traditional dancing.

We travelled all the next day, with the Pamir Mountain range to our left. The scenery was spectacular. We ended up in Kashgar, again staying in a hotel that lacked fully functional plumbing and electricity. I understand that today, modern hotels are available there. In 1987, things looked very much as they would have looked in 1887 or 1787. We saw relatively few members of China's predominant Han group. The majority of the local people were Uyghurs, Muslims who were members of a Turkic ethnic minority. They were dressed in the traditional attire of the "stans," and had carts pulled by horses or donkeys. Theirs was a traditional agrarian society; they are culturally quite different from the Han.

The big experience was the Kashgar Sunday market, and it was unbelievable: acres and acres and acres of anything you could imagine, all manner of food, clothing, furs, and primitive electronic appliances. We had pleasant visits to several mosques and also had a chance to talk with some Uyghurs who had a modern education. There was no sense, in that very distant time, of the kinds of events that were to take place later.[2]

From Kashgar, we flew to Urumqi, a much larger city that is the capital of Xinjiang. We stayed there overnight, and then flew to Beijing. On that flight, it seemed there were more Hami melons than people. The melons, grown in the region, are the most delicious I have ever tasted. They are somewhat like cantaloupes, but oblong and with a paler yellow-orange flesh, and a lighter taste. It seemed each of the passengers had several of the melons in mesh bags.

In Beijing that evening, there was a banquet at the Great Hall of the People in Pierre's honour, and among those present were all China's former ambassadors to Canada, whom Pierre knew, of course. There were many speeches and marvellous discussions about Canada-China relations, Canada's role in assisting China to take its place in international organizations, and how appreciative they were. It was sort of a big thank you for the role he had played. The host of the evening was China's first ambassador to Canada, Huang Hua, also a major party figure. From his Canadian post, he became Communist China's first ambassador to the United Nations and after that, China's foreign minister.

Pierre went off to see Deng Xiaoping on his own, a meeting that had been arranged by the Chinese side. None of the rest of us accompanied him. Pierre was very discreet about his meetings with heads of state or other powerful people, but I was able to persuade him to give me his impression of Deng. The one point Pierre made to me was that Deng was focused on building the Chinese economy and engaging the entrepreneurial passions of the people. Deng emphasized that the policy objective was to create a society whose security and stability could not be threatened. Without a modern economy, China would remain weak and dependent.

From there we flew to Chongqing, in order to take a cruise down the Yangtze River. This was before the construction of the Three Gorges Dam. We spent three days on the boat, getting off here and there, seeing villages that hadn't changed in hundreds, if not thousands of years, some of which were going to be flooded when the dams were built.

It was a lovely boat ride, but I was preoccupied. I was busy writing the speech that I was to deliver at the University of East Asia in Macao, where Pierre and I were to be awarded honorary doctorates. It was to be a major policy statement about Canada-China relations. Pierre had agreed to accept the doctorate, but wanted me to be the one to make the speech. I did discuss key points with him. The boat took us to Yichang, and from there we continued on a chartered airplane, a Second World War–vintage DC-3, to Guangzhou for a short visit, and then to Hong Kong.

Pierre was incredibly pleased with the trip. We all were.

After the success of our Silk Road travels, the consensus was that we should plan another trip. Pierre expressed a strong interest in going to South America and Central America. Leo Kolber and I discussed it, and I expressed concern about the complications of arranging internal travel. There were very few, if any, commercial routes we could take to follow our itinerary and the time that would be added would be considerable. Kolber said that he would contribute the use of a private airplane, which he did.

Our trip began in early February 1989, and our first stop was Belém, the capital of the Brazilian state of Pará, where we were received by the state officials, including the governor. The city is at the mouth of the

Amazon River and our interest was essentially to be briefed on the Amazon region and the country's environmental measures to protect the Amazon rainforest as the lungs of the world. There were concerns even at that time about deforestation, the burning down of trees by illegal settlers clearing the land. There were also concerns about illegal mining by people who were going into Indigenous lands reserved under Brazilian law and just ignoring the laws, ignoring the Indigenous people, and mining using cyanide for leeching the rock. The cyanide is highly toxic, poisoning both land and water, with destructive effects on both people living downstream and aquatic life. We saw several signs of dead fish and amphibians. We wanted briefings on how that was happening, and why the government only haphazardly interceded.

The Brazilians were very much on the defensive in terms of their environmental stewardship but also their societal stewardship, and that sensitivity expressed itself in many ways during our visit. During a conversation in Belém with the senior staff of an organization there, I asked whether it would be possible for foreign money to be invested in environmental programs, to take over an area and manage it environmentally, for example. I said I thought quite a bit of money could be raised in the West for this purpose, because of concerns and a realization of the importance to the world of the Amazon. The answer was, essentially, no thank you, we'll look after our own interests. This was at the very beginning of the trip, and it was said rather sharply. Perhaps they thought we were coming with a superior attitude, to tell them what to do, although we didn't have that attitude at all. They harboured a deep resistance and antagonism particularly toward the Americans. I had scratched that sensitivity very thinly, and the reaction had been firm. So that type of comment was not repeated by anyone during the trip; we just observed the culture and society, rather than discussing it or debating it.

From there, we flew down to Rio de Janeiro. Experiencing the city's famous carnival was high on our agenda. The Canadian ambassador, John Bell, had arranged seats for us in one of the permanent viewing booths that line the main street where the famous parade takes place. It was quite an exciting evening. It was also a time when Pierre became the subject of international media coverage. In the viewing stands next to us was a very attractive woman, a model. Somehow Pierre struck up a conversation with her, and she came over to our booth where the two of them danced to the carnival samba music. A photo ended up in several Canadian newspapers. I don't think Pierre minded that at all. I think he recognized it might be a news story of a kind that would show him in a light he would favour, seventy years old and still interesting to women. This was the provocative Pierre who loved to defy social convention, who slid down a banister, who pirouetted behind the queen, who wore a Spanish cape to a CFL football game. For the record, he didn't go anywhere with her. He came back to the hotel with the rest of us.

From Rio, John Bell had arranged for us to see a big iron mining operation in the interior, the Vale Mine site. And then we went to Manaus, the capital of Amazonas state, which became our base for exploring the Amazon region. The city was very much a Portuguese community that had been implanted in the middle of the Amazon forest. Its European opera house was internationally famous.

From Manaus, we rode in a motorized canoe for about two hours up a tributary of the Amazon and visited an illegal gold mining operation. We saw how people were using shovels and tools to cut into the bank of a river. Officials had arranged for us to visit the site, to see what they were doing. This may sound paradoxical, but while the operation was illegal, it was tolerated. It was understood that poverty was at the base of illegal economic activities, and the government took a pragmatic approach, recognizing people had to make a living somehow, that in the absence of social programs and without modern employment skills, people would resort to whatever measures they could. These activities did environmental damage, but it was an acceptable cost, in their thinking.

Another excursion from Manaus was by air, to Boa Vista, not far from the border with Venezuela. From the airport, we were driven part of the way and then we walked for a couple of hours to visit a Yanomami village. These were Indigenous people who had made little adaptation to Western society. They wore a mix of traditional and Western clothes. We visited their straw huts and through translators chatted with some of the male elders.

From Manaus, we flew west to visit the Galapagos Islands, which are part of Ecuador. We were impressed by the care the Ecuadorean government was taking to preserve the natural beauty and the animal and plant life. Lima, the capital of Peru, was our next stop, to prepare for Bolivia, where we met President Víctor Paz Estenssoro and several ministers. We discussed the challenges facing their country, including the dichotomy in their society between the Indigenous people and those of European origin. Pierre wanted to see Lake Titicaca, one of the highest lakes in the world, which straddles the Bolivia-Peru border. It was one more experience to check off his list. We rented reed boats and paddled around.

Our next destination was San Jose, Costa Rica. Flying at about 35,000 feet over Panama, we were able to see the whole of that country, with the Pacific Ocean on one side and the Atlantic on the other. It was an amazing sight. When we were planning the trip, I had suggested we stop in Panama, but Trudeau hadn't been interested. He saw it as merely an American colony. Our purpose in Costa Rica was to meet with President Óscar Arias, who two years previously had won the Nobel Peace Prize for his work in ending armed conflicts that had been under way in Central America at that time. Our talks with Arias revolved around the politics of Central America and some of the work he was doing, although they also touched on other international issues. He gave us a backgrounder on Daniel Ortega and life in Nicaragua, our next stop.

Ortega's image at that time was much better than it is today. He was a revolutionary from the left who had overthrown a corrupt dictatorship. Trudeau was very interested in Ortega, trying to understand who he was and what he was trying to accomplish. We didn't stay in Nicaragua long, just for the day. Then we headed home, via Miami. I had recommended a stop in Mexico, but Pierre declined. He had been there a few times as prime minister, and his focus was seeing places that were new to him.

I came away with a better understanding of the political and social realities in South and Central America, of their challenges and their attitudes, particularly toward the United States. Our trip came just as I was beginning my involvement with Mexico – about three months after the founding of the NAMI – and it did enhance considerably my starting point for understanding the structure of Mexican society. The social, political, and economic profiles of the countries we visited were not dissimilar. Mexico's political organization, however, was stronger and more stable than that of the other countries in the region, which, to varying degrees, with the exception of Costa Rica, had all suffered from the caudillo factor.[3]

When talking to government officials in Bolivia about their society and economy, little did I know that my mining interests after finally leaving Ottawa would focus so significantly on that country's economic aspirations.

After retiring from the Senate and returning to Vancouver and private life, my fascination with mining and the people who risk their talents and their capital to discover new resources found a happy relationship with Dr Rui Feng. Born in China, he obtained his PhD in geological sciences from the University of Saskatchewan. Feng went on to build a number of companies based on his passion for discovery. In 2002, he discovered the Jinshan Gold's csh gold mine in China. This led to his founding of Silvercorp in 2003, a Canadian mining company that acquired and developed a series of silver properties in China and is China's leading silver producer.

With the Silvercorp success in China behind him, Feng had Silvercorp organize a subsidiary company, New Pacific Metals, to carry out exploration and development opportunities in Canada and elsewhere in the Western Hemisphere. In early 2008, I met Feng, and after some discussion I agreed to join New Pacific as a director and as non-executive chair of the board of directors. In the years since, I have admired the professionalism, integrity, and mine-finding skills of Feng and not least his business knowledge and entrepreneurial talents. As I write this, he has again made what is being called a world-class discovery. Leading New Pacific to Bolivia, he has under exploration a potential high-grade silver property.

At another of our lunches at the Ritz-Carlton, Pierre asked me whether I was interested in continuing to travel, even though the Kolbers were no longer in a position to join us because Sandra was suffering from serious health issues. I said, yes, that Natalie and I would look forward to another trip.

Africa, more specifically South Africa, was next on Pierre's agenda. Momentous changes were under way there. An end to apartheid – South Africa's repugnant doctrine of racial classification and separation, based on a belief in white supremacy – was around the corner, but whether that change would occur without large-scale violence was still in question. Pierre was interested to engage with key people in South African society to gain a better understanding of where things were heading. As well, he wanted to visit the southern tip of the continent, to see the point where the Atlantic and Indian Oceans meet. On all our trips, one major focus was visiting geographically and culturally important places in order to check them off what some might call a bucket list, though Pierre would never have used that term.

We met in London and flew to Cape Town in March 1992. There were four of us: myself, Natalie, Pierre, and Nancy Southam, a good friend of Trudeau and member of his social circle in Montreal. Our visit coincided with a particularly dynamic and fluid period in South Africa. While we were there, the country held a referendum in which white voters authorized the government to continue the reform process that would lead to the negotiation of a new constitution, one that would bring about the end of apartheid and rule by the white minority.

Especially from Vancouver, it was a long journey, and we spent a few days in Cape Town adjusting to the time change and doing some touristy things, like seeing Table Mountain and going out on a sailboat. We rented a car and drove to Cape Agulhas, which is actually the southernmost point – not the Cape of Good Hope. Whenever we travelled by car, Pierre did the majority of the driving. He loved to drive, insisting that we drive rather than fly to Johannesburg, despite our having been advised of security risks. We arrived without incident.

Pierre, of course, was not an ordinary tourist. He was a distinguished visitor, and the Canadian embassy in Johannesburg, led by Ambassador Christopher Westdal, helped us with our itinerary and arrangements and set up meetings for us with prominent South Africans. Our first visit in Johannesburg was with Helen Suzman, at whose home we had lunch. Suzman had served in the South African Parliament for thirty-six years, representing an opposition party, and she had consistently opposed apartheid. Known both for her principles and her wit, she had been a thorn in the side of the governing white supremacist National Party, a Jewish woman tenaciously and courageously standing her ground as she was subjected to all manner of misogynistic and anti-Semitic abuse. By the time we met her, she had retired from Parliament. I had thought she would be the ideal person to provide us with an initial overview before we met all the important active players, and we were not disappointed. She discussed with us the problems of reconciliation and her opinion of Nelson Mandela – her impression of him was very positive – and the African National Congress (ANC) that he led, which was not nearly so positive.

We had the pleasure of meeting with Mandela and Walter Sisulu, another prominent ANC official, at the party's offices. By this point, Mandela had been free for more than a year, after his long imprisonment on Robben Island. At the time, there was considerable violence, perpetrated both by the state and the ANC. Mandela knew we would be meeting with President F.W. de Klerk a day later, and he asked Trudeau to tell de Klerk to call off the violence and the ANC would do the same. Mandela asked Trudeau to convince de Klerk that he sought reconciliation and would oppose the forces within the ANC that sought a violent accounting.

I spent nearly two hours listening to their exchanges. These touched on world issues but mostly were about the history of the ANC and the contemporary struggle with the de Klerk regime. That encounter with Mandela impressed me greatly. He was a man of deep insight into the psychology of his nation and its peoples and committed to reconciliation as the only way to raise the standard of living of the Black communities. He believed democracy was the best system for delivering on his ideal of equality for all. He expressed thanks to Canadians for showing what a multicultural society could achieve and for Canada's role in opposing apartheid. It was the Diefenbaker and Mulroney governments that had led the way in this respect. He also recalled his visit to Ottawa in mid-1990, only months after his release from prison, and the warm welcome he received.

Trudeau was guarded in his conversation with Mandela, however, and disappointed him in refusing to speak out publicly against the government's fomenting violence against the ANC and in favour of a more rapid transition to majority rule. As a retired politician, Trudeau explained that he felt it was not appropriate for him to engage publicly on the issues, that Canadian policy on South Africa was a matter for the current

Brian Mulroney government. Mandela accepted that, but with a tone of disappointment. It was clear he expected more help from Trudeau than he got. But I understood Trudeau's caution completely.

At the meeting with de Klerk that followed, the South African president asked us what Mandela had said. Trudeau conveyed Mandela's messages. De Klerk said he understood, but it wasn't so easy to act on. He said he was moving toward an offer for a transitional constitution and an elected parliament. However, he wasn't offering any immediate say in the government, a position unacceptable to Mandela and the ANC as far less than their political power required.

De Klerk showed a very respectful attitude toward Trudeau. He said he appreciated the visit and that Trudeau had come to learn and was willing to hear his point of view. He expressed the hope that Trudeau, when he returned to Canada or had meetings with other retired world leaders, would show patience and concern for the issues of transition. De Klerk was aware that Trudeau was a member of a group of former world leaders called the InterAction Council.

We had the opportunity to meet another ANC leader, Cyril Ramaphosa. At the time, he was the party's secretary general. In 2018, he would become South Africa's president. Ramaphosa had not been available for our meeting with Mandela, so we invited him to dinner at one of Johannesburg's upscale restaurants. Mandela had told us Ramaphosa would be playing an important role, both at that time and into the future, and when we met him, I could see why. His insight and broad perspective were clearly communicated in the discussions, which among other things centred on how to foster the development of a Black entrepreneurial class. We had an exchange of views on how to bring individuals from the Black communities onto boards of directors to gain experience and into management, including accounting and legal roles, and in particular, how to build equity behind Black entrepreneurs. One of the issues Ramaphosa raised was the importance of Black business people becoming equity partners with white business people, and, in answer to a question, he argued that equity should be funded by white businesses by means of loans to purchase equity. I found the discussion fascinating, but I'm not sure Trudeau, who was less interested in business than the political issues, was as focused on it. During our meal, another diner approached our table. It was famous English entrepreneur Richard Branson. He had recognized Pierre and came over to introduce himself.

We also met with Archbishop Desmond Tutu, the leader of the Anglican Church in South Africa, a man of great energy who welcomed us warmly. Tutu was an ardent supporter of Mandela (although they sometimes had differences) and critical of the de Klerk regime and its predecessors. He told us he believed that South Africa was well on the way to its next stage in resolving the relationship between the majority Black communities and the minority white communities. (Tutu would go on to lead South Africa's Truth and Reconciliation Commission.) Pierre was more animated in his discussion with Tutu than he had been with either Mandela or de Klerk. Trudeau asked Tutu about how influential Christianity could be in bringing about reconciliation among South Africans. After that meeting, Natalie and Trudeau conversed over dinner about the concept of justice in Western philosophy.

Near the end of our visit, we attended a dinner at the home of Julian Ogilvie Thompson, chair of De Beers diamonds. Among the other guests were some important members of the white business elite. By and large, they had accepted that changes were taking place. They had a certain confidence in Mandela, but much less confidence in other ANC leaders. The conversation focused on what would happen after Mandela, and whether South Africa would be a stable place for business. They were happy about the prospect of the end of international economic sanctions. Looking ahead, one guest suggested South Africa would need a robust stock exchange for venture capital companies in order to stimulate small- and medium-sized businesses. I said we had such a venture capital exchange in my hometown, Vancouver. I was asked how that worked. What they probably didn't know was that the Vancouver Stock Exchange did not have a great reputation. I replied, "Well, basically, you get the venture, and they keep the capital." Everybody laughed. Then Pierre said to me, "I've never heard you say that before, that's very interesting." He was laughing, too.

One excursion that was Trudeau's initiative, not the embassy's, was our trip to a bar in Soweto, the biggest Black suburb, or township, of Johannesburg. Under apartheid, most Blacks were not permitted to live in the city itself. The embassy wasn't keen about the risk, because it was a violent time for both political and economic reasons, but they weren't overly concerned, given that we would be travelling in embassy cars accompanied by security, and everybody was aware we had been received by Mandela and Tutu. The bar we visited was told in advance by the South African security people that we were coming. When we arrived, the bar was nearly full, and the people in it had been screened. Accompanying us was a Canadian journalist, Jonathan Manthorpe, then covering South Africa from his base in Harare. He had got wind of Trudeau's visit and had contacted us at the hotel. He had been hoping to interview him. Trudeau declined the interview but we invited Manthorpe to come along with us to the bar.

Another visit was to the University of the Witwatersrand, where the embassy had arranged, at the request of the faculty of political science and law, a discussion on the Canadian constitution. We met with the faculty members over lunch. They were well aware Trudeau had led constitutional change in Canada. And they knew I was in the Senate, that it was an important part of the Canadian governance system, and had been the subject of much discussion as well. Trudeau gave them a history of patriation, with the Charter of Rights emphasized. There was discussion about the timing for a charter of rights in South Africa. I talked about the role of the Senate and the bicameral system. They were quite familiar with all the issues. There were a lot of good exchanges, and it made for an interesting day.

Having done all the political heavy lifting in Johannesburg, we moved on to Namibia, a neighbouring former German colony that had been run by South Africa, first as a League of Nations mandate and later in defiance of the international community. South Africa had not wanted to give up its control of the abundant mineral resources there, including diamonds. The country had gained its independence only two years before our visit.

Including Namibia in our itinerary had been my idea. My interest in that country had been piqued by conversations I had had in Ottawa with Sam Hanson, a Canadian diplomat who had served there in 1989–90, just as the internationally supervised transition to independence was under way. Sam, originally from Calgary, is the son of my cousin Zelda. He had come back really impressed with Namibia and the people there. He lent me some books on the country, which I found quite fascinating. It turned out to be one of the most exciting parts of the world we visited – and we visited a lot of exciting parts.

In the capital, Windhoek, we had lunch with President Sam Nujoma. He and Trudeau had an open discussion about international affairs. Nujoma told us about the political movement he had led, the South West Africa People's Organisation, and their long struggle to break free of South Africa's rule. While in Windhoek, we also visited the newly established campus of the University of Namibia.

From Windhoek we flew to the Skeleton Coast in a small single-engine plane: the four of us, the pilot, our luggage. The area, in the northwestern part of the country, owes its name to the history of shipwrecks there. The coast was completely desert. Indeed, much of Namibia is desert, the Namib, for which the country is named. We stayed for two nights on the northern part of the coast. Each person had their own little hut, just big enough for a single bed. Our location was not far from the Angolan border. In fact, our guide took us in a rowboat across the river that formed the border so that we could say we had been there. Pierre was pleased to be able to state that he had visited Angola.

Later, we travelled toward the interior to a famous vantage point for seeing elephants. The van brought us to one end of a wide valley and picked us up at the other end, where there was a small oasis. We were told to walk through and assured the elephants would not pose any danger. Indeed, the elephants ignored us completely. It was a spectacular walk. Another area we visited featured "singing sands." We would climb to the top of a huge sand dune and then the four of us would hold hands and run down. The contact of our shoes with the sand produced the singing, groaning sound.

We ended up at a resort in Etosha National Park, after about four days of living either in single huts or tents parked on the desert. This area had more water and vegetation, and there were lots of animals to see. We stayed a day or two, and then the plane picked us up and took us back to Windhoek.

After transiting through South Africa and Kenya, we arrived in Ethiopia, our final stop. This was a country that Pierre was interested in visiting, primarily because he wanted to see its ancient Christian churches and monasteries.

In Addis Ababa, we were received at the presidential palace by President Meles Zenawi, a meeting the Canadian embassy had arranged. He had come to power the previous year, after a civil war had resulted in the overthrow of the Derg, a repressive socialist military junta. Its leader, Mengistu Haile Mariam, had then fled the country. The president discussed with us his country's problems and his government's quest for financial support from foreign governments and agencies. The security situation was still quite unstable, with various conflicts under way. The United Nations had a big presence in Addis, and we also met with UN officials there to talk about their issues and problems, which were profound.

The Hilton hotel we stayed in was in a compound enclosed by a high wire fence and was well protected by local police. At our hotel, we attended a dinner with several English-speaking local people who had international educations, an event set up by the embassy so that we could gain further insights into the country. The surprising feature of the dinner was that we were expected to eat with our hands, using the injera bread to scoop up the stews, as is the Ethiopian practice. So, we washed our hands very carefully, and we had wet towels to wipe our hands constantly at the dinner table. I made a comment to the effect that I understood that this was the traditional practice, but wondered whether in modern times it might be considered unsanitary. The response was, "I don't know where a fork has been, but I know where my hands have been." Touché. We laughed. The food, a lamb stew as I recall it, was delicious.

To see the Christian religious sites, we had to drive into the countryside, which posed security issues. We had about four jeeps provided by the Ethiopian government and military armed guards on each one. At that time in Ethiopia, there were both governmental and nongovernmental toll booths and barriers, and every few kilometres we were stopped by people carrying machine guns. We would stop, there would be a conversation between our head guard and whatever group was manning these roadblocks, and then we would drive on. These sorts of roadblocks are often used to shake down travellers for money, but I never saw any money exchanged.

We visited monasteries and churches at Lake Tana, the famous churches carved of living stone nearby, and also visited churches in Gondar. Pierre chatted through translators with the monks and local people who had come to pray. He was doing what he came to do and seeing what he came to see. It was a very satisfying excursion for him.

My own interest was piqued by similarities I saw, particularly at one church, to Orthodox Jewish synagogues. There was a bimah in the centre of the church, a raised area where the priests stood with what looked like prayer shawls around their shoulders and read from books. I was aware that historically there had been a Jewish population in the area. In the preceding years, many Ethiopian Jews had immigrated to Israel. I asked one of our guides about the Jewish community. He said some had left; he clearly did not want to discuss the subject. I later learned these similarities were not only due to the historic presence of a Jewish community but also the influence of Judaism on the Ethiopian Orthodox Tewahedo Church.

We travelled back to Addis, and then flew to London. Before we went our separate ways, I said to Pierre, "Where next?" He answered, "I'll let you know."

By the time we were in Africa, Pierre and I had more or less had our chats about past events, but after our visit to the University of the Witwatersrand, we reflected further on the constitution. We talked about Michael Pitfield, his work and our admiration for him; the Senate-House committee on the constitution; Trudeau's negotiations on patriation and the constitution with the provinces; and a little about Lévesque and Lougheed. We also reflected on how Margaret Thatcher handled the legislation in the United Kingdom. She had faced a difficult situation in the British Parliament, but she had been supportive of Trudeau's initiative. Trudeau also mentioned how well informed and insightful the queen was about Canadian politics, but he did not disclose what she said. While our discussion did not amend the story as I had known and lived it, a number of details filled in my understanding of what had occurred.

Most of our discussions about the constitution, which also took place during our lunches at the Ritz-Carlton, were those of two lawyers talking about how transferring interpretive power to the Supreme Court of Canada would change the social fabric of the country over time. Patriation and the Charter had launched a process that would move Canada from parliamentary democracy to constitutional democracy, and we considered where that process could and would go. We talked, too, about Bora Laskin, whom Trudeau had appointed chief justice of the Supreme Court of Canada in 1973. I had the impression that Trudeau had consulted Laskin privately on the directions the court might take once the Constitution Act of 1982 had been proclaimed. Unfortunately, Laskin died before the court acted in any significant way on its new responsibilities.

The new chief justice, also appointed by Trudeau, was Brian Dickson, from Manitoba. After Trudeau retired, he began to express some concern about the Dickson court and its interpretation of its role concerning the Charter. Trudeau also famously took exception to the Supreme Court's earlier ruling in the patriation reference. A year before our trip to Africa, Trudeau delivered a harsh attack on that decision in his speech marking the opening of the Bora Laskin Law Library at the University of Toronto. Essentially, Trudeau accused the majority, which found that convention weighed against unilateral patriation, of having manipulated the evidence in order to arrive at the desired political result. Awkwardly, Dickson, who had been part of that majority and was by then retired, was in the audience. Dickson had been upset at the criticism, and I recall asking Trudeau about that. He had no regrets.

I remember raising section 35, the provision entrenching Aboriginal rights. He was well aware that it would enhance the constitutional, legal, and political position of the First Nations in their drive for recognition and a different relationship. He had originally resisted entrenchment because he was wary of entrenching rights that had not yet been defined. Moreover, he did not believe the premiers would agree to patriation on that basis. But he accepted it. He knew that it clarified a legal principle, and that even without it, the courts might have found that rights existed in any event.

Certainly, Trudeau's attitude had evolved from the time of the 1969 white paper, which had proposed to abolish the Indian Act and consider

First Nations people to have the same rights as everybody else. It had been received with shock and anger by First Nations people, who, for all of their unhappiness with the Indian Act, saw the proposal as simply a government effort to abandon its obligations to them and assimilate them. At the time, I was in Vancouver working in the private sector and not a party to any discussions in Ottawa on the subject. However, in retrospect, knowing Trudeau, I think it was a case of his having grown tired of hearing criticism of the Indian Act and having said, in effect, fine, stop complaining about it, I'll remove it. But he didn't offer an alternative, and he soon came to realize it was a much more fundamental Canadian issue. He put the issue largely on the back burner during the 1970s as his focus was first on navigating through the issues of minority government, and in the latter part of the decade, on Quebec.

For our next trip, Pierre expressed an interest in Indonesia, a large and significant country he had previously visited as prime minister but wished to see more of. Given Pierre's background with multiculturalism and bilingualism, he was particularly interested in Indonesia's foundational principle of Pancasila, a doctrine of pluralism and tolerance that sought to reconcile the predominantly Muslim country's many different cultures, religions, and languages into a secularist society. He was also interested in Indonesia's creation of a common language, Bahasa Indonesia, in order for Indonesians to better communicate with each other. This language did not supplant Indonesia's multiple native languages but offered common ground, without having to maintain the use of the colonial language, Dutch.

In preparation for this trip, I did a lot of background reading and research. I also talked to the Indonesian ambassador in Ottawa, to tell him we were planning a private visit to his country. I wanted to confirm that we would be welcome. I assured him we were not intending to make any political statements or seek publicity in any way; we simply wanted to experience the diversity and culture of the country, to gain information and insights. The ambassador was highly receptive to our plan and wanted to know whether Trudeau would like to meet President Suharto. I replied he would certainly be available if Suharto wished to meet with him. In fact, Trudeau was anything but excited about the prospect of meeting Suharto, who was a dictator at the head of a government that had committed many human rights abuses. And as it turned out, Suharto evidently was not in a rush to chat with Trudeau either. Ultimately, the Indonesians told us they just couldn't find a time, and that was more than fine.

Ahead of our trip, I also went to the Department of External Affairs to inform them of our plans. I want to give the department and embassy their due with respect to the arrangements, which turned out to be fantastic. Of course, in addition to helping us, they wanted to use us, too, which was understood. It was a benefit to the mission that a former prime minister, world famous, would come to visit. This honoured the bilateral relationship and presented a golden opportunity for the embassy to get face time with senior Indonesian officials, who generally did not pay much attention to Canada, but turned out in full force when invited to a reception to meet Trudeau. The embassy also set up other events for Canadians and Indonesian business figures, meetings that afforded insights for us but also served the embassy's purposes.

The four of us – me, Natalie, Pierre, and Nancy Southam – were in Indonesia for about three weeks in the late summer of 1994, during which time we travelled to several islands. From Jakarta, we flew east to the island of Sulawesi, to the large city on the south end. It was then called Ujung Pandang, but has since reverted to its previous name, Makassar. We met our tourist guide and drove north, taking about five or six days to get to Palu, and from there we flew to Manado, in the far northeast, where we stayed another couple of days. Sulawesi is enormous, about 180,000 square kilometres. (As a point of comparison, Vancouver Island, which is not small, is 31,285 square kilometres.) We were introduced to a culture of Sulawesian people who buried their dead in the trees. We talked to their chiefs, our guide serving as an interpreter. At mid-island, Inco had a nickel mining operation of some importance run by Canadians, and we stopped for a visit. We talked with the managers about their operation and the challenges of operating in Indonesia. There was a nine-hole golf course there, which Natalie, an avid golfer, was keen to try. She had the opportunity to play a round with some of the managers' wives, just after dawn. Any later in the day would have been too hot.

In Manado, Pierre's objective was to go scuba diving. He was an experienced diver and the area had a reputation as a diver's paradise. There was no one to dive with him, so he rented gear and went alone to explore some underwater caves. As we watched him disappear into the depths, yes, I was concerned. When he came back up, he described it as spectacular, and said it was one of the best dives he'd ever had. Natalie, Nancy, and I went snorkelling. The tropical fish we could see were phenomenal.

From there, we flew to Ternate, in the Moluccas, the capital of a former sultanate. We learned the story of the notorious Moluccan pirates. Then, on to Papua, the Indonesian western part of an enormous island whose eastern half is the country of Papua New Guinea. Pierre had a particular interest in the island's culture, and it was at his suggestion that we included it in our itinerary. We flew into Jayapura, and from there we travelled in an old single-engine De Havilland Beaver southwest to the Baliem Valley. I had been fascinated but not really surprised to see the Canadian-made plane so far from home. The rugged plane was suited to the purpose. It held the four of us, our groceries, and our luggage, and two tourist service officials who were looking after us. It was an unusual flight. Normally, when you take off, you climb, then you level off, and eventually you descend. On this flight, we were climbing, climbing, climbing, climbing, and then in the highlands, there was a landing strip. At the time, the Indonesian part of the island was a restricted military zone and not open to tourism, except for selected visitors; travelling with Pierre had its privileges. There was only one place for us to stay, it was like a tiny motel with about six bedrooms and a small dining room. It in fact was some sort of Indonesian military or police outpost.

Papua was a closed area partly because of the long-running dispute over sovereignty there. When the Dutch had ended their colonial rule of Indonesia in 1949, they had sought to hold onto what then was called Netherlands New Guinea, maintaining its Melanesian population, different from the other ethnic groups in Indonesia, should be allowed to decide its own fate. Indonesia, meanwhile, moved into the territory, which it claimed as its own. The status of West Irian, as it was also called by Indonesia, became a major international issue in the 1960s. The upshot was that the international community accepted Indonesia's control after a deeply flawed vote was held in the territory in 1969 that went in Indonesia's favour; however, insurgents fighting for independence, or union with Papua New Guinea, have remained active.

From our base in the Baliem Valley, we visited villages where people wore their traditional attire: loin cloths and not much else. This was not for the benefit of tourists– there were practically none – but how they lived. Historically, they had been cannibals. We hiked in the area for several days. At one point, we were on a trail that led across a fast-flowing river to a village our guides wanted to show us. There was a bridge, but part of it was in the water, and that was a problem for me. Somewhere along the way, I had got an infected toe. We had brought antibiotics and I was taking them, but I didn't think it was a good idea for me to risk putting my toe in that water, so they offered to lead Pierre and me to cross farther downstream, where there was a bridge above the water. Before setting out, we stayed to watch Natalie and Nancy cross. The guide told them to be careful to stay on the bridge, but Natalie stepped off and fell into the river. I was shocked and felt helpless. The guides pulled her out immediately, and she was fine, although her camera was lost. I later joked that Natalie was one to always blaze her own trail, but the mishap left me shaken. The women continued to the village, while Pierre and I took the other route with one of the guides, and then waited for the others to join us.

While we were waiting, Pierre and I sat on an outcrop of rock and chatted. Three local men arrived, hunters, wearing only penis gourds and carrying machetes. One of them started gesturing vigorously. I had no idea what he was trying to tell us, but Pierre figured it out, saying "He wants a cigarette," just as our guide whipped out a pack. Neither Pierre nor I smoked. Pierre said, "Jack will buy the pack." So I did. Pierre then distributed the cigarettes. I happened to have matches, as we had been advised these could come in handy if we needed to light a fire to dry out, and I offered them up. Our guide was able to translate, so Pierre took the opportunity to ask the hunters questions about how many wives they had and whether they recently had fought wars. They were friendly and offered to take us to see the mummified remains of their ancestors. We politely declined; we weren't sure what we might be getting ourselves into, and it would have disrupted our schedule. After the men went on their way, I said to Pierre, "At any point, were you concerned they might go for their machetes?" He replied, "With your sore toe, I can run faster than you can."

We flew back to Jayapura in the Beaver, and then caught a commercial flight to Ambon, a city on an island of the same name, which had once been a major centre for the Dutch. It looked more European than the other places we had visited, with a clear Christian presence. From Ambon we made a side trip to the Banda Islands, known as the place where nutmeg comes from. The spice historically had a high value, attracting European colonizers to the area. It may have been the first global commodity.

From Banda, we flew to Bali, via Ambon. At that point, we had been travelling for about three weeks. I had arranged for us to stay at a Four Seasons Hotel. It was a series of cottages, each with its own swimming pool. The contrast with our conditions over the previous three weeks was incredible. We had lived with no showers, wearing mainly the same clothes, walking through rainstorms, bugs, and underbrush. This experience made the luxury of our hotel in Bali all the more striking. We stayed there for two or three days, enjoyed a bit of the Bali scenery – the gorgeous beaches, beautiful hotels, rice paddies – and then we returned to Jakarta.

The Canadian embassy had asked us whether Pierre would be interested in attending a reception the owners of the Aman Hotel group would host at their home. He had agreed. Our host was Adrian Zecha, an Indonesian businessman. It was a beautiful home on a large estate, with tea rooms and bridges and a large central house. It was our last event in Indonesia, and we had a wonderful time. Pierre was quite animated that evening, though I remember none of the conversation. The guests included the top of Indonesian society, business and political, along with some diplomats from the Canadian embassy. As in Bali, we could not help but compare the luxury we encountered there with the rudimentary conditions we experienced in so many places we had visited in the island nation.

Then we headed home.

In fact, our travels did not end with the Indonesia trip, at least not those involving just Pierre and myself. The mention during the meeting with F.W. de Klerk of Pierre's involvement in the InterAction Council had piqued my curiosity. I asked him about it afterward. The organization had been founded in 1983 by former Japanese prime minister Takeo Fukuda to allow former national leaders to meet, pool their collective wisdom, and engage in strategic thinking on global issues. The organization is not a mere discussion club, but produces policy recommendations and reports. After Trudeau retired, he was invited to join.

Trudeau was not one to reach out to people, but he would respond to expressions of interest. So, when I expressed interest, he invited me to accompany him to the council's May 1993 meeting in Shanghai. It was chaired by former West German chancellor Helmut Schmidt, and much of the focus was on the international consequences of the breakup of the Soviet Union.

Pierre and I continued to meet for lunch at the Ritz when I was in Montreal, and at some point, probably in late 1994 or early 1995, he mentioned that it was his turn to host a meeting of the InterAction Council. He asked whether I would take on its organization. I said, of course, so long as we could hold it in Vancouver, where I would be better able to bring everything together. He said that would be fine.

The meeting took place 19–22 May 1996, at the Pan Pacific Hotel. The main topic was globalization, and in their final communique, the leaders expressed concern: "A most disturbing consequence of the present trends toward globalization and privatization [is] the increasing disparities in income and economic well-being among countries and within countries. These must be contained." They noted that globalization of the world's economy was being matched by globalization of many other of the world's problems. Pierre chaired the meeting, and I sat next to him, assisting with the agenda. The fourteen former national leaders in attendance included Schmidt, former French president Valéry Giscard d'Estaing, and former Polish president Lech Walesa. Canada's prime minister at the time, Jean Chrétien, made a dinner keynote speech to the conference. A future prime minister was also in attendance: Justin

Trudeau, then a twenty-four-year-old university student. (The younger Trudeau was quoted in a 23 May 1996 *Vancouver Sun* news report about the meeting as saying, "I'm just here because I'm finally old enough to appreciate what my father does." He told the reporter he did not foresee a future in politics for himself.)

I attended two more InterAction Council meetings with Trudeau: in the Netherlands in June 1997 and in Rio de Janeiro in May 1998. One of those at the meeting in the Netherlands was a radical Swiss Roman Catholic priest and theologian named Hans Küng, whom Trudeau considered an important Catholic thinker. Küng's theology was a topic Trudeau and I would discuss from time to time. Küng played an influential role in that meeting's work on a *Universal Declaration of Human Responsibilities*, to complement the 1948 *Universal Declaration of Human Rights*. That the report issued by the InterAction Council on responsibilities did not receive the interest or attention of global leaders, including at the United Nations, was one of the real disappointments Trudeau and many of the members of the council felt at that time.

The Rio meeting was Trudeau's last. Later that year, his youngest son, Michel, died, at age twenty-three, in an avalanche while skiing in southeastern British Columbia. That ended Pierre's interest in a lot of things. By then, he wasn't well, either. He was suffering from both Parkinson's disease and prostate cancer. He died on 28 September 2000. I didn't see him again after Michel's death. He had withdrawn, and I didn't press. It was very clear he was not interacting with people outside his innermost circle.

Attending Trudeau's funeral was one of the saddest occasions of my life. As Natalie and I sat in Notre-Dame Basilica in Montreal, I reflected on my personal interactions with him, my admiration for his brilliance, his leadership of Canada, his social conscience, his caring about the organization of the global community, all wrapped up in a deeply held passion for life, experiences, and camaraderie. I knew I was going to miss him greatly.

Conclusion

SINCE DEPARTING POLITICAL LIFE more than a decade ago, I have maintained a keen interest in the issues on which I have had a lifetime of focus. I have both studied and discussed with others the progress of Canadians in coping with our ongoing challenges and the way in which we go about our internal negotiations for progress. I remain confirmed in my belief that Canadians are committed to a tolerant, democratic, and socially progressive society.

While I share Martin Luther King Jr's optimism that the "arc of the moral universe is long but it bends toward justice," and along with Pierre Trudeau tend to believe "Desiderata," that "the universe is unfolding as it should," I am as well a realist in recognizing there are many forces at work to shape history and human development in anti-democratic and anti-social directions. Canadians must remain clear in our objectives for the well-being of our society and determined in our efforts.

What happens outside our borders affects us as much as, and sometimes even more than, what we do at home. Canadians look on with alarm as authoritarian nations increasingly assert their power and influence, posing challenges to the US-established post–Second World War international order in which Canada has a vital stake. This is written as the Russian invasion of Ukraine is under way – a deplorable event. European and perhaps global stability is threatened by a regime determined to remain authoritarian and be the dominant power in Eastern Europe and increasingly in the Middle East. Are these events defining a new reality, a world of competition between the authoritarian and liberal democracies as US president Joe Biden is alleging? Are we seeing a new definition of sovereignty emerging that assigns different levels of entitlement to nations? Are the old spheres of influence to resurface as the way of the future?

For a long time after the Second World War, the United States was respected globally for its democracy, economic strength, and capacity to bring stability to a world badly in need of it. Access to the wealthiest market in the world allowed Canada to share in the growing prosperity of its neighbour. Canada has also benefited from the US defence umbrella. However, in recent times, the United States has grown less committed to the international system that it created and is focusing more on narrower self-interest. Along with many Canadians, I watch with growing concern the increasing political, economic, social, and racial divisions that are raising the adversarial tenor of life in the United States, as well as greatly harming American prestige in the global community.

China is, and will be for a very long time, a world power; its economy one of the driving forces of global economic growth. As it grows in strength and relevance, China seeks to alter some of the rules and relationships of the existing system to its own advantage. The obvious contradictions between China's ambitions, values, and practices and those of the West are emerging as a focal point of rivalry and, indeed, conflict. As an optimist and a realist, and with a half-century's experience as an interlocutor with China, I hold to my original conviction that we have to maintain the strongest possible and most open communication between the two systems. We must tackle issues day by day, working toward common interests, accepting differences where we can, and avoiding conflict where differences are irreconcilable. In the arc of history, a century is but the flicker of a moment.

Today, there are challenges from many quarters to the global supply system and long-standing rules for international trade in goods and services. Regionalism and protectionism, which are growing in strength and practice, are undermining multilateralism in trade – a key to Canada's prosperity. In particular, of concern in Canada is that successive US administrations seem increasingly willing to erect barriers to trade, all the while displaying indifference to the impact of their actions on the economic stability of their northern neighbour.

At the same time, we face an array of challenges in the management of our own society. Whatever is happening internationally, Canadians must maintain a focus as well on our key domestic priorities. First and foremost is maintaining a healthy economy and the capacity for economic growth, the source of the revenues that underpin the progressive society Canadians want to be. Energy is the lifeblood of any economy, and we must see to it that we have adequate sources at competitive costs. And we must achieve these goals while moving rapidly to a regime of environmental management in step with the climate threat and our global responsibility.

In building the new Canada, we must bring into our national family more of the world's best talents and those who seek new opportunities for a better life. Immigration is essential to maintain and grow our workforce and remain a competitive player in the world economy. Canada is a society unlike most others in the nature of its diversity, which is both regional and demographic. It is multicultural, with no dominant ethnic makeup. More than 20 per cent of Canadians were not born in Canada, a proportion unknown in any other country. Our fellow citizens and their forebears have come from every part of the globe, bringing with them diverse cultures, interests, and ambitions. My own province of British Columbia is fortunate to have a strong community of Asian Canadians, people who bring to us new knowledge of a part of the world so significant to today and of increasing importance in the years to come. These communities are a bridge for all Canadians to new opportunities for relationships, historical and cultural understanding, and Canada's economic growth. British Columbians and Canadians have come from everywhere and are creating a society of diversity, of unparalleled multiculturalism, in which we share a devotion to our democratic values and the welfare of our society without forcing assimilation into the mainstream culture.

Admittedly, our embrace of diversity so far has fallen short. Racism, hatred of "the other," and social discord remain open sores, as Asian Canadians, Muslim Canadians, and Black Canadians are so aware. Anti-Semitism lingers. And Canadians are belatedly coming to recognize this country's shameful history of colonialism toward Indigenous Peoples and realize that they are not merely tiles in the multicultural mosaic but the original inhabitants of this land and thus continuing rights-holders. Indigenous people and nations are in the process of reconstituting their cultures, social networks, and legal and governance systems, moving away from forced dependence to become significant partners in Canada's economic growth.

While a new relationship between Indigenous Peoples and other Canadians is only now starting to take shape, Canadians have long understood that homogeneity is not necessary or even desirable. Canada was founded as a partnership between English and French Canadians, and protections for linguistic and religious minorities (at the time, Protestants or Roman Catholics) were built into our laws and system of governance. The presence in Canada of a sizable French-Canadian minority, forming a majority in the province of Quebec, has meant that from the beginning, there have been different ways of being Canadian. Quebec has a fair claim to be a nation within a nation, a continuing reality that English-speaking Canadians, whether for reasons of pragmatism or principle, have ultimately chosen to accommodate.

For me, Canada's accommodation of diversity, its progress in becoming a more inclusive society, is not only political theory, it is personal. I had the good fortune to be born in Canada, protected from the ravages of a raging war and genocide in Europe, and then to come of age after the Second World War in a confident and outward-looking nation. Canadian Jews have become accepted and have assumed our place in all walks of Canadian life. While in the Trudeau cabinet, I served with two other Jewish ministers: Herb Gray and Bob Kaplan, both from Ontario. In the Martin cabinet, there were two others: Irwin Cotler and Jacques Saada, both from Quebec. In British Columbia, we have had a Jewish premier, Dave Barrett.

Canada's continuing challenge is to remove remaining systemic inequalities and biases to ensure we have truly equal opportunities and all are treated fairly. In this, our legal and political systems have key roles to play. As a young university student, I had been impressed with John Stuart Mill's dictum that society should be organized to foster the greatest good for the greatest number. That seemed to me a simple truth, but as life's experiences evolved, I came to see it was not a complete approach to the human condition and the governance of a democratic society. In issues such as those that affected First Nations communities and other minority communities, including my own, I began to see that the "greatest number," exerting their power in their own self-interest, could possibly infringe on the rights of minorities. Hence the need for the Charter of Rights and Freedoms, a project to which I devoted more than a year as a member of the special joint committee on the constitution.

Among many significant provisions, the Charter introduced legal constraints and judicial review of the dominant powers of the majority. Leveraging the power of law to overcome biases and repair injustices is essential to achieve successful governance of a society whose diversity over the years to come can only grow more significant.

The way in which we govern ourselves is central in building a successful society. All must have confidence that our political system takes into account their views and interests. Our Parliament in Ottawa and our provincial and territorial capitals are the places where Canadians come together to articulate their aspirations and negotiate compromises, based on the best interests of the whole. Essential to our common good is the clear understanding that our way of life depends on continuous and open dialogue and negotiation between people in government, business, the social sector, and among all Canadians. The optimum system of governance achieves a harmonious balance between public power, expressed through our democratic forms of governance, and sufficient private power in the hands of our citizens to oppose an arbitrary use of public power. A free and responsible press plays a crucial role in this system, holding politicians of all sectors to account for their ideas and behaviour. From time to time through my forty years of public life, this has not always been pleasant for me or for the governments in which I served, but the necessity remains. Journalism, when performed impartially and ethically, is as necessary as dentistry, and sometimes has felt like it.

A majority of Canadians, however they vote, demonstrate their respect and desire for a society that recognizes equality of citizenship under the law, and respect for diversity and the encouragement to seek the role they wish to play in Canadian society. This is an incredible achievement of which most Canadians are still consciously unaware, although at some level they are operating to move these values forward.

Understanding one another is at the base of our sense of fairness and achieving compromise. Trusting one another as jointly committed for the well-being of Canadian society and the Canadian nation is the ultimate ingredient in national success.

Trust was one of the key themes in my last major public speech, delivered at SFU's June 2017 convocation as I accepted an honorary degree:

Trust is the glue that holds our society together. Our willingness to trust allows us to act as a community to deal with the issues that are too great for the individual or any single group. Trust is a learned behaviour based on millennia of human experience. We distrust first, and then learn to trust for the sake of our advancement.

International security is based on the willingness of nations to build trust in their relationships. Commercial behaviour is based on trust in our institutions to constrain negative behaviour. We have trust in the rule of law and an impartial judicial system. And trust in government in our liberal democracy brings policies to address social and economic inequality.

I am old enough to remember the experiences of my parents in Calgary during the Depression of the 1930s. These were trying times for many Canadians. The result was a determination by Canadians in all regions and of all political persuasions to order our society to protect the vulnerable and build a competitive Canadian economy. No Canadian value stands higher than social justice, education, health care, security of the person, access to a proper old age, and an effective social safety net. These are now the rights of all Canadian citizens.

While Canadians are proud to belong to a society that claims rights for the individual, we cannot ignore the duty of each one of us to understand we also have responsibilities, as individuals and collectively. One day, Canadians should adopt a charter of responsibilities. The need for such a charter was made clear by the events of February 2022: the occupation of the core of Ottawa, including Wellington Street in front of the Parliament Buildings and the blockades of several border crossings to the United States. The process of analysis, reflection, and debate on the responsibilities of citizenship that would accompany the drafting and adoption of such a charter would be a major step in knitting together Canadian society.

Our history is one of accommodation, negotiation, and effective and pragmatic resolution of our differences. These skills and attributes will be more needed than ever as we turn to the considerable challenges of the coming decades.

To quote the 1950s comic strip character Pogo, highly popular when I was a student at Harvard, "We have met the enemy, and he is us." None can do us more harm than we can do to ourselves, if we lose collective sight of who we are and what we have.

Acknowledgments

First and foremost, I would like to thank my daughter Edie, without whom this book would not have been written. I mean that literally.

For the last decade or so, Edie, Natalie, other members of my family, colleagues at the University of British Columbia, former colleagues in Ottawa, and several others had been urging me to write a memoir. And for many years, I resisted. Once you get to your eighties, you realize you only have so many years left, and there are choices to be made about how you want to use them. My own strong preference was to remain active in the present, working to advance various forward-looking initiatives, rather than focus on past accomplishments and events.

At a certain point, Edie declared that if I wouldn't write my memoirs, she would, and launched into the project despite her own busy schedule. As the early chapters started taking shape, I was astounded by how well she was capturing my voice and my perspectives. As the manuscript progressed, my own participation in the project steadily increased.

I also owe a debt of gratitude to several others for their insights, encouragement, and help along the way, in particular my daughters Shari Austin and Barbara Austin for their frank feedback on earlier versions of the manuscript; my wife of more than forty-five years Natalie Veiner Freeman; her children Richard Freeman and Jody Freeman; Ron Stern; Professor Paul Evans of UBC; Mark Abley; Trevor Boyd; Philip Cercone and Emily Andrew of McGill-Queen's University Press; copy editor Paula Sarson; and the three anonymous peer reviewers. My gratitude also to the highly efficient team at MQUP who transformed the manuscript into this handsome volume.

Public service is a team sport. It would not have been possible for me to accomplish what I have without the support and contributions of many others. I would not want to overlook the all too often under-recognized contributions of the staffers and advisers with whom I have served and whose hard work and devotion to public service have been no less than my own. In addition to those named in the preceding pages, my deepest thanks to: Joan Ablett, Jonathan Ablett, Russell Anthony, Doug Beaton, Edith Clippingdale, Allan T. Collier, Jack Croll, Bill Cunningham, Netty DeWit, Jennifer Dickson, Korry Duckworth, Nicole Edwards, Cindy Grauer, Louise Haddock, Jennifer Hatton, Christine Hearn, Dove Hendren, Bev Hendrickson, Alice Hill, Mike Hillman, Adam Johnson, Lilliane Johnstone, Justyna Jonca, Barbara Kagedan, Ray Lucas, David Martin, Heather Martin, Ian McKay, Deborah Palumbo, David Parkinson, Forrest Parlee, Tom Pitfield, Mary Alice Ryan, Michael Scandiffio, Ann Wicks, Mike Witherly, and Bruce Young. If there is anyone I have missed here, my deepest apologies, it was not intentional.

Notes

Chapter One

1 As for my maternal grandparents, they died when I was young, so I have few memories of them.

2 One important reminder of the Montefiore Colony remains. In 1916, my maternal grandfather provided the land for the construction of the community's synagogue/library/community centre, which was called the Montefiore Institute. Sometime after the colony folded, the small wooden building was moved to another site and became a private home. Decades later, it was located by members of the Calgary Jewish community, purchased, restored, and then moved with great care to Heritage Park, where it remains as testament to the Jewish community's long-standing presence in Alberta. In 2011, our family gathered there as my youngest grandson, Alex Austin-Boyd – whose middle name is Joseph, like his great-great-grandfather – arrived from Toronto to celebrate his bar mitzvah in this historic building.

3 In czarist Russia, Jews were not allowed to own land. The Chetners had been innkeepers.

4 The building is now home to the highly popular Vendome Cafe.

5 This was the term Scots applied to English people, usually with a disparaging tone.

6 My sister Eva became a registered nurse with a specialty in psychiatry. My sister Josie attended UBC and went on to become an Alberta civil servant in the department dealing with higher education.

7 Harold became a meteorologist and worked across Canada for the federal government, including on Vancouver Island. He eventually settled in Nanaimo.

8 Learning by analysis of actual cases, not by studying first principles.

Chapter Two

1 Jack Cahill, "Art Laing Stays, Says Irate Pearson," *Vancouver Sun*, 20 November 1964, 3.

2 My account of our trip was published in the 18 September 1965 edition of *Maclean's* magazine.

Chapter Three

1 After operations were finished, the mine was redeveloped into Brenda Lake, a recreational area.

Chapter Four

1 In her 1995 book *Cloak of Green*, Elaine Dewar writes that Maurice Strong recruited me for the job. While I cannot be certain that Strong had no role to play in my appointment, he had no role to my knowledge.

2 The name was chosen by Prime Minister Trudeau himself.

3 I had improved my credentials with Quebecers by taking Jean-Guy Fredette, whom I had first met in Ottawa in the Pearson years and who was then Quebec's deputy minister of energy and mining, to sit as an observer at an OECD oil committee meeting in Paris. Premier Robert Bourassa was thrilled and called Trudeau to express his gratitude. Trudeau later expressed a feigned annoyance to me that he wasn't consulted, but actually he was quite happy I did it on my own so that he couldn't be held responsible. When I reported on the OECD oil committee session to a meeting of cabinet, he said to me, with a smile, "And so, you have your own Quebec policy."

Chapter Six

1 The Supreme Court of Canada ruled in 2005 that the denial of timely health care was an infringement on the Quebec charter of rights. It opened the way for Quebecers to buy private health insurance.

2 Bruce Hutchison, "Conservatism vs. Liberalism – A Daring Duo Duel," *Vancouver Sun*, 15 January 1983, A4.

3 Some of the press coverage about my post, for example, a 21 July 2004 story in the *Vancouver Sun*, said that on Parliament Hill I was known as the Yoda of the Liberal Party. It was a very nice image to have.

Chapter Seven

1 Examples abounded, especially from Quebec and the Atlantic region. A British Columbia example was the successful work done starting in 1964 by Sen. J.W. de B. Farris to persuade the Pearson government to incorporate the Bank of British Columbia as a full-service bank. (Premier W.A.C. Bennett had created it to focus on BC business development and trade with Asia and as a means of ending a Central Canadian monopoly over banking.)

2 A Tanach is a Hebrew Bible that includes the five books of Moses as well as the prophets and other scriptures.

3 Quoted in Jim Lyon, "Jack Austin: Lonely Liberal Whiz in the West," *Financial Post*, 7 April 1984, 9.

4 The designation B-C did not refer to the name of the province; the twin pier was part of a series named for letters of the alphabet.

5 In addition to being sensible, Bud Olson had a colourful way with words. Speaking on 1 April 1982 at the event announcing the agreement, he said, "Negotiating a deal with Bill Bennett is something like doing the roundup back at my ranch in Alberta. You're apt to get your teeth rattled a bit while it's going on, but when it's over you know for sure it was all worthwhile." (Quoted in Michael Bocking, "Ottawa, Lottery to Pay for Twin Project," *Vancouver Sun*, 2 April 1982, A1.)

6 I had first met Jim Pattison more than twenty years earlier, when I had stopped at Marshall Motors on Cambie Street, near City Hall, for gas and to have a look at the cars for sale there. He came out of the office to talk to me and introduced himself. He was famous for his flamboyance even then. He was wearing some outlandish sports jacket, probably yellow, with green pants. For years, he dressed in an eccentric way in order to build an identity, a brand. He was a marketing guy who understood branding right from the beginning. Our first meeting was brief, but you never forgot Jim Pattison once you met him. We had crossed paths a few more times over the years, so by this time we had a very good working relationship.

Chapter Eight

1 Although CDC was created by Parliament, it was not a Crown corporation.

2 The Joe Clark government, during its brief time in office, had introduced an Expenditure Management System; however, it was more limited in that it did not really incorporate policy.

3 Timely care was an essential principle and came to be tested in the courts with the Chaoulli case, in which it was ruled that Quebec's failure to provide timely medical care was a violation of a patient's rights under the province's human rights charter (which is why the decision only applies to Quebec).

4 In an article in the *Vancouver Sun* on 18 August 1983, Prince Rupert port authority chair Joe Scott said he was looking forward to local control: "What a relief it will be. We haven't been able to get a roll of toilet paper without getting permission from Ottawa first."

5 The BC fishing community and provincial government always alleged that fisheries ministers who didn't come from the province paid no attention to British Columbia, that the Atlantic coast was always given more importance. There was indeed some truth to this.

6 Peter H. Pearse and the Commission on Pacific Fisheries Policy, *Turning the Tide: A New Policy for Canada's Pacific Fisheries – Final Report*, 1982, 79.

Chapter Nine

1   Taiwan, which calls itself the Republic of China, is the large island about 150 kilometres from the Chinese mainland, to which the Nationalists had fled when the Communists took power. The Nationalist government there maintained it was the legitimate government of all of China, and for some three decades was largely recognized as such by Western countries.

2   An antimacassar was a piece of lace cloth intended to protect the top of a chair from grease or dirt.

3   The institution had no connection to the Japanese university of the same name.

4   In my speech, I noted, "At the heart of this self-assurance is China's belief that modernization and technological reform can be achieved 'with Chinese characteristics,' as Deng Xiaoping has repeatedly stated. Chinese leadership is clear that modernization is not Westernization. The rest of us understand this proposition less well."

Chapter Ten

1   By then I had joined the Boughton Peterson Yang Anderson law firm and was working with their Hong Kong–based partner, Victor Yang, on gaining a representative law firm licence in China. We were successful. That licence was awarded to the firm in 1993, making it the first Canadian law firm authorized to have a representative office in China.

2   Anthony Wilson-Smith, "The China Deal," *Maclean's*, 21 November 1994, 14.

3   This was the riding where I had run unsuccessfully in 1965.

4   The members of our group each paid their own way.

5   Evans later followed up with a book titled *John Fairbank and the American Understanding of Modern China*, published in 1988.

Chapter Eleven

1   The poll is quoted in Jonathon Gatehouse, "America Lite: Is That Our Future?," *Maclean's*, 25 November 2002.

2   Making the suggestion was David Winfield, then Canada's ambassador to Mexico. He had previously served as economic and commercial minister at Canada's embassy in Japan.

3   Kenneth "Ken" Courtis went on to become vice-chair of Goldman Sachs Asia and then chair of Starfort Investment Holdings.

4   Zebulon Pike was an American brigadier general and explorer, for whom Pikes Peak in Colorado is named. He died during an attack by US forces on Fort York, in present-day Toronto, during the War of 1812.

5   Tertiary recovery involves injecting chemicals into a declining oil field in order to extract more oil.

Chapter Twelve

1 Dave Porter, now a BC Indigenous leader, spent two years covering those meetings for the CBC. I met Dave Porter, after I retired from the Senate, when we talked about First Nations' mining industry interests, ambitions, and objectives. We also negotiated a successful agreement on behalf of a BC mining company, Silvercorp.

2 The term "Aboriginal" is used here instead of Indigenous, as that is the term used in the constitution.

3 Peter Ittinuar later crossed the floor to become a Liberal.

4 The other BC First Nations that joined initially were the Squamish just north of Vancouver; Westbank in the Okanagan; Lheidli T'enneh near Prince George; and N'Quatqua near Whistler.

5 Bill Reid, an important Haida artist, designed a carving that is an amazing depiction of this traditional story. It is a major feature in UBC's Museum of Anthropology.

Chapter Thirteen

1 Senator Kolber and I did not have the problem of Trudeau's international prominence and, obviously, we did not represent the Mulroney government. We travelled as private citizens.

2 In February 2021, Canada's House of Commons labelled as a genocide China's imprisonment of Uyghur people in "re-education" camps and its attempts to reduce Uyghur birth rates, including by sterilization. China's actions are a response to its concerns about an independence movement in the region and possible influence on the population by radical Islamist political movements. China's behaviour clearly does not meet international human rights standards. Interesting, however, is that there isn't a squeak from the Muslim world. China is not shy to use its economic power for political reasons, and many of these countries are dependent on China economically and, in Pakistan's case also, militarily. It is the Western world, with its human rights sensitivities, that is sounding the alarm.

3 By the caudillo factor, I mean strongman government by boss figures with a power base in the armed forces or their own private militias.

Index

Abbreviations: JA, Jack Austin; PET, Pierre Elliott Trudeau

Ablett, Joan, 320
Ablett, Jonathan, 320
Aboriginal rights, constitutional entrenchment of (section 35), 8, 139, 260–5, 275, 282–3, 303–4
abortion issue, 104–5
African National Congress (ANC), 296–8
Ainsworth, Allan, 117
Alberta: childhood in, 12–17; federal energy policies and, 59, 69, 73–6, 87, 99, 249; provincial resource ownership, 73; representation in Ottawa, 81, 83, 92, 120, 122–3, 130, 136
Alcock, Reg, 210, 216
Alkali Lake Band. *See* Esk'etemc First Nation
Allmand, Warren, 262
Amazon region, Brazil, 291–2
Anderson, David, 79, 127
Anderson, Ray, 190
Andre, Harvie, 92
Anthony, Russell, 320
anti-Semitism, 13, 23, 97, 109, 137, 255, 295, 313
apartheid, 294–5, 298
Applebaum-Hébert report (*Report of the Federal Cultural Policy Review Committee*), 169–70
Applebaum, Louis, 169

Arenstein or Arnstein, Gershon Zelig (later known as Jacob Austin, JA's paternal grandfather), 12
Argue, Hazen, 136
Arias, Óscar, 293
Asia Pacific Foundation of Canada: creation of, ix, 188–91; endowment for, 215–17, 227
Asia Pacific Initiative, 191
Assembly of First Nations, 278
Atlantic Canada, ix, 3, 69, 73, 119, 122–3, 177, 323
Atleo, Shawn, 281
Atomic Energy of Canada, 237
Austin, Barbara (daughter), 18, 319
Austin (née Chetner), Clara (JA's mother), 13–14
Austin, Edie (JA's daughter), 18, 28, 284, 319
Austin, Harold (JA's cousin), 17, 321
Austin, Jack, academic involvement after Senate retirement: Royal Roads University, 228–9; Simon Fraser University, 227–8; University of British Columbia, 222–7
Austin, Jack, business activities: Brameda, 53, 55–6, 97, 101, 141; Brenda group, on behalf of, 51–3, 126; Giant Mascot, 53–6; New Pacific, 294; Oceanic Wind, 276–7; Westcoast Energy, consultant to, 249–51

Austin, Jack, Canada-China relations, involvement in: advancing academic relations with, 222, 225–8; Canada China Business Council/ Team Canada missions, x, 6, 204–8; Canada-China Legislative Association, 6, 209–11, 221; Expo 86, China's participation in, 186–8; first visit in 1971, 6, 183–5; general, 6, 211; meetings with Chinese leaders, 6, 153–4, 184, 202, 207, 209, 214, 221, 289; opening of relations, 181–2; role in facilitation of China-Indigenous relations, 281–2; second visit to China, 186–8

Austin, Jack, civil service career as deputy minister of Energy, Mines and Resources: comprehensive energy study (*An Energy Policy for Canada*), 58, 62, 67, 70–1, 74, 79; implementing change in EMR's mandate, 60–1; job interview with PET, 58–9; loss of water division, 61–2; Mackenzie Valley Pipeline Commission, creation of, 76–8; moratorium on west coast oil exploration, 79; oil crisis, 68–9, 73–5, 81; Petro-Canada, creation of, 59, 70–3, 75–6; uranium "cartel," 62–6

Austin, Jack, early career: interest in foreign service, 23–4; as law lecturer, 20–3; legal practice, 24–5, 45–6; mining law, early involvement in, 24, 46–8, 50

Austin, Jack, early life and education: in Calgary, 12–17; involvement in Young CCF in high school, 16–17; studies at Harvard, 20, 22–3, 26, 47, 71, 194, 235, 317; studies at University of British Columbia, 17–20; studies at University of California (Berkeley), 7, 28, 49

Austin, Jack, honours and awards: honorary doctorate from Royal Roads University, 229; honorary doctorate from Simon Fraser University, 228; honorary doctorate from the University of British Columbia, 226; honorary doctorate from the University of East Asia, 198; Order of the Aztec Eagle, 248; SFU President's Distinguished Leadership Award, 228

Austin, Jack, in Paul Martin cabinet (2003–05): Asia Pacific Foundation of Canada, endowment for, 215–17; ethics legislation, passage in the Senate, 128–9; Kelowna Accord x, 277–80; Leader of the Government in the Senate, x, 126–30; Pacific Gateway Strategy, x, 218–19

Austin, Jack, in Pierre Trudeau cabinet (1981–84): appointment and swearing in, 137–8; Asia Pacific Foundation of Canada, creation of, ix, 188–91; Canada Development Corporation, responsibility for, 157–61; Canada Development Investment Corporation (CDIC), responsibility for, 160–1, 163–5; Canada Place, construction of, 146–8, 151, 155; China, visit to finalize participation in Expo, 152–3; dropped from cabinet by John Turner, 178; Expo 86, obtaining federal support for, 3–5, 142–6; fisheries legislation, 176–7; minister of state, 138–40; New Orleans, visit to, 149–50; Northern Native Fishing Corporation, creation of, 266–7; Ridley Island port project, obtaining federal support for, 140–2; royal visit to British Columbia (1983), minister in attendance for,

148–9; shipbuilding, obtaining federal funding for, 173–4; social development committee of cabinet, chair of, 165–70; Social Development ministry, 165, 172; Zhao Ziyang, visit to Vancouver, 153–4, 202

Austin, Jack, Prime Minister's Office as principal secretary: cabinet and caucus attitudes and issues, 83–4, 88–9; council of economic advisers, 95–6; operation of PMO, 84–6; PET's work habits, 94; Michael Pitfield (Clerk of Privy Council), role of, 92–4; Quebec, 86–8; swimming pool at 24 Sussex, 94–5; Margaret Trudeau, 89–92

Austin, Jack, Senate, service in: appointments, suggestions to Paul Martin about, 131–2; appointment to, x, 101–2; early years in, 106–11; first speech in, 107–8; introduction in, 106; Leader of the Government in the Senate, x, 126–30; role in ensuring passage of First Nations Fiscal and Statistical Management Act, 274; role in ensuring passage of First Nations Land Management Act, 272–3; role in ensuring passage of Nisga'a Final Agreement legislation, 269–72; role in ensuring passage of Westbank First Nation Self-Government Act, 273–4; special joint committee on the Constitution, service on, 8, 124–5, 260–3

Austin, Jack, travel outside Canada and United States: Bhutan, 162, 284–5; Bolivia, 293; Brazil, 290–2, 310; China, x, 5, 152–3, 183–8, 195, 203, 206–8, 210, 213, 221–2, 225, 250, 288–90, 309; Costa Rica, 293; Croatia (as Yugoslavia), 22; Ecuador, 292; Ethiopia, 301–2; France, 22, 65;

Hong Kong (under British rule), 48, 193–4, 196, 198–200, 203; India, 285; Indonesia, 305–8; Iran, 67; Italy, 22; Japan, x, 47–8, 54, 64, 67, 151, 212–13; Macao (under Portuguese rule), 197–200; Mexico, 247–8, 250; Namibia, 299–300; Netherlands, 22, 310; Nicaragua, 293; Pakistan, 286–8; Peru, 292; Russia (as Soviet Union), 38–9; South Africa, 65, 294–9; United Kingdom, 170–1

Austin, Morris (JA's father), 12–16, 18

Austin, Shari (JA's daughter), 18, 28, 99, 319

Austin, Sheila, née Toban (JA's first wife), 18, 22, 81, 101

Axworthy, Lloyd, 246

Axworthy, Tom, 245

Aztec Eagle, Order of the, 248

Babbitt, Bruce, 242

Baillie, Jim, 160, 164

Bank of British Columbia, 115, 191–6, 322

Baosteel co-generation plant, 250

Barber, Tim, 115

Barclay, Ian, 147

Barrett, Dave, 87, 149, 153–4, 314

Basford, Ron, 88–9, 107, 141

Baxter, Clive, 96

Beaton, Doug, 320

Beaudoin, Laurent, 247

Beck, Stewart, 217

Bégin, Monique, 169

Beichuan, Sichuan province, China, 281

Beigie, Carl, 95

Beijing, 184, 187–8, 201–3, 205, 207–8, 210, 213, 220–1, 229–30, 243, 286, 289

Bell, Joel, 100, 159–61, 163

Bell, John, 291–2

Bennett, Bill, 4, 123, 140–1, 143–5, 149, 153–4, 277, 323

Bennett, W.A.C., 27, 30–3, 43, 51, 59, 87, 122

Bentsen, Lloyd, 244

Berger, Tom, 8, 78, 257–9

Berger Commission. *See* Mackenzie Valley Pipeline Inquiry

Bhutan, 162, 284

Bhutto, Zulfikar Ali, 287

Bird, Florence, 110

Blaikie, Bill, 210

Blom, Paul, 281

Blondin-Andrew, Ethel, 279

Bolivia, 293–4

Borden line (also known as Ottawa Valley line), 68–9

Bouchard, Lucien, 205

Boughton Peterson Yang Anderson (law firm), 324

Boundary Waters Treaty of 1909, 21

Bourassa, Robert, 86, 322

Bow, Henry, 193

Brameda mining group, 53–7, 97, 101, 141

Brazil, 290–2, 310

Bream, Ken, 146–7, 151, 155

Bream, Leslie, 151

Brenda mining group, 51–3, 126

Breton, Albert, 95

Britannia, royal yacht, 148–9

British Columbia: alienation felt by, 4–5, 29–30, 155; economy of, 4, 7, 31, 45–6, 55, 140, 143–4, 156, 175–8, 193, 217, 242, 270; fed-bashing, 3, 30, 143, 145; federal-provincial relations, 30–3, 37, 127, 142, 145–6, 177; importance of Asia to, 5, 48, 55, 101, 181, 189, 193, 219, 313; Indigenous Peoples in, 8, 34, 78, 140, 222, 266–9, 272–3, 275, 281; JA's advocacy for, ix–xi, 3–5, 11, 107–8, 119, 144–5, 161, 173–4, 235, 269; legal system discrimination against Indigenous people, 254–5, 263; provincial governments, 3, 5, 31, 43, 87, 144, 156, 191, 272, 279; representation in federal cabinet, 3, 11, 32, 35, 88–9, 107, 126–7, 136–8, 140, 145, 151, 165, 218–19; under-representation in Senate, 9, 123–4. *See also* Bennett, Bill; Bennett, W.A.C.; Campbell, Gordon; Esk'etemc First Nation; Haida Gwaii; Haida Nation; Harcourt, Mike; Ktunaxa First Nation; Lheidli T'enneh; Liberal Party (federal): in British Columbia; Merritt, BC; Musqueam Nation; Nisga'a advocacy; Nisga'a Final Agreement; Northern Native Fishing Corporation; Nuu-chah-nulth people; Okanagan Indian Band; Pacific Gateway Strategy, Bill C-68; Peace River power development; Prince Rupert, BC; Royal Roads University; Simon Fraser University (SFU); Tk'emlups te Secwepemc; Tl'azt'en Nation; University of British Columbia (UBC); Westbank First Nation

British Columbia Packers, 266

Bronfman, Samuel, 54, 56

Brooks, David, 76–7

Bruk, John, 25, 189–90, 216

Brynelson, Bern, 51–2, 56

Burns, Mike, 277

Burns Fry, 53, 55–6

Bush, George W., 246

Business Council on National Issues, 247

Cadario, Michele, 127

Cahoon, Allan, 228

Calder, Frank, 78, 268, 271

Calgary, 12–17, 22, 26, 100, 254, 264, 299, 316, 321

Calgary Stampede, 254

Calla, Harold, 275

Callbeck, Catherine, 112

Campbell, Donald, 231

Campbell, Gordon, 191, 217–18, 245, 271, 279

Campbell, Kim, 105

Canada China Business Council: challenges ahead, 231; consultations about possible trade deal with China, 230; early involvement with, 203–4; end of JA's presidency, 208–9; recognition from, 230–1; Team Canada missions to China, x, 6, 204–9

Canada-China Economic Forum, 227

Canada-China Legislative Association, 6, 209–11, 221

Canada Development Corporation (CDC), 157–61, 163, 323

Canada Development Investment Corporation (then CDIC), 160–1, 163–5, 237

Canada Harbour Place Corporation, 146–7, 155

Canada Health Act (1984), 169

Canadair, 161, 163–5, 192, 195, 237

Canada-Mexico Business Retreat, 247–8, 250

Canada Place: construction of, 146–8, 151, 155; sale of air rights, 151; significance of, ix, 5, 156. *See also* Canada Harbour Place Corporation

Canada Ports Corporation (formerly National Harbours Board), 145, 173

Canada Steamship Lines, 211

Canadian Consortium on Asia Pacific Security, 224

Canadian National Committee for Pacific Economic Cooperation (CANCPEC), 231

Canadian Security Intelligence Service, 113

Canadian sovereignty, 11, 240–1, 253, 256

Canadian Wheat Board, 237

CANDU nuclear reactor, 188, 208, 237

Canol pipeline, 77, 256

Cantarell Nitrogen Project, 250

Carney, James, 41

Carney, Pat, 123, 136

Caron, Joseph, 231

Carrillo, Emilio, 245, 248

Carstairs, Sharon, 126

Castañeda, Jorge, 245

Centre for First Nations Governance, 275

Chamberlin, Bob, 281

Chan, Raymond, 127

Chaoulli case, 114, 323

Charter of Rights and Freedoms: constitutional committee hearings, 124–5, 260; importance of, 314–15; Indigenous rights, relationship to, 261, 263, 268; lack of agreement about, 263; Magna Carta, possible related purchase of, 170–1; PET, discussions with, 299, 301

Cheek, Tim, 223

Cheng, Albert, 231

Chetner, Joseph and Fanny (JA's maternal grandparents), 13, 321

China: academic links with, 225–8; Chinese participation in Expo 86, 152–3; De Havilland, sale of airplanes to, 195; engagement, importance of, 180, 182–3, 185, 202, 204, 231–2, 234; first Canadian mission to China (1971), 6, 183–5; free trade deal, discussion of under PM Justin Trudeau, 229; global economy, participation in, 180–1, 199, 212, 233–4, 312; Harper government attitude to, 220–1; human rights, 185, 213, 231–2, 325; Meng Wanzhou and Two Michaels issue, 230, 236; opening of Canadian relations with, 5, 180–2; Team Canada missions, x, 6, 204–9;

Tiananmen Square, 154–5, 183, 201–4, 206, 209–10, 213; visit to Canada by Hu Jintao (2005), 214–15; visit to China by Prime Minister Paul Martin (2005), 213–14; Xi Jinping, changes under, 225–7, 232. *See also* Canada China Business Council; Canada-China Legislative Association; Interdepartmental Committee on External Relations (ICER)

China Council for the Promotion of International Trade, 205

China National Petroleum Corporation, 250

China Reform Foundation, 228

Chinese Academy of Social Sciences, 228

Chongqing, China, 184, 225, 290

Chrétien, Jean: China, leading role in relations with, x, 6, 204–11; dedication to public service, 9; Indigenous issues, positions on, 261–3, 269; InterAction Council, speech to, 309; Iraq, refusal to send troops to, 236; Liberal leadership bid (1984), 178; Senate business, intervention in, 125–6; tensions with Paul Martin supporters, 125–7, 208

Christie, Norma, 25

Churchill Copper, 53, 55

Civil Aviation Administration of China (CAAC), 195

civil service, role of, 61

Clancy, Bill, 31–2, 59

Clark, Joe and Clark government, 118, 136, 153–4, 323

Clarkson, Adrienne, 271

Clarkson, Stephen, 241

climate change, 277, 313

Clippingdale, Edith, 320

coal: in China, 208; in northeastern BC (Sukunka/Tumbler Ridge area, metallurgical), 53, 55–6, 70, 79, 140–2; in southeastern BC (metallurgical), 191; in Soviet Union, 38

Cohen, Bruce, 177

Collier, Allan T., 320

Columbia River Treaty, x, 7, 25, 29, 31, 56, 86, 235

Comprehensive and Progressive Agreement for Trans-Pacific Partnership, 199

Connaught Laboratories, 159

Conservative Party (federal), 105, 121, 124, 132, 134, 213–14, 219, 280. *See also* Progressive Conservative Party

constitution, patriation of, 120, 123, 170, 260–5, 299, 302–3. *See also* Constitution, special joint committee on

constitution, special joint committee on: Charter discussions, 124–5, 260, 314; creation of, 124; entrenchment of Aboriginal rights, 8, 125, 260–3; service on, 8, 124, 260; televising of hearings, 261–2; testimony by Indigenous people at, 260–2

Cools, Anne, 112

Co-operative Commonwealth Federation (CCF), 17, 42, 108

Copithorne, Maurice, 23

Costa Rica, 293

Côté, Ernest (E.A.), 39

Cotler, Irwin, 314

Courtis, Ken, 243, 324

Coutts, Jim, 80, 82–3, 90, 95, 99

Cowan, Jim, 130

Craigmont (mine), 46–52, 54

Croll, David, 109–10, 112

Croll, Jack, 320

Cunningham, Bill, 320

Curtis, George, 19–20, 23
Cyprus Anvil Mining, 189

Danson, Barney, 137, 164, 245
d'Aquino, Tom, 247–8
Davey, Keith, 35–6, 80–2, 90, 95, 99, 107
Davis, Jack, 175, 177
Davis, Merv, 51, 53, 55–6, 96
Day, Joe, 211
De Bané, Pierre, 176–7
De Havilland: Dash 7 aircraft sales to
    China, 195; Dash 8 aircraft, 164–5;
    De Havilland products, 164, 306;
    problems at, 164; public ownership
    of, 161, 164; sale of, 165
de Klerk, F.W., 296–8, 309
Delgamuukw case, 271
Delworth, Tom, 188–90
Deng Xiaoping, 152, 154, 183, 196, 201,
    234, 289–90, 324
Denison Mines, 63, 65
Department of Indian Affairs and
    Northern Development (DIAND), 77
Desmarais, André, 203–4, 208
Desmarais, Paul, Sr, 203–4
Dewar, Elaine, 322
DeWit, Netty, 320
Dewitt, David, 224
Dickson, Brian, 303
Dickson, Jennifer, 320
Dobell, Ken, 218, 244–5
Dobell, Rod, 244–5
Document Number Nine, 226
Dosanjh, Ujjal, 127, 272
Drake, Earl, 203–4
Drury, Charles "Bud," 71
Duckworth, Korry, 320
Dyck, Lillian, 112

Earnscliffe Strategies, 127
economy, state role in, 157–8, 237–8.
    See also Canada Development

Corporation (CDC); Canada Develop-
    ment Investment Corporation (then
    CDIC); Canadair; De Havilland;
    Eldorado Resources (formerly
    Eldorado Nuclear); Petro-Canada
Edwards, Nicole, 320
Eldorado Resources (formerly
    Eldorado Nuclear), 63, 161, 165, 237
elections, federal: (1958), 26, 28; (1962),
    27–8; (1963), 28; (1965), 33, 40–4, 57,
    324; (1972), 72, 80, 83, 118; (1974), 80,
    83, 89, 99; (1976), 34; (1979), 136; (1980),
    3, 136; (1984), 104, 147, 155, 179; (2004),
    126, 128, 129, 272; (2006), 219, 280
Elizabeth II, Queen: PET and, 292, 302;
    visit in 1983 to British Columbia,
    JA role, 148–9; visit in 2005 to
    Saskatchewan, 149
Elliot Lake, 63
Emerson, David, 127, 212, 215, 218–19
energy: coal, 70; hydro-electric, 31–2,
    45, 70; nuclear, 65, 70, 188, 208, 214,
    237; oil and gas, 7, 50–1, 58–60, 62,
    67–79, 81, 183, 214, 237–8, 249, 256,
    258–9, 322, 324; wind power, 276–7.
    See also CANDU nuclear reactor;
    Energy, Mines and Resources (EMR),
    federal department of; energy crisis
    (1973); *Energy Policy for Canada, An*;
    Imperial Oil; Oceanic Wind; Peace
    River power development; Petro-
    Canada
Energy, Mines and Resources (EMR),
    federal department of, x, 7, 57–81, 99,
    107, 186, 198, 257–8
energy crisis (1973), 7, 66, 69, 73–6, 80–1,
    87, 186, 198, 235
Energy Policy for Canada, An, 58–60, 62,
    67, 70–2, 74, 79, 100
Eng, Peter, 196–7
envelope system. *See* Policy and
    Expenditure Management System

environment: Amazon, 291–2;
awareness of, 22, 77, 161; creation
of federal department, 62;
environmental costs of resource
development, 76–8, 139, 162, 258–9.
See also Baosteel co-generation
plant; climate change; oil and gas:
west coast exploration moratorium
Esk'etemc First Nation, 266
ethics rules and conflict of interest:
creation of blind trust as deputy
minister, 59; in the Senate, 115–16,
128–9
Ethiopia, 300–2
Ethiopian Orthodox Tewahedo
Church, 302
Evans, Paul, 217, 220, 223–4, 319, 324
Expo 84 (Louisiana), 149–50
Expo 86: announcement of deal with
BC government, 145; appointed
minister of state for, 146; Chinese
participation in, 186–8; construction
of Canada Place, 146–8, 151, 155;
contribution to, ix, 3–5, 142–6;
legacy, 3, 156; US participation in,
149–50. *See also* Austin, Jack, in
Pierre Trudeau cabinet (1981–84);
Canada Harbour Place Corporation;
Canada Place; Bennett, Bill;
Mitchell, Keith; Olson, H.A. "Bud";
Pattison, Jim; Perrault, Ray
Eyton, Trevor, 247–8

Fairbairn, Joyce, 84, 112, 114, 125–6, 130
Fan Gang, 228
Farris, Senator John Wallace de Beque,
24, 322
"fed-bashing," ix, 3, 30, 143–5
Feng, Dr Rui, 294
First Nation Panel on Fisheries, 267
First Nations Commercial and
Industrial Development Act, 280

First Nations Energy and Mining
Council, 281
First Nations Finance Authority, 274
First Nations Financial Management
Board, 274–5
First Nations Fiscal and Statistical
Management Act (2005), 274, 278
First Nations Land Management Act,
272–3
First Nations Oil and Gas and Moneys
Management Act, 280
First Nations Summit, 274, 279, 281
First Nations Tax Commission, 274–5
Fishery Products International, 161, 165
fishing and fisheries, west coast: Cohen
report, 177–8; Davis plan, 175–6; First
Nation Panel on Fisheries (*Our Place
at the Table*), 267; Northern Native
Fishing Corporation, 266–7; Pacific
Fisheries Restructuring Act (1984, died
on the Order Paper), 176–7; Pearse
report (*Turning the Tide: A New Policy
for Canada's Pacific Fisheries*), 175–7
Fitterman, Herb, 221–2
Fitterman, Shirley, 187, 221–2
Flynn, Jacques, 109
Fontaine, Phil, 278
Forsey, Eugene, 108
Fotheringham, Allan, 96–9, 101, 106–7
Fox, Francis, 127
Fox, Marie-Hélène, 90–1
Fox, Vicente, 245–6, 248
Fraser, Joan, 112
Fraser, John, 118
Freeman, Jody, 18, 319
Freeman, Natalie Veiner (wife of
JA, wed in 1978): and Asia-Pacific
Foundation, 189, 191; first meeting,
18; influence of, 18, 105, 319;
married, 18, 162; reaction to cabinet
appointment, 137; travels with, 149,
151, 187–8, 221–2, 284–308

Freeman, Richard, 18, 319
free trade with the United States: Auto
  Pact, 239, 252; Canada-US Free Trade
  Agreement, 104, 240–1, 247; election
  of 1911, 240; election of 1988, 240; PET
  cabinet discussions of, 239. *See also*
  United States: protectionism
Frolic, B. Michael, 231
Fulton, Davie, 32, 61
Fukuda, Takeo, 309
Fung, Dr David T., 251

Getty, Don, 75
Giant Mascot (mine), 53–6, 59
Gibson, Gordon, Jr, 44, 118
Gillespie, Alastair, 107
Gitanyow First Nation, 271
Gitwinksihlkw, 272
Gitxsan Wet'suwet'en Tribal Council,
  267
Glassco Commission (Royal
  Commission on Government
  Organization), 60, 62
Goldenberg, Carl, 109–10
Goldenberg, Eddie, 261
Goodale, Ralph, 149, 216
Gordon, Gerry, 47–8
Gosnell, Joseph, 271
Gotoh, Noboru, 151
Grafstein, Jerry, 129
Grauer, Cindy, 320
Gray, Herb, 110, 137, 314
Green, Rosario, 246
Greene, Joe, 63–4, 67–8
Guangdong (province of China), 188
Guangzhou (Canton), 184, 188, 198, 290
Guest, Gowan, 147
Guujaaw, 276

Haddock, Louise, 320
Haida Gwaii, 79, 276
Haida Nation, 276, 283

Hamilton, Alvin, 96
Hampson, Tony, 159–60
Hangzhou, 184, 208
Hansen, Colin, 191
Hanson, Sam, 299
Harcourt, Becky, 206
Harcourt, Mike, 149, 153–4, 205–6
Harper, Stephen: and China, 214,
  220–1; and fisheries, 177; and the
  Kelowna Accord, 8, 280–1; and the
  Senate, 121, 132; recruitment of
  David Emerson, 219
Harrison, Jim, 60
Hartt, Stanley, 196
Harvard University, JA's studies there,
  20, 22–3, 26, 47, 71, 194, 235, 317
Hatton, Jennifer, 320
Hays, Dan, 130
Head, Ivan, 84–5, 153
Hearn, Christine, 320
Hearne Copper Mine, 53
Hébert, Jacques, 10, 169
Hecate Strait, 276
Helliwell, John, 95
Hendren, Dove, 320
Hendrickson, Bev, 320
Herle, David, 127
Herter, Susan, 243
Hervieux-Payette, Céline, 112, 245
Herzog, Jesús Silva, 242
Hill, Alice, 320
Hillman, Mike, 320
Ho, Robert (Fairmont Shipping), 195
Ho, Robert (Vancouver
  philanthropist), 195
Hong Kong, 48, 154, 183, 188, 191,
  193–200, 290, 324
Hopper, Bill, 71, 100
Horvath, Thérèse, 127
Huang Hua, 289
Huberman, David, 25
Hu Jintao, 213–15, 225–6, 234, 281

Hunza Valley, Pakistan, 287
Hurtig, Mel, 240–1
Hutchison, Bruce, 118, 322
Hu Yaobang, 183, 188, 201

immigration, 12, 34, 313
Imperial Oil, 50, 60, 76, 78
Inco, 305
Indian Act, 8, 254, 268, 272–3, 275, 278, 303–4
Indian Claims Commission of Canada, 280
Indigenous Peoples in Canada: advocacy by, 261–2, 265, 267; constitutional recognition of rights, 8, 260, 282; dispossession of, 254, 259, 261, 267; First Nations, 8, 34, 79, 111, 140, 260, 264, 266–7, 269–283, 303–4, 314, 325; Inuit, 34–5, 88, 111, 256, 260, 262–3, 283; JA's early awareness of, 254–6; Métis, 111, 260, 262–3; prejudicial attitudes toward, 8, 254–5, 257, 269, 282. *See also* Aboriginal rights, constitutional entrenchment of (section 35); Assembly of First Nations; Centre for First Nations Governance; Delgamuukw case; Esk'etemc First Nation; First Nation Panel on Fisheries; First Nations Commercial and Industrial Development Act; First Nations Energy and Mining Council; First Nations Finance Authority; First Nations Financial Management Board; First Nations Fiscal and Statistical Management Act (2005); First Nations Land Management Act; First Nations Oil and Gas and Moneys Management Act; First Nations Summit; First Nations Tax Commission; Gitanyow First Nation; Gitxsan Wet'suwet'en Tribal Council; Haida Nation; Indian Act;

Indian Claims Commission of Canada; Kelowna Accord; Ktunaxa First Nation; Kwanlin Dün First Nation; Lheidli T'enneh; Mackenzie Valley Pipeline Inquiry (Berger Commission); Musqueam Nation; Nisga'a advocacy; Nisga'a Final Agreement; Northern Native Fishing Corporation; Nuu-chah-nulth people; Okanagan Indian Band; residential schools; Royal Commission on Aboriginal Peoples; Sixties Scoop; Tk'emlups te Secwepemc; Tl'azt'en Nation; Westbank First Nation; Westbank First Nation Self-Government Act (2004)
Indonesia, 10, 304–8
InterAction Council, 297, 309–10
Interdepartmental Committee on External Relations (ICER), 181–2
International Joint Commission, 21
Inuit, 34–5, 88, 111, 256, 260, 262–3, 283
Ittinuar, Peter, 262

Jack Austin Centre for Asia Pacific Business Studies (at Simon Fraser University), 227
Jaffer, Mobina, 112
Jammu and Kashmir, 286
Japan: as market for BC resources, 5, 37, 48, 53–6; as market for Canadian uranium, 64; Canadian relationship with, 101–2, 182, 188–9, 212, 231, 233, 243, 324; JA's visits to, x, 47–8, 54, 64, 67, 151, 212–13. *See also* Sumitomo; Tokyo Electric; Tokyu Corporation; Toyota investment in Woodstock, ON
Jews, in western Canada, 12–18, 23, 321; participation in Canadian political life, 11, 41, 109–10, 137, 314. *See also* anti-Semitism
Jiang Xinxiong, 210
Jiang Zemin, 207, 209

Job, Brian, 223–4
John, Ed, 274, 279, 281
Johnson, Adam, 320
Johnston, Donald, 166, 178
Johnstone, Lilliane, 320
Jonca, Justyna, 320
Joyal, Serge, 129
Juan Carlos, King, and Queen Sophia
    of Spain, 149
Jules, Manny, 274–5

Kadoorie, Lawrence, 208
Kagedan, Barbara, 320
Kaiser, Edgar, Jr, 191–3, 195–6
Kan, Michael Y.L. and Morgiana,
    194
Kaplan, Bob, 137, 314
Keenleyside, Hugh, 242
Keevil, Norman, Jr, 48, 56
Kelleher, James, 204
Kelly, Charles, 245
Kelowna Accord, x, 8, 278–81
Kenney, Jason, 213
Kenny, Colin, 85, 114
Kirby, Michael, 84, 113, 116, 166
Kissinger, Henry, 162, 186, 198–200
Kitimat, 31
Koerner, Walter, 241–2
Koizumi, Junichiro, 212
Kolber, Jonathan, 286
Kolber, Leo, 125, 284–6, 290, 294, 325
Kolber, Sandra, 284–6, 294
Komatsu, Kazuko, 212
Kovrig, Michael, 230
Kroeger, Arthur, 127
Kroft, Richard, 129
Kruyt, Peter, 204
Ktunaxa First Nation, 283
Kuchar, Len, 129–30
Küng, Hans, 310
Kuujjuaq, PQ (formerly Fort Chimo), 35
Kwanlin Dün First Nation, 256

Laing, Arthur "Art": appointment as
    minister of northern affairs and
    national resources, 28; attitudes
    toward Indigenous people, 34–5,
    50, 256–7, 283; bridge named for, 26,
    33; first meeting with, 26; influence
    on JA, 26–44, 251, 257; 1962 election
    campaign, 27–8; 1963 election
    campaign, 28; opposition to fresh
    water exports, 36, 235; political
    background of, 27; rivalry with
    W.A.C. Bennett, 31–3, 43; trip to
    Soviet Arctic with, 37–9
Lalonde, Marc, 4, 80, 165, 168, 173, 249
Lamb, Jamie, 118
Lapierre, Jean, 218
Laskin, Bora, 303
LeBlanc, Roméo, 146, 174
Lee, Bob, 192
Lee, Ted, 23
Lévesque, René, 35, 302
Lewis, David, 72–3, 75, 99
Lheidli T'enneh, 325
Li, Jing, 227
Liberal leadership race and convention
    (1968), x, 41, 57, 67, 126, 180
Liberal Party (federal): in British
    Columbia, 3–4, 27–8, 40–4, 79,
    88–9, 98, 107, 118, 136, 138–9, 145,
    147, 269, 272; candidacy of JA in
    Vancouver Kingsway (1965), 40–4;
    early involvement of JA in, 26, 90,
    174; nationally, 35, 41, 72, 81–3, 105–9,
    111–14, 116–17, 119–20, 124–30, 132–4,
    159–60, 165, 168, 177–9, 180, 189–91,
    193, 204, 229, 239–40, 261–2, 269–72;
    philosophy, 42–3, 118, 322
Lighthizer, Robert, 252
Lin, Justin Yifu, 226
Lin, Paul, 200
Li Peng, 183, 206–8, 210
Long, Russell, 149–50

Losier-Cool, Rose-Marie, 112
Lougheed, Peter, 75, 302
Louie, Robert, 273
Lucas, Ray, 320
Lu Congmin, 210, 221
Lu Shumin, 215

Macao, 197–200
Macdonald, Donald, 68, 74, 99
Macdonald, John A., 104, 108, 133
MacEachen, Allan, 129, 160, 189, 193
MacInnis, Angus, 42
MacInnis, Grace, 42, 44
MacIntyre, Malcolm, 19
MacKay, Elmer, 97–8
MacKenzie, Norman, 20–1
Mackenzie Valley Pipeline Inquiry
    (Berger Commission), 7, 76–9, 139,
    257–60
MacLaren, Roy, 205
Made in China 2025 plan, 233
Magna Carta, 170–2
Mandela, Nelson, 10, 296–9
Manley, John, 248
Manning, Paul, 85
Manthorpe, Jonathan, 299
Mao Zedong, 152, 180–1, 184, 186, 188,
    201, 223
maquiladora system, 252
Marchand, Jean, 10, 30
Marchand, Len, 34
Marsden, Lorna, 112, 114, 245
Martin, David, 320
Martin, Heather, 320
Martin, Paul, Sr: appearance on
    behalf of JA's election campaign in
    1965, 40; Columbia River Treaty
    negotiations, x, 29; creation
    of Canadian International
    Development Agency (CIDA), 162;
    Liberal leadership bid (1968), x, 57,
    126; mentorship by, 9

Martin, Paul E.: appointment of JA to
    cabinet by, 126; character, 9, 126;
    China, relations with, 211–14, 221; as
    finance minister, 127; first meeting
    with, 126; foreword by, ix–xi; gov-
    ernment of, x, 8, 72, 126–32, 216, 272,
    314; Indigenous Peoples and recon-
    ciliation, commitment to, 8, 277–81,
    283; JA's support for, 125–7, 208; re-
    sponse to JA's proposals on Senate,
    132; transition team of, 127; visit to
    Japan, 212–13; visit to Vancouver,
    248. See also Kelowna Accord; Pacific
    Gateway Strategy, Bill C-68
Massey Ferguson, 161, 165
Mazankowski, Don, 155
McArthur, John H., 71, 216
McCann, Sheila, 130
McDiarmid, Neil, 46–7
McKay, Ian, 320
McNabb, Gordon, 70
McNaughton, Andrew, 21–2, 45
Mei Ping, 231
Meng Wanzhou, 230, 236
Menzies, Merrill, 96
Menzies, Morris, 51, 53, 55–6, 96–7
Merritt, BC, 46, 255
Métis, 111, 260, 262–3
Mexico, 7, 22, 28, 116, 218, 229, 235, 241–
    52, 293. See also Aztec Eagle, Order
    of the; Canada-Mexico Business
    Retreat; Cantarell Nitrogen
    Project; North American Free
    Trade Agreement (NAFTA); North
    American Institute (NAMI); Partido
    Acción Nacional (PAN); Partido
    Revolucionario Institucional (PRI)
Mina, Parviz, 67
mining, involvement in: Brameda, 53–
    7, 97, 101, 141; Craigmont, 46–52, 54;
    Giant Mascot, 53–6, 59; New Pacific
    Metals, 294

minority governments and challenges
  stemming from, 28, 37, 42–3, 72, 78,
  83–4, 126, 129, 149, 213, 280, 304
Mitchell, Andy, 279
Mitchell, Keith, 147, 156
Moltchanov, Vladimir, 37
Montefiore Colony, 13, 321
Montefiore Institute at Heritage Park,
  321
Mulroney, Brian, 104, 139, 155, 179,
  239–40
Mulroney government: abortion bill,
  104–5; apartheid, leadership against,
  296; Asia Pacific Foundation of
  Canada, 190–1, 215; cabinet ministers
  in, 118, 123, 204, 270; China, relations
  with, 202, 220; and Expo 86, 147,
  155–6; free trade with US, 104, 239–
  40; Indigenous policy, 275; North
  American Free Trade Agreement,
  246; sale of Canadair and De
  Havilland, 165; sale of Connaught
  Laboratories, 159
multiculturalism, 111, 304, 313
Munro, John, 137–40, 264, 267
Murphy, Tim, 127
Murray, Lowell, 109, 123–4
Musqueam Nation, 272–3, 283

Namibia, 299–300
National Energy Board (NEB), 58, 60, 69
National Energy Program, 249
National Harbours Board. See Canada
  Ports Corporation
National People's Congress, China, 6,
  209–10, 215, 221
national unity (Canadian), 4, 9, 93, 120
Nault, Robert, 272
Nemetz, Nathan, 23–7, 31, 45–6, 49, 90,
  149, 174
New Democratic Party (NDP):
  influence on Liberal minority

government (1972–74), 73–4, 76,
  78, 80; provincial party in BC, 143,
  153, 206, 272; rejection of free trade
  pact, 240; Senate, policy on, 103,
  108–9; in Vancouver Kingsway,
  40, 42, 219; worldview, 42–3. See
  also Co-operative Commonwealth
  Federation (CCF)
Newman, Peter C., 35–6
New Orleans, 149–50
New Pacific Metals, 294
Nicaragua, 293
Nichol, John, 41
Nichols, Marjorie, 154
Nicholson, Jack, 27
Nicholson, Peter, 127
Nielsen, Arne, 100
Nippon Mining, 47
Nisga'a advocacy, 78, 255, 268
Nisga'a Final Agreement, xi, 268–73,
  279
Nixon Shock, 66–7, 69
Noranda (mining company), 47, 51–2
North, Canadian: economic
  development in, 34, 39, 50, 53, 70, 76,
  257–8; environmental and social
  threats to, 62, 70, 77, 139, 256–7;
  governance of, 34, 50, 122, 259–60;
  JA's education about, 7, 33–5, 256.
  See also Mackenzie Valley Pipeline
  Inquiry (Berger Commission)
North American Free Trade
  Agreement (NAFTA), 243–8, 252–3
North American Institute (NAMI),
  243–6, 248
northeast coal. See coal
Northern Native Fishing Corporation,
  266–7
North Star Grocery, Calgary, 14–15, 22
Northwest Territories (pre-1999), 34, 50,
  53, 77, 86, 256, 259–60
N'Quatqua, 325

Nujoma, Sam, 300
Nuu-chah-nulth people, 149

Oceanic Wind, 277
O'Connell, Martin, 80
October Crisis, 88
O'Hagan, Richard, 35–6
oil and gas: Canadian market, 68–9,
    73, 75–6; Canadian reserves, 58, 60,
    62, 70; export tax, 74–5, 79; national
    oil companies, 59, 67, 71, 72–3,
    249–50; US dominance of Canadian
    industry, 7, 49, 58, 60, 76, 235, 237–8;
    west coast exploration moratorium,
    79. *See also* Borden line (also known
    as Ottawa Valley line); energy;
    energy crisis (1973); *Energy Policy for
    Canada, An*; Imperial Oil; Panarctic
    Oils Ltd; Petro-Canada
oil crisis (1973). *See* energy crisis (1973)
Okanagan Indian Band, 34
O'Leary, Terrie, 127
Olson, H.A. "Bud," 136, 144–5, 166, 323
O'Neil, Pierre, 85
Ontario, 3, 62–3, 68, 69, 73, 75, 81, 83,
    107, 109, 116, 119, 121–3, 137, 165, 190,
    212–14, 314
Ontario Hydro, 65–6
Oregon Treaty of 1846, 21
Organization of the Petroleum
    Exporting Countries (OPEC), 66
Ortega, Daniel, 293
Owen, Stephen, 127

Pacific Fisheries Restructuring Act
    (1984), 176–7
Pacific Gateway Strategy, Bill C-68, x,
    218–19
Padilla, Ezequiel, 248
Pakistan, 285–8
Paley Commission report (*Resources for
    Freedom*) (1952), 7, 49

Palumbo, Deborah, 320
Panarctic Oils Ltd, 258
Pan Pacific Hotel, 148, 151, 155, 215, 309
Parkinson, David, 320
Parlee, Forrest, 320
Partido Acción Nacional (PAN),
    or National Action Party (Mexico),
    248
Partido Revolucionario Institucional
    (PRI), or Institutional Revolutionary
    Party (Mexico), 244
Pattison, Jim, 154, 323
Paz Estenssoro, Víctor, 293
Peace River power development, 31–2,
    51, 79
Pearse, Peter, 175–7, 323
Pearse report, 1982 (*Turning the Tide:
    A New Policy for Canada's Pacific
    Fisheries*), 175–6
Pearson, Lester B., 28, 30, 35–6, 40,
    42–3, 86, 116
Pearson government, 28–39, 63, 72,
    82–3, 322
Pelletier, Gérard, 10
PEMEX, 249
Pépin, Jean-Luc, visit to China with
    (1971), 6, 183–5
Perrault, Ray, 3, 40–1, 89, 106–7, 136, 138,
    140–1, 143–5, 149, 151, 153
Peterson, Leslie, 59
Petro-Canada, x, 7, 59, 72–3, 75–6,
    78–80, 99–100, 157, 162–3, 216, 235,
    238
Petter, Andrew, 228
Pharmacare, 168, 172
Phelps, Michael, 249–50
Philip, Prince, 148–9
Phillip, Joan, 281
Phillip, Stewart, 281
Phillips, Art, 136
Phillips, Don, 140
Pickens, T. Boone, 195

Pitfield, Michael, 9, 61–2, 78, 80, 84–5, 92–4, 101–2, 112–13, 115, 120, 159, 166, 168, 172, 302

Pitfield, Tom, 320

Placer Development, 24, 47–8, 52

Policy and Expenditure Management System, also known as the envelope system, 166–9, 172, 323

Poole, Jack, 192

Porter, Dave, 281, 325

ports: Prince Rupert, 140–2, 323; Vancouver, 192. *See also* Canada Ports Corporation (formerly National Harbours Board); Pacific Gateway Strategy, Bill C-68

Potter, Pitman, 222

Power Corporation, 52, 126, 161–2, 203–4

Prentice, Jim, 280–1

Prime Minister's Office (PMO): operation of, 84–6, 94, 166; role of, 82, 93, 167–8; switchboard, 98. *See also* Austin, Jack, Prime Minister's Office as principal secretary

Prince Rupert, BC, 140–2, 173–4, 217–18, 267, 323

Priorities and Planning Committee of cabinet (P&P), 4, 71, 75, 145, 165–6, 168, 170

Privy Council Office (PCO), 61, 85, 113, 137, 160, 166–8, 172, 189, 279

Progressive Conservative party: governments, 27–8, 61, 104, 136, 155, 176; in the House of Commons, 72, 76, 96, 98–9, 105 118; position on Petro-Canada, 73; in Senate, 106, 109, 113, 123–4, 270–1; worldview, 43. *See also* Clark, Joe and Clark government; Mulroney government

Quebec: and Asia, 190, 205; Indigenous Peoples, 35, 261, 263, 270–1; JA and, 30, 57, 81, 86–8, 322; mining in, 53, 55; nation within a nation, 314, oil market, 69, 74; Quebecers in Ottawa, 3, 10, 85, 90, 109, 112, 165, 176, 218, 314; and the Senate, 103, 112, 119–23; PET and, 86, 93, 120, 304. *See also* Martin, Paul E.; Trudeau, Justin; Trudeau, Pierre Elliott

Rae, Bob, 130

Ramaphosa, Cyril, 297

Raybould, Tim, 273

Reid, Patrick, 152, 154

Reid, Scott, 127

Reisman, Simon, 96

Report of the Federal Cultural Policy Review Committee. See Applebaum-Hébert report

residential schools, 8, 90, 256–7

Reyes-Heroles, Jesús, 245

Reynolds, John, 219

Richardson, Miles, 276

Ridley Island, 140–2

Rivard, Jean, 267

Robertson, Gordon, 9, 57–8, 61–2, 85–6, 93–4

Robinson, Basil, 77–8, 257

Robinson, Mike, 127

Rogers, Robert, 146–7

Roman, Stephen, 65

Rompkey, Bill, 126

Rowley, Graham, 39

Royal Commission on Aboriginal Peoples, 283

Royal Commission on Bilingualism and Biculturalism, 30

Royal Commission on Canada's Economic Prospects (led by Walter Gordon), 157

Royal Commission on Government Organization. *See* Glassco Commission

Royal Commission on the Status of Women, 110

Royal Roads University, 228–9
Rozental, Andrés, 246
Rudd, Kevin, 231
Ryan, Mary Alice, 320

Saada, Jacques, 314
Sabia, Michael, 172
Salinas de Gortari, Carlos, 244, 246–7
Salisbury Convention, 104
Satsan (Herb George), 275
Saul, John Ralston, 100
Sauvé, Pauline, 172
Schreyer, Edward "Ed," 149
Scott, Andy, 279
Scow, Alfred, 266
section 35 (in the constitution). *See*
  Aboriginal rights, constitutional
  entrenchment of (section 35)
Senate of Canada: attendance
  requirement, 116, 193; BC
  underrepresentation in, 9, 122–4;
  changes by Justin Trudeau to, 132;
  constitutional role of, 9, 103–6,
  111–12, 114–15, 119, 125, 130, 133, 240;
  diversity in, 110–12; ethics in, 115–16,
  128–9; future of, 11, 130–5; NDP
  position on, 108–9; policy work of,
  110, 112–14; reform efforts, 120–2;
  resources available to senators, 114–
  15; role in regional representation,
  119–20, 122–3; women in, 110, 112. *See
  also* Austin, Jack, Senate, service in
Shapiro, Daniel, 227
Sharp, Mitchell, 72, 182, 245
Sheng Huaren, 221
Shenzhen, 183
shipbuilding contracts for BC, 173
Sibbald, AB, 13
Sichuan, China, 250, 281
Silvercorp, 294, 325
Simon Fraser University (SFU),
  227–8, 315

Sinclair, James: career, 27, 174; early
  influence on author, 26, 90, 174;
  naming of Sinclair Centre, 174–5
Sinclair, Murray, 283
Sisulu, Walter, 296
Sixties Scoop, 257
SkyTrain, 143, 145
Sloan, Gordon, 46
Smith, Elijah, 256
Smith, Gordon, 172
Smith, Stewart, 46
Social Credit Party, or Socreds: in
  Alberta, 15; in BC, 27, 32, 41, 144, 153;
  federal, 144, 238
Social Development ministry,
  165–9, 171–2. *See also* Policy and
  Expenditure Management System
softwood lumber trade dispute,
  235, 239. *See also* United States:
  protectionism
South Africa, 10, 65, 294–9
Southam, Nancy, 295, 305–7
sovereignty, Canadian, 11, 72, 240–1,
  251, 253, 256
Soviet Arctic, tour of (1965), 37–9
Sparrow, Herb, 112
Spavor, Michael, 230
Squamish Nation, 275, 283, 325
Starck, Lou, 54
Stern, Janet, 221
Stern, Ron, 221–2, 266–7, 319
Stewart, Jane, 273
Stewart, Michael, 250
St Germain, Gerry, 270
St-Laurent, Louis, 26, 109
St Lawrence Seaway, 237
Strong, Hanne, 284
Strong, Maurice, 52, 77, 100, 159–62, 221,
  242–3, 284, 322
Suharto, 304–5
Sukunka coal deposit. *See* coal
Sullivan, Sean, 164

Sumitomo, 54, 56
Supreme Court of Canada:
appearances by JA at, 27, 48; Charter
impact, 303; Delgamuukw case,
271; Nisga'a case, 78, 268; patriation
reference, 120, 263, 303; suggested
role in Senate nominations, 131
Suzman, Helen, 295–6
swimming pool at 24 Sussex, 94–5

Tait, Neil, 204
Taiwan, 180, 182, 192, 194, 281, 324
Taylor, Vernon "Moose," 47
Team Canada trade missions to China,
x, 6, 204–9. *See also* Canada China
Business Council
Teck Resources, 48, 56, 97, 141
Teleglobe, 161, 165
Tellier, Paul, 139
Thompson, Andrew, 116
Thompson, Julian Ogilvie, 298
Thompson, Robert, 238
Tiananmen Square, 154–5, 183, 201–4,
206, 209–10, 213
Tiberghien, Yves, 223
Tk'emlups te Secwepemc, 274
Tl'azt'en Nation, 274
Tokyo Electric, 64
Tokyu Corporation, 148, 151
Toope, Stephen, 224–5
Toyota investment in Woodstock, ON,
212–13
Trudeau, Justin, 132–4, 177, 217, 229–30,
309–10
Trudeau, Margaret, 89–94, 174
Trudeau, Pierre Elliott: and China,
180–3, 186, 198–9, 202, 220, 223, 288–
90; disarmament tour, 153; focus
on Quebec, 86, 120, 304; funeral,
310; governance style, 83, 124, 138;
impact of marital problems, 92, 94;
and Indigenous Peoples, 261, 265,

303–4; InterAction Council, 297,
309–10; interest in architecture, 148;
JA's first impression of, 57–8; JA's first
meeting with, 58–9; patriation of the
constitution, 260, 302–3; personality,
9–10, 84, 99, 107; travels with, 10,
285–310; work habits, 9, 94. *See also*
Austin, Jack, civil service career as
deputy minister of Energy, Mines
and Resources; Austin, Jack, in
Pierre Trudeau cabinet (1981–84);
Austin, Jack, Prime Minister's Office
as principal secretary
Trump, Donald, 229–30, 252
Truth and Reconciliation Commission
(Canada), 8, 283
Turner, Bill, 52
*Turning the Tide: A New Policy for
Canada's Pacific Fisheries. See* Pearse
report, 1982
Turner, John, 38–9, 96, 168–9, 177–9,
239–40
Tutu, Desmond, 298

United States: Canadian relationship
with, 6–7, 11, 29, 45, 66–7, 104, 233, 235–
6, 238, 240–1; participation in Expo
86, 149–50; protectionism, 63, 235–6,
239, 252; relations with China, 182,
198, 230, 232, 236, 252; relations with
Mexico, 242, 247; tax laws favouring
foreign investment, 49, 237. *See also*
Boundary Waters Treaty of 1909;
Canadian sovereignty; Columbia
River Treaty; free trade with the
United States; Nixon Shock; North
American Free Trade Agreement
(NAFTA); Oregon Treaty of 1846; Paley
Commission report (*Resources for
Freedom*) (1952); Trump, Donald
United States-Mexico-Canada
Agreement (USMCA), 252–3

University of British Columbia (UBC): developing China relationships for UBC, 224–6; honorary degree from, 226; JA as honorary professor, 222–4; JA as law lecturer, 20–3; JA as student, 17–20, 78, 192; UBC China Council, 224–6

University of California (Berkeley), 7, 28, 49

University of East Asia (later University of Macao), 197–200, 324

University of the Witwatersrand, 299, 302

Uranium Canada, 65, 238

uranium industry in Canada and uranium "cartel," 62–6, 157, 235

Vancouver, ix, x, 3, 5, 17–18, 23–4, 26–9, 36, 40, 44, 49–51, 58, 81, 88, 101–2, 105, 107, 115–18, 121, 136–8, 140, 142–3, 146–9, 151, 153, 156, 157, 161, 173–4, 179, 181, 184, 190, 192–3, 199, 202–3, 215, 217–19, 221–2, 224, 228, 230, 236, 241, 243, 248, 249, 251, 266, 272–3, 281, 294–5, 298, 309. *See also* Canada Place; Expo 86; Pan Pacific Hotel; ports: Vancouver; Sinclair, James: naming of Sinclair Centre; University of British Columbia (UBC); Vancouver Art Gallery; *Vancouver Sun*

Vancouver Art Gallery, 173

Vancouver Sun, 35, 37, 59, 96–7, 107, 117–18, 138, 153–4, 241, 310, 321–3

Van Roggen, George, 106

Veiner, Harry (JA's father-in-law), 18, 144

Volpe, Joe, 210

Waring, Gerald, 37–8

Wasson, Evans, 48

water, fresh: clean water for Indigenous communities, 20, 278; EMR loses responsibility for, 62; for hydroelectricity, 21, 31–2, 45, 70; US interest in imports, 36, 235. *See also* Columbia River Treaty

Watson, John, 279

Watt, Charlie, 34–5

Wen Jiabao, 212–13, 220

Westbank First Nation, 273–4, 283, 325

Westbank First Nation Self-Government Act (2004), 273–4

Westcoast Energy, 249–51

Westdal, Christopher, 295

Wicks, Ann, 320

Wiebe, John, 217

Witherly, Mike, 320

Williams, Bryan, 51

Wilson, Bill, 265–6

Wilson, Graham, 250

Wilson-Raybould, Jody, 265

wind power, 276–7

Winfield, David, 324

Wirth, John, 242–3, 246

Wolfensohn, James, 194

Wong, K.K., 196–7

Woo, Edward, 196

Woo, Yuen Pau, 217

Woodsworth, J.S., 42

World Trade Organization (WTO), 182, 212, 214, 234, 236

Wright, Robert, 221

Xianjiang province (1987 visit), 288–9

Xi Jinping, 154, 183, 226, 232

Yang, Victor, 221, 324

Young, Bruce, 320

Yukon, 31, 34, 50, 53, 77, 178, 189, 256, 258

Zecha, Adrian, 308

Zedillo, Ernesto, 244, 248

Zhang Wenpu, 286

Zhang Yijun, 206
Zhao Ziyang, 153–5, 183, 188, 202, 213
Zha Peixin, 209

Zhou Enlai, 6, 181, 184–5
Zhu Rongji, 206–7
Zia-ul-Haq, Muhammad, 286–7